Fodo

Moscow, St. Petersburg, Kiev

"When it comes to information on regional history, what to see and do, and shopping, these guides are exhaustive."

—*USAir Magazine*

"Valuable because of their comprehensiveness."
—*Minneapolis Star-Tribune*

"Fodor's always delivers high quality...thoughtfully presented...thorough."

—*Houston Post*

"An excellent choice for those who want everything under one cover."

—*Washington Post*

Fodor's Travel Publications, Inc.
New York • Toronto • London • Sydney • Auckland
http://www.fodors.com/

Fodor's Moscow, St. Petersburg, Kiev

Editors: Fionn Davenport, Anto Howard

Contributors: Steven Amsterdam, Chris Billy, Robert Blake, David Brown, Lauri del Commune, Sam Lardner, Linda K. Schmidt, M.T. Schwartzman, Katherine Semler, Juliette Shapland, Natalya Tolstoya

Creative Director: Fabrizio La Rocca

Associate Art Director: Guido Caroti

Photo Researcher: Jolie Novak

Cartographer: David Lindroth

Cover Photograph: Jeffrey Aaronson/Network Aspen

Text Design: Between the Covers

Copyright

Third Edition

ISBN 0–679–03401–3

Special Sales

Fodor's Travel Publications are available at special discounts for bulk purchases for sales promotions or premiums. Special editions, including personalized covers, excerpts of existing guides, and corporate imprints, can be created in large quantities for special needs. For more information, contact your local bookseller or write to Special Markets, Fodor's Travel Publications, 201 East 50th Street, New York, NY 10022. Inquiries from Canada should be directed to your local Canadian bookseller or sent to Random House of Canada, Ltd., Marketing Department, 1265 Aerowood Drive, Mississauga, Ontario L4W 1B9. Inquiries from the United Kingdom should be sent to Fodor's Travel Publications, 20 Vauxhall Bridge Road, London SW1V 2SA, England.

PRINTED IN THE UNITED STATES OF AMERICA

10 9 8 7 6 5 4 3 2 1

CONTENTS

ON THE ROAD WITH FODOR'S

A GOOD TRAVEL GUIDE is like a wonderful traveling companion. It's charming, it's brimming with sound recommendations and solid ideas, it pulls no punches in describing lodging and dining establishments, and it's consistently full of fascinating facts that make you view what you've traveled to see in a rich new light. In the creation of *Moscow, St. Petersburg, Kiev '97,* we at Fodor's have gone to great lengths to provide you with the very best of all possible traveling companions—and to make your trip the best of all possible vacations.

About Our Writers

The information in these pages has been compiled by three extraordinary writers.

Christopher J. Billy is an editor and writer at Fodor's and a longtime student of Eastern European languages and cultures.

Lauri del Commune has lived in Moscow since 1993. She previously worked for 12 years in U.S. book publishing, the last six years in the international department of Alfred A. Knopf in New York.

Writer **Natalya Tolstaya** was born in St. Petersburg. She has a Ph.D. in Scandinavian and Russian literature and is an associate professor at St. Petersburg University. She is author of short stories and a book, *St. Petersburg: City of White Nights,* a history of the city that includes essays on contemporary life there.

What's New

Big things are happening at Fodor's—and in Moscow, St. Petersburg, and Kiev.

A New Design

If this is not the first Fodor's guide you've purchased, you'll immediately notice our new look. More readable and easier-to-use than ever? We think so—and we hope you do, too.

Travel Updates

Just before your trip, you may want to order a Fodor's Worldview Travel Update. From local publications all over Ireland, the lively, cosmopolitan editors at Worldview gather information on concerts, plays, opera, dance performances, gallery and museum shows, sports competitions, and other special events that coincide with your visit. See the order blank in the back of this book for more information, call 800/799–9609, or fax 800/799–9619.

How to Use this Book

Organization

Up front is **The Gold Guide,** comprised of two sections on gold-colored paper chock-full of information about traveling in general and specifically at your destination. Both are in alphabetical order by topic. **Important Contacts A to Z** gives you addresses and telephone numbers of organizations and companies that offer detailed information and publications, plus information about getting to Russia and Ukraine and back again. **Smart Travel Tips** gives you specific tips on how to get the most out of your travels as well as information on how to accomplish what you need to in your destination.

Stars

Stars in the margin denote the most highly recommended sights, attractions, hotels, and restaurants.

Hotel Facilities

Note that in general you incur charges when you use many hotel facilities; we wanted to let you know what facilities the hotel has to offer, but don't always specify whether or not there's a charge, so when planning a resort vacation that entails a stay of several days, it's wise to ask what's included in your rates.

Credit Cards

The following abbreviations are used: **AE,** American Express; **DC,** Diners Club; **MC,** MasterCard (called Access in Ireland and Northern Ireland), and **V,** Visa. Discover is not accepted outside the U.S.

Please Write to Us

Everyone who has worked on *Moscow, St. Petersburg, Kiev* has worked hard to make the text accurate. All prices and opening times are based on information supplied to us at press time, and the publisher cannot accept responsibility for any errors that may have occurred. The passage of time will bring changes, so it's always a good idea to call ahead and confirm information when it matters—particularly if you're making a detour to visit specific sights or attractions. When making reservations at a hotel or inn, be sure to speak up if you have a disability or are traveling with children, if you prefer a private bath or a certain type of bed, or if you have specific dietary needs or any other concerns.

Were the restaurants we recommended as described? Did our hotel picks exceed your expectations? Did you find a museum we recommended a waste of time? Positive and negative, we would love your feedback. If you have complaints, we'll look into them and revise our entries when the facts warrant it. If there's a special place you've happened upon that we haven't included, we'll pass the information along to the writers so they can check it out. So please send us a letter or post card (we're at 201 East 50th Street, New York, New York 10022). We'll look forward to hearing from you. And in the meantime, have a wonderful trip!

Karen Cure
Editorial Director

European Russia and Ukraine

0   300 miles
0   400 km

KEY
Rail Lines

Barents Sea

NORWAY

Nike
Murmansk

Pechora

SWEDEN

Kozhva

White Sea

Arkhangelsk
Vendenga
Mikun
Syktyvkar

Severnaya Dvina

Yushkozero
Kimasozero

FINLAND

Petrozavodsk

RUSSIA

Kotlas

Kirov

Gulf of Bothnia

N

Lake Ladoga

Helsinki
Tallinn
Gulf of Finland
St. Petersburg
Vologda
Cherepovets

Vyatka

Baltic Sea
Gulf of Riga

ESTONIA
Novgorod
Yaroslavl
Nizhniy Novgorod

Kazan

Riga

Pskov
Tver

Vladimir
Volga

Simbirsk
Saransk

LATVIA

LITHUANIA
Kaunas
Vitsyebsk
Moscow
Ryazan
Oka

Kaliningrad
RUSSIA
Vilnius
Smolensk
Kaluga

Penza

Warsaw

Minsk
Mahilyow
Oka
Lipetsk
Tambov

Saratov

BELARUS
Bryansk
Orel
KAZAKHSTAN

POLAND
Homyel
Kursk
Voronezh

Volga

Belgorod

UKRAINE
Kiev
Kharkiv
Don
Volgograd

L'viv

Vinnytsya
Dnieper
Donets

SLOVAKIA
Dnipropetrovsk

HUNGARY
MOLDOVA
Kherson
Rostov na Donu

Chisinau
Sea of Azov
Krasnodar
Stavropol

ROMANIA
Odesa

Bucharest
Sevastopol

YUGOSLAVIA
Danube
BULGARIA
Black Sea
GEORGIA

Europe

Reykjavík
ICELAND

NORWAY
Bergen

SCOTLAND

NORTHERN
IRELAND
Edinburgh

*North
Sea*

Skagerrak

Belfast

IRELAND *Irish
Sea*   DENMARK

Dublin   UNITED
KINGDOM

WALES   Hamburg

Cardiff   ENGLAND   NETHERLANDS
London   The Hague Amsterdam
Rotterdam

*ATLANTIC
OCEAN*

English Channel   Brussels   GERM
BELGIUM   Bonn

Paris   Frankfurt
LUXEMBOURG

FRANCE   Zürich   Munich
Bern
SWITZERLAND
LIECHTENSTEIN
Lyon
Milan   Venice

Monte
Carlo   Florence
Nice
Marseille   MONACO

PORTUGAL   Madrid   ANDORRA
Corsica

Lisbon   Barcelona

SPAIN   *Sardinia*

Seville   Granada   *Balearic
Islands*   *Tyrrhenian*

Gibraltar   *Mediterranean Sea*

MOROCCO   ALGERIA
0   400 miles
0   600 km   TUNISIA

World Time Zones

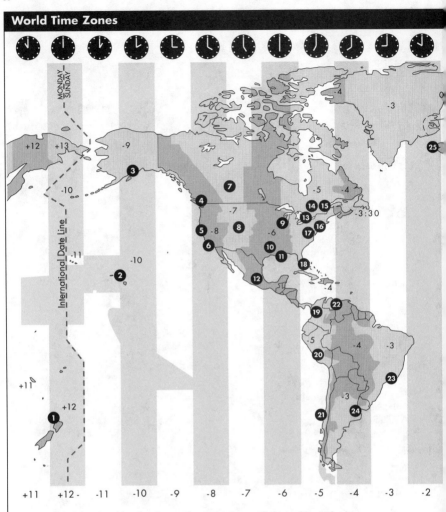

Numbers below vertical bands relate each zone to Greenwich Mean Time (0 hrs.).
Local times frequently differ from these general indications,
as indicated by light-face numbers on map.

Algiers, **29**

Anchorage, **3**

Athens, **41**

Auckland, **1**

Baghdad, **46**

Bangkok, **50**

Beijing, **54**

Berlin, **34**

Bogotá, **19**

Budapest, **37**

Buenos Aires, **24**

Caracas, **22**

Chicago, **9**

Copenhagen, **33**

Dallas, **10**

Delhi, **48**

Denver, **8**

Djakarta, **53**

Dublin, **26**

Edmonton, **7**

Hong Kong, **56**

Honolulu, **2**

Istanbul, **40**

Jerusalem, **42**

Johannesburg, **44**

Lima, **20**

Lisbon, **28**

London (Greenwich), **27**

Los Angeles, **6**

Madrid, **38**

Manila, **57**

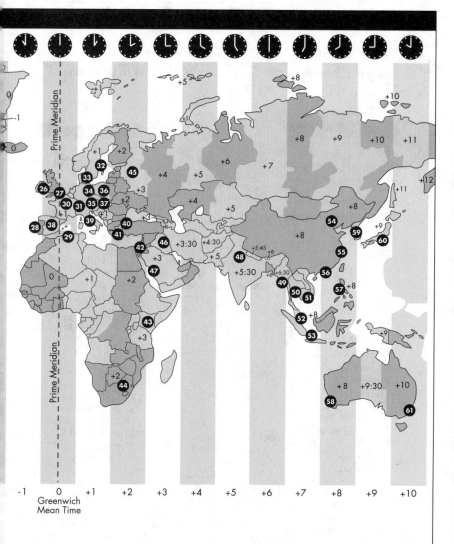

THE GOLD GUIDE / IMPORTANT CONTACTS

IMPORTANT CONTACTS A TO Z

An Alphabetical Listing of Publications, Organizations, and Companies that Will Help You Before, During, and After Your Trip

A

AIR TRAVEL

The major gateways are **Sheremetyevo II Airport** in Moscow (☎ 578–5633 or 578–5614), **Pulkovo II Airport** in St. Petersburg (☎ 104 34 44), and **Borispol Airport** in Kiev. Flying time is 8½ hours from New York, 10–11 hours from Chicago, and 12 hours from Los Angeles.

CARRIERS

Carriers serving Russia and Ukraine include **Aeroflot** (✉ 630 5th Ave., New York, NY 10011, ☎ 212/265–1185 or 800/995–5555), **Air France** (☎ 800/237–2747), **British Airways** (☎ 800/247–9297), **Delta** (☎ 800/241–4141), **Finnair** (☎ 800/950–5000), **KLM** (☎ 800/374–7747), **Lufthansa** (☎ 800/645–3880), **Northwest Airlines** (☎ 800/447–4747), **SAS** (☎ 800/221–2350), and **Swissair** (☎ 800/221–4750).

COMPLAINTS

To register complaints about charter and scheduled airlines, contact the U.S. Department of Transportation's **Aviation Consumer Protection Division** (✉ C-75, Washington, DC 20590, ☎ 202/366–2220). Complaints about lost baggage or ticketing problems and safety concerns may also be logged with the **Federal Aviation Administration (FAA) Consumer Hotline** (☎ 800/322–7873).

CONSOLIDATORS

For the names of reputable air-ticket consolidators, contact the **United States Air Consolidators Association** (925 L St., Suite 220, Sacramento, CA 95814, tel. 916/441–4166, fax 916/441–3520). For discount air-ticketing agencies, *see* Discounts & Deals, *below.*

PUBLICATIONS

For general information about charter carriers, ask for the Department of Transportation's free brochure **"Plane Talk: Public Charter Flights"** (✉ Aviation Consumer Protection Division, C-75, Washington, DC 20590, ☎ 202/366–2220). The Department of Transportation also publishes a 58-page booklet, **"Fly Rights,"** available from the Consumer Information Center (✉ Supt. of Documents, Dept. 136C, Pueblo, CO 81009; $1.75).

For other tips and hints, consult the Consumers Union's monthly **"Consumer Reports Travel Letter"** (✉ Box 53629, Boulder, CO 80322, ☎ 800/234–1970; $39 1st year).

B

BETTER BUSINESS BUREAU

For local contacts in the hometown of a tour operator you may be considering, consult the **Council of Better Business Bureaus** (✉ 4200 Wilson Blvd., Suite 800, Arlington, VA 22203, ☎ 703/276–0100, FAX 703/525–8277).

C

CAR RENTAL

The major car-rental companies represented in Moscow are **Avis** (☎ 800/331–1084; in Canada, 800/879–2847), **Budget** (☎ 800/527–0700; in the U.K., 0800/181181), and **Hertz** (☎ 800/654–3001; in Canada, 800/263–0600; in the U.K., 0345/555888). Rates begin at $100 a day and $350 a week for an economy car plus 45¢ per kilometer. This does not include tax on car rentals, which is 21.5%.

INSURANCE

Ingosstrakh (12 Pyatniskaya ulitsa, Moscow, ☎ 095/231–1677, FAX 095/230–2518, telex 411144).

CHILDREN & TRAVEL

FLYING

Look into **"Flying with Baby"** (✉ Third Street Press, Box 261250,

Littleton, CO 80163, ☎ 303/595–5959; $4.95 includes shipping), cowritten by a flight attendant. **"Kids and Teens in Flight,"** free from the U.S. Department of Transportation's Aviation Consumer Protection Division (✉ C-75, Washington, DC 20590, ☎ 202/366–2220), offers tips on children flying alone. Every two years the February issue of *Family Travel Times* (☞ Know-How, *below*) details children's services on three dozen airlines. **"Flying Alone, Handy Advice for Kids Traveling Solo"** is available free from the American Automobile Association (AAA) (✉ send stamped, self-addressed, legal-size envelope: Flying Alone, Mail Stop 800, 1000 AAA Dr., Heathrow, FL 32746).

KNOW-HOW

Family Travel Times, published quarterly by Travel with Your Children (✉ TWYCH, 40 5th Ave., New York, NY 10011, ☎ 212/477–5524; $40 per year), covers destinations, types of vacations, and modes of travel.

CUSTOMS

U.S. CITIZENS

The **U.S. Customs Service** (✉ Box 7407, Washington, DC 20044, ☎ 202/927–6724) can answer questions on duty-free limits and publishes a helpful brochure, "Know Before You Go." For information on registering foreign-made articles, call 202/927–0540 or write U.S. Customs Service, Resource Management,

1301 Constitution Ave. NW, Washington DC, 20229.

COMPLAINTS➤ Note the inspector's badge number and write to the commissioner's office (✉ 1301 Constitution Ave. NW, Washington, DC 20229).

CANADIANS

Contact **Revenue Canada** (✉ 2265 St. Laurent Blvd. S, Ottawa, Ontario K1G 4K3, ☎ 613/993–0534) for a copy of the free brochure **"I Declare/Je Déclare"** and for details on duty-free limits. For recorded information (within Canada only), call 800/461–9999.

U.K. CITIZENS

HM Customs and Excise (✉ Dorset House, Stamford St., London SE1 9NG, ☎ 0171/202–4227) can answer questions about U.K. customs regulations and publishes a free pamphlet, **"A Guide for Travellers,"** detailing standard procedures and import rules.

D
DISABILITIES & ACCESSIBILITY

COMPLAINTS

To register complaints under the provisions of the Americans with Disabilities Act, contact the U.S. Department of Justice's **Disability Rights Section** (✉ Box 66738, Washington, DC 20035, ☎ 202/514–0301 or 800/514–0301, 𝖥𝖠𝖷 202/307–1198, TTY 202/514–0383 or 800/514–0383). For airline-related problems, contact the U.S. Department of Transportation's **Aviation Consumer**

Protection Division (☞ Air Travel, *above*). For complaints about surface transportation, contact the Department of Transportation's **Civil Rights Office** (✉ 400 7th St., SW, Room 10215, Washington DC, 20590 ☎ 202/366–4648).

ORGANIZATIONS

TRAVELERS WITH HEARING IMPAIRMENTS➤ The **American Academy of Otolaryngology** (✉ 1 Prince St., Alexandria, VA 22314, ☎ 703/836–4444, 𝖥𝖠𝖷 703/683–5100, TTY 703/519–1585) publishes a brochure, "Travel Tips for Hearing Impaired People."

TRAVELERS WITH MOBILITY PROBLEMS➤ Contact **Mobility International USA** (✉ Box 10767, Eugene, OR 97440, ☎ and TTY 541/343–1284, 𝖥𝖠𝖷 541/343–6812), the U.S. branch of a Belgium-based organization (☞ *below*) with affiliates in 30 countries; **MossRehab Hospital Travel Information Service** (☎ 215/456–9600, TTY 215/456–9602), a telephone information resource for travelers with physical disabilities; the **Society for the Advancement of Travel for the Handicapped** (✉ 347 5th Ave., Suite 610, New York, NY 10016, ☎ 212/447–7284, 𝖥𝖠𝖷 212/725–8253; membership $45); and **Travelin' Talk** (✉ Box 3534, Clarksville, TN 37043, ☎ 615/552–6670, 𝖥𝖠𝖷 615/552–1182) which provides local contacts worldwide for travelers with disabilities.

TRAVELERS WITH VISION IMPAIRMENTS➤ Contact

THE GOLD GUIDE / IMPORTANT CONTACTS

the **American Council of the Blind** (✉ 1155 15th St. NW, Suite 720, Washington, DC 20005, ☎ 202/467–5081, FAX 202/467–5085) for a list of travelers' resources or the **American Foundation for the Blind** (✉ 11 Penn Plaza, Suite 300, New York, NY 10001, ☎ 212/502–7600 or 800/232–5463, TTY 212/502–7662), which provides general advice and publishes "Access to Art" ($19.95), a directory of museums that accommodate travelers with vision impairments.

IN THE U.K.

Contact the **Royal Association for Disability and Rehabilitation** (✉ RADAR, 12 City Forum, 250 City Rd., London EC1V 8AF, ☎ 0171/250–3222) or **Mobility International** (✉ rue de Manchester 25, B-1080 Brussels, Belgium, ☎ 00–322–410–6297, FAX 00–322–410–6874), an international travel-information clearing-house for people with disabilities.

PUBLICATIONS

Several publications for travelers with disabilities are available from the **Consumer Information Center** (✉ Box 100, Pueblo, CO 81009, ☎ 719/948–3334). Call or write for its free catalog of current titles. The Society for the Advancement of Travel for the Handicapped (☞ Organizations, *above*) publishes the quarterly magazine **"Access to Travel"** ($13 for 1-year subscription).

The 500-page **Travelin' Talk Directory** (✉ Box 3534, Clarksville, TN

37043, ☎ 615/552–6670, FAX 615/552–1182; $35) lists people and organizations who help travelers with disabilities. For travel agents worldwide, consult the **Directory of Travel Agencies for the Disabled** (✉ Twin Peaks Press, Box 129, Vancouver, WA 98666, ☎ 360/694–2462 or 800/637–2256, FAX 360/696–3210; $19.95 plus $3 shipping).

TRAVEL AGENCIES & TOUR OPERATORS

The Americans with Disabilities Act requires that all travel firms serve the needs of all travelers. That said, you should note that some agencies and operators specialize in making travel arrangements for individuals and groups with disabilities, among them **Access Adventures** (✉ 206 Chestnut Ridge Rd., Rochester, NY 14624, ☎ 716/889–9096), run by a former physical-rehab counselor.

TRAVELERS WITH MOBILITY PROBLEMS➤ Contact **Flying Wheels Travel** (✉ 143 W. Bridge St., Box 382, Owatonna, MN 55060, ☎ 507/451–5005 or 800/535–6790), a travel agency specializing in European cruises and tours; **Hinsdale Travel Service** (✉ 201 E. Ogden Ave., Suite 100, Hinsdale, IL 60521, ☎ 630/325–1335), a travel agency that benefits from the advice of wheelchair traveler Janice Perkins; and **Wheelchair Journeys** (✉ 16979 Redmond Way, Redmond, WA 98052, ☎ 206/

885–2210 or 800/313–4751), which can handle arrangements worldwide.

TRAVELERS WITH DEVELOPMENTAL DISABILITIES➤ Contact the nonprofit **New Directions** (✉ 5276 Hollister Ave., Suite 207, Santa Barbara, CA 93111, ☎ 805/967–2841).

TRAVEL GEAR

The **Magellan's** catalog (☎ 800/962–4943, FAX 805/568–5406), includes a section devoted to products designed for travelers with disabilities.

DISCOUNTS & DEALS

AIRFARES

For the lowest airfares to Moscow, St. Petersburg, and Kiev, call 800/FLY–4–LESS.

CLUBS

Contact **Entertainment Travel Editions** (✉ Box 1068, Trumbull, CT 06611, ☎ 800/445–4137; $28–$53, depending on destination), **Great American Traveler** (✉ Box 27965, Salt Lake City, UT 84127, ☎ 800/548–2812; $49.95 per year), **Moment's Notice Discount Travel Club** (✉ 7301 New Utrecht Ave., Brooklyn, NY 11204, ☎ 718/234–6295; $25 per year, single or family), **Privilege Card International** (✉ 3391 Peachtree Rd. NE, Suite 110, Atlanta, GA 30326, ☎ 404/262–0222 or 800/236–9732; $74.95 per year), **Travelers Advantage** (✉ CUC Travel Service, 49 Music Sq. W, Nashville, TN 37203, ☎ 800/548–1116 or 800/648–

4037; $49 per year, single or family), or **Worldwide Discount Travel Club** (✉ 1674 Meridian Ave., Miami Beach, FL 33139, ☎ 305/534–2082; $50 per year for family, $40 single).

PUBLICATIONS

Consult *The Frugal Globetrotter,* by Bruce Northam (✉ Fulcrum Publishing, 350 Indiana St., Suite 350, Golden, CO 80401, ☎ 800/992–2908; $16.95 plus $4 shipping). For publications that tell how to find the lowest prices on plane tickets, *see* Air Travel, *above.*

STUDENTS

Members of Hostelling International–American Youth Hostels (☞ Students, *below*) are eligible for discounts on car rentals, admissions to attractions, and other selected travel expenses.

G
GAY & LESBIAN
TRAVEL

ORGANIZATIONS

The **International Gay Travel Association** (✉ Box 4974, Key West, FL 33041, ☎ 800/448–8550, FAX 305/296–6633), a consortium of more than 1,000 travel companies, can supply names of gay-friendly travel agents, tour operators, and accommodations.

Two organizations in Moscow serve as clearing houses for information about gay life in Russia: the **International Gay and Lesbian Human Rights Commission** (21/15 Bolshevistskaya

ul., ☎ 252–3316) and the **Rainbow Foundation** (4 Malomoskovskaya ul., ☎ 489–2543).

PUBLICATIONS

The 16-page monthly newsletter **"Out & About"** (✉ 8 W. 19th St., Suite 401, New York, NY 10011, ☎ 212/645–6922 or 800/929–2268, FAX 800/929–2215; $49 for 10 issues and quarterly calendar) covers gay-friendly resorts, hotels, cruise lines, and airlines.

TOUR OPERATORS

Toto Tours (✉ 1326 W. Albion Ave., Suite 3W, Chicago, IL 60626, ☎ 773/274–8686 or 800/565–1241, FAX 773/274–8695) offers group tours to worldwide destinations.

TRAVEL AGENCIES

The largest agencies serving gay travelers are **Advance Travel** (✉ 10700 Northwest Fwy., Suite 160, Houston, TX 77092, ☎ 713/682–2002 or 800/292–0500), **Club Travel** (✉ 8739 Santa Monica Blvd., W. Hollywood, CA 90069, ☎ 310/358–2200 or 800/429–8747), **Islanders/Kennedy Travel** (✉ 183 W. 10th St., New York, NY 10014, ☎ 212/242–3222 or 800/988–1181), **Now Voyager** (✉ 4406 18th St., San Francisco, CA 94114, ☎ 415/626–1169 or 800/255–6951), and **Yellowbrick Road** (✉ 1500 W. Balmoral Ave., Chicago, IL 60640, ☎ 773/561–1800 or 800/642–2488). **Skylink Women's Travel** (✉ 2460 W. 3rd St., Suite 215, Santa Rosa, CA 95401, ☎ 707/

570–0105 or 800/225–5759) serves lesbian travelers.

H
HEALTH

FINDING A DOCTOR

For its members, the **International Association for Medical Assistance to Travellers** (✉ IAMAT, membership free; 417 Center St., Lewiston, NY 14092, ☎ 716/754–4883; 40 Regal Rd., Guelph, Ontario N1K 1B5, ☎ 519/836–0102; 1287 St. Clair Ave. W., Toronto, Ontario M6E 1B8, ☎ 416/652–0137; 57 Voirets, 1212 Grand-Lancy, Geneva, Switzerland, no phone) publishes a worldwide directory of English-speaking physicians meeting IAMAT standards.

MEDICAL ASSISTANCE COMPANIES

The following companies are concerned primarily with emergency medical assistance, although they may provide some insurance as part of their coverage. For a list of full-service travel insurance companies, *see* Insurance, *below.*

Contact **International SOS Assistance** (✉ Box 11568, Philadelphia, PA 19116, ☎ 215/244–1500 or 800/523–8930; Box 466, Pl. Bonaventure, Montréal, Québec H5A 1C1, ☎ 514/874–7674 or 800/363–0263; 7 Old Lodge Pl., St. Margarets, Twickenham TW1 1RQ, England, ☎ 0181/744–0033), **Medex Assistance**

THE GOLD GUIDE / IMPORTANT CONTACTS

THE GOLD GUIDE / IMPORTANT CONTACTS

Corporation (✉ Box 5375, Timonium, MD 21094, ☎ 410/453–6300 or 800/537–2029), **Near Travel Services** (✉ Box 1339, Calumet City, IL 60409, ☎ 708/868–6700 or 800/654–6700), **Traveler's Emergency Network** (✉ 1133 15th St. NW, Suite 400, Washington DC, 20005, ☎ 202/828–5894 or 800/275–4836, FAX 202/828–5896), **TravMed** (✉ Box 5375, Timonium, MD 21094, ☎ 410/453–6380 or 800/732–5309), or **Worldwide Assistance Services** (✉ 1133 15th St. NW, Suite 400, Washington, DC 20005, ☎ 202/331–1609 or 800/821–2828, FAX 202/828–5896).

PUBLICATIONS

The Safe Travel Book, by Peter Savage (✉ Jossey-Bass Publishers, Inc., 350 Sansome St., San Francisco, CA 94104 ☎ 800/956–7739, FAX 800/605–2665; $12.95 plus $5 shipping) is authoritative.

WARNINGS

The hot line of the **National Centers for Disease Control** (✉ CDC, National Center for Infectious Diseases, Division of Quarantine, Traveler's Health Section, 1600 Clifton Rd., M/S E-03, Atlanta, GA 30333, ☎ 404/332–4559, FAX 404/332–4565) provides information on health risks abroad and vaccination requirements and recommendations. You can call for an automated menu of recorded information or use the fax-back service to request printed matter.

I
INSURANCE

IN CANADA

Contact **Mutual of Omaha** (✉ Travel Division, 500 University Ave., Toronto, Ontario M5G 1V8, ☎ 800/465–0267(in Canada) or 416/598-4083).

IN THE U.S.

Travel insurance covering baggage, health, and trip cancellation or interruptions is available from **Access America** (✉ 6600 W. Broad St., Richmond, VA 23230, ☎ 804/285–3300 or 800/334–7525), **Carefree Travel Insurance** (✉ Box 9366, 100 Garden City Plaza, Garden City, NY 11530, ☎ 516/294–0220 or 800/323–3149), **Tele-Trip** (✉ Mutual of Omaha Plaza, Box 31716, Omaha, NE 68131, ☎ 800/228–9792), **Travel Guard International** (✉ 1145 Clark St., Stevens Point, WI 54481, ☎ 715/345–0505 or 800/826–1300), **Travel Insured International** (✉ Box 280568, East Hartford, CT 06128, ☎ 203/528–7663 or 800/243–3174), and **Wallach & Company** (✉ 107 W. Federal St., Box 480, Middleburg, VA 22117, ☎ 540/687–3166 or 800/237–6615).

IN THE U.K.

The **Association of British Insurers** (✉ 51 Gresham St., London EC2V 7HQ, ☎ 0171/600–3333) gives advice by phone and publishes the free pamphlet **"Holiday Insurance and Motoring Abroad,"** which sets out typical policy provisions and costs.

L
LODGING

HOME EXCHANGE

One clearinghouse is **Loan-a-Home** (✉ 2 Park La., Apt. 6E, Mount Vernon, NY 10552, ☎ 914/664–7640; $40–$50 per year), which specializes in long-term exchanges.

M
MONEY

ATMS

For specific foreign **Cirrus** locations, call 800/424–7787; for foreign **Plus** locations, consult the Plus directory at your local bank.

CURRENCY EXCHANGE

If your bank doesn't exchange currency, contact **Thomas Cook Currency Services** (☎ 800/287–7362 for locations). **Ruesch International** (☎ 800/424–2923 for locations) can also provide you with foreign banknotes before you leave home and publishes a number of useful brochures, including a "Foreign Currency Guide" and "Foreign Exchange Tips."

WIRING FUNDS

Funds can be wired via **MoneyGram**[SM] (for locations and information in the U.S. and Canada, ☎ 800/926–9400) or **Western Union** (for agent locations or to send money using MasterCard or Visa, ☎ 800/325–6000; in Canada, 800/321–2923; in the U.K., 0800/833833; or visit the Western Union office at the nearest major post office).

P

PACKING

For strategies on packing light, get a copy of *The Packing Book,* by Judith Gilford (✉ Ten Speed Press, Box 7123, Berkeley, CA 94707, ☎ 510/559–1600 or 800/841–2665, FAX 510/524–4588; $7.95 plus $3.50 shipping).

PASSPORTS & VISAS

U.S. CITIZENS

For fees, documentation requirements, and other information, call the State Department's **Office of Passport Services** information line (☎ 202/647–0518).

For visa applications, contact the **Russian Consulate General** (11 E. 91st St., New York, NY 10128, ☎ 212/348–0926 or 800/634–4296) and the **Ukrainian Consulate** (3350 M St., NW Washington, D.C. 20007, ☎ 202/333–7507) for more information.

CANADIANS

For fees, documentation requirements, and other information, call the Ministry of Foreign Affairs and International Trade's **Passport Office** (☎ 819/994–3500 or 800/567–6868).

For visa applications, contact the **Russian Consulate General** (3655 Avenue du Musée, Montréal, Québec, H3G 2E1, ☎ 514/843–5901) and the **Ukrainian Consulate** in Ottawa (☎ 613/230–8015 or 613/235–8214).

U.K. CITIZENS

For fees, documentation requirements, and to request an emergency passport, call the **London Passport Office** (☎ 0990/210410).

For visa applications, contact the **Russian Consulate General** (Kensington Palace Gardens 5, London W8, ☎ 0171/229–32–15) and the **Ukrainian Consulate** (☎ 0171/727–6312).

PHOTO HELP

The **Kodak Information Center** (☎ 800/242–2424) answers consumer questions about film and photography. The *Kodak Guide to Shooting Great Travel Pictures* (available in bookstores; or contact Fodor's Travel Publications, ☎ 800/533–6478; $16.50 plus $4 shipping) explains how to take expert travel photographs.

S

SAFETY

"**Trouble-Free Travel,**" from the AAA, is a booklet of tips for protecting yourself and your belongings when away from home. Send a stamped, self-addressed, legal-size envelope to Trouble-Free Travel (✉ Mail Stop 75, 1000 AAA Dr., Heathrow, FL 32746).

SENIOR CITIZENS

EDUCATIONAL TRAVEL

The nonprofit **Elderhostel** (✉ 75 Federal St., 3rd Floor, Boston, MA 02110, ☎ 617/426–7788), for people 55 and older, has offered inexpensive study programs since 1975.

Courses cover everything from marine science to Greek mythology and cowboy poetry. Costs for two- to three-week international trips—including room, board, and transportation from the United States—range from $1,800 to $4,500.

ORGANIZATIONS

Contact the **American Association of Retired Persons** (✉ AARP, 601 E St. NW, Washington, DC 20049, ☎ 202/434–2277; annual dues $8 per person or couple). Its Purchase Privilege Program secures discounts for members on lodging, car rentals, and sightseeing.

STUDENTS

HOSTELING

In the United States, contact **Hostelling International–American Youth Hostels** (✉ 733 15th St. NW, Suite 840, Washington, DC 20005, ☎ 202/783–6161, FAX 202/783–6171); in Canada, **Hostelling International–Canada** (✉ 205 Catherine St., Suite 400, Ottawa, Ontario K2P 1C3, ☎ 613/237–7884); and in the United Kingdom, the **Youth Hostel Association of England and Wales** (✉ Trevelyan House, 8 St. Stephen's Hill, St. Albans, Hertfordshire AL1 2DY, ☎ 01727/855215 or 01727/845047). Membership (in the U.S., $25; in Canada, C$26.75; in the U.K., £9.30) gives you access to 5,000 hostels in 77 countries that charge $5–$40 per person per night.

ORGANIZATIONS

A major contact is the **Council on International**

THE GOLD GUIDE / IMPORTANT CONTACTS

Educational Exchange (✉ mail orders only: CIEE, 205 E. 42nd St., 16th Floor, New York, NY 10017, ☎ 212/822–2600, FAX 212/822–2699, info@ciee.org). The **Educational Travel Centre** (✉ 438 N. Frances St., Madison, WI 53703, ☎ 608/256–5551 or 800/747–5551, FAX 608/256–2042) offers rail passes and low-cost airline tickets, mostly for flights that depart from Chicago.

In Canada, also contact **Travel Cuts** (✉ 187 College St., Toronto, Ontario M5T 1P7, ☎ 416/979–2406 or 800/667–2887).

T

TELEPHONES

The country code for Russia is 7; for Ukraine, 380. For local access numbers abroad, contact **AT&T** USADirect (☎ 800/874–4000), **MCI** Call USA (☎ 800/444–4444), or **Sprint** Express (☎ 800/793–1153).

TOUR OPERATORS

Among the companies that sell tours and packages to Moscow, St. Petersburg, and Kiev, the following are nationally known, have a proven reputation, and offer plenty of options.

GROUP TOURS

SUPER-DELUXE➤ **Abercrombie & Kent** (✉ 1520 Kensington Rd., Oak Brook, IL 60521-2141, ☎ 708/954–2944 or 800/323–7308, FAX 708/954–3324) and **Travcoa** (✉ Box 2630, 2350 S.E. Bristol St., Newport Beach, CA 92660, ☎ 714/476–

2800 or 800/992–2003, FAX 714/476–2538).

DELUXE➤ **Globus** (✉ 5301 S. Federal Circle, Littleton, CO 80123, ☎ 303/797–2800 or 800/221–0090, FAX 303/795–0962) and **Maupintour** (✉ Box 807, 1515 St. Andrews Dr., Lawrence KS 66047, ☎ 913/843–1211 or 800/255–4266, FAX 913/843–8351).

FIRST-CLASS➤ **Collette Tours** (✉ 162 Middle St., Pawtucket, RI 02860, ☎ 401/728–3805 or 800/832–4656, FAX 401/728–1380), **Delta Dream Vacations** (☎ 800/872–7786), **General Tours** (✉ 53 Summer St., Keene, NH 03431, ☎ 603/357–5033 or 800/221–2216, FAX 603/357–4548), **Isram World of Travel** (✉ 630 Third Ave., New York, NY 10017, ☎ 212/661–1193 or 800/223–7460), **Rahim Tours** (✉ 12 S. Dixie Hwy., Lake Worth, FL 33460, ☎ 407/585–5305 or 800/556–5305), **Russian Travel Bureau** (✉ 225 E. 44th St., New York, NY 10017, ☎ 212/986–1500 or 800/847–1800), **Trafalgar Tours** (✉ 11 E. 26th St., New York, NY 10010, ☎ 212/689–8977 or 800/854–0103, FAX 800/457–6644), and **Uniworld** (✉ 16000 Ventura Blvd., #200, Encino, CA 91436, ☎ 818/382–7820 or 800/733–7820).

BUDGET➤ **Cosmos** (☞ Globus, *above*) and **Trafalgar** (☞ Group Tours, *above*).

ORGANIZATIONS

The **National Tour Association** (✉ NTA,

546 E. Main St., Lexington, KY 40508, ☎ 606/226–4444 or 800/755–8687) and the **United States Tour Operators Association** (✉ USTOA, 211 E. 51st St., Suite 12B, New York, NY 10022, ☎ 212/750–7371) can provide lists of members and information on booking tours.

PACKAGES

Independent vacation packages are available from major tour operators and airlines. Contact **Abercrombie & Kent** (☞ Group Tours, *above*), **General Tours** (☞ Group Tours, *above*), **Five Star Touring** (✉ 60 E. 42nd St., New York, NY 10165, ☎ 212/818–9140 or 800/792–7827, FAX 212/818–9142), **ITS Tours & Travel** (✉ 1055 Texas Ave., #104, College Station, TX 77840, ☎ 409/764–9400 or 800/533–8688), **MIR Corp.** (✉ 85 South Washington, #210, Seattle, WA 98104, ☎ 206/624–7289 or 800/424–7289), **Rahim Tours** (☞ Group Tours, *above*), and **Russian Travel Bureau** (☞ Group Tours, *above*).

New Solutions (✉ 912 S. Juanita Ave., Redondo Beach, CA 90277, ☎ 800/768–9535) specializes in custom-designed tours with a religious, historical, academic, or genealogical theme.

PUBLICATIONS

Contact the USTOA (☞ Organizations, *above*) for its **"Smart Traveler's Planning Kit."** Pamphlets in the kit include the "Worldwide Tour and Vacation Package Finder," "How to Select a Tour or Vacation Package," and information on the organization's consumer protection plan. Also get a copy of the Better Business Bureau's **"Tips on Travel Packages"** (✉ Publication 24-195, 4200 Wilson Blvd., Arlington, VA 22203; $2).

THEME TRIPS

ART➤ For tours of Moscow and St. Petersburg's art and architecture, look into **Esplanade Tours** (✉ 581 Boylston St., Boston, MA 02116, ☎ 617/266–7465 or 800/426–5492, FAX 617/262–9829), **Five Star Touring** (☞ Group Tours, *above*), and **Russian Travel Bureau** (☞ Group Tours, *above*).

CRUISES➤ For a cruise on the Volga River between Moscow and St. Petersburg, contact the group-tour operators listed above. Also contact **EuroCruises** (✉ 303 W. 13th St., New York, NY 10014, ☎ 212/691–2099 or 800/688–3876), which represents more than 20 European-based cruise lines and 60 ships, ranging from 32-passenger yachts to 2,500-passenger ocean liners.

HOME STAYS➤ To stay with a Russian or Ukrainian family in Moscow and St. Petersburg, contact **American-International Homestays** (✉ Box 1754, Nederland, CO 80466, ☎ 303/642–3088 or 800/876–2048, FAX 303/642–3365).

MUSIC➤ For packages that include tickets to the ballet, opera, and classical concerts, call **Dailey-Thorp Travel** (✉ 330 W. 58th St., #610, New York, NY 10019-1817, ☎ 212/307–1555 or 800/998–4677, FAX 212/974–1420).

RAIL➤ **Abercrombie & Kent** (☞ Group Tours, *above*) can arrange excursions aboard a five-passenger private railcar, the Anna Karenina, between Moscow and St. Petersburg. Sumptuous meals, champagne, and personal attendants are part of the ride. These rail trips must be combined with a longer A&K tour or package.

TRAVEL GEAR

For travel apparel, appliances, personal-care items, and other travel necessities, get a free catalog from **Magellan's** (☎ 800/962–4943, FAX 805/568–5406), **Orvis Travel** (☎ 800/541–3541, FAX 540/343–7053), or **TravelSmith** (☎ 800/950–1600, FAX 415/455–0554).

ELECTRICAL CONVERTERS

Send a self-addressed, stamped envelope to the **Franzus Company** (✉ Customer Service, Dept. B50, Murtha Industrial Park, Box 142, Beacon Falls, CT 06403, ☎ 203/723–6664) for a copy of the free brochure "Foreign Electricity Is No Deep, Dark Secret."

TRAVEL AGENCIES

For names of reputable agencies in your area, contact the **American Society of Travel Agents** (✉ ASTA, 1101 King St., Suite 200, Alexandria, VA 22314, ☎ 703/739–2782), the **Association of Canadian Travel Agents** (✉ Suite 201, 1729 Bank St., Ottawa, Ontario K1V 7Z5, ☎ 613/521–0474, FAX 613/521–0805), or the **Association of British Travel Agents** (✉ 55-57 Newman St., London W1P 4AH, ☎ 0171/637–2444, FAX 0171/637–0713).

U

U.S.
GOVERNMENT
TRAVEL BRIEFINGS

The U.S. Department of State's American Citizens Services office (✉ Room 4811, Washington, DC 20520; enclose SASE) issues **Consular Information Sheets** on all foreign countries. These cover issues such as crime, security, political climate, and health risks as well as listing embassy locations, entry requirements, currency regulations, and providing other useful information. For the latest information, stop in at any U.S. passport office, consulate, or embassy; call the interactive hot line (☎ 202/647–5225, FAX 202/647–3000); or, with your PC's modem, tap into the department's computer bulletin board (☎ 202/647–9225).

V

VISITOR
INFORMATION

Intourist-USA, Inc. (✉ 620 5th Ave., Suite 868, New York, NY 10111, ☎ 212/757–3884) can provide information about traveling in Russia and assist with some travel arrangements. The **Russian Consulate General** (⊠ 11 E. 91st St., New York, NY, ☎ 212/348–0926; in Canada, 3655 Ave. du Musée, Montréal, Québec H3G 2E1, ☎ 514/843–5901; in the U.K., ⊠ 5 Kensington Palace Gardens, London W8, ☎ 0171/229–8027) can also provide some assistance with travel plans. For information about Kiev, contact the **Ukrainian Consulate** (⊠ 3350 M St., NW, Washington, D.C. 20007, ☎ 202/333–7507; in Canada, ⊠ 331 Metcalfe St., Ottawa, Ontario K2P 1S3, ☎ 613/230–8015 or 613/235–8214).

W
WEATHER

For current conditions and forecasts, plus the local time and helpful travel tips, call the **Weather Channel Connection** (☎ 900/932–8437; 95¢ per minute) from a Touch-Tone phone.

The *International Traveler's Weather Guide* (⊠ Weather Press, Box 660606, Sacramento, CA 95866, ☎ 916/974–0201 or 800/972–0201; $10.95 includes shipping), written by two meteorologists, provides month-by-month information on temperature, humidity, and precipitation in more than 175 cities worldwide.

SMART TRAVEL TIPS A TO Z

Basic Information on Traveling in Moscow, St. Petersburg, and Kiev and Savvy Tips to Make Your Trip a Breeze

A

AIR TRAVEL

Nonstop flights from the United States are available only to Moscow, originating in New York or Los Angeles. To St. Petersburg and Kiev, either a direct flight, which requires at least one stop, or a connecting flight, which requires a change of airplanes, will be your only choice. Some flights, especially nonstops, may be scheduled only on certain days of the week. Depending upon your destination and originating city, you may need to make more than one connection. Your best bet is to **use Helsinki for the greatest number of connecting flights.** Helsinki is less than an hour from St. Petersburg and less than two hours from Moscow or Kiev.

CUTTING COSTS

Shop around, since you never know who may have the best deal. Make sure to call the airlines directly, get price quotes from a travel agent or tour operator who is experienced in booking travel to Moscow, St. Petersburg, and Kiev, and contact a few consolidators. The Sunday travel section of most newspapers is a good place to look for deals.

MAJOR AIRLINES

Major airlines usually require that you **book 14–21 days in advance and stay at least seven days**—and no more than 30—to get the lowest fares. These fares generally allow no stopovers en route and are nonrefundable. Airlines generally allow you to change your return date for a $150 fee. If you don't use your ticket, you can apply the cost toward the purchase of a new ticket—but at a higher fare. If you plan to stay longer than 30 days, fares are a little more costly—about $100–$200 per round-trip, but you may be allowed one or two stopovers. These higher-fare tickets are usually refundable, minus a fee of $150 in most cases. Before you book, **call a number of airlines** and **check different routings.**

FROM THE U.K.➤ To save money on flights, **look into an APEX or Super-Pex ticket.** APEX tickets must be booked in advance and have certain restrictions. Super-PEX tickets can be purchased right at the airport.

CONSOLIDATORS

Consolidators buy tickets for scheduled flights at reduced rates from the airlines, then sell them at prices below the lowest available from the airlines directly—usually without advance restrictions. Sometimes you can even get your money back if you need to return the ticket, although you usually have to pay a refund fee of $150–$200. Carefully read the fine print detailing penalties for changes and cancellations. If you doubt the reliability of a consolidator, **confirm your reservation with the airline.**

ALOFT

AIRLINE FOOD➤ If you hate airline food, **ask for special meals when booking.** These can be vegetarian, low-cholesterol, or kosher, for example; commonly prepared to order in smaller quantities than standard fare, they can be tastier.

JET LAG➤ To avoid this syndrome, which occurs when travel disrupts your body's natural cycles, try to maintain a normal routine. At night, **get some sleep.** By day, move about the cabin to **stretch your legs, eat light meals, and drink water—not alcohol.**

SMOKING➤ Smoking is not allowed on flights of six hours or less within the continental United States. Smoking is also prohibited on flights within Canada. For U.S. flights longer than six hours or international flights, **contact your carrier regarding their smoking policy.** Some carriers have prohibited smoking throughout their system; others allow smoking only on certain routes or even certain departures of that route.

WITHIN EUROPE

If you plan to make more than one stopover on your way to or from Moscow, St. Petersburg, or Kiev, **look for a "European Multi-Coupon Airpass,"** which is good for discounted flights between points within Europe, including Russia and Ukraine. Each flight generally costs $99–$175, depending on the season and length of the flight. Often, you can use the pass on more than one airline within Europe. Some passes require that your transatlantic carrier be one of the participating carriers, but not all—so ask.

Single-coupon discounted flights may also be available to travelers with an international air ticket. You can purchase these in the United States or in Europe. However, it's best to **compare the cost of a single ticket versus multiple tickets before leaving home.** Sometimes, a single fare that includes all stopovers is the better deal.

WITHIN RUSSIA AND UKRAINE

The airline industry in the former Soviet Union is in a state of flux. Aeroflot, once the Soviet Union's only airline, is now being given a run for its money by a new company called Transaero, which flies to all the major destinations within Russia and the CIS (as well as to major cities in Western Europe). Flying only Boeing aircraft (as opposed to Russian-made Ilyushin planes) and reportedly refusing to hire anyone who previously worked for Aeroflot, Transaero is establishing new standards for safety and service on flights within the old Soviet territory. Most of Aeroflot's domestic routes use the same outdated aircraft and offer the same abominable service that the airline has long been famous for; its international flights, however, are today considered to be on a par with those offered by major Western carriers.

Since the collapse of the Soviet Union, many routes have been abandoned, smaller airports have been closed permanently, and the scheduled flights that remain are often canceled due to fuel shortages. Because of unpredictable service, many tour operators are now chartering flights for their groups. Seasoned business travelers frequently choose to fly circuitous routes on international carriers (i.e., Moscow–Helsinki–Kiev), which often proves faster and certainly more reliable than flying direct on Aeroflot.

If you are flying as an independent traveler within the CIS, it's best to **purchase your ticket in hard currency before you leave home.** Foreigners are not always allowed to fly on tickets purchased in rubles, though this may be changing; hard-currency tickets are available in-country and this is now easier to do than it was a few years ago. Be forewarned, however, that delays and outright cancellations are common, and you should **reconfirm your booking in person as soon as you arrive in the country.**

On the day of your departure, **get to the airport early to avoid being bumped.** Bring some snacks and beverages with you—after a meal on Aeroflot, Western airline food will seem gourmet. On flights shorter than four hours the only refreshment served is vile-tasting mineral water. Planes are usually boarded with no regard for assigned seats; passengers either take a bus or walk en masse across the runway to their waiting plane and then push and shove their way aboard. If you are traveling with a group of foreign tourists, you may be granted the courtesy of boarding ahead of the Russian passengers. If you are traveling independently, it is likely that you will be completely ignored and left to your own defenses. If you encounter any difficulties, assert your rights and make it clear to everyone that you paid for your ticket in hard currency.

The rules regulating carry-on luggage are strict but often disregarded. Since checked luggage is frequently lost and/or pilfered, **pack as much as you can in your carry-on,** including all of your valuables. Many airports have a special section set aside for foreign travelers, a holdover from the days when foreigners received preferential treatment by Soviet authorities. These sections are usually more comfortable and often have a hard-currency shop or café where you can buy snacks and refreshments.

B
BUSINESS HOURS

State banks are usually open 9:30–2; some of the new private banks have slightly longer hours. Private exchange offices and those in hotels are usually open 9–6 daily, with an hour break for lunch between 1 and 3 PM. Museums keep varying hours; many are closed on Mondays and Tuesdays. Last entry is usually an hour before closing time, and museums often close an hour earlier the day before their closed day. Stores likewise keep varying hours, with grocery stores normally opening at 8 or 9 AM and department stores opening at 11 AM. Closing times also vary; stores are rarely open past 8 or 9 PM. Many shops are closed on Sunday, and almost every store closes for an hour at lunchtime between 1 and 3 PM. Restaurants usually open around noon and often close by midnight, although many are staying open until 2 AM and even later these days. Many restaurants, especially those that are state-run, close for a "dinner" break somewhere between 4 and 6 PM.

C
CAMERAS, CAMCORDERS, & COMPUTERS

IN TRANSIT

Always **keep your film, tape, or disks out of the sun;** never put these on the dashboard of a car. Carry an extra supply of batteries, and **be prepared to turn on your camera, camcorder, or laptop computer for security personnel** to prove that it's real.

X-RAYS

Always **ask for hand inspection at security.** Such requests are virtually always honored at U.S. airports, and are usually accommodated abroad. Photographic film becomes clouded after successive exposure to airport x-ray machines. Videotape and computer disks are not harmed by X-rays, but **keep your tapes and disks away from metal detectors.**

CUSTOMS

Before departing, **register your foreign-made camera or laptop with U.S. Customs.** If your equipment is U.S.-made, call the consulate of the country you'll be visiting to find out whether it should be registered with local customs upon arrival.

CAR RENTAL

CUTTING COSTS

To get the best deal, **book through a travel agent who is willing to shop around.** Ask your agent to **look for fly-drive packages,** which also save you money, and **ask if local taxes are included** in the rental

or fly-drive price. These can be as high as 20% in some destinations. Don't forget to find out about required deposits, cancellation penalties, drop-off charges, and the cost of any required insurance coverage.

Also **ask your travel agent about a company's customer-service record.** How has it responded to late plane arrivals and vehicle mishaps? Are there often lines at the rental counter, and—if you're traveling during a holiday period—does a confirmed reservation guarantee you a car?

Always **find out what equipment is standard** at your destination before specifying what you want; automatic transmission and air-conditioning are usually optional—and very expensive.

INSURANCE

When driving a rented car, you are generally responsible for any damage to or loss of the rental vehicle, as well as any property damage or personal injury that you cause. Before you rent, **see what coverage you already have** under the terms of your personal auto insurance policy and credit cards.

If you do not have auto insurance or an umbrella insurance policy that covers damage to third parties, purchasing CDW or LDW is highly recommended.

LICENSE REQUIREMENTS

In Russia and Ukraine your own driver's license is not acceptable. An International Driver's Permit is necessary; it's available from the American or Canadian automobile associations, or, in the United Kingdom, from the AA or RAC.

SURCHARGES

Before you pick up a car in one city and leave it in another, **ask about drop-off charges or one-way service fees,** which can be substantial. Note, too, that some rental agencies charge extra if you return the car before the time specified on your contract. To avoid a hefty refueling fee, **fill the tank just before you turn in the car**—but be aware that gas stations near the rental outlet may overcharge.

CHILDREN & TRAVEL

When traveling with children, **plan ahead** and **involve your youngsters** as you outline your trip. When packing, **include a supply of things to keep them busy** en route (☞ Children & Travel *in* Important Contacts A to Z). On sightseeing days, try to **schedule activities of special interest to your children,** like a trip to a zoo or a playground. If you **plan your itinerary around seasonal festivals,** you'll never lack for things to do. In addition, **check local newspapers for special events** mounted by public libraries, museums, and parks.

BABY-SITTING

For recommended local sitters, **check with your hotel desk.**

DRIVING

If you are renting a car, don't forget to **arrange for a car seat when you reserve.** Sometimes they're free.

FLYING

As a general rule, infants under two not occupying a seat fly at greatly reduced fares and occasionally for free. If your children are two or older **ask about special children's fares.** Age limits for these fares vary among carriers. Rules also vary regarding unaccompanied minors, so again, check with your airline.

BAGGAGE➤ In general, the adult baggage allowance applies to children paying half or more of the adult fare. If you are traveling with an infant, **ask about carry-on allowances** before departure. In general, for infants charged 10% of the adult fare you are allowed one carry-on bag and a collapsible stroller, which may have to be checked; you may be limited to less if the flight is full.

SAFETY SEATS➤ According to the FAA, it's a good idea to **use safety seats aloft** for children weighing less than 40 pounds. Airline policies vary. U.S. carriers allow FAA-approved models but usually require that you buy a ticket, even if your child would otherwise ride free, since the seats must be strapped into regular seats. However, some U.S. and foreign-flag airlines may require you to hold your baby during takeoff and landing—defeating the seat's purpose. Other foreign carriers may not allow infant seats at all, or may charge a child rather than an infant fare for their use.

FACILITIES➤ When making your reservation, **request for children's meals or freestanding bassinets** if you need them; the latter are available only to those seated at the bulkhead, where there's enough legroom. If you don't need a bassinet, **think twice before requesting bulkhead seats**—the only storage space for in-flight necessities is in inconveniently distant overhead bins.

GAMES

Milton Bradley and Parker Brothers have travel versions of some of their most popular games, including Yahtzee, Trouble, Sorry, and Monopoly. Prices run $5 to $8. Look for them in the travel section of your local toy store.

LODGING

Most hotels allow children under a certain age to stay in their parents' room at no extra charge; others charge them as extra adults. Be sure to **ask about the cutoff age.**

CUSTOMS & DUTIES

To speed your clearance through customs, **keep receipts for all your purchases abroad** and **be ready to show the inspector what you've bought.** If you feel that you've been incorrectly or unfairly charged a duty, you can **appeal assessments in dispute.** First ask to see a supervisor. If you are still unsatisfied, **write to the port director** at your point of entry, sending your customs receipt and any other appropriate documentation. The address will be listed on your receipt. If you still don't get satisfaction, you can take your case to customs headquarters in Washington.

ON ARRIVAL

Upon arrival, you first pass through passport control, where a border guard will carefully examine your passport and visa, and retain one sheet of your Russian visa. The procedure in Ukraine is similar, except that the Ukrainian visa is actually stamped in your passport.

After retrieving your luggage, you fill out a customs form that you must keep until departure, when you will be asked to present it again. You may import free of duty and without special license any articles intended for personal use, including clothing, food, tobacco and cigarettes, alcoholic drinks, perfume, sports equipment, and camera. One video camera and one laptop computer per person are allowed. Importing weapons and ammunition, as well as opium, hashish, and pipes for smoking them, is prohibited. The punishment for carrying illegal substances is severe. You should write down on the customs form the exact amount of currency you are carrying (in cash as well as traveler's checks); you may enter the country with any amount of money, but you cannot leave the country with more money than you

had when you entered. You should also **include on your customs form any jewelry (particularly silver, gold, and amber) as well as any electronic goods (cameras, personal tape recorders, computers, etc.) you have.** It is important to include any valuable items on the form to ensure that you will be allowed to export them, but beware that you are expected to take them with you, so you cannot leave them behind as gifts. If an item included on your customs form is stolen, you should obtain a police report to avoid being questioned upon departure.

IN THE U.S.

You may bring home $400 worth of foreign goods duty-free if you've been out of the country for at least 48 hours and haven't already used the $400 allowance, or any part of it, in the past 30 days.

Travelers 21 or older may bring back 1 liter of alcohol duty-free, provided the beverage laws of the state through which they reenter the United States allow it. In addition, regardless of their age, they are allowed 100 non-Cuban cigars and 200 cigarettes. Antiques, which the U.S. Customs Service defines as objects more than 100 years old, are duty-free. Original works of art done entirely by hand are also duty-free. These include, but are not limited to, paintings, drawings, and sculptures.

Duty-free, travelers may mail packages valued at up to $200 to them-

selves and up to $100 to others, with a limit of one parcel per addressee per day (and no alcohol or tobacco products or perfume valued at more than $5); on the outside, the package must be labeled as being either for personal use or an unsolicited gift, and a list of its contents and their retail value must be attached. Mailed items do not affect your duty-free allowance on your return.

IN CANADA

If you've been out of Canada for at least seven days, you may bring in C$500 worth of goods duty-free. If you've been away for fewer than seven days but for more than 48 hours, the duty-free allowance drops to C$200; if your trip lasts between 24 and 48 hours, the allowance is C$50. You cannot pool allowances with family members. Goods claimed under the C$500 exemption may follow you by mail; those claimed under the lesser exemptions must accompany you.

Alcohol and tobacco products may be included in the seven-day and 48-hour exemptions but not in the 24-hour exemption. If you meet the age requirements of the province or territory through which you reenter Canada, you may bring in, duty-free, 1.14 liters (40 imperial ounces) of wine or liquor *or* 24 12-ounce cans or bottles of beer or ale. If you are 16 or older, you may bring in, duty-free, 200 cigarettes, 50 cigars or cigarillos, and 400 tobacco sticks or 400 grams of manufactured tobacco. Alcohol and tobacco must accompany you on your return.

An unlimited number of gifts with a value of up to C$60 each may be mailed to Canada duty-free. These do not affect your duty-free allowance on your return. Label the package "Unsolicited Gift—Value Under $60." Alcohol and tobacco are excluded.

IN THE U.K.

From countries outside the EU, including Russia and Ukraine, you may import, duty-free, 200 cigarettes, 100 cigarillos, 50 cigars, or 250 grams of tobacco; 1 liter of spirits or 2 liters of fortified or sparkling wine or liqueurs; 2 liters of still table wine; 60 milliliters of perfume; 250 milliliters of toilet water; plus £136 worth of other goods, including gifts and souvenirs.

D

DINING

IN HOTELS

If you are traveling on an organized tour, you can **expect your hotel meals to be hearty and ample but far from gourmet.** If you depend on coffee to wake you up in the morning, **bring a small jar of instant coffee with you;** sometimes only tea is available in the morning and sometimes hotel restaurants use "coffee-flavored drink" instead of genuine coffee.

EATING OUT

When you tire of the traditional hotel cuisine,

you can explore the many new private restaurants and joint-venture establishments that have recently opened in all three cities. You should always **make reservations in advance.** Even if the restaurant is half-empty, you may be refused a table if you don't have a reservation. Be prepared to **set aside an entire evening for your restaurant meal;** Russians and Ukrainians consider dining out to be a form of entertainment, and table turnover is virtually an unknown concept.

Drinks are normally ordered by grams (100 or 200) or by the bottle. An average bottle holds about three-quarters of a liter. In foreign-run establishments you will often find an impressive wine list with imported wine and foreign liquors, but the state-run restaurants and smaller cooperatives usually have only vodka and wine available. Georgian wine is excellent, although supplies have become limited (distribution has been disrupted by the ongoing ethnic strife in that country).

Getting a quick snack on the go is getting easier to do in all three cities. Though some of the old state-run cafés and *stolovayas* are still open, they're being steadily replaced by new chains of fast-food restaurants (Russian-, Ukrainian-, and foreign-owned) that offer a much more appetizing variety of sandwiches, snacks, light meals, and beverages at fairly inexpensive prices.

DISABILITIES & ACCESSIBILITY

Provisions for disabled travelers in Russia and Ukraine are extremely limited. Traveling with a nondisabled companion is probably the best solution. Some of the new, foreign-built hotels in Moscow offer wheelchair-accessible rooms, but beyond that special facilities at public buildings in all three cities are rare. Public transportation is especially difficult for the disabled traveler to maneuver.

When discussing accessibility with an operator or reservationist, **ask hard questions.** Are there any stairs, inside *or* out? Are there grab bars next to the toilet *and* in the shower/tub? How wide is the doorway to the room? To the bathroom? For the most extensive facilities, meeting the latest legal specifications, **opt for newer accommodations,** which more often have been designed with access in mind. Older properties or ships must usually be retrofitted and may offer more limited facilities as a result. Be sure to **discuss your needs before booking.**

DISCOUNTS & DEALS

You shouldn't have to pay for a discount. In fact, you may already be eligible for all kinds of savings. Here are some time-honored strategies for getting the best deal.

LOOK IN YOUR WALLET

When you **use your credit card to make**

travel purchases, you may get free travel-accident insurance, collision damage insurance, medical or legal assistance, depending on the card and bank that issued it. American Express, Visa, and MasterCard provide one or more of these services, so **get a copy of your card's travel benefits.** If you are a member of the AAA or an oil-company-sponsored road-assistance plan, always **ask hotel or car-rental reservationists for auto-club discounts.** Some clubs offer additional discounts on tours, cruises, or admission to attractions. And don't forget that auto-club membership entitles you to free maps and trip-planning services.

SENIOR CITIZENS & STUDENTS

As a senior-citizen traveler, you may be eligible for special rates, but you should mention your senior-citizen status up front. If you're a student or under 26 you can also get discounts, especially if you have an official ID card (☞ Senior-Citizen Discounts *and* Students on the Road, *below*).

DIAL FOR DOLLARS

To save money, **look into "1-800" discount reservations services,** which often have lower rates. These services use their buying power to get a better price on hotels, airline tickets, and sometimes even car rentals. When booking a room, always **call the hotel's local toll-free number** (if one is available) rather than the central reservations number—you'll often get a better price. Ask the reservationist about special packages or corporate rates, which are usually available even if you're not traveling on business.

JOIN A CLUB?

Discount clubs can be a legitimate source of savings, but you must use the participating hotels and visit the participating attractions in order to realize any benefits. Remember, too, that you have to pay a fee to join, so **determine if you'll save enough to warrant your membership fee.** Before booking with a club, **make sure the hotel or other supplier isn't offering a better deal.**

GET A GUARANTEE

When shopping for the best deal on hotels and car rentals, **look for guaranteed exchange rates,** which protect you against a falling dollar. With your rate locked in, you won't pay more even if the price goes up in the local currency.

DRIVING

Due to poor and sometimes even dangerous conditions, you should **avoid driving in Russia and Ukraine.** Even the main highways are potholed and in poor condition. Repair stations are few and far between, and there is a severe shortage of gasoline. In addition, you should not underestimate the risk of crime; highway robbery and car theft are on the rise, and foreign drivers are number-one targets. Russian drivers routinely remove their window blades, side mirrors, and anything else removable when parking their car for the evening, since theft of these items is common. Also, you should never **leave anything of value inside your car.**

GASOLINE & REPAIRS

The gasoline shortage in Russia, and especially in Ukraine, is severe. You should **fill up your tank at every opportunity.** In rubles, gasoline is very inexpensive, but you will have to wait in long lines; often drivers line up hours before an expected delivery of gasoline. In all three cities you can find foreign-currency gasoline stations, where lines are much shorter, but even these are not immune to the local shortages. It's also difficult to find unleaded gasoline. Finally, since repair stations are few and poorly stocked, tourists are advised to **bring a complete emergency repair kit,** including a set of tools, a towing cable, a pressure gauge, a pump, a spare wheel, a repair outfit for tubeless tires, a good jack and one or two tire levers, gasoline can, a spare fan belt, spare window-screen blades, and spark plugs. You should also have a set of lamp bulbs and fuses, a set of contact-breaker points for the ignition distributor, a spare condenser, a box of tire valve interiors, and a roll of insulating tape.

POLICE

Traffic control in Russia and Ukraine is exercised by traffic inspectors

(GAI) who are stationed at permanent posts; they also patrol in cars and on motorcycles. They may stop you for no apparent reason other than simply to check your documentation. Information on rules and road conditions can be obtained from them; they will also supply directions to motels, campsites, restaurants, and filling and service stations.

REQUIREMENTS

Tourists driving in Russia or Ukraine will need an international driver's license and an international certificate of registration of the car in the country of departure. You will also need a certificate of obligation promising to take the car out of the country, to be registered with customs at the point of entry.

RULES OF THE ROAD

Driving regulations are strict, but they are often broken by local drivers; a good rule of thumb is to **drive defensively.** Traffic keeps to the right. The speed limit on highways is 90 kph (56 mph); in towns and populated areas it is 60 kph (37 mph), although on the wide streets of Moscow few people observe this rule. You can proceed at traffic lights only when the light is green—this includes left and right turns. You must wait for a signal—an arrow—permitting the turn, and give way to pedestrians crossing. Wearing front seat belts is compulsory; driving while intoxicated carries very heavy fines,

including imprisonment. Do not consume any alcohol at all if you plan to drive. You should also **keep your car clean**—drivers can be fined for having a dirty car.

H
HEALTH

The Russian and Ukrainian medical systems are far below world standards. Anyone visiting these countries runs the risk of encountering the horrors of their medical facilities, and individuals in frail health and those who suffer from a chronic medical condition should take this risk into careful consideration. You may want to **purchase traveler's health insurance,** which would cover medical evacuation. Sometimes even minor conditions cannot be treated adequately in-country due to the severe and chronic shortage of basic medicines and medical equipment.

These warnings aside, as long as you don't get sick, a visit to Russia or Ukraine poses no special health risk. The U.S. government affirms that the fallout from the 1986 Chernobyl nuclear accident no longer poses any risk to either short- or long-term visitors to Kiev.

You should **drink only boiled or bottled water.** The water supply in St. Petersburg is thought to contain an intestinal parasite called Giardia Lamblia, which causes diarrhea, stomach cramps, and nausea. The gestation period is two–three weeks, so

that symptoms usually arise after the traveler has already returned home. The condition is easily treatable, but be sure to let your doctor know that you may have been exposed to this parasite. Avoid ice cubes and use bottled water to brush your teeth. In Moscow and St. Petersburg, imported, bottled water is freely available in hard-currency shops, but this is not always true in Kiev. You may want to **consider bringing a small supply of bottled water with you.** Hotel floor attendants always have a samovar in their offices and will provide boiled water if asked.

Food poisoning is common in Russia and Ukraine, so **be wary of dairy products and ice cream that may not be fresh.** The pirozhki (meat and cabbage-filled pies) sold everywhere on the streets are cheap and tasty, but they can give you a nasty stomach ache.

I
INSURANCE

Travel insurance can protect your monetary investment, replace your luggage and its contents, or provide for medical coverage should you fall ill during your trip. Most tour operators, travel agents, and insurance agents sell specialized health-and-accident, flight, trip-cancellation, and luggage insurance as well as comprehensive policies with some or all of these coverages. Comprehensive policies may also reimburse you for delays due to weather—an important consideration if you're traveling during the winter months. Some health-insurance policies do not cover preexisting conditions, but waivers may be available in specific cases. Coverage is sold by the companies listed in Important Contacts A to Z; these companies act as the policy's administrators. The actual insurance is usually underwritten by a well-known name, such as The Travelers or Continental Insurance.

Before you make any purchase, **review your existing health and homeowner's policies** to find out whether they cover expenses incurred while traveling.

BAGGAGE

Airline liability for baggage is limited to $1,250 per person on domestic flights. On international flights, it amounts to $9.07 per pound or $20 per kilogram for checked baggage (roughly $640 per 70-pound bag) and $400 per passenger for unchecked baggage. Insurance for losses exceeding the terms of your airline ticket can be bought directly from the airline at check-in for about $10 per $1,000 of coverage; note that it excludes a rather extensive list of items, shown on your airline ticket.

COMPREHENSIVE

Comprehensive insurance policies include all the coverages described above plus some that may not be available in more specific policies. If you have purchased an expensive vacation, especially one that involves travel abroad, comprehensive insurance is a must; **look for policies that include trip delay insurance,** which will protect you in the event that weather problems cause you to miss your flight, tour, or cruise. A few insurers will also sell you a waiver for preexisting medical conditions. Some of the companies that offer both these features are Access America, Carefree Travel, Travel Insured International, and TravelGuard (☞ Insurance *in* Important Contacts A to Z).

FLIGHT

You should **think twice before buying flight insurance.** Often purchased as a last-minute impulse at the airport, it pays a lump sum when a plane crashes, either to a beneficiary if the insured dies or sometimes to a surviving passenger who loses his or her eyesight or a limb. Supplementing the airlines' coverage described in the limits-of-liability paragraphs on your ticket, it's expensive and basically unnecessary. Charging an airline ticket to a major credit card often automatically provides you with coverage that may also extend to travel by bus, train, and ship.

HEALTH

Medicare generally does not cover health care costs outside the United States; nor do many privately issued policies. If your own health insurance policy does not cover you outside the United States, **consider buying supplemental medical coverage.** It can reimburse you for $1,000–$150,000 worth of medical and/or dental expenses incurred as a result of an accident or illness during a trip. These policies also may include a personal-accident, or death-and-dismemberment, provision, which pays a lump sum ranging from $15,000 to $500,000 to your beneficiaries if you die or to you if you lose one or more limbs or your eyesight, and a medical-assistance provision, which may either reimburse you for the cost of referrals, evacuation, or repatriation and other services, or automatically enroll you as a member of a particular medical-assistance company. (☞ Health Issues *in* Important Contacts A to Z.)

U.K. TRAVELERS

You can buy an annual travel insurance policy valid for most vacations during the year in which it's purchased. If you are pregnant or have a preexisting medical condition make sure you're covered before buying such a policy.

TRIP

Without insurance, you will lose all or most of your money if you cancel your trip regardless of the reason. Especially if your airline ticket, cruise, or package tour is nonrefundable and cannot be changed, it's essential that you **buy trip-cancellation-and-interruption insurance.** When considering how much coverage you need, look for a policy that will cover the cost of your trip plus the nondiscounted price of a one-way airline ticket should you need to return home early. Read the fine print carefully, especially sections that define "family member" and "preexisting medical conditions." Also **consider default or bankruptcy insurance,** which protects you against a supplier's failure to deliver. Be aware, however, that if you buy such a policy from a travel agency, tour operator, airline, or cruise line, it may not cover default by the firm in question.

L

LANGUAGE

Russian and Ukrainian are closely related East Slavic languages. Russian is still spoken widely in Ukraine, although its use has become a controversial political issue. With the rise of Ukrainian nationalism, Russian street signs are being replaced and public announcements are now recorded in Ukrainian. But if you speak Russian, you will have no problem getting by in Kiev. Both languages use the Cyrillic alphabet, which makes them particularly intimidating for English-speakers.

If you make an effort to learn the Russian alphabet, you will be able to decipher many words; with just a rudimentary knowledge of the alphabet you will be able to navigate the streets and subways on your own. You may want to **learn a few basic words** in both languages, but don't

expect to become conversant overnight. Hotel staff almost always speak good English, and the many restaurants and shops catering to foreigners are also staffed with English-speakers. Outside these places a good grasp of English is uncommon, though most people know at least a few words and phrases since they all took English in grade school. German is the second most common language in both countries.

LODGING

Detailed information about the hotels available can be found in the individual city chapter. In most instances you can book reservations (and request visa support for your Russian visa) directly with the hotel (in the past, all hotel reservations had to be made through Intourist, the official state tourist agency of the Soviet Union). But it is difficult to communicate with the CIS. In addition to the language barrier, placing a call to Russia or Ukraine can be extremely time-consuming. International telephone lines are often overloaded and once you get through, you may find that no one answers the phone. To save time and avoid language problems, **book your hotel through a travel agent or sign on for an organized tour.**

Until the early 1990s, hotels catering to foreign tourists were controlled by Intourist and Sputnik, a branch of the Komsomol specializing in youth

tourism. Most of the hotels built and owned by Intourist and Sputnik are now operating as independent establishments, but capitalism is catching on slowly, and service and accommodations have improved only slightly. If you are traveling with an organized tour, you will probably land in one of the old Intourist hotels, most of which are bleak, modern high rises. Accommodations at these hotels are adequate but far from luxurious. Standard items found in most Western hotels, such as soap, shampoo, and even sink stoppers, are rarely provided. Rooms usually come with telephone and televisions, but don't expect room service or in-room movies. The hot-water supply may be interrupted, a problem that occurs most frequently in summer.

Many hotels still have key attendants on each floor to whom you are supposed to relinquish your room key every time you leave the hotel. Since only one key is given out for a double room, you may find this a convenient system. But the key attendant often leaves the key unattended (in an open box on the desk in front of the stairwell), so if you can coordinate your schedule with your roommate, you're better off "attending" to the key yourself. The key attendants—usually rather stern elderly women—can be quite friendly and helpful, however. They can provide extra blankets or help get a leaky faucet fixed. They almost always have a samovar in their office and will provide hot water for tea or coffee.

HOME EXCHANGE

If you would like to find a house, an apartment, or some other type of vacation property to exchange for your own while on holiday, **become a member of a home-exchange organization,** which will send you its updated listings of available exchanges for a year, and will include your own listing in at least one of them. Arrangements for the actual exchange are made by the two parties involved, not by the organization.

HOME STAYS

Visa restrictions make it virtually impossible for Western tourists to make their own arrangements to stay in a private home. In order to obtain a Russian visa, you must first have a confirmed hotel reservation or an official invitation from a Russian organization. But if you're interested in a more native experience, home-stay options are now available as part of package tours. If you opt for this choice, **ask lots of questions when arranging your home stay.** How are the families chosen and screened? What are the living conditions? Will you have your own room? Do your hosts speak English? If you book a tour through a travel agency, the Russian visa should be included as part of the package.

HOSTELS

Accommodations at Sputnik hotels, the Soviet Union's answer to youth hostels, vary tremendously but are often just as good as the more expensive Intourist hotels. Rooms are usually doubles or triples with only the basic necessities provided (bath and bed but little else). Sputnik hotels are most commonly found on the city outskirts.

M
MAIL

Postal rates increase at nearly the same rapid pace as inflation, but again the advantageous exchange rate vis-à-vis the dollar keeps rates low for foreigners. You can **buy international envelopes and postcards at post offices and in hotel-lobby kiosks.** Beware that the postal system in all parts of the CIS and Ukraine is notoriously inefficient and mail is often lost. DHL and Federal Express have offices in Moscow and St. Petersburg if you need to send something important back home. Postcards generally have a better chance of reaching their destination than letters.

RECEIVING MAIL

Mail from outside the CIS takes approximately four weeks to arrive, sometimes longer, and sometimes it never arrives at all. If you absolutely must receive something from home during your trip, **consider using an express-mail service, such as DHL or Federal Express.**

MEDICAL ASSISTANCE

No one plans to get sick while traveling, but it happens, so **consider signing up with a medical assistance company.** These outfits provide referrals, emergency evacuation or repatriation, 24-hour telephone hot lines for medical consultation, cash for emergencies, and other personal and legal assistance. They also dispatch medical personnel and arrange for the relay of medical records. Coverage varies by plan, so **read the fine print carefully.**

MONEY

IN RUSSIA

The national currency in Russia is the ruble. There are paper notes of 100, 200, 500, 1,000, 5,000, 10,000, 50,000, and 100,000 rubles. Until the early 1990s, the highest denomination was the 100-ruble note. New, larger notes were added to keep up with spiraling inflation. Except for newspapers and single pieces of fruit, all purchases in Russia today are made in terms of thousands of rubles; 100-, 200-, 500-, and 1,000-ruble notes have become the equivalent of small change. At press time, there was talk of another possible currency reform.

Rubles cannot be obtained outside Russia, and it is illegal to import or export them. There is no limit, however, on the amount of foreign currency you may bring in with you. Most establishments these days (hotels,

THE GOLD GUIDE / SMART TRAVEL TIPS

stores, and restaurants) accept payment in rubles and/or credit cards. You'll find that street artists and vendors often prefer payment in dollars. Major credit cards (American Express, Diners Club, Eurocard, JCB, Master-Card, and Visa) are now widely accepted. Of course it is safest to carry your money in traveler's checks, but you will want to have at least $100 in cash (in tens and twenties). If you don't mind the risk of theft or loss, bring more; you are bound to need it. Worn or torn bills are often refused by Russian merchants, so **make sure your bills are crisp and clean.** On your way out of Russia and Ukraine, you can change excess rubles back into dollars at any bank or at the airport. For this you will need your passport, and some banks will insist on seeing your customs declaration.

IN UKRAINE

As in Russia, Ukraine has a two-tiered, predominantly cash economy. Dollars (cash) and major credit cards are accepted at many restaurants, stores, and hotels; as in Russia, many establishments accept only foreign currency. Traveler's checks are almost impossible to cash. The Russian ruble—once the only currency throughout the former Soviet Union—is gradually being replaced by the Ukrainian "coupon." The coupon was originally introduced as a ration card to prevent the sale of Ukrainian goods to non-Ukrainian residents and

has gradually acquired the status of a national currency. Its value decreases on a daily basis, and you should never exchange more money than you expect to need in the next day or so. The inflation rate in Ukraine has outpaced Russia's, and by press time, one ruble would buy approximately 46 coupons. You can exchange rubles or dollars for coupons at banks and all major hotels. As in Russia, the black market is a thriving business, and again you are advised to stay away from it.

ATMS

CASH ADVANCES➤ Before leaving home, **make sure that your credit cards have been programmed for ATM use in Moscow, St. Petersburg, and Kiev.** Note that Discover is accepted mostly in the United States. Local bank cards often do not work overseas either; **ask your bank about a MasterCard/Cirrus or Visa debit card,** which works like a bank card but can be used at any ATM displaying a MasterCard/Cirrus or Visa logo.

TRANSACTION FEES➤ Although fees charged for ATM transactions may be higher abroad than at home, Cirrus and Plus exchange rates are excellent, because they are based on wholesale rates offered only by major banks.

COSTS

Russians talk about prices in much the same way Americans talk about weather. The inflation rate is mind-

boggling, but so far the exchange rate vis-à-vis the dollar has kept pace. In November 1989, when the Soviet government relaxed the strict regulations controlling exchange rates, one ruble was worth approximately $1.50; by the fall of 1996, one dollar was worth more than 5,500 rubles. You can find some incredible bargains for rubles, but you will have to **search for ruble-priced values.**

Goods and services aimed at foreigners are as expensive as anywhere in Western Europe. A cup of coffee in a foreign-run hotel will cost around $3; in a stand-up café dealing in rubles, around 10¢. A ride on the subway is less than a penny and a pass for the entire month costs around a dollar. Taxi rates are generally fairly low, but as soon as the driver realizes that you are a foreigner, the rate goes up. In general, it's best only to deal with taxis that have been ordered for you by the staff of your hotel. Some museums, such as the Armory Palace in the Kremlin and St. Basil's Cathedral on Red Square, have instituted special, hard-currency fees for foreign tourists, but tickets for Russians, in rubles, are incredibly inexpensive. An evening of classical music at one of Russia's many concert halls can cost less than a dollar if you buy the tickets in rubles, but if you order them through a tourist agency, the cost rises significantly. The price discrimination against foreigners is particularly prevalent in Moscow.

EXCHANGING CURRENCY

You can exchange foreign currency for rubles (and vice versa) at state-run exchange offices and at any of the numerous currency exchange booths (*obmen valyuty*). Traveler's checks can be cashed at the state-run offices, at private banks, and at most major hotels. You may be approached by people on the streets, in your hotel, or by waiters in state-run restaurants, offering to exchange money at more advantageous rates. These unofficial currency-exchange activities, commonly referred to as the black market, are now legal under Russian law, but only the foolhardy engage in them. Your chances of being shortchanged are extremely high, and the savings are hardly worth the risk.

TRAVELER'S CHECKS

Whether or not to buy traveler's checks depends on where you are headed; **take cash to rural areas and small towns, traveler's checks to cities.** The most widely recognized checks are issued by American Express, Citicorp, Thomas Cook, and Visa. These are sold by major commercial banks for 1%–3% of the checks' face value—it pays to **shop around.** Both American Express and Thomas Cook issue checks that can be countersigned and used by either you or your traveling companion. So you won't be left with excess foreign currency,

buy a few checks in small denominations to cash toward the end of your trip. Before leaving home, **contact your issuer for information on where to cash your checks** without incurring a transaction fee. Record the numbers of all your checks, and keep this listing in a separate place, crossing off the numbers of checks you have cashed.

WIRING MONEY

For a fee of 3%–10%, depending on the amount of the transaction, you can have money sent to you from home through Money-Gram[SM] or Western Union (☞ Money Matters *in* Important Contacts A to Z). The transferred funds and the service fee can be charged to a Master-Card or Visa account.

P
PACKING FOR MOSCOW, ST. PETERSBURG, AND KIEV

No matter what time of year you visit, **bring a sweater.** St. Petersburg especially can be unexpectedly cold in summer. A raincoat and fold-up umbrella are also musts. Since you will probably be doing a lot of walking outdoors, bring warm, comfortable clothing, and be sure to **pack a pair of sturdy walking shoes.**

Russians and Ukrainians favor fashion over variety in their wardrobes, and it is perfectly acceptable to wear the same outfit several days in a row.

Be sure to **pack one outfit for dress-up occasions,** such as theater events. Coat-check attendants at theaters and restaurants will scold you if you do not have a hook sewed into the back of your coat for hanging. The layer system works well in the unpredictable weather of fall and spring; wear a light coat with a sweater that you can put on and take off as the weather changes. If you visit in winter you will of course need to prepare for the cold. Take heavy sweaters, warm boots, a wool hat, a scarf and mittens, and a heavy coat. Woolen tights or long underwear are essential during the coldest months. Russian central heating can be overly efficient, so you'll use the layer system again to avoid sweltering in an overheated building or train.

Local shortages are common. The hard-currency stores (especially those in Moscow) are well stocked, but certain items still disappear periodically and may be hard for passing tourists to find. To avoid running out of the essentials, **bring all your own toiletries and personal hygiene products with you.** Women should bring a supply of sanitary napkins or tampons. Of course you'll want to pack as light as possible, but consider whether you might want any of the difficult or impossible-to-find items: ball-point pens, insect repellent (in summer and fall mosquitoes can be a serious problem), film, camera batteries, laxatives, antidiarrhea pills, travel-sickness medicine, aspirin, and any over-the-counter medicine or prescription drug you take regularly.

Toilet paper is plentiful in hotels but less so in public buildings, so **bring small packages of tissue paper** to carry around with you. If you're a stickler for cleanliness and you are staying in one of the old Intourist hotels, bring disinfectant spray for the bathroom. Premoistened cleansing tissues will also come in handy, especially if you are traveling by train. A small flashlight may also prove useful, since streets are often dimly lit at night. Laundry facilities in hotels are unpredictable, so you will probably end up washing some clothes by hand. Bring your own laundry detergent and a round sink stopper (not always provided in hotel rooms). If you're a coffee drinker, **bring some instant coffee with you**; when the restaurant runs out of coffee, you can ask for a cup of hot water and make your own.

If you meet any Russians, chances are they will give you something; Russians tend to give small gifts even on short acquaintance. You may want to be prepared to reciprocate with souvenirs from your hometown or state, such as postcards, pens, or pins.

Bring an extra pair of eyeglasses or contact lenses in your carry-on luggage, and if you have a health problem, **pack enough medication**

to last the trip or have your doctor write you a prescription using the drug's generic name, because brand names vary from country to country (you'll then need a duplicate prescription from a local doctor). It's important that you **don't put prescription drugs or valuables in luggage to be checked,** for it could go astray. To avoid problems with customs officials, carry medications in the original packaging. Also, don't forget the addresses of offices that handle refunds of lost traveler's checks.

ELECTRICITY

To use your U.S.-purchased electric-powered equipment, **bring a converter and an adapter.** The electrical current in Russia and Ukraine is 220 volts, 50 cycles alternating current (AC); wall outlets take continental-type plugs, with two round prongs.

If your appliances are dual-voltage, you'll need only an adapter. Hotels sometimes have 110-volt outlets for low-wattage appliances near the sink, marked FOR SHAVERS ONLY; don't use them for high-wattage appliances like blow-dryers. If your laptop computer is older, carry a converter; new laptops operate equally well on 110 and 220 volts, so you need only an adapter.

LUGGAGE

Airline baggage allowances depend on the airline, the route, and the class of your ticket; ask in advance. In

general, on domestic flights and on international flights between the United States and foreign destinations, you are entitled to check two bags. A third piece may be brought on board, but it must fit easily under the seat in front of you or in the overhead compartment. In the United States, the FAA gives airlines broad latitude regarding carry-on allowances, and they tend to tailor them to different aircraft and operational conditions. Charges for excess, oversize, or overweight pieces vary.

If you are flying between two foreign destinations, note that baggage allowances may be determined not by piece but by weight—generally 88 pounds (40 kilograms) in first class, 66 pounds (30 kilograms) in business class, and 44 pounds (20 kilograms) in economy. If your flight between two cities abroad *connects* with your transatlantic or transpacific flight, the piece method still applies.

SAFEGUARDING YOUR LUGGAGE➤ Before leaving home, **itemize your bags' contents** and their worth, and label them with your name, address, and phone number. (If you use your home address, cover it so that potential thieves can't see it readily.) Inside each bag, **pack a copy of your itinerary.** At check-in, **make sure that each bag is correctly tagged** with the destination airport's three-letter code. If your bags arrive damaged—or fail to arrive at all—file a written report with the airline before leaving the airport.

PASSPORTS & VISAS

PASSPORTS & VISAS

If you don't already have one, **get a passport.** It is advisable that you **leave one photocopy of your passport's data page** with someone at home and keep another with you, separated from your passport, while traveling. If you lose your passport, promptly call the nearest embassy or consulate and the local police; having the data page information can speed replacement.

U.S. CITIZENS

All U.S. citizens, even infants, need only a valid passport to enter Russia or Ukraine for stays of up to 90 days. Application forms for both first-time and renewal passports are available at any of the 13 U.S. Passport Agency offices and at some post offices and courthouses. Passports are usually mailed within four weeks; allow five weeks or more in spring and summer.

U.S. citizens traveling to Russia and Ukraine are also required to obtain a visa for each country. For a Russian visa, you will need to submit the following items to the Russian Consulate at least 14 days before departure: a completed application, a copy of the signed page(s) of your passport, three photos, reference numbers from the hotels you'll be staying at (to prove that you have confirmed reservations),

a self-addressed stamped envelope, and a $20 application fee. The fee is higher if you need a faster turn-around time ($30 for 2–14 days, $60 for 48 hours). Requirements vary slightly if you'll be staying as a guest in a private home or if you're traveling on business.

The requirements for obtaining a visa to Ukraine are similar: an application form, copy of your passport, three photos, confirmation of hotel bookings, and the fee ($20 for a single-entry visa, $40 for a double-entry visa, and $100 for a multiple-entry visa).

CANADIANS

You need only a valid passport to enter Russia or Ukraine for stays of up to 90 days. Passport application forms are available at 28 regional passport offices, as well as post offices and travel agencies. Whether for a first or a renewal passport, you must apply in person. Children under 16 may be included on a parent's passport but must have their own to travel alone. Passports are valid for five years and are usually mailed within two to three weeks of application.

Canadian citizens are required to obtain a visa to enter either Russia or Ukraine. Requirements are very similar to those outlined above for U.S. citizens.

U.K. CITIZENS

Citizens of the United Kingdom need only a valid passport to enter Russia or Ukraine for stays of up to 90 days. Applications for new

and renewal passports are available from main post offices and at the passport offices in Belfast, Glasgow, Liverpool, London, Newport, and Peterborough. You may apply in person at all passport offices, or by mail to all except the London office. Children under 16 may travel on an accompanying parent's passport. All passports are valid for 10 years. Allow a month for processing.

S

SENIOR-CITIZEN DISCOUNTS

To qualify for age-related discounts, **mention your senior-citizen status up front** when booking hotel reservations, not when checking out, and before you're seated in restaurants, not when paying the bill. Note that discounts may be limited to certain menus, days, or hours. When renting a car, **ask about promotional car-rental discounts**—they can net even lower costs than your senior-citizen discount.

STUDENTS ON THE ROAD

To save money, **look into deals available through student-oriented travel agencies.** To qualify, you'll need to have a bona fide student ID card. Members of international student groups are also eligible (☞ Students *in* Important Contacts A to Z).

T

TELEPHONES

Most coin-operated telephones in Moscow

and St. Petersburg now take the plastic subway tokens (*zhetony*), which you can purchase at all subway stations and at some kiosks for 1,500 rubles a piece (at press time, a price increase had been threatened). (There are also still a few phones around that take coins (*monety*), but these are gradually being replaced, since the old ruble coins have gone out of circulation.

In Ukraine, where rubles in general are no longer in circulation, public telephones work without any coin at all. This situation is likely to change, however, as soon as the Ukrainian government introduces a bona fide Ukrainian currency complete with metal coins.

LONG-DISTANCE

The long-distance services of AT&T, MCI, and Sprint make calling home relatively convenient, but in many hotels you may find it impossible to dial the access number. The hotel operator may also refuse to make the connection. Instead, the hotel will charge you a premium rate—as much as 400% more than a calling card—for calls placed from your hotel room. To avoid such price gouging, travel with more than one company's long-distance calling card—a hotel may block Sprint but not MCI. If the hotel operator claims that you cannot use any phone card, ask to be connected to an international operator, who will help you to access your phone card. You can also dial the interna-

tional operator yourself. If none of this works, try calling your phone company collect in the United States. If collect calls are also blocked, call from a pay phone in the hotel lobby. Before you go, **find out the local access codes** for your destinations.

Most hotels offer satellite telephone booths where for several dollars a minute you can make an international call in a matter of seconds. If you want to economize, you can visit the main post office and order a call for rubles (sometimes there is a wait of up to 3 days). The per-minute rate increases frequently to keep pace with inflation but in recent years has never exceeded more than a dollar a minute. From your hotel room or from a private residence, you can dial direct. To place your call, dial 8, wait for the dial tone, then dial the country code (for the United States, 101) followed by the number you are trying to reach. In the new joint-venture hotels, rooms are often equipped with international, direct-dial (via satellite) telephones, but beware that the rates are hefty.

TIPPING

In the postcommunist era, tipping is rapidly becoming an accepted practice, so **when in doubt, tip.** Cloak-room attendants, waiters, porters, and taxi drivers will all expect a tip, preferably in foreign currency. Add an extra 10% to 15% to a restaurant bill or taxi fare. Some restaurants

are now adding a service charge to the bill automatically, so double-check before you leave a big tip. If you're paying by credit card, leave the tip in cash—the waiter will never see it if you add it to the credit-card charge.

TOUR OPERATORS

A package or tour to Moscow, St. Petersburg, and Kiev can make your vacation less expensive and more hassle-free. Firms that sell tours and packages reserve airline seats, hotel rooms, and rental cars in bulk and pass some of the savings on to you. In addition, the best operators have local representatives available to help you at your destination.

A GOOD DEAL?

The more your package or tour includes, the better you can predict the ultimate cost of your vacation. Make sure you know exactly what is covered, and **beware of hidden costs.** Are taxes, tips, and service charges included? Transfers and baggage handling? Entertainment and excursions? These can add up.

Most packages and tours are rated deluxe, first-class superior, first class, tourist, or budget. The key difference is usually accommodations. If the package or tour you are considering is priced lower than in your wildest dreams, **be skeptical.** Also, **make sure your travel agent knows the accommodations** and other services. Ask about the hotel's location, room size, beds, and whether it has a pool, room service, or programs for children, if you care about these. Has your agent been there in person or sent others you can contact?

BUYER BEWARE

Each year a number of consumers are stranded or lose their money when operators—even very large ones with excellent reputations—go out of business. To avoid becoming one of them, take the time to **check out the operator**—find out how long the company has been in business and ask several agents about its reputation. Next, **don't book unless the firm has a consumer-protection program.** Members of the USTOA and the NTA are required to set aside funds for the sole purpose of covering your payments and travel arrangements in case of default. Nonmember operators may instead carry insurance; look for the details in the operator's brochure—and for the name of an underwriter with a solid reputation. Note: When it comes to tour operators, **don't trust escrow accounts.** Although there are laws governing those of charter-flight operators, no governmental body prevents tour operators from raiding the till.

Next, **contact your local Better Business Bureau and the attorney general's offices** in both your own state and the operator's; have any complaints been filed? Finally, **pay with a major credit card.** Then you can cancel payment, provided that you can document your

complaint. Always **consider trip-cancellation insurance** (☞ Insurance, *above*).

BIG VS. SMALL➢ Operators that handle several hundred thousand travelers per year can use their purchasing power to give you a good price. Their high volume may also indicate financial stability. But some small companies provide more personalized service; because they tend to specialize, they may also be more knowledgeable about a given area.

USING AN AGENT

Travel agents are excellent resources. In fact, large operators accept bookings made only through travel agents. But it's good to **collect brochures from several agencies** because some agents' suggestions may be skewed by promotional relationships with tour and package firms that reward them for volume sales. If you have a special interest, **find an agent with expertise in that area**; ASTA can provide leads in the United States. (Don't rely solely on your agent, though; agents may be unaware of small-niche operators, and some special-interest travel companies only sell direct.)

SINGLE TRAVELERS

Prices are usually quoted per person, based on two sharing a room. If traveling solo, you may be required to pay the full double-occupancy rate. Some operators eliminate this surcharge if you agree to be matched up with a roommate of the same

sex, even if one is not found by departure time.

TRAIN TRAVEL

In Russia and the Ukraine, **take the train for the most reliable and convenient transportation.** Remarkably, most trains leave exactly on time; there is a broadcast warning five minutes before departure, but no whistle or "all aboard!" call, so be careful not to be left behind.

Trains are divided into four classes. The highest class, "deluxe," is usually only available on trains traveling international routes. The deluxe class offers two-berth compartments with soft seats and private washrooms; the other classes have washrooms at the end of the cars. The first-class service is called "soft-seat," with spring-cushioned berths; there are two berths in each compartment. There is no segregation of the sexes and no matter what class of service you choose, chances are good that you will find yourself sharing a compartment with someone of the opposite sex. The second, or "hard-seat," class has a cushion on wooden berths, with four berths to a compartment. The third class—wooden berths without compartments—is rarely sold to foreigners unless specifically requested. Most compartments have a small table, limited room for baggage (including under the seats) and a radio that can be turned down, but not off. In

THE GOLD GUIDE / SMART TRAVEL TIPS

soft class there is also a table lamp. The price of the ticket may or may not include use of bedding; sometimes this fee (which increases daily with the inflation rate) is collected by the conductor.

All the cars are also equipped with samovars. Back in the days of communism, the conductor would offer tea to passengers before bedtime. These days the train is often out of tea and sometimes even out of water, so **bring your own snacks and beverages onto the train.** Most conductors run their own small businesses selling champagne and caviar, so don't be surprised if you're approached with such an offer. The communal bathrooms located at both ends of each car are notoriously dirty, so **bring premoistened cleansing tissues for washing up and water for brushing your teeth.** Definitely pack toilet paper. Also be sure to pack a heavy sweater. The cars are often overheated and toasty warm, but sometimes they are not heated at all, so in winter it can get very cold.

There are numerous day and overnight trains between St. Petersburg and Moscow and between Moscow and Kiev. There is also train service between Kiev and St. Petersburg, but the trip is a long one (over 30 hours). The past few years have witnessed increased crime on the overnight trains; the safest option for travel between Moscow and St. Peters-

burg is the high-speed day-train *Avrora*, which makes the trip in just under six hours. If you are traveling alone on an overnight train, you should take extra security precautions. The doors to the compartments can be locked, but the locks can be picked, so you might consider bringing a bicycle chain. You may also want to buy out the entire compartment so as not to risk your luck with unknown compartmentmates.

Train travel in Russia may be primitive by Western standards, but it offers an unrivaled opportunity to glimpse the quaint Russian countryside, which is dotted in places with colorful wooden cottages. If you are traveling by overnight train, be sure to set your alarm and get up an hour or so before arrival so that you can watch at close hand the workers going about their morning rounds in the rural areas just outside the cities.

Purchasing a domestic train ticket outside the CIS can be difficult, but tickets are easily purchased within the country. Tickets go on sale 10 days prior to departure. Train tickets sold to foreigners for travel within Russia must be paid for with foreign currency. A one-way ticket between Moscow and St. Petersburg on an overnight train now costs just under $50.

TRAVEL GEAR

Travel catalogs specialize in useful items that

can **save space when packing** and make life on the road more convenient. Compact alarm clocks, travel irons, travel wallets, and personal-care kits are among the most common items you'll find. They also carry dual-voltage appliances, currency converters, and foreign-language phrase books. Some catalogs even carry miniature coffeemakers and water purifiers.

U

U.S. GOVERNMENT

The U.S. government can be an excellent source of travel information. Some of this is free and some is available for a nominal charge. When planning your trip, **find out what government materials are available.** For just a couple of dollars, you can get a variety of publications from the Consumer Information Center in Pueblo, Colorado. Free consumer information also is available from individual government agencies, such as the Department of Transportation or the U.S. Customs Service. For specific titles, see the appropriate publications entry in Important Contacts A to Z, *above.*

W

WHEN TO GO

The climate in Russia and Ukraine changes dramatically with the seasons. All three cities are best visited in late spring or early autumn, just before and after the peak tourist season. The weather is always unpredictable, but you are most apt to encounter pleasantly warm and sunny days in late May and late August. In Moscow summers tend to be hot, although thunderstorms and heavy rainfall are common in July and August. In St. Petersburg, on the other hand, it rarely gets very hot, even at the height of summer. If this maritime city is your only destination, try to **visit St. Petersburg during the White Nights** (mid-June to early July), when the northern day is virtually endless.

The Ukrainian climate is milder than the Russian one; spring comes earlier to Kiev than to Moscow and St. Petersburg, and summer lasts longer. In winter months all three cities are covered in an attractive blanket of snow.

But only the hardiest tourists should visit between late November and early February, when the days are short and dark, extremely so in St. Petersburg, and the weather is often bitterly cold.

CLIMATE

Below are the average daily maximum and minimum temperatures for Moscow.

Jan.	16F	− 9C	May	67F	19C	Sept.	61F	16C
	4	−16		47	8		45	7
Feb.	22F	− 6C	June	70F	21C	Oct.	49F	9C
	7	−14		52	11		38	3
Mar.	32F	0C	July	74F	23C	Nov.	36F	2C
	18	− 8		56	13		27	− 3
Apr.	50F	10C	Aug.	72F	22C	Dec.	23F	− 5C
	34	1		54	12		14	−10

1 Destination: Moscow, St. Petersburg, Kiev

THE RUSSIAN PARADOX

SUCH EXTREMES CHARACTERIZE Russia—extremes of geography, of politics, of temperament, and even of weather—that it ultimately defies characterization. Winston Churchill's observation that "Russia is a riddle wrapped in a mystery inside an enigma" is itself a masterfully Russian pronouncement, adamant in its opaqueness. And if it was accurate in 1939, it is no less so now, when the situations that "characterized" Russia then—devotion under Stalin to the communist purpose, a centralized economy, a nation-state comprising 15 republics welded into the monolith of the USSR—have been overturned as radically as what had come before.

Today, after perestroika and glasnost, many in the West had hoped that Russia would stand revealed, that it would be comprehensible and accessible. Eager to embrace her, engage and understand her, perhaps even indulge her, we visit wondering if we may finally decipher that mysterious, fabled "Russian-ness." While there is indeed a new kind of Russian daily world, it is not the one we were expecting. It is likely to surprise us; some will be disappointed, others exhilarated. No one will go away unstimulated.

Stretching across 10 time zones, from the Pacific Ocean to the Baltic Sea, Russia remains the world's largest country. Even as a single ex-republic, its realms extend to the Arctic Circle and to subtropical resorts. Its western border is Europe; its eastern, the Orient. In between them the Russian people comprise over 100 distinct ethnic groups. How, then, can we speak in sweeping generalizations of a monolithic empire?

It helps to understand that Russia's power, as well as its charm, resides in paradox, and perhaps never before has its dual nature been so evident. Extremes and contrasts—these will form the bulk of your impressions as you tour these three cities.

The first, very difficult transitions are already far behind, but the path ahead can still look rocky. Sweeping changes in politics and economics, as well as in media, law, and entertainment, have transformed the lives of most Russians. Those left disenfranchised by the demise of the communist system have been set adrift for at least two generations, with no relief in sight.

Russia exists as if in a time warp. White-aproned clerks still calculate change on a wooden abacus; eggs are sold on the street; gas is peddled from trucks on the side of the road. Clothes are still washed mostly by hand; scythes are the Russian lawnmowers. Meanwhile, at least in the cities, sales of fax machines and personal computers outstrip nearly all others; there is a booming market for Mercedes-Benzes and Volvos. You see more cellular phones on the street than anywhere except Los Angeles. In Moscow, beneath a giant neon sign flashing the dollar-exchange rate, the very Soviet *gai* (traffic police) signal the tinted-glass limousine and the battered Lada laden with refrigerators, cigarettes, juice, and crates of possessions. On the corner a young mother taking her child to school waits to cross the busy intersection, along with recent arrivals from Armenia or Azerbaijan (a wave of immigration has convulsed Russia), an old man in a shabby suit laden with war medals and ribbons, a teenager in black leather and sneakers listening to a Walkman, and a kerchiefed grandmother in for the day from the village, struggling with a rusted cart filled with potatoes (or carrots or jars of homemade sour cream) to sell at the market.

Special words are reserved for Kiev's nation, Ukraine. Inextricably bound up in Russia's history during the last 70 years as an integral part of the Soviet Union, Ukraine has struck off in determined pursuit of its own destiny. While the two nations share many post-Soviet struggles, they are different, too. In their intertwined genealogy, it is Kiev that is said to have given birth to Russia. It was in Kiev, more than 1,000 years ago, that the Kievan-Rus civilization is considered to have begun. Eventually, power shifted to the north, but the Ukrainian capital continued to thrive and grow on its own cultural, religious, and political terms. It is a separateness that it has now proclaimed wholly on its own.

Explored together, these cities will enrich and fascinate. Their monuments and people will command your interest, attention, and respect—and perhaps win your affection, too. In 1919 the American journalist Lincoln Steffens, back from a trip to the young Soviet Union, said to Bernard Baruch, "I have been over into the future, and it works." Perhaps it did, at least for a while. As you witness the future that is unfolding in Russia and Ukraine, judge for yourself if one could say the same today. But remember that, if the collapse of the empires here proves anything, it is that anything about this part of the world is averse to prediction. Welcome to the enigma. Enjoy the surprises.

WHAT'S WHERE

Moscow

The end of communism has undoubtedly affected the ancient capital of Russia. The central streets have largely reverted to their old pre-revolutionary names, and the number of places named after Lenin has been drastically reduced. The new advertising billboards, many in English as well as Russian, point to real and profound economic change. Western investment and cooperative agreements have led to a rash of new building, notably of hotels and business complexes. Yet for all this, the face of Moscow appears curiously impervious to change. Its Stalinist physionomy, born in the 1930s, continues to brazen it out; the Gothic skyscrapers of the old Ukraine Hotel and the Foreign Ministry look contemptuously down on the modest Western-style shops down below. Building after building, made redundant by the demise of communism with its vastly over-swollen bureaucracy and now taken over by new organizations, refuses to budge. Although Moscow has now much in common with its great Western counterparts—Paris, London, New York—it still has a stubbornly Russian stamp.

St. Petersburg

Planned from the first brick as a great capital, St. Petersburg has not fallen short of Peter the Great's original vision. It has not been the capital of Russia since the Bolshevik Revolution, but it still carries itself as though it were. Indeed, the imposing grandeur of its most important landmarks—Palace Square and the Winter Palace—and the stylish sophistication of its residences make this 300-year-old city one of the great urban centers in the world. Czar Peter's intention was to reorient Russia to the West by making the city a "window looking into Europe," and indeed the geometric elegance of its layout and the perfect planning of its architecture owe more to the grand cities of Europe than to its Russian counterparts to the east. It has also been called the northern Venice, for it is a city built on more than a hundred islands cradled in the watery lap of the winding Neva and the intricate network of canals carved into the soft ground at the mouth of the Gulf of Finland.

Kiev

Although it is the capital of the recently independent Ukraine, Kiev is known as the Mother of Russia, for it was here in the 9th century that Russian civilization began and Rus, the land of the eastern Slavs, was founded. For centuries it was an important cultural, political, and economic center until it was razed to the ground by Mongol invaders in 1240. The city has seen its fair share of violence and tragedy: in this century alone, it witnessed a bitter struggle at the time of the Bolshevik Revolution, an 800-day occupation by the Germans during World War II, and, most recently, in 1986, the tragedy of Chernobyl, only 60 miles away. It is perhaps this combination of ancient glory and modern disaster that best define Kiev's struggle to re-establish itself as an urban center of importance; one need visit for only a few days to become aware of this dual identity, as the city proudly displays the elegance of its glorious past alongside the uncertain fervor of a newly independent capital tackling the problems inherited from 70 years of bureaucratic rule.

PLEASURES AND PASTIMES

Ballet

There have been few *corps de ballet* to match the Russians over the last 150 years. The Bolshoi and Kirov ballets have produced some of the world's greatest dancers; indeed, the names Pavlova, Nijinsky, Nureyev, Barishnikov, and Diaghilev, all home-grown talents, are synonymous with ballet excellence. Unfortunately, faltering standards due to chronic underfunding and the attraction of the West led to a seemingly unstoppable hemorrhaging of Russia's greatest dancers, beginning with the defection of Rudolf Nureyev in 1961. The demise of communism has exposed decades of complacency and lack of innovation, and has done little to stop the bleeding—the British Royal Ballet poached Russia's current great, Irek Mukhamedov, in 1991. Despite such problems, a night at the Kirov or the Bolshoi can be a unique experience for those wishing to take a peek at the heart of some of the world's greatest dance venues.

Bath Houses

A visit to the Russian *banya,* or bath, should not be missed. It has been part of the national culture for centuries; indeed, the bath houses of Moscow and St. Petersburg were once the last word in luxury. Yegerov's in St. Petersburg, for example, had a tented disrobing room, decked out in Moorish style with cushions and settees, and a swimming pool traversed by a grottolike bridge and rockery, classical-style statues, and trailing greenery.

Bring a towel, shampoo, and plastic shoes or sandals. You may be given a plastic bathing robe and offered a *venik,* the bundle of birch twigs without which no visit to the bath is complete. By brushing the soaked twigs lightly across the body, striking more boldly with each turn, one stimulates the circulation of the blood and draws out toxins. Most Russians finish with a glass of tea or water or even a shot of vodka, but be careful not to overindulge: sip, don't gulp, any liquids.

Dining

The dining scene in all three cities has changed dramatically in the past few years. In terms of sheer numbers and types of restaurants, Moscow is far ahead of St. Petersburg and Kiev, but in all three cities you'll find a variety of cuisines and price ranges.

In Russia, breakfast is often a familiar omelet or fried eggs, but don't be surprised if the meal includes cabbage salad, fish, or hot dogs (served with cold peas), which are all standard breakfast fare. The main meal of the day is served in midafternoon and usually consists of a starter, soup, and a main course. Supper is traditionally a lighter meal, with just an appetizer and a main course. The main course will be either meat or fish; the fish you are most likely to be served are sturgeon, halibut, or herring. A favorite meat dish is beef Stroganoff, beef stewed in sour cream and served with mushrooms and fried potatoes. The soup is likely to be borscht, a beet soup, or *shchi,* cabbage soup. Other national dishes include piroshki, fried rolls filled with cabbage or meat, and blini, small, light pancakes rolled and filled with caviar, fish, melted butter, jam, or sour cream.

In Ukraine, you may be lucky enough to be served a well-cooked chicken Kiev—fried chicken breast filled with melted butter that shoots forth when you pierce the chicken with your fork. Another Ukrainian specialty is *vareniky,* sweet dumplings filled with fruit or cheese.

Nature

If you ask Russians what they think most identifies them as Russian, do not be surprised to hear that it is their close association with nature. At the turn of the century, it was estimated that 90 percent of the population was rural, and while this figure has dropped over the course of the century, the Russian attachment to the natural world has not. Every major city has at least one large park where citizens can spend entire days enjoying the greenery in the company of friends and family. At weekends, families stream out of the cities to their countryside *dachas* or to a low-budget hotel complex. There they can indulge in one of the greatest of Russian pastimes, *mushrooming.* From early June to mid-October, the countryside is awash with genuflecting men and women picking mushrooms, which are then eaten at a *shashlik,* or barbecue.

Sports and Outdoor Activities

Skiing and hunting packages to Moscow and St. Petersburg are available, some through Intour Service. Cross-country skiing is a particularly popular sport in Russia and Ukraine, and all three cities have acres of wooded parkland perfect for it. Outdoor skating rinks also abound, and there are downhill skiing facilities just outside of Moscow. Rentals of skis and skates are available only sporadically, so you should bring your own equipment or make prior arrangements. If you plan to go hunting, you may bring your own hunting gun provided you carry a voucher issued by an accredited travel agent attesting to the fact that you intend to hunt. All sporting rifles must be presented for customs inspection and the serial numbers declared on the customs form.

Vodka

The Russian national drink is an inseparable part of Russian social life. It is drunk literally everywhere, with the effect of breaking down inhibitions and producing a state of conviviality that the Russians refer to as *dusha-dushe* (heart-to-heart). When a Russian taps his throat, beware: It's impossible to refuse this invitation to conviviality.

Vodka is often flavored and colored with herbs and spices. *Limonaya,* lemon-flavored vodka, is particularly popular with American tourists, as is *pertsovka,* pepper-flavored vodka. Other varieties include *starka* (a dark, smooth "old" vodka), *pshenichnaya* (made from wheat), *ryabinovka,* in which ashberries have been steeped, and *tminaya* (caraway-flavored vodka). Be wary of the *krepkaya* vodka, which at 110 proof is the strongest variety. In Ukraine, try *khorilka s pertsem* (with hot peppers).

Normally served from an ice bucket, vodka is drunk neat in one gulp and "chased" with a mouthful of food. It goes down particularly well with *zakuski* (hors d'oeuvres)—smoked salmon, salted herring, marinated mushrooms, salami, caviar, etc. To quell the fiery taste, some Russians advise exhaling before gulping, while others recommend deep inhalation. Many Russians swear by a shot of vodka with a dash of pepper as a cure for the common cold.

NEW AND NOTEWORTHY

Events have moved on a long way since the world watched in fascination at the fiery attack on Moscow's parliament building in October 1993. A vocal and energized Boris Yeltsin defiantly braved the conservative backlash and won a great political—and moral—victory. Three years later, and despite an election victory, the image of Yeltsin the revolutionary democrat has been replaced by that of Yeltsin the stumbling autocrat, battling increasing popular dissatisfaction with the pace of his reforms, the disastrous campaign to subjugate Chechnya, his insistence on governing by decree, and a personal illness that has left him a shadow of the man who catapulted himself and his reformist supporters onto the international stage. Paradoxically, the pace of change has been both remarkable and nonexistent; although the monolith of communist rule has been radically overhauled, the fledgling market system that has replaced it has not resulted in the widespread improvement of living conditions it had so vociferously promised. Indeed, although reforms and the introduction of a crude market system have brought tangible increases in the lifestyles of entrepreneurs and market players, most ordinary Russians and Ukrainians have been unable to escape the poverty and economic confinement they suffered during the Soviet years.

Although the economic reforms begun by Mikhail Gorbachev and continued by Yeltsin have met with dubious success, one area where the improvements have been dramatic is the tourist industry. In the past five years, dozens of new hotels, many of them foreign-owned and -managed, have opened in the major cities, reintroducing, for the first time since the Bolshevik Revolution, the concept of luxury accommodations. The tourist industry has also shifted its focus from group to individual travel. If in the past the Soviet tourist industry frowned upon individual tourists, encouraging foreigners to travel in groups by giving them preferential treatment and discount rates, today the situation has been reversed. In 1997 tourists will discover that there is now a direct correlation between what you pay for and what you get.

What is certain, however, is that the economy will continue to remain in a state of flux for the time being. At the time this book goes to print Yeltsin's health has taken a turn for the worse and Kremlinologists are once again busy guessing who will succeed him if it becomes necessary. The doves and the hawks, the reformists and the traditionalists, are all maneuvering to seize power in that slow, secret way the Russians have always carried out their politics.

Moscow

In this, the most Russian of all Russian cities, change is a question of perspective. For most, life continues as it always did, despite additions to the skyline of new, flashing neon advertisements encouraging the purchase of domestic and foreign goods (and one that shows the dollar exchange rate). The mayor has made radical municipal changes, turning buildings that once housed the labyrinthian Soviet bureaucracy into new agencies charged with accelerating economic reform. Indeed, economic activity is in evidence literally everywhere, from the small-time entrepreneurs hawking folk art on street corners to massive international ventures that have resulted in the construction of business centers and hotels, as well as the emergence from out of the woodwork of an extremely well-organized—and often ruthless—industry of organized crime. There is no one in Moscow who does not have a take on the activities of the Mafia; the problem has gotten so bad that many Muscovites have thrown up their hands in despair, unable to distinguish between what is a legitimate business venture from what has been obtained by extortion, bribery, and violence.

St. Petersburg

The 50th anniversary of the end of World War II was celebrated in 1995, amid much pomp and circumstance (including the presence of many world leaders at the official celebrations) and much emotion, as citizens looked back fifty years to the devastating siege of their beloved city by the Nazis that symbolized the struggle of all of the Soviet Union during the War. Today, St. Petersburg's struggles continue, albeit in a different way: Like its urban counterparts in Russia and Ukraine, the city has mobilized itself to make the market system work for its citizens. Although it continues to lag behind Moscow in terms of general prosperity, the positive growth resulting from the introduction of a market economy has had tangible effects. Like the capital, St. Petersburg is full of new projects for hotels and business centers, and it has been relatively successful in attracting foreign business. Prices are lower in this genteel city, and the nouveau riche that are very much in evidence in Moscow seem to be absent here, even if the plague of organized crime is as widespread—some say more so—as in Moscow.

Kiev

The rebirth of Kiev as the capital of a sovereign state has led to the establishment of foreign embassies and an influx of businesspeople from Eastern and Western Europe. Although tourist facilities are still relatively limited, restaurants catering to the growing foreign community are opening, and hotels are being refurbished to approach Western standards. Tense relations between Russia and Ukraine are having a direct impact on the struggling Ukrainian economy. Oil and gas are in short supply, and public buildings tend to be poorly heated in winter.

FODOR'S CHOICE

No two people will agree on what makes a perfect vacation, but it's fun and helpful to know what others think. We hope you'll have a chance to experience some of Fodor's Choices yourself while visiting Moscow, St. Petersburg, and Kiev. For detailed information about each entry, refer to the appropriate chapters within this guidebook.

Churches and Monasteries

★**Alexander Nevsky Lavra, St. Petersburg.** One of only four highest-ranking monasteries in Russia and the Ukraine, the burial place of St. Alexander Nevsky—and many other famous names—was built in 1710 by Peter the Great.

★**Donskoy Monastery, Moscow.** The once secret archives at this 16th-century monastery are a fascinating memorial to Russian architecture and art.

★**Monastery of the Caves, Kiev.** An entire day should be set aside for discovering the intricate mazes of this 11th-century monastery, which was once the center of the Ukrainian Orthodox Church.

⭐ **New Maiden's Convent and Cemetery, Moscow.** This immaculately preserved ensemble of 16th- and 17th-century architecture borders a fascinating cemetery where some of Russia's greatest literary, political, and miliatry figures are buried.

⭐ **St. Andrew's Cathedral, Kiev.** The green, blue, and gold cupolas of this magnificent cathedral high on a bluff overlooking the Dnieper River, are a fine example of the Ukrainian baroque.

⭐ **St. Sophia's Cathedral, Kiev.** The city's oldest church was consecrated in 1037 and is richly decorated with mosaics and frescoes dating from the 11th and 12th centuries.

⭐ **Smolny Convent and Cathedral, St. Petersburg.** This magnificent five-domed, blue-and-white masterpiece by Bartolomeo Rastrelli seems to have leapt off the pages of a fairy tale.

⭐ **Zagorsk (Sergyev Posad), Moscow.** Pilgrims have been worshipping at the monastery here, Russia's most important center of pilgrimage, for over 500 years.

Historical Buildings and Sites

⭐ **Armory Palace, Moscow.** A wide selection of imperial regalia and historical artifacts is stored in the vast galleries of the Kremlin's oldest and richest museum.

⭐ **Babi Yar, Kiev.** The Nazi's execution of over 100,000 Jews and partisans at this pretty ravine during World War II is commemorated by a dramatic monument that is a moving testament to the victims' suffering.

⭐ **Catherine Palace, Pushkin.** This dazzling example of Russian baroque architecture was the summer residence of the imperial family from the days of Peter the Great.

⭐ **Kremlin, Moscow.** There are few buildings in the world that can match the historical importance of the Kremlin, *the* symbol of Russia's mystery and power since the 15th century.

⭐ **Maria's Palace, Kiev.** This delightful mixture of Russian and Ukrainian baroque has a magnificent facade with balustrades decorated with vases and sculptures of lions that lead down majestically to the formally landscaped park.

⭐ **Pavlovsk, St. Petersburg.** High on a bluff overlooking the river and a 1,500-acre park, the Great Palace was built as a summer residence for Paul I.

⭐ **Petrodvorets, St. Petersburg.** This former imperial palace on the shores of the Baltic sea, complete with lush parks, monumental cascades, and gilded fountains, will leave a lasting impression.

⭐ **Red Square, Moscow.** Surprisingly, the Bolshevik Revolution did not give this magnificent and beautiful square its name; the Russian word for "beautiful," strangely enough, comes from the word "red."

⭐ **Strelka, St. Petersburg.** The easternmost tip of Vasilievsky Island, lined with brightly colored houses, affords a dazzling view of the city and its glorious architecture.

⭐ **Winter Palace, St. Petersburg.** Created by Bartolomeo Rastrelli for the Empress Elizabeth I, the former imperial residence has over 1,000 rooms replete with works of art and historical objects.

Hotels

⭐ **Dnipro, Kiev.** The business traveler will find this centrally located hotel a popular and well-organized stopover, and the staff are charming and extremely helpful. *$$$$*

⭐ **Grand Hotel Europe, St. Petersburg.** The service shines in the midst of prerevolutionary splendor, making it the finest hotel in town. *$$$$*

⭐ **Metropole, Moscow.** One of the capital's most elegant hotels, it successfully combines the opulence of its 19th-century decor with the efficiency of its late 20th-century service and amenities. *$$$$*

Monuments

⭐ **Bronze Horseman, St. Petersburg.** This city landmark, depicting Peter the Great astride a rearing horse, is a symbol of Russia rising up to crush its enemies, shown here as a serpent.

⭐ **Egyptian Sphinxes, St. Petersburg.** It may have taken the Russians over a year to transport them from Thebes, but it was worth it, if only for the magnificent view of the old city from the supporting quay.

⭐ **Monument to the Baptism of Russia, Kiev.** A 66-foot bronze of Prince Vladimir holding a cross in his right hand dominates a hilltop overlooking the Dnieper.

Museums

★**Chernobyl Museum, Kiev.** The somber display here commemorates the victims of the devastating nuclear explosion at the infamous power plant.

★**Hermitage, St. Petersburg.** One of the world's richest repositories of art will be found here, with the Italian Renaissance, Spanish, and Dutch masters well represented.

★**Kolomenskoye Estate Museum, Moscow.** This estate, once a favorite summer residence of Moscow's grand dukes and czars, has been turned into an impressive open-air museum that includes a Siberian prison tower and Peter the Great's cottage.

★**Museum of Historical Treasures, Kiev.** The highlight of the impressive collection here is a massive gold pectoral, or chest ornament, decorated with scenes from Scythian life in the 4th century BC.

★**Pushkin Museum of Fine Arts, Moscow.** After St. Petersburg's Hermitage, this is the largest museum of fine art in Russia, with a veritable smorgasbord of world-class art.

★**State Museum of Russian Art, St. Petersburg.** The scores of Russian masterpieces on display here have made this one of the country's most important art galleries.

★**Tretyakov Art Gallery, Moscow.** Russia's largest and most important repository of its national art is housed in a fanciful building designed in the Russian art nouveau style.

Parks and Gardens

★**Gidro Park, Kiev.** This pretty park on an island near the left bank is a popular spot in summer for boating and bathing.

★**Gorky Park, Moscow.** The 110-acre park is Moscow's most popular, and in summer families throng to its many attractions, including a giant Ferris wheel.

★**Kirovsky Park on Yelagin Island, St. Petersburg.** An open-air theater, boating stations, and a beach are among the attractions at this park, which covers an entire island.

★**Summer Gardens, St. Petersburg.** Pavilions, ponds, and an intricate network of fountains, along with sculptures and statues from all over the world, make up this

brainchild of Peter the Great, who wanted to create the Russian Versailles.

Restaurants

★**Europe, St. Petersburg.** The opulent dinner served at this elegant restaurant is fit for a czar. $$$$

★**Glazur, Moscow.** The subdued atmosphere and exquisite cuisine at this upscale establishment are geared toward the city's foreign community. $$$$

★**Savoy, Moscow.** This might be the only restaurant where you can truly eat like a czar: It features a re-creation of one of the menus served at the coronation of Czar Nicholas II in 1896. $$$$

★**Apollo, Kiev.** This elegant restaurant with a beautifully restored interior and an exquisite European cuisine has set a standard for fine dining in Kiev. $$$

★**Gostinny Dvor, Kiev.** Great food and atmosphere—as well as the affordable prices—make this restaurant attractive to both locals and foreigners, who are guaranteed to eat well in convivial surroundings. $

Special Moments

★**Red Square at night.** The best time to view the impressive square is when the red stars of the Kremlin towers light up the night and the entire area is floodlit.

★**Your first glimpse of St. Basil's Cathedral.** The eight onion-shaped domes of this distinctive cathedral are one of the great architectural symbols of Russia and will not disappoint.

★**An evening of classical music at the Tchaikovsky Conservatory.** Fine performances can be enjoyed at this auditorium named after one of Russia's greatest composers.

★**A midnight cruise along the Neva River during the White Nights.** In June and July, when the northern day is virtually endless, the imperial palaces sparkle along the embankments and the colorful facades of the riverside estates glow gently as you wind your way around this northern Venice.

★**Kiev in spring.** The climate is milder than in Moscow, and the end of winter means the shutters can reopen, the trees are in bloom, and all of the colors of this beautiful city come to life.

HOLIDAYS AND FESTIVALS

With the demise of the Soviet Union and the accompanying religious revival, church holidays are now more widely celebrated than the traditional political holidays. These days November 7, the anniversary of the Bolshevik Revolution, merits only a minor military parade in Moscow. The date goes by virtually unnoticed in Kiev, while in St. Petersburg November 7 is now celebrated as the anniversary of the city's renaming from Leningrad back to St. Petersburg. Listed below are the current major holidays celebrated in Russia and Ukraine.

WINTER

DEC.➤ **New Year's Eve** is a favorite holiday marked by merrymaking and family gatherings. Friends and family exchange small gifts, putting them under a New Year's tree, a tradition that began when Christmas and other religious holidays were not tolerated by the Soviet authorities. December Nights is a month-long festival of music, dance, theater, and art held in Moscow.

JAN.➤ **New Year's Eve** is celebrated twice—first on December 31, with the rest of the world, and then again on January 13, "Old" New Year's Eve (according to the Julian calendar used in Russia until the revolution). Russian Orthodox Christmas is celebrated on January 7.

FEB.➤ February 23, **Soviet Army Day,** is somewhat similar to Father's Day in the United States. Since just about every male ends up in the army, the holiday traditionally honors all men, not just members of the military. In recent years the holiday—whose name has not changed despite the fact that the Soviet Army no longer exists—has acquired political significance for Communists and nationalists who want the Soviet Union back. The day is celebrated with fireworks in the evening.

SPRING

MAR.➤ March 8, **International Women's Day,** is a popular holiday similar to Mother's Day.

MAR.–APR.➤ **Orthodox Easter** is a major national holiday in both Russia and Ukraine. Visitors should attend the festive services, which begin at midnight and run through the night.

MAY➤ May 1, formerly **International Labor Day,** has in recent years turned into a celebration of spring (in Russian, *Prazdnik Vesny*). May 9, **Victory Day,** is one of the country's most important holidays; World War II veterans appear on the streets decked out in their medals and are honored throughout the day at open-air festivals and parades. **Moscow Stars,** a music and dance festival, is held in Moscow May 5 to 13.

SUMMER

JUNE➤ In Kiev, **Ivan Kupallo Day** (June 6) is a celebration of Mid-Summer's Night that dates from the city's pagan days. June 12 is **Russian Independence Day.** In St. Petersburg, the **White Nights Music Festival** is held during the last two weeks of June.

AUG.➤ August 24 is **Ukrainian Independence Day.**

AUTUMN

NOV.➤ November 7 and 8, the **Anniversary of the Bolshevik Revolution,** still inspire unofficial celebrations in some quarters.

2 MOSCOW

Prerevolutionary Moscow has woken from a long sleep and in every district work is under way to restore the splendor of the city's ancient monasteries and palaces. Statues have fallen, street names have changed, and everywhere Moscow is a hive of new restaurants, advertising offices, dance clubs, and supermarkets. Capitalism has not come lightly here, or cheaply, but at last the city's streets and squares bustle with the activity and color of commerce.

By Lauri del
Commune

Updated by
Christopher J.
Billy

IT IS DIFFICULT FOR WESTERNERS to comprehend what an important place Moscow holds in the Russian imagination as a symbol of spiritual and political power. Through much of its history the city was known as Holy Moscow and was regarded by Russians as a place of pilgrimage not unlike Jerusalem, Mecca, or Rome. Founded more than 850 years ago as the center of one of several competing minor principalities, Moscow eventually emerged as the center of a unified Russian state in the 15th century. One hundred years later it had grown into the capital of a strong and prosperous state, one of the largest in the world. Although civil war and Polish invasion ravaged the city in the early 17th century, a new era of stability and development began with the establishment of the Romanov dynasty in 1613.

The true test for Moscow came under Peter the Great. Profoundly influenced by his exposure to the West, Peter deliberately turned his back on the old traditions of Moscow, establishing his own new capital— St. Petersburg—on the shores of the Baltic Sea. Yet Western-looking St. Petersburg never replaced Moscow as the heart and soul of the Russian nation. Moscow continued to thrive as an economic and cultural center, despite its demotion. More than 200 years later, within a year of the Bolshevik Revolution in 1917, the young Soviet government restored Moscow's status as the nation's capital. In a move just as deliberate as Peter the Great's, the new Communist rulers transferred their government back to the Russian heartland, away from the besieged frontier and away from Russia's imperial past.

Moscow thus became the political and ideological center of the vast Soviet empire. And even though that empire itself has now broken apart, the city retains its political, industrial, and cultural sway. Although the several republics are now politically independent, no one challenges Moscow's status as capital of Russia or as the effective if not official center of that loosely defined political formation known as the Commonwealth of Independent States. Russia's largest city, with a population of more than 9 million, Moscow is home to the country's most renowned theaters, film studios, and cultural institutions. It is the country's most important transportation hub (even today most flights to the former Soviet republics are routed through Moscow's airports). And it is still the center of the continuing power struggles within the Russian government.

During the Soviet years, when all things foreign were regarded with deep suspicion, Moscow was the embodiment of the extreme isolationism of the Russian Communist regime. Sweeping political changes have dramatically changed this. To salvage and propel its giant economy, the Russian government and business community are actively pursuing foreign investment, even turning to foreign governments for assistance and advice, and everywhere setting their own economic plans and agendas into action.

As a result, today's Moscow is awash with construction sites and many of the city's historical structures are surrounded by scaffolding as the Russians attempt to reclaim and refurbish their pre-revolutionary past. Electronic billboards atop Stalinist-era socialist-realist buildings broadcast an eclectic array of messages, including the daily exchange rate, and a site just west of Red Square is under excavation for the construction of an indoor shopping mall. In stores and on endless rows of makeshift tables on some streets are a mix and breadth of products unthinkable in years past. A huge swelling in the number of cars means that traffic jams and their attendant noise—not to mention exhaust fumes—form a constant backdrop to the lively new street life. But all of it vividly reflects the commotion and excitement (as well as the pain and struggle) involved in the ongoing transition from a centralized economic system to a fluid free market.

Pleasures and Pastimes

The Arts
Gone are the days when the Bolshoi Theater and the Moscow Arts Theater ruled the cultural life of the Russian capital. Since the fall of Communism, Moscow's arts scene has taken a decidedly adventurous turn, and smaller, innovative theater companies and musical ensembles are giving the old standbys a run for their money. One feisty opera troupe, for example, appropriately called the **Novaya Opera** (New Opera), is challenging the Bolshoi Opera's ascendancy by staging fresh new productions of the old warhorses, many from the Russian repertoire. As is the case with a lot of these upstarts, the New Opera has no permanent home of its own; they mount their productions at various host venues throughout the city, usually at several different places within one season. Musicians, writers, directors are all flexing their muscles after years of working under strict state-imposed guidelines of what constitutes art.

Churches and Monasteries
All over Moscow churches are being painted, refurbished, polished, resurfaced, and in some cases, entirely rebuilt from the ground up. At almost every turn you'll run into another church surrounded by scaffolding and diligent artisans tending to the rebirth of Orthodoxy in the Russian capital. Many of these restoration projects are already finished and one of the joys of meandering through the city is turning a corner and suddenly happening upon the gleaming cupolas and brightly painted facade of a church from the Moscow Baroque. Most of these churches are also open to the public—brief services are conducted throughout the day. In addition to viewing the city's churches, visitors to Moscow with an interest in Orthodoxy and architecture will also enjoy touring one or more of the area's splendid monastery complexes. A few are within the city limits; others, including the venerated Sergyev Posad (Zagorsk) are just a day trip away.

Dining
The dining scene in the Russian capital continues to change, almost convulsively. From the state-run restaurants, once the only kind available, to the collectively owned cooperatives that followed perestroika, to the private-enterprise restaurants proliferating now, the changes are nothing short of astonishing. Whereas only two years ago, one was hard-pressed to find anything decent—let alone outstanding—there is no such shortage now: You may pick and choose among all three types of establishments. The contrasts, however, may leave you a bit wobbly. At a small restaurant or *stolovaya* you can experience the discomforts of Soviet management techniques. But right up the street you'll find an establishment so elegant it could compete in Paris or New York.

Lodging
A number of world-class luxury hotels have opened their doors in Moscow in the last few years, and for the traveler who is able and willing to splurge, they offer a level of amenities and pampering that were unavailable to tourists in the Russian capital just a few years ago. Gourmet restaurants, business centers, cafés and cocktail bars, health clubs, and attentive service are now the norm rather than the exception at Moscow's top hotels. (Mid-level establishments seem to be get-

ting the message, and there's evidence that they, too, are working hard to upgrade their facilities and level of service.) Leading the pack of deluxe properties today are the National, the Metropole, the Savoy, the Radisson Slavyanskaya, and the Baltschug Kempinski.

Nightlife

Moscow's after-hours scene has virtually created itself in the past few years. It may still have a long way to go, but there are already a fair number of choices despite predictable lapses of taste (many clubs and bars feature erotic floor shows that rival those of Times Square). Casinos, with their special brand of flashy tackiness, abound, but those interested in less overdone entertainment may take heart. As incomes rise and exposure to new types of leisure activity spreads, a wider range of night spots is opening. Nowadays you'll find clubs that specialize in particular kinds of music—jazz, country music, blues, rock. And there are now a few gay and lesbian venues to choose from. No matter what your taste or inclination, you'll be sure to find something to keep you out late. And in Moscow, late is very late: most clubs and bars are open until dawn.

When to Tour Moscow

The spring and fall, when temperatures are moderate, remain the optimal times for a visit. Unless your favorite season is winter and you feel you simply must have a picture of the Kremlin under freshly fallen snow, it's best to stay away during November, December, and January. Although the winter air in Moscow is dry and crisp, these months are by and large fairly miserable. The dead of summer, on the other hand, can actually be stiflingly hot; one advantage of visiting in July and August, though, is that on the weekends the streets are relatively uncrowded and you'll generally have no problem gaining access to museums and sights since most Muscovites abandon the city from Friday to Monday.

EXPLORING MOSCOW

Though the layout of the city may look confusing when you first look at a map, you'll soon see it has a logic of its own: Moscow is a series of concentric circles radiating out from the Kremlin at the center. The main streets of downtown Moscow extend out like spokes from a wheel starting at the Kremlin and intersecting the so-called Boulevard Ring and then the Garden Ring. Moscow's downtown proper, and most of the city's famous sights, are within the Garden Ring. You can walk most of the areas below on foot, but to be efficient in your touring of the city, especially if you're only in the city for a few days and you want to make sure you hit the highlights, you will have to familiarize yourself with the subway system (☞ Moscow A to Z, *below*).

Great Itineraries

To see all of the main sights of Moscow and its environs you need at least two weeks. Add another week to that if you want to do a thorough job of exploring the city's many museums along the way. Short-term visitors will have to be very selective in what they see.

IF YOU HAVE 3 DAYS
Start with a stroll across **Red Square,** a tour of **St. Basil's Cathedral,** the shopping arcades of **GUM,** and, if you're a devoted student of Soviet history and/or embalming techniques, the **Lenin Mausoleum.** Then walk through **Aleksandrovsky Sad** (the Alexander Gardens) to reach the tourist entrance to the **Kremlin.** Plan on spending the better part of your first day exploring the churches, monuments, and exhibits within the grounds of this most famous of Russian fortresses. The must-see

sights on a brief visit to the Kremlin include the **Archangelsky Sobor** (Cathedral of Archangel Michael), the **Uspensky Sobor** (Cathedral of the Assumption), the **Blagoveshchensky Sobor** (Cathedral of the Annunciation), the **Almazny Fond** (Diamond Fund), and, of course, the world's largest cannon (the Czar Cannon) and the world's largest bell (the Czar Bell). On the second day, spend the morning sightseeing and shopping on **Tverskaya Ulitsa** and the afternoon exploring **Kitai Gorod** and the churches and historical buildings on **Varvarka Ulitsa,** which extends from the eastern edge of Red Square, just behind St. Basil's. Try also toward the end of the day to squeeze in a stroll across **Teatralnaya Ploshchad** to see the **Bolshoi** and **Maly** theaters. Devote the third morning to the **Tretyakovskaya Gallery,** which has the finest collection of Russian art in the country, and in the afternoon go for a stroll down the **Arbat,** where you'll find plenty of options for sampling good food and haggling for Russian souvenirs.

IF YOU HAVE 7 DAYS
Follow the three-day itinerary above, then take our tour of the **Old Moscow of Bolshaya Nikitskaya Ulitsa** on day four. Devote day five to the **Pushkin Museum of Fine Arts** and an exploration of some of the streets in the surrounding **Kropotkinsky** District. Come back the next day and walk **from the Russian State Library to the Kropotkinsky District,** being sure to include the **Pushkin Memorial Museum** and a walk along the **Kremlyovskaya Naberezhnaya** (the embankment of the Moscow River) in the late afternoon for the spectacular views of the cupolas and towers of the Kremlin. On the final day, depending on whether your interests tend to the religious or the secular, spend the morning visiting either the Novodevichy Convent and Cemetery or complete the rest of our tour of the **Gorky Park Area,** which includes the Tretyakovskaya Gallery and the **Tolstoy House Estate Museum.** On your last afternoon finish up whatever shopping you still need to do on the **Novy Arbat.**

IF YOU HAVE 10 DAYS
In this amount of time it is possible to see most of the seven-day itinerary above, then travel farther afield on day trips to visit the cathedrals and museums of **Kolomenskoye, Zagorsk (Sergyev Posad),** the **Arkhangelskoye Estate Museum, and the New Jerusalem Monastery.** Depending on your interests, you could also use this extra time to visit some of the smaller museums devoted to the lives and accomplishments of prominent Russians; these include the **Pushkin Apartment Museum** and the **Chaliapin House Museum,** as well as museums devoted to the writers **Chekhov, Dostoevsky, Lermontov,**and **Mayakovsky,** the composers **Tchaikovsky, Glinka,** and **Scriabin,** and the artist **Viktor Vaznetsov.**

The Kremlin and Red Square

There are few buildings in the world that can match the historical importance of the Kremlin, *the* symbol of Russia's mystery and power for nearly five hundred years. The first wooden structure was erected on this site sometime in the 12th century. As Moscow grew, it followed the traditional pattern of Russian cities, developing in concentric circles around the elevated fortress at its center (the Russian word *kreml* means citadel or fortress). After Moscow emerged as the center of a vast empire in the late 15th century, the Kremlin came to symbolize the mystery and power of Russia. In the 20th century the Kremlin became synonymous with the Soviet government, and "Kremlinologists," Western specialists who studied the movements of the politicians in and around the fortress, made careers out of trying to decipher Soviet Russian policies. Much has changed in the last decade, as the former Soviet Union has unraveled. But despite the dramatic changes, the Kremlin remains mysteriously alluring. You'll find many signs of the old—and new—Russian enigma as you tour the ancient Kremlin grounds, where, before the black-suited men of the Bolshevik Revolution took over, czars were crowned and buried.

You can buy tickets for the Kremlin grounds and cathedrals for rubles at the kiosk in the **Aleksandrovsky Sad** (Alexander Garden) outside the Kremlin walls. There is a two-tiered price system for admission to the cathedrals and museums; foreigners pay significantly more than Russians. There are separate fees for seeing the Kremlin, each of its churches, the Armory Museum, and the Diamond Fund. Although you can purchase the Armory and Diamond Fund tickets inside as well, tickets to the cathedrals are only sold here, so be sure to get all the tickets you need now and save yourself the trip back. If you've decided that you want to visit all of the sights, tell the clerk that you want "fsye bil-YE-ti" (all tickets). Also, for entrance to the Armory and Diamond Fund, foreigners must pay in hard currency, a rule that is strictly enforced. Beware of scalpers offering tickets to the Armory at reduced prices; they are usually invalid for foreigners.

Numbers in the text correspond to numbers in the margin and on the Moscow and Kremlin maps.

A Good Walk

The oldest part of the city, the **Kremlin** ① is situated at the very center of Moscow, atop Borovitsky (Pine Grove) Hill. Start at the **Aleksandrovsky Sad** (Alexander Garden) subway stop, or from **Teatralnaya** station, both outside the fortress walls, in order to visit a few sights on your way to the Kremlin gates. To the right as you emerge from the **Teatralnaya** stop are the Kremlin's battlemented walls. In some places 65 feet high and 10 to 20 feet thick, they have stood in their present form practically unchanged since the end of the 15th century. At the northernmost point of the battlements is the so-called **Sobakina (Arsenal) Tower** ②. Adjacent to the tower is the monumental, wrought-iron gate that marks the entrance to the **Aleksandrovsky Sad.** Just beyond the garden entrance, to your left against the Kremlin wall, is the **Tomb of the Unknown Soldier** ③. Looking up from the garden to the Kremlin walls, you see a large yellow building, the **Arsenal.**

Continuing along the garden's path, you reach a double bastion lined by a stone bridge on nine pillars. The outer tower is the **Kutafya** ④, the massive tower at the far side is the **Troitskaya Bashnya** ⑤. Up to the right is the exit for the Alexandrovsky Sad subway stop, and farther up, as you ascend around to the right toward the tower, you will find the kiosk where you purchase tickets to the Kremlin grounds and cathedrals. After you have your tickets, go back to the path and continue through the garden to its end at the western corner of the Kremlin. To your left a path leads up a steep incline to the pyramid-shaped **Borovitskaya Tower** ⑥, the main entrance to the fortress. The yellow building to your immediate left as you enter the Kremlin houses the **Oruzheynaya Palata** ⑦, the oldest and richest museum in the Kremlin. In the same building is the **Almazny Fond.** As you exit the Oruzheynaya Palata, you will see a courtyard to your left, closed off by a wrought-iron railing. On the right-hand side of the courtyard, adjoining the armory, is the **Bolshoi Kremlyovsky Dvorets** ⑧, a cluster of buildings that includes the Terem and the the 15th-century Granovitaya Palata (Palace of Facets). Although most of the buildings are closed to the public, a portion of the Granovitaya Palata's facade is visible from the Square of Cathedrals. Continue up the steps to the historical heart of the Kremlin, **Cathedral Square** ⑨. To your immediate left as you enter the square

16

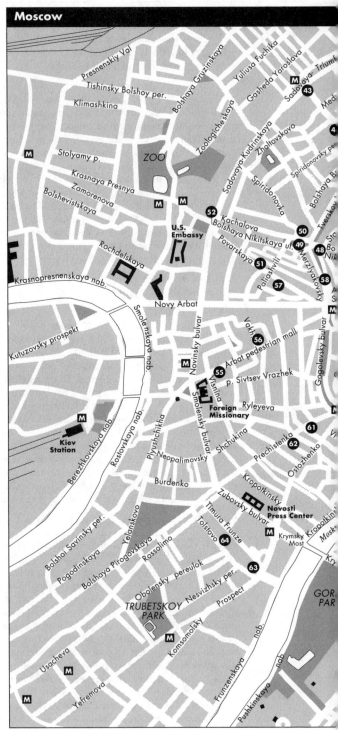

Moscow

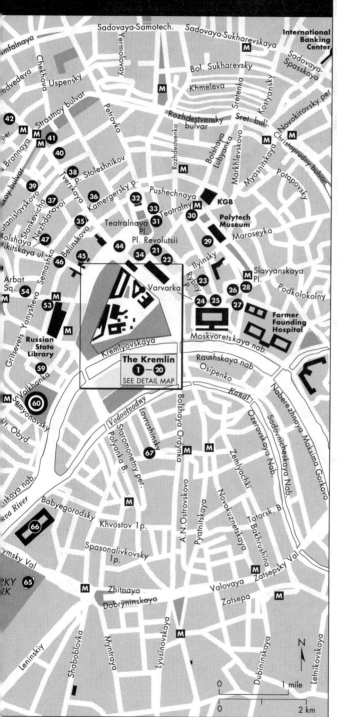

The Kremlin

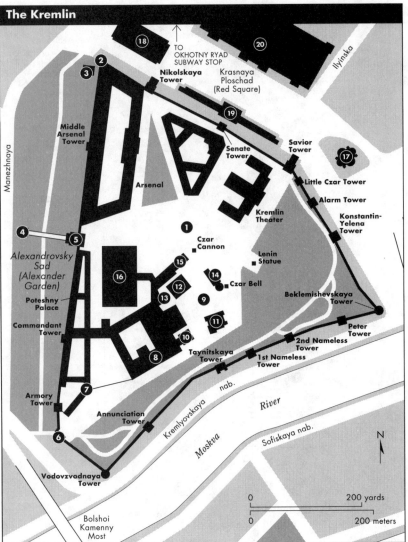

TO OKHOTNY RYAD SUBWAY STOP

Nikolskaya Tower

Krasnaya Ploschad (Red Square)

Ilyinska

Middle Arsenal Tower

Manezhnaya

Arsenal

Senate Tower

Savior Tower

Little Czar Tower

Alarm Tower

Konstantin-Yelena Tower

Kremlin Theater

Czar Cannon

Lenin Statue

Alexandrovsky Sad (Alexander Garden)

Czar Bell

Beklemishevskaya Tower

Poteshny Palace

Commandant Tower

Peter Tower

2nd Nameless Tower

1st Nameless Tower

Armory Tower

Taynitskaya Tower

Annunciation Tower

Kremlyovskaya nab.

River

Moskva

Sofiskaya nab.

Vodovzvodnaya Tower

N

0   200 yards
0   200 meters

Bolshoi Kamenny Most

Arkhangelsky Sobor, **11**

Blagoveshchensky Sobor, **10**

Bolshoi Kremlyovsky Dvorets, **8**

Borovitskaya Tower, **6**

Cathedral Square, **9**

Dvorets Syezdov, **16**

GUM, **20**

Istorichesky Muzey, **18**

Kremlin, **1**

Kolokolnya Ivan Veliky, **14**

Kutafya Tower, **4**

Mavzolei Lenina, **19**

Oruzheynaya Palata, **7**

St. Basil's Cathedral, **17**

Sobakina Tower, **2**

Sobor Dvenadtsati Apostolov, **15**

Tomb of the Unknown Soldier, **3**

Troitskaya Bashnya, **5**

Tserkov Rizopolozheniya, **13**

Uspensky Sobor, **12**

is the **Blagoveshchensky Sobor** ⑩. Standing opposite, to your right as you enter the square, is the **Arkhangelsky Sobor** ⑪. The dominating structure of the square is the massive **Uspensky Sobor** ⑫ bordering the north side (to your right as you exit the Arkhangelsky Sobor). All three cathedrals here are open to the public as museums. To the left of Uspensky Sobor is the smaller, single-domed **Tserkov Rizopolozheniya** ⑬. Cross the square to the eastern side, which is bordered by a massive bell tower, the **Kolokolnya Ivan Veliky** ⑭.

Leave Cathedral Square by walking through the open space to the left of the bell tower. You will come out to the road where vehicular traffic passes; across the road are the working buildings of the Russian government. They are off-limits to the public, and uniformed policemen blow whistles at trespassers. To your immediate left is the huge **Czar Cannon.** Nearby, mounted on a stone pedestal at the foot of the Ivan the Great Bell Tower (on the opposite side, to your right), is the **Czar Bell,** the world's largest bell. Follow the path along the road leading to your left out of the Kremlin. The last of the buildings open to the public is the **Sobor Dvenadtsati Apostolov** ⑮, to the north of Uspensky Sobor. Return to the road, bear left, and return to the Kutafya Tower. As you exit, you will notice, on your left, the horribly out-of-place **Dvorets Syezdov** ⑯.

Turn right after passing through the Kutafya Tower and walk back down to the Alexander Garden. Retrace your steps through the garden past the Tomb of the Unknown Soldier. Turn right once again, following the wall of the Kremlin. Climb the slight incline and you have reached **Krasnaya Ploshchad**–in English, Red Square. As you reach the square, you will not miss the multicolored onion domes of **St. Basil's Cathedral** ⑰ as they slowly come into view. Outside the cathedral doors is the **Lobnoye Mesto;** to the left is the **Spassky Tower.** Opposite St. Basil's, at the north end of Red Square, stands the redbrick **Istorichesky Muzey** ⑱. On the west side of the square, running along the Kremlin wall, is the **Mavzolei Lenina** ⑲, the world-famous and much-visited last resting place of Communism's greatest icon. Bordering the east side is the long facade of the **GUM** ⑳ department store.

TIMING
There are four daily tours of the Kremlin: at 10, noon, 2:30, and 4:30. The tour lasts about two hours. Join the line that forms outside the Armory entrance about 15 minutes before the tour. If you don't want to tackle all of this solo, you should consider a tour of the Kremlin grounds that includes the Armory, available from virtually any tour service that you prefer in Moscow. The Kremlin grounds and cathedrals are open every day except Thursday, 10–6. The Armory and Diamond Fund are also closed on Thursday. Admission to the Diamond Fund is by its own separate ticket; the highest priced of all of them, it is available at the entrance to the vaulted chambers. Again, joining a tour is recommended, if only because there are no signs, in any language, explaining the displays. If you wish to see Red Square in all its splendor, come back in the evening, when the square and its surrounding buildings are beautifully lit up.

Sights to See
Aleksandrovsky Sad (Aleksander Garden). Laid out in the 19th century by the Russian architect Osip Bove, the garden stretches along the northwest wall of the Kremlin, where the Neglinnaya River once flowed. The river now runs beneath the garden, through an underground pipe. ⊠ *Manezhnaya ul. Metro: Aleksandrovsky Sad.*

★ **Almazny Fond** (Diamond Fund). This amazing collection of diamonds, jewelry, and precious minerals was established in 1922 by the young Soviet government. The items on display date from the 18th century to the present. Highlights of the collection are the Orlov Diamond, a present from Count Orlov to his mistress, Catherine the Great; and the Shah Diamond, which was given to Czar Nicholas I by the Shah of Persia as a sign of condolence after the assassination in 1829 of Alexander Griboyedov, the Russian ambassador to Persia and a well-known poet. ⊠ *Kremlin.*

⓫ **Arkhangelsky Sobor** (Cathedral of the Archangel). This five-domed cathedral was commissioned by Ivan III (also known as Ivan the Great), whose reign witnessed much new construction in Moscow and in the Kremlin in particular. The cathedral was built in 1505–09 to replace an earlier church of the same name. The architect was the Italian Aleviso Novi, who came to Moscow at the invitation of the czar. You will notice distinct elements of the Italian Renaissance in the cathedral's ornate decoration, particularly in the scallop-shaped gables on its facade. Until 1712, when the Russian capital was moved to St. Petersburg, the cathedral was the burial place of Russian princes and czars. Inside you will find 46 tombs, including that of Ivan Kalita (Ivan Moneybags), who was buried in the earlier cathedral in 1340. Ivan Moneybags, who earned his nickname because he was so good at collecting tribute, was the first Russian ruler to claim the title of grand prince. The tomb of Ivan the Terrible is hidden behind the altar; that of his young son Dmitry is under the stone canopy to your right as you enter the cathedral. Dmitry's death at the age of seven is one of the many unsolved mysteries in Russian history. He was the last descendent of Ivan the Terrible, and many believe he was murdered, since he posed a threat to the ill-fated Boris Godunov (who at the time ruled as regent). A government commission set up to investigate Dmitry's death concluded that he was playing with a knife and "accidentally" slit his own throat. The only czar to be buried here after 1712 was Peter II (Peter the Great's grandson), who died of smallpox while visiting Moscow in 1730.

The walls and pillars of the cathedral are covered in frescoes that tell the story of ancient Russian history. The original frescoes, painted right after the church was built, were repainted in the 17th century by a team of more than 50 leading artists from several Russian towns. Restoration work in the 1950s uncovered some of the original medieval frescoes, fragments of which can be seen in the altar area. The pillars are decorated with figures of warriors; Byzantine emperors; the early princes of Kievan Rus, Vladimir, and Novgorod; as well as the princes of Moscow, including Vasily III, the son of Ivan the Great. The frescoes on the walls depict religious scenes, including the deeds of Archangel Michael. The carved Baroque iconostasis is 13 meters (43 feet) high and dates from the 19th century. The icons themselves are mostly 17th-century, although the revered icon of Archangel Michael is believed to date back to the 14th century. ⊠ *Kremlin.*

Arsenal. Begun in 1701 by Peter the Great, it was finished only at the end of the 18th century; its present form dates from the early 19th century, when it was reconstructed by Bove (the same architect who designed the Alexander Garden), after it was partially destroyed in the 1812 fire. The simple yet impressive two-story building was originally commissioned by Peter the Great as a weapons arsenal; today it houses government offices. ⊠ *Kremlin.*

⓾ **Blagoveshchensky Sobor** (Annunciation Cathedral). This remarkable monument of Russian architecture, linking three centuries of art and religion, was the private chapel of the royal family. Its foundations were laid in the 14th century, and in the 15th century a triangular brick church in the early Moscow style was erected on this site. Partially destroyed by fire, it was rebuilt during the reign of Ivan the Terrible, when six new gilded cupolas were added. Czar Ivan would enter the church by the porch entrance on the southeast side, which was built especially for him. He was married three times too many (for a total of six wives) under the bylaws of the Orthodox religion and was therefore not allowed to enter the church through its main entrance. The interior is decorated by brilliant frescoes painted in 1508 by the Russian artist Feodosy. The polished tiles of agate jasper covering the floor were a gift from the Shah of Persia. Most striking of all is the chapel's iconostasis. The fine icons of the second and third tiers were painted by some of Russia's greatest masters—Andrei Rublyov, Theophanes the Greek, and Prokhor of Gorodets. ⊠ *Kremlin.*

❽ **Bolshoi Kremlyovsky Dvorets** (Great Kremlin Palace). The palace actually consists of a group of buildings. The main section is the newest, built between 1838 and 1849. Its 375-foot-long facade faces south, overlooking the Moskva River. This was for centuries the site of the palace of the grand dukes and czars, but the immediate predecessor of the present building was badly damaged in the 1812 conflagration. For a few years it was the seat of the Russian parliament, which has now changed locations. It is not currently open to the general public.

The other buildings of the Great Kremlin Palace include the **Terem**, one of the oldest parts of the Kremlin, where the czarina received visitors, and the 15th-century **Granovitaya Palata** (Palace of Facets). Both building are also closed to the public. ⊠ *Kremlin.*

❻ **Borovitskaya Tower.** This pyramid-shaped tower, the main entrance to the Kremlin, rises to more than 50 meters (150 feet). At its foot a gate pierces its thick walls, and you can still see the slits for the chains of the former drawbridge. Black Volgas carrying government employees to work go whizzing through the vehicular entrance. Uniformed security guards stand at the separate pedestrian entrance, which opens promptly at 10 AM every day except Thursday. Tourists are usually admitted a few, or a group, at a time. The guards may ask where you are from and check inside your bags; sometimes there is a small security checkpoint to walk through, similar to those at airports. ⊠ *Kremlin. Manezhnaya ul. Metro: Borovitskaya.*

❾ **Cathedral Square.** The paved square, the ancient center of the Kremlin complex, is framed by three large cathedrals in the old Russian style, the imposing Ivan Bell Tower (☞ *below*), and the Granovitaya Palata (☞ Bolshoi Kremlyovsky Dvorets, *above*). ⊠ *Kremlin.*

Czar Bell. The world's largest bell is also the world's most silent: It has never rung once. Commissioned in the 1730s, the bell was damaged when it was still in its cast. It weighs more than 200 tons and is 20 feet high. The bas-reliefs on the outside show Czar Alexei Mikhailovich and Czarina Anna Ivanovna. ⊠ *Kremlin.*

Czar Cannon. This huge piece of artillery has the largest caliber of any gun in the world, but like the Czar Bell that was never rung, it has never fired a single shot. Cast in bronze in 1586 by Andrei Chokhov, it weighs 40 tons and is 17½ feet long. Its present carriage was cast in 1835, purely for display purposes. ⊠ *Kremlin.*

⓰ **Dvorets Syezdov** (State Kremlin Palace). This rectangular structure of glass and aluminum was built in 1962 to accommodate meetings of Communist Party delegates from across the Soviet Union. Today it is affiliated with the Bolshoi Theater and is used exclusively for concerts and ballets. ⊠ *Kremlin.*

㉑ GUM. Pronounced "goom," the initials are short for *Gosudarstvenny Universalny Magazin* or State Department Store. Formerly called the Upper Trading Rows, it was built in 1889–93 on the site where rows of trading stalls once stood. Three long passages with three stories of shops run the length of the building. Each passage is covered with a glass roof, and there are balconies and bridges on the second and third tiers. Another series of passages runs perpendicular to the three main lines, creating a mazelike mall. In feel, it resembles a cavernous turn-of-the-century European train station. There are shops aplenty here now, Western and Russian, and you may enjoy a saunter down at least one of its halls. ⊠ *3 Red Sq.* ☉ *Mon.–Sat. 8–8, Sun. 10–6. Metro: Ploshchad Revolutsii.*

⑱ Istorichesky Muzey (Historical Museum). This redbrick museum was built in 1874–83 in the pseudo-Russian style, which combined a variety of architectural styles. You may remember the building's twin towers from watching Soviet military parades on television. Against the backdrop of the towers' pointed spires, the tanks and missiles rolling through Red Square seemed to acquire even more potency. The museum was closed in 1986 for restoration, and no date has been set for its reopening. Before it closed, its extensive archaeological and historical materials outlined the development of Russia as well as that of the peoples of the former Soviet Union. In typical Soviet fashion, the exhibits focused on the growing political unrest in prerevolutionary Russia, which culminated (naturally, according to Marx) in the Bolshevik Revolution. Much has changed since 1986, and when it finally opens again, the museum's exhibits may be altered to reflect the new Russian political order. The museum also contains a rich collection of Russian arms and weaponry. ⊠ *1/2 Red Sq.,* ☎ *095/228–8452. Closed for restoration. Metro: Ploshchad Revolustsii.*

⑭ Kolokolnya Ivan Veliky (Ivan the Great Bell Tower). This is the tallest building in the Kremlin. The octagonal main tower is 263 feet high— 3 feet higher than the Hotel Rossiya (on the opposite side of Red Square), in accordance with the tradition established by Boris Godunov that the bell tower remain the tallest building in Moscow. The first bell tower was erected on this site in 1329. It was replaced in the early 16th century, during the reign of Ivan the Great (hence the bell tower's name). But it was during the reign of Boris Godunov that the tower received its present appearance. In 1600, the main tower was rebuilt, crowned by an onion-shaped dome, and covered with gilded copper. For many years it served as a watchtower; Moscow and its environs could be observed for a radius of 32 kilometers (20 miles). Altogether, the towers have 52 bells, the largest weighing 70 tons. The annex of the bell tower is used for temporary exhibits of items from the Kremlin collection, tickets for which are purchased at the entrance. ⊠ *Kremlin.*

★ Krasnaya Ploshchad (Red Square). World-famous for the grand military parades staged here during the Soviet era, it was originally called the Torg, the Slavonic word for marketplace. You may think that the name "Red Square" has something to do with Communism or the Bolshevik Revolution. In fact, however, the name dates back to the 17th century. The adjective *krasny* originally meant "beautiful," but over the centuries the meaning of the word changed to "red," hence the square's present name. The square is most beautiful at night. It is both romantic and impressive when entirely illuminated by floodlights, its ruby-red stars atop the Kremlin towers glowing against the dark sky. There are five stars in all, one for each of the tallest towers. They made their appearance in 1937 to replace the double-headed eagle, a tsarist symbol that is again finding favor as an emblem of Russia. The glass stars, which are lighted from inside and designed to turn with the wind, are far from fragile: The smallest weighs a ton. *Metro: Ploshchad Revolutsii.*

❹ **Kutafya.** This white bastion once defended the approach to the drawbridge that linked Aleksandrovsky Sad (☞ *above*) to the Kremlin. In Old Slavonic *kutafya* means "clumsy" or "confused"; this adjective was applied to the tower because it differs so in shape and size from the other towers of the Kremlin. ✉ *Manezhnaya ul. Metro: Aleksandrovsky Sad.*

Lobnoye Mesto. The name of the strange, round, white-stone platform in front of St. Basil's Cathedral (☞ *below*) literally means "place of the forehead," but it has come to mean "execution site," for it was right next to the platform where public executions were carried out. The platform was built in 1534 and was used by the czars as a podium for public speeches. Imperial *ukazy* (decrees) were proclaimed from here, and when the heir apparent reached the age of 16, he was presented to the people from this platform. ✉ *Red Sq. Metro: Ploshchad Revolutsii.*

⓳ **Mavzolei Lenina** (Lenin Mausoleum). Except for a brief interval during World War II, when his body was evacuated to the Urals, Lenin has lain in state here since his death in 1924. Whether it is really Lenin or a wax look-alike is probably one of those Russian mysteries that will go down in history unanswered. From 1924 to 1930 there was a temporary wooden mausoleum, replaced by the pyramid-shaped mausoleum you see now. It is made of red, black, and gray granite, with a strip of black granite near the top level symbolizing a belt of mourning. It was from the balcony of the mausoleum that Soviet leaders watched parades.

In the past, there were notoriously endless lines of people waiting to go in, but this is no longer the case. A visit to the mausoleum, however, is still treated as a serious affair. The surrounding area is cordoned off during visiting hours, and all those entering are observed by uniformed policemen. It is forbidden to carry a camera or any large bag. Inside it is cold and dark. It's considered disrespectful to put your hands inside your pockets (the same applies when you visit an Orthodox church), and the guards have been known to reprimand people for unbuttoned collars or sweaters. If you are inclined to linger at all, they will gently but firmly move you along. Before you know it you are ushered out of the mausoleum to the special burial grounds outside the mausoleum. When Stalin died in 1953, he was placed inside the mausoleum alongside Lenin, but in the early 1960s, during Khrushchev's tenure, the body was removed and buried here, some say encased in heavy concrete. Also here are such communist leaders as Zhdanov, Dzerzhinsky, Brezhnev, Chernenko, and Andropov, now mostly discredited. The American journalist John Reed is buried alongside the Kremlin wall. Urns set inside the wall contain ashes of the Soviet writer Maxim Gorky; Lenin's wife and collaborator, Nadezhda Krupskaya; Sergei Kirov, the Leningrad Party leader whose assassination in 1934 (believed to have been arranged for Stalin), was followed by enormous purges; the first Soviet cosmonaut, Yuri Gagarin; and other Soviet eminences.

The hourly changing of the guard outside Lenin's tomb, once a staggeringly formal event, has been eliminated. Local policemen, much more jocular in demeanor, have replaced the ramrod-stiff soldiers who once guarded the way into the tomb. ✉ *Red Sq.* ☉ *Tues.–Thurs. and Sat. 10 to 1, Sun. 10 to 2. Metro: Ploshchad Revolutsii.*

★ ❼ **Oruzheynaya Palata.** The Armory Palace is the oldest and richest museum in the Kremlin. It was originally founded in 1806 as the Imperial Court Museum, which was created out of three royal treasuries: the Court Treasury, where the regalia of the czars and ambassadorial gifts were kept; the Stable Treasury, which contained the royal harnesses and carriages used by the czars during state ceremonies; and the Armory, a collection of arms, armor, and other valuable objects gathered from the country's chief armories and storehouses. The Imperial Court Museum was moved to the present building in 1851. It was further enhanced and expanded after the Bolshevik Revolution with valuables confiscated and nationalized from wealthy noble families as well as from the Patriarchal Sacristy of the Moscow Kremlin. It now contains some 4,000 exhibits dating from the 12th century to 1917, including a rare collection of 17th-century silver. The museum tour begins on the second floor, which may cause some confusion if you visit the Armory on your own. Halls VI–IX are on the first floor, Halls I–V on the second.

Hall I displays works of goldsmiths and silversmiths of the 12th through 19th centuries, and **Hall II** contains a collection of 18th- to 20th-century jewelry. One of the most astounding exhibits is the collection of Fabergé eggs on display in Hall II (case 23). Among them is a silver egg whose surface is engraved with a map of the Trans-Siberian Railroad. The "surprise" inside the egg, which is also on display, was a golden clockwork model of a train with a platinum engine, windows of crystal, and a headlight made of a tiny ruby.

Hall III contains Oriental and Western European arms and armor, including heavy Western European suits of armor from the 15th to 17th centuries, pistols, and firearms.

Hall IV has a large collection of Russian arms and armor from the 12th to early 19th centuries, with a striking display of helmets. The earliest helmet here dates from the 13th century and is ascribed to Prince Yaroslav, father of Alexander Nevsky. Here, too, you will find the helmet of Prince Ivan, the son of Ivan the Terrible. The prince was killed by his father at the age of 28, an accidental victim of the czar's unpredictable rage. The tragic event has been memorialized in a famous painting by Ilya Repin (now in the Tretyakov Gallery; ☞ Gorky Park Area, *below*) showing the frightened czar holding his mortally wounded son. Russian chain mail, battle-axes, maces, harquebuses, ceremonial armor, and Russian and Oriental sabers are also in this hall. A highlight of the collection is the large Greek quiver belonging to Czar Alexei, his Oriental saber, and a heavy golden mace presented to him by the Persian Shah Abbas. Among the sabers on display here are those of Kuzma Minin and Dmitry Pozharsky, the national heroes who led the battle to oust the Polish forces from Moscow during the Time of Troubles in the early 17th century. Later you will see their statue on Red Square.

Hall V is filled with foreign gold and silver objects, mostly ambassadorial presents to the czars. History buffs will be interested in the "Olympic Service" of china presented to Alexander I by Napoléon after the signing of the Treaty of Tilsit in 1807.

Hall VI has vestments of silk, velvet, and brocade, embroidered with gold and encrusted with jewels and pearls. They were once worn by the czars, patriarchs, and metropolitans.

Hall VII contains the regalia and the imperial thrones. The oldest throne, veneered with carved ivory, belonged to Ivan the Terrible. The throne of the first years of Peter the Great's reign, when he shared power with his older brother Ivan, has two seats in front and one hidden in the back. The boys' older sister Sophia, who ruled as regent from 1682 to 1689, sat in the back, prompting the young boys to give the right answers to the queries of ambassadors and others. Another throne, covered with thin plates of gold and studded with more than 2,000 precious stones and pearls, was presented to Czar Boris Godunov by Shah Abbas of Persia. The throne of Czar Alexei, also from Persia, is decorated with 876 diamonds and 1,223 other stones. Among the crowns, the oldest is the sable-trimmed Cap of Monomakh, which dates to the 13th century. Ukraine is now asking for it back, since it originally belonged to the Kievan prince Vladimir Monomakh. It was a gift to the prince from his grandfather, the Byzantine emperor, and is revered as a symbol of the transfer of religious power from Byzantium to Russia. Also on display in this section are several coronation dresses, including the one Catherine the Great wore at her coronation in 1762.

Hall VIII contains dress harnesses of the 16th through 18th centuries. On display are Russian saddles, including one used by Ivan the Terrible, and other items once belonging to the Moscow Kremlin Equestrian Department.

Hall IX has a marvelous collection of court carriages. The oldest one came from England and is believed to have been presented to Czar Boris Godunov by King James I. Here you will find the Winter Coach that carried Elizabeth Petrovna (daughter of Peter the Great and someone who clearly liked her carriages) from St. Petersburg to Moscow for her coronation. Catherine the Great's French carriage, painted by François Boucher, is arguably the most attractive of the collection. ⊠ *Kremlin.*

② **Sobakina (Arsenal) Tower.** More than 180 feet high, the Sobakina Tower at the northernmost part of the thick battlements that encircle the Kremlin, was an important part of the Kremlin's defenses. Its thick walls concealed a secret well, which was of vital importance during times of siege. ⊠ *Kremlin. Manezhnaya ul. Metro: Ploshchad Revolutsii.*

⑮ **Sobor Dvenadtsati Apostolov** (Cathedral of the Twelve Apostles). Built in 1655–56 by Patriarch Nikon, this was used as his private church. Since 1963 the buildings have housed the **Museum of 17th-Century Applied Art.** The exhibits were taken from the surplus of the State Armory Museum and include books, tableware, clothing, and household linen. Next door to the church is the **Patriarshy Dvorets** (Patriarch's Residence), which is also open to the public. ⊠ *Kremlin.*

Spassky Tower (Tower of the Savior). Until Boris Yeltsin's presidency this tower served as the main entrance to the Kremlin. Indeed, in the centuries before Communist power, all who passed through it were required to doff their hat and bow before the icon of the Savior that hung on the front of the tower. The icon was removed, but you can see the outlines of where it was. ⊠ *Red Sq., Kremlin. Metro: Ploshchad Revolutsii.*

⑰ **St. Basil's Cathedral.** Although it is popularly known as St. Basil's Cathedral, the proper name of this whimsical structure is Pokrovsky Sobor (Church of the Intercession). It was commissioned by Ivan the Terrible to celebrate his conquest of the Tatar city of Kazan on October 1, 1552, the day of the feast of the Intercession. The central chapel, which rises 107 feet, is surrounded by eight towerlike chapels linked by an elevated gallery. Each chapel is topped by an onion dome carved with its own distinct pattern and dedicated to a saint on whose day the Russian army won battles against the Tatars. The cathedral was built between 1555 and 1560 on the site of an earlier Trinity Church where the Holy Fool Vasily (Basil) had been buried in 1552. Basil was an adversary of the czar, publicly reprimanding Ivan the Terrible for his cruel and bloodthirsty ways. He was protected from the czar by his status as a Holy Fool, for he was considered by the Church to be an emissary of God. Ironically, Ivan the Terrible's greatest creation came to be known by the name of his greatest adversary. In 1558 an additional chapel was built in the northeast corner over Basil's remains, and from that time on the cathedral has been called St. Basil's.

Very little is known about the architect who built the cathedral. It may have been the work of two men—Barma and Postnik—but now it seems more likely that there was just one architect, Postnik Yakovlyev, who went by the nickname Barma. Legend has it that upon completion of the cathedral, the mad czar had the architect blinded to ensure he would never create such a masterpiece again.

After the Bolshevik Revolution, the cathedral was closed and in 1929 turned into a museum dedicated to the Russian conquest of Kazan. Although services are occasionally held here on church holidays, the museum is still open. The antechamber contains displays outlining the various stages of the Russian conquest of Kazan as well as examples of 16th-century Russian and Tatar weaponry. Another section details the history of the cathedral's construction, with displays of the building materials used. After viewing the museum exhibits, you are free to wander through the cathedral. Compared to the exotic exterior, the dark and simple interiors are a disappointment. The brick walls are decorated with faded flower frescoes. The most interesting chapel is the main chapel, which contains a 19th-century Baroque iconostasis. ⊠ *Red Sq.,* ☏ *095/298–3304.* ☉ *Wed.–Mon. 11–3:30. Closed 1st Mon. of month. Metro: Ploshchad Revolutsii.*

The **statue** just outside St. Basil's originally stood in the center of the square. It depicts Kuzma Minin, a Nizhni-Novgorod butcher, and Prince Dmitry Pozharsky, who liberated Moscow in October 1612 from Polish-Lithuanian occupation. The work of Ivan Martos, it was erected in 1818, paid for by public subscription.

❸ Tomb of the Unknown Soldier. Dedicated on May 9, 1967, the 22nd anniversary of the Russian victory over Germany, this red granite monument contains the body of an unidentified Soviet soldier, one of those who, in the autumn of 1941, stopped the German attack at the village of Kryukovo, just outside Moscow. To the right of the grave there are six urns holding soil from the six "heroic cities" that so stubbornly resisted the German onslaught: Odessa, Sevastopol, Volgograd (Stalingrad), Kiev, Brest, and Leningrad (St. Petersburg). Very likely, no matter what time of year you are visiting, you'll see at least one wedding party. The young couple in full wedding regalia, along with friends and family, customarily stops here after getting married, leaving behind flowers and snapping photographs along the way. The gray obelisk just beyond the Tomb of the Unknown Soldier was erected in 1918 to commemorate the Marxist theoreticians who contributed to the Bolshevik Revolution. It was created out of an obelisk put up three years earlier, in honor of the 300th anniversary of the Romanov Dynasty. The arched "ruins" along the Kremlin wall, opposite the Obelisk, were designed by Osip Bove when he created the park. In the 19th century it was fashionable to include authentic-looking ruins in a landscaped park. ⊠ *Manezhnaya ul., Aleksandrovsky Sad. Metro: Ploshchad Revolutsii.*

❺ Troitskaya Bashnya (Trinity Tower). Rising 240 feet above the garden, this is the tallest tower in the Kremlin wall. Its deep, subterranean chambers were once used as prison cells. It is said that Napoléon lost his hat when he entered the Kremlin through this gate in 1812. ⊠ *Aleksandrovsky Sad, Kremlin. Metro: Aleksandrovsky Sad.*

⑬ **Tserkov Rizopolozheniya** (Church of the Deposition of the Virgin's Robe). This single-domed church was built in 1484–86 by masters from Pskov. Once the private church of the Moscow patriarch, it was rebuilt several times and restored to its 15th-century appearance by Soviet experts in the 1950s. The building boasts brilliant frescoes dating from the mid-17th century covering all of its walls, pillars, and vaults. Its most precious treasure is the iconostasis by Nazary Istomin. On display inside the church is an exhibit of ancient Russian wooden sculpture from the Kremlin collection. ⊠ *Kremlin.*

⑫ **Uspensky Sobor** (Assumption Cathedral). The dominating structure of Cathedral Square is one of the oldest edifices of the Kremlin. Designed after the Uspensky Sobor of Vladimir, it was built in 1475–79 by the Italian architect Aristotle Fiorovanti, who had spent many years in Russia studying traditional Russian architecture. Topped by five gilded domes, it is both austere and solemn. The ceremonial entrance faces Cathedral Square; the visitor's entrance is on the west side (to the left). After visiting the Archangel and Annunciation cathedrals (☞ *above*), you will be struck by the spacious interior here, unusual for a medieval church. Light pours in through two rows of narrow windows. The cathedral contains rare ancient paintings, including the icon of the Virgin of Vladimir (the work of an 11th-century Byzantine artist), the 12th-century icon of St. George, and the 14th-century Trinity. The carved throne in the right-hand corner belonged to Ivan the Terrible, and the gilt wood throne to the far left was the seat of the czarina. Between the two is the patriarch's throne. Until the 1917 Revolution, Uspensky Sobor was Russia's principal church. This is where the crowning ceremonies of the czars took place, a tradition that continued even after the capital was transferred to St. Petersburg. Patriarchs and metropolitans were enthroned and buried here. After the Revolution the church was turned into a museum, but in 1989 religious services were resumed here on major church holidays. ⊠ *Kremlin.*

Kitai Gorod

★ This tour explores the twisting and winding streets of **Kitai Gorod,** the oldest section of Moscow outside the Kremlin. The literal translation of Kitai Gorod is Chinatown, but there has never been a Chinese settlement here. The origin of the word *kitai* is disputed; it may come from the Tatar word for fortress, but most likely it derives from the Russian word *kita*, in reference to the bundles of twigs that were used to reinforce the earthen wall that once surrounded the area.

Kitai Gorod begins where Red Square ends. Settlement of this area began in the 12th century, around the time that the fortified city of Moscow was founded on Borovitsky Hill (the site of the present-day Kremlin). By the 14th century Kitai Gorod was a thriving trade district, full of shops and markets. At that time it was surrounded by earthen ramparts, which were replaced in the 16th century by a fortified wall. Remnants of that wall remain, and we will pass them later. As Moscow grew, so did Kitai Gorod. At the time of the Bolshevik Revolution it was the city's most important financial and commercial district, with major banks, warehouses, and trading companies concentrated here. These days, with the multitude of shops and new banks springing up throughout it, the area seems intent on inventing itself all over again.

A Good Walk

A good starting point for your tour is Nikolskaya ulitsa, which begins at the corner opposite the Historical Museum and runs along the north side of GUM. If you are coming from St. Basil's, walk down to the opposite side of Red Square. If you are coming from outside of Red Square, enter through the passageway to the right of the Teatralnaya subway station (as you are facing it). It is crowded, easily spotted, and is lined with the now ubiquitous *babushki* selling their wares. You can haggle over anything from lingerie to perfume to loaves of bread; unfortunately, their numbers testify to the ugly side of today's new freedom to trade, which in their case is not a matter of freedom but of survival. Taking a right out of the passageway, you find yourself on Nikolskaya ulitsa. Go a short way farther, to the cobblestone edge of Red Square, to begin your walk.

Named after the Kremlin's Nikolskaya Gate Tower, Nikolskaya ulitsa is one of the oldest streets in Moscow. At the corner with Red Square is the church **Kazansky Sobor.** Leaving the church, take a left to make your way through the teeming crowds of shoppers on Nikolskaya ulitsa to No. 7, the **Zaikonospassky Monastery** ㉑, the former Slavonic-Greco-Latin Academy. Farther down the street, also on the left-hand side, is a once brightly painted white-and-aqua building with an elaborate facade (No. 15). The building was erected in 1810–14 on the site of the 16th-century Pechatny Dvor (Printing Yard), where Russia's first printed book was assembled in 1553. Today the building is home to the Moscow Institute of Historical Records. Cross the street to go down Kuibyshevsky pereulok. Halfway down the block, opposite the entrance to the Ploshchad Revolutsii subway, is the **Bogoyavlensky Sobor** ㉒. Continue down the street to where it intersects with Ilinka Ulitsa. Before the 1917 revolution, this was Moscow's Wall Street. It is lined with the impressive facades of former banks. On the left-hand corner is the former **Ryabushinsky Bank.** As you cross the street, look to your right; Ilinka ulitsa leads directly to the Kremlin's Savior Gate Tower. Continue down Ilinka to Khrustalny pereulok, one of the border streets of the **Gostinny Dvor** ㉓ merchant's arcade (now being refurbished). Turn left and walk the length of Khrustalny pereulok to reach one of the oldest streets in Moscow, Varvarka ulitsa (Barbara Street). The opposite side of the street is lined with quaint old churches and buildings, but the first thing you notice is the gray bulk of the massive **Rossiya Hotel.**

At the farthest corner of the street, to your right, is the **Tserkov Velikomuchenitsy Varvary** ㉔. Adjacent is the **Old English Court.** Next comes the white-stone **Tserkov Maksima Blazhennovo.** The pointed bell tower situated just before the semicircle sidewalk leading to the upper-level entrance to the Rossiya Hotel was once attached to the redbrick **Znamensky Sobor** ㉕ on the other side of the sidewalk; with its foundation on the slope below, it is set back from the street. At No. 10 is the **Palace of the 16th and 17th centuries in Zaryadye** ㉖, considered the birthplace of Czar Mikhail Romanov. Before leaving this street of museums and churches, take note of the last one, the blue **Tserkov Georgiya na Pskovskoy Gorke** ㉗ at No. 12. If you stand to the left of the church (on the walkway leading to the Rossiya Hotel) you can glimpse a remnant of the 16th-century brick fortification wall. It is to your left, opposite the hotel's eastern facade. Return now to Varvarka ulitsa and cross to the other side, going a short hop past the final church. With your back to the Kremlin, take a left and climb the narrow Ipatevsky pereulok, which will lead up to a number of governmental and administrative buildings. At the top of the incline to the right, you will find one of Moscow's best-preserved 17th-century churches, the **Tserkov Troitsy v Nikitnikach** ㉘.

Continue down the lane to the right of the church to reach **Novaya Ploshchad,** or New Square, which is more like a boulevard than a square. To your right, at the far bottom of the hill, **Slavyanskaya Ploshchad**

(Slavic Square) opens up. At the bottom of the hill is the redbrick **Church of All-Saints in Kulishki.** From Novaya Ploshchad, stroll for a long block or two past the governmental buildings, where the Central Committee of the Communist Party once sat. Now they house the Duma of the Moscow Region. Soon you will come to the beginning of a busy intersection. To your right, in the median strip that divides Novaya Ploshchad, is a park that holds the Plevna Memorial, an octagonal, towerlike monument commemorating the Russian soldiers who fell in the Battle of Plevna in the Russo-Turkish War (1878). Keep walking up the street on the left side to go to the **Museum of the History of Moscow** ㉙.

Before you reach it, you will notice a building on the opposite side of the street that takes up the entire block. This is the **Polytechnical Museum.** A short distance from the museum, Novaya Ploshchad intersects with the circular **Lubyanskaya Ploshchad** ㉚, where you can behold the Lubyanka Prison and KGB headquarters. The store on the west side of the square is **Detsky Mir** (Children's World), a large department store that used to specialize in toys.

Still bearing left, walk past Lubyanka Square to the west side, down to where it converges with the broad street of **Teatralny proyezd.** In a side street to your right stands the recently refurbished Savoy Hotel (3 Rozhdestvenka ul.), which, like the Metropol Hotel, was built in connection with the celebrations honoring 300 years of the Romanov Dynasty. On the left-hand side of the street you will pass a statue of Ivan Fyodorov, the printer who produced Russia's first book at the Old Printing House you passed earlier on Nikolskaya ulitsa. The arched gateway just beyond the statue links Teatralny proyezd with Nikolskaya ulitsa in Kitai Gorod, the street on which you started the tour. Theater Passage leads into Theater Square, where three of Moscow's most important theaters are located.

The first building you will encounter, taking up the block on the southeast corner, to your left as you approach Theater Square, is the **Metropol Hotel** ㉛. Reaching the square, you will see at the center a large monument to Karl Marx, carved on the spot from a 200-ton block of granite and unveiled in 1961. Across the boulevard stands the **Bolshoi Theater** ㉜, flanked on the left, on the corner farthest away from you, by the Central Children's Theater, and, to the right, by the **Maly Theater** ㉝. Turn left at the corner of the Savoy Hotel, walk by the park and the hotel's main entrance. The fragmented brick wall ahead is the other surviving remnant of the 16th-century fortification wall that once surrounded Kitai Gorod. When you reach the Teatralnaya subway station, you may want to take a moment to admire the exterior of the massive redbrick building on the corner—the **Tsentralny Muzey V. I. Lenina** ㉞ (Lenin Museum, now closed).

TIMING

Taken at a leisurely pace, with stops to at least glance at the interiors of the many churches along the route, this walk should take about five hours. If you intend to have at least a quick look at the exhibits in the museums along the way, you'll need an entire day. Both the English Court and the Museum of the History of Moscow are worth coming back to for a more leisurely look at their holdings.

Sights to See

㉒ **Bogoyavlensky Sobor** (Cathedral of the Epiphany). This church is all that remains of the monastery that was founded on this site in the 13th century by Prince Daniil of Moscow. A good example of the Moscow Baroque style, the cathedral is now undergoing a long overdue renovation, and, unfortunately for tourists, much of the structure will remain hidden by scaffolds for at least another year. It is, however, open for services (Sun. 7 and 9:30 AM) and there's a shop in the foyer that sells icon cards, religious objects, and books about the Russian Orthodox faith (entry is from the courtyard around back). ⊠ *Bogoyavlensky pereulok. Metro: Ploshchad Revolutsii.*

★ ☼ ㉜ **Bolshoi Theater.** Formerly known as the Great Imperial Theater, Moscow's "big" (*bolshoi* means big) and oldest theater was completely rebuilt after a fire in 1854. Its opera and ballet companies are world-famous and its 2,155 seats are often sold out. The building itself is remarkable: its monumental colonnade is topped by a quadriga of bronze horses pulling the chariot of Apollo, patron of music. Its crimson-and-gold interior is similarly grand. If you have the pleasure of seeing a performance at the Bolshoi, don't leave before the stage curtain is lowered at the end of the performance. It falls resplendent, in a thick weave of hammers and sickles. An interesting footnote in the theater's and the Soviet Union's history: Lenin made his last public speech here, in 1922. To the left of the Bolshoi is the **Central Children's Theater,** which puts on traditional performances for a younger audience. This is also where you'll find the Bolshoi's main ticket office. ⊠ *Teatralnaya Ploshchad,* ☎ *095/292–0050. Metro: Teatralnaya.*

Detsky Mir (Children's World). This large store used to specialize exclusively in toys and clothing for children, but these days you'll find just about anything in its crowded aisles. ⊠ *2 Teatralny proyezd. Metro: Lyubyanka.*

NEED A BREAK? The small lobby bar at the **Savoy Hotel** (⊠ 3 Rozhdestvenka ul.) is a favorite spot with Moscow's foreign community. Join them in its gilt interior for a spicy-hot bowl of French onion soup or a club sandwich. The hotel also has a famous—and very expensive—restaurant. The bar menu, although by no means cheap, is more reasonably priced than the one you'll find in the hotel's famous restaurant. The service is professional, and it's a great place to take a break after fighting the crowds of downtown Moscow.

English Court. Built in the mid-16th century, this white-stone building with a steep shingled roof and narrow windows became known as the English Court because Ivan the Terrible—wanting to encourage foreign trade—presented it to English merchants trading in Moscow. Reopened as a branch of the Museum of the City of Moscow in late 1995, its displays about Russian-British trade relations over the centuries may be particularly interesting to visitors from the U.K. ⊠ *4 Varvarka ul.,* ☎ *095/298–3952/3961.* ☼ *Tues., Thurs., and weekends 10–6; Wed. and Fri. 11–7. Metro: Ploshchad Revolutsii or Kitai-Gorod.*

㉓ **Gostinny Dvor** (Merchants' Arcade). This market, which takes up an entire block between ulitsa Ilinka and Varvarka ulitsa, just east of Red Square, is made up of two imposing buildings: running the length of Khrustalny pereulok is the Old Merchant Arcade, erected by the Italian architect Quarenghi in 1791–1805; on the other side of the block, bordering Rybny pereulok, is the New Merchant Arcade, built in 1838–40 on the site of the old fish market. The entire complex is being renovated and will not be open until early 1998. ⊠ *Ulitsa Ilinka. Metro: Ploshchad Revolutsii or Kitai-Gorod.*

Ivanovsky Monastery (St. John's Convent). Built in the 16th century and restored in the 19th, this monastery was used as a prison in the Stalinist era and was in shambles for many years after that. Fortunately, it is once again being refurbished. Among the noble women who were forced to take the veil here were Empress Elizabeth's illegitimate daughter, Princess Tarankova, and the mad serf-owner Dariya Saltykova, who was imprisoned here after she murdered 138 of her serfs, most of them young women. ⊠ *Zabelina ul. and Maly Ivanovsky pereulok. Metro: Kitai-Gorod.*

Kazansky Sobor (Cathedral of Our Lady of Kazan). Built in 1633–36 to commemorate Russia's liberation from Polish occupation during the Time of Troubles, this church was purposely blown up in 1936 and not rebuilt and fully restored until 1993. Its salmon-and-cream painted brick and gleaming gold cupolas are now a colorful magnet at the northeast corner of Red Square, between the Historical Museum and GUM. Inside and outside hang icons of Our Lady of Kazan; the small chapel affords an excellent look at the traditional iconostasis and interior design of Russian churches. In the front vestibule, you can buy candles to light a prayer; you'll also find other religious articles for sale. Many faithful visit throughout the day. ⊠ *Nikolskaya ul., at Red Sq.* ☉ *Daily 8–7, except Mon., when it closes is at the end of the 5 PM vespers service. Sun. services at 7 and 10 AM. Metro: Ploshchad Revolutsii.*

㉚ Lubyanskaya Ploshchad. This circular "square" was recently returned to its prerevolutionary name. In 1926 it had been renamed Dzerzhinsky Square, in honor of Felix Dzerzhinsky, a Soviet revolutionary and founder of the infamous CHEKA, the forerunner to the KGB. His statue once stood in the center of the square, but was toppled in August 1991, along with the old regime. A huge round flower bed has replaced it. The large yellow building facing the square, with bars on the ground-floor windows, was once the notorious Lubyanka Prison and KGB headquarters. *Metro: Lubyanka.*

㉝ Maly Theater. Opened in 1824 and formerly known as the Little Imperial Theater (*maly* means "little"), this house is famous for its productions of Russian classics. Maxim Gorky once called the Maly "the Russian people's university." Out front stands a statue of a beloved and prolific playwright whose works are often performed here, the 19th-century satirist Alexander Ostrovsky. ⊠ *1/6 Teatralnaya Ploshchad,* ☎ *095/923–2621. Metro: Teatralnaya.*

Mayakovsky Library and Museum. This museum of Russia's great revolutionary poet is in his former home. ⊠ *3/6 Proeyzd Serova,* ☎ *095/ 255–0186.* ☉ *Tues., Fri.–Sun. 10–6; Mon. noon–6; Thurs. 1–9. Metro: Lubyanka.*

㉛ Metropol Hotel. Built in the early 20th century in preparation for the anniversary celebrations commemorating 300 years of the Romanov dynasty, the Metropol was reconstructed in the late 1980s, and its brilliant Art Nouveau facade is now being restored to its original appearance. The venue of many a historical speech, including a few by Lenin, the hotel was the focus of heavy fighting during the revolution, and for some time the Central Committee of the Russian Soviet Federal Republic met here under its first chairman, Yakov Sverdlov. Until 1990, Theater Square, the wide-open space across from the hotel, facing the Bolshoi Theater, was named Sverdlov Square, in his honor. (☞ Lodging, *below,* for more information.)

㉙ Museum of the History of Moscow. Housed in the former **Church of St. John the Baptist** (1825), this museum presents Moscow's architectural history using paintings and artifacts. It's a small, manageable museum, and it's worth stopping in for a brief visit to get a fuller view of the Moscow you've been getting glimpses of while exploring the city's older districts. ⊠ *12 Novaya Pl.,* ☎ *095/924–8490.* ☉ *Tues., Thurs.,* *weekends 10–6; Wed., Fri. 11–7. Closed last day of month. Metro: Lubyanka.*

㉖ Palaty Romanovych v Zaryadye (Romanov Palace Chambers in Zaryadye). It is believed that Mikhail Romanov was born in this house. Today the mansion houses a lovely museum devoted to the *boyar* (nobleman) lifestyle of the 16th and 17th centuries. The rooms are furnished to show how the boyars lived, with period clothing, furniture, and household items on display. During the week, the museum is generally open only to groups with advance reservations, but if you ask, you may be allowed to join a group. On Sunday the museum is open to the general public. Once again, tourists can visit only in groups, but after a short wait, enough people will gather to form a tour. You'll find the entrance downstairs, opposite the lower doorway of the hotel. ✉ *10 Varvarka ul.,* ☎ *095/298–3706.* ⊘ *Mon., Thurs.–Sun. 10–6; Wed. 11–5. Metro: Kitai-Gorod.*

Polytechnical Museum. This museum, which takes up the entire block and was opened in 1872 (it was originally called the Museum of Applied Knowledge), today houses exhibits devoted to achievements in science and technology. ✉ *3/4 Novaya Pl.,* ☎ *095/923–0756.* ⊘ *Tues.–Sun. 10–6. Closed last Thurs. of month. Metro: Lubyanka.*

Rossiya Hotel. With accommodation for 6,000, the Rossiya is one of Europe's largest hotels. Russians often joke that the Soviets chose this site for the hotel because foreign tourists wouldn't ever have to leave their room: Varvarka Ulitsa, with its rich mixture of architecture, was all they would ever need to see. (☞ Lodging, *below,* for more information.) ✉ *6 Varvarka ul. Metro: Kitai-Gorod.*

Ryabushinsky Bank. This Art Nouveau masterpiece was designed by Fyodor Shekhtel at the turn of the century for the rich merchant Ryabushinsky. The pale-orange building on the opposite side of the street is the former Birzha (Stock Exchange). Built in the classical style at the end of the 19th century, it now houses Russia's Chamber of Commerce and Industry. ✉ *Birzhevaya Pl. at Ilinka ul.*

㉞ Tsentralny Muzey V. I. Lenina. The Lenin Museum, once a solemn and sacred place in Soviet Russia, is now closed, but the magnificent exterior is well worth a look.

㉗ Tserkov Georgiya na Pskovskoy Gorke (Church of St. George on Pskov Hill). The graceful five-domed blue church, built in 1657 by merchants from Pskov, stands right next to the Romanov Mansion, in front of the Rossiya Hotel. The bell tower was an addition from the 19th century. ✉ *12 Varvarka ul. Metro: Kitai-Gorod.*

Tserkov Maksima Blazhennovo (Church of St. Maxim the Blessed). Built in 1698 on the site where the Holy Fool Maxim was buried, this white-stone church between St. Barbara's and the Znamensky Sobor (in front of the northern side of the Rossiya Hotel) contains a folk-art exhibit of wood carvings, embroidery, and other handicrafts. All the art work is for sale. ✉ *6 Varvarka ul.,* ☎ *095/298–1312.* ⊘ *Daily 11–6. Metro: Kitai-Gorod.*

㉘ Tserkov Troitsy v Nikitnikach (Church of the Trinity in Nikitniki). This lovely redbrick creation—one of the most striking churches in the city—mixes Baroque decoration with the principles of ancient Russian church architecture. Painted with white trim and topped by five green cupolas, the church was built in 1635–53 for the merchant Grigory Nikitnikov. The private chapel on the south side was the family vault. The murals and iconostasis were the work of Simon Ushakov, a famous icon painter whose workshop was located nearby, in the brick building across the courtyard. Unfortunately the structure is now closed for restoration, but it's still worth seeking out for a look at its exterior. ⊠ *3 Nikitnikov pereulok,* ☎ *095/298–5018. Metro: Kitai-Gorod.*

㉔ Tserkov Velikomuchenitsy Varvary (St. Barbara's Church). This pink-and-white church, built in the classical style at the end of the 18th century, lends its name to the street. It is now once again an active church, with daily services. Its gift shop sells religious items as well as souvenirs. ⊠ *Varvarka ul. off of Red Sq. Metro: Ploshchad Revolutsii.*

Tserkov Vsekh Svyatykh na Kulishkakh (Church of All-Saints in Kulishki). This graceful church, a fine example of 17th-century religious architecture, is one of the few survivors of the Soviet reconstruction of the area. It was recently returned to the Orthodox Church and is now open for services (Sun. 10 AM and 5:30 PM). ⊠ *Pl. Varvarskych Vorot. Metro: Kitai-Gorod.*

Victor Vasnetsov Museum. This house-museum was the home of the Russian artist Victor Vasnetsov from 1894 to 1926. Built by the artist himself, it is a charming example of the "fairy-tale" architectural style that was popular at the end of the 19th century. Inside the house, Vasnetsov's paintings of Russian fairy tales are on display. ⊠ *13 pereulok Vasnetsova,* ☎ *095/281–1329.* ☉ *Wed.–Sun. 10–4:30. Closed last Thurs. of month. Metro: Sukharevskaya.*

㉑ Zaikonospassky Monastery (Monastery of the Savior Behind the Icons). Russia's first institution of higher learning, the Slavonic-Greco-Latin Academy, was opened in this building in 1687. The monastery itself was founded at the beginning of the 17th century by Boris Godunov. Hidden inside the courtyard between buildings No. 7 and No. 8 is the monastery's cathedral, built in 1717–42 in the style of Moscow Baroque. It is currently under *"remont,"* but a Sunday service is still held here, and on other days you can usually gain access. ⊠ *7 Nikolskaya ul. Metro: Pl. Revolutsii.*

㉕ Znamensky Sobor (Cathedral of the Sign). This was part of the monastery of the same name, built on the estate of the Romanovs in the 16th century, right after the establishment of the Romanov dynasty. After the death of the last heir to Ivan the Terrible, a dark period set in, marked by internal strife and foreign intervention. That period, commonly known as the Time of Troubles, ended in 1613, when the Boyar Council elected the young Mikhail Romanov czar.

Tverskaya Ulitsa

Tverskaya ulitsa is Moscow's version of New York's Fifth Avenue. The city's main shopping artery, it attracts out-of-towners searching hungrily for a good buy, as well as the foreign investor looking for a lucrative place to set up shop. The street is lined with massive apartment buildings whose ground floors house some of the city's best and biggest stores. In recent years, many of the old state-run enterprises have been ousted and replaced with neon-lit private and foreign ventures dealing in credit cards and pricey goods. A stroll up Tverskaya these days promises window shopping of a very fancy order and a look at some of Moscow's attractive buildings, several graced by a fine Art Nouveau style. It is a lovely, wide boulevard lined with perfumeries, banks and exchanges, eateries, and bookshops. On a sunny day, it is an especially pleasant walk. Keep an eye out for plaques etched in stone on building walls. These will tell you about the famous people, usually artists, politicians, or academicians, who lived or worked there.

Tverskaya ulitsa was given its present form in the mid '30s, during the first plan of reconstruction, though it had been an important route for centuries—the line of the road that led from the Kremlin to the ancient town of Tver. Later that road was extended all the way to the new capital on the Baltic Sea, St. Petersburg. From 1932 to 1990 Tverskaya was known as Gorky Street, in honor of the writer Maxim Gorky, the father of Soviet socialist realism. In 1990, the first section of the street, leading from the heart of town to Triumfalnaya Square, was given back its prerevolutionary name. The renaming was completed a year later, when the second section, ending at the Belorussian Railway Station, was also returned to its old name—Tverskaya Yamskaya. Until the rebuilding in the 1930s, Tverskaya ulitsa was narrow and twisting, lined in places with wooden houses. Today it is a broad, busy avenue, a tribute to the grandiose reconstruction projects of the Stalinist era.

A Good Walk

Walking up the left-hand side of the street, you pass, at No. 5, the **Yermolova Theater.** One short block farther, on the same side of the street, you come to the **Central Telegraph Office** ㉟. On the opposite side of the avenue, Kamergersky pereulok leads off to the right. The small green building on the left-hand side of this street houses the **Moscow Art Theater** ㊱. If you're interested in antiquarian bookshops, you'll find some here.

Returning to Tverskaya, continue up on the left-hand side of the street. If you want to take a break from the hustle and bustle of Tverskaya, wander down ulitsa Nezhdanovoi, a side street to the left. You enter the street through the arched passageway of No. 11, which is the **Russian Federation of Science and Technology.** This street has long been home to many of Moscow's successful artists. At the end of the block, you come upon the pretty **Tserkov Voskreseniya** ㊲. Go back to Tverskaya ulitsa. The handsome red building just ahead with its impressive iron gates to its adjacent side street is the **Moscow City Council** (Mossoviet). Across the street, another short stretch brings you to the small square **Tverskaya Ploshchad** ㊳. Farther up the street, again on the left-hand side, you pass ulitsa Stanislavskovo. At No. 7 is the **Russian Folk Art Museum** ㊴. At No. 14 you find **Yeliseyevsky's** ㊵, the most dazzling of all of Moscow's stores. Back outside you're likely to encounter lots of construction (destined, it would seem, to go on for years), as you head farther up the street, toward **Pushkinskaya Ploshchad** ㊶, named after the revered poet and writer. Bordering the west side of the square is the **Rossiya Movie Theater.**

Bordering the square to the right and left of the park are the offices of some of Russia's largest and most influential newspapers. Easily spotted is *Izvestia* (*News*), once the mouthpiece of the Soviet government and now considered a liberal newspaper. Between 18 and 20 Tverskaya, if you look down the alley, you'll see the striking facade of *Trud* (*Labor*), the official newspaper of the trade unions and of late a conservative voice. Looking back to the far corner that you came from, you'll see the building of *Moscow News,* the newspaper that helped give *glasnost* true meaning back in the early years of *perestroika*. Its brave editor allowed articles on topics then considered extremely controversial, from Stalinist collectivization to the ethnic strife in Armenia and Azerbaijan.

Continuing along Tverskaya ulitsa, you reach the attractive railings of the former **English Club** ㊷, now the Museum of the Revolution. As you continue in the same direction, you'll pass the Moscow Drama Theatre, another bearing the name of Stanislavsky. The next major intersection is **Triumfalnaya Ploshchad** ㊽. On the north side of Triumfalnaya Ploshchad, Tverskaya ulitsa becomes **Tverskaya-Yamskaya ulitsa.**

TIMING

Allow at least three hours for this tour, five or six if you plan to visit the museums along the route.

Sights to See

㉟ Central Telegraph Office. The striking semicircular entrance is adorned with a large, illuminated, and constantly revolving globe. Inside, you can buy stamps, send a fax home, or even make a phone call abroad. You will find currency-exchange counters in the lobby and the main post office as well. ⊠ *7 Tverskaya ul.* ☏ *095/924–9004.* ☉ *Mon.–Sat. 9 AM–7 PM. Metro: Okhotny Ryad.*

㊷ English Club. The onetime social center of the Moscow aristocracy has an entrance flanked by two smirking lions. Built by Giliardi in 1787, the mansion was rebuilt in the classical style after the Moscow Fire of 1812. Since 1926, it has housed the **Museum of the Revolution.** Although it retains many of its former exhibits—heavily imbued with Soviet propaganda—the museum has been updated to reflect the changing political situation in Russia. The permanent exhibit, located on the second floor, begins with a review of the first workers' organizations in the 19th century. The exhibits outlining the 1905 and 1917 revolutions include the horse-drawn machine-gun cart of the First Cavalry Army, the texts of the first decrees of the Soviet government on peace and land, dioramas and paintings portraying revolutionary battles, and thousands of other relics. The next rooms outline the history of Soviet rule, with extensive material devoted to Stalin's rise to power. The final exhibit is dedicated to the August 1991 coup. It features a reconstructed version of the barricades set up outside the Russian Parliamentary Building, where Yeltsin made his famous appeals to the Russian people. Explanations of the exhibits are only in Russian, but you can arrange for a guided tour in English by calling ahead. The entrance fee is low, even though foreigners pay more than Russians. You will also find interesting temporary exhibits on the first floor of the museum. Snoop through their gift shop, which features standard Russian souvenirs (including some beautiful amber) and great vintage items like flags and political-rally posters. ⊠ *21 Tverskaya ul.,* ☏ *095/299–6724.* ☉ *Tues., Thurs.–Sat. 10–6; Wed. 11–7; Sun. 10–5. Closed last Fri. of month. Metro: Tverskaya.*

Glinka Museum. This museum is devoted to the history of music, with a special emphasis on Russian composers of the 19th century. There is a fine collection of musical instruments. ⊠ *4 ul. Fadeyeva,* ☏ *095/ 972–3237.* ☉ *Wed., Fri., weekends 11–6:30; Tues., Thurs. 1–7:30. Closed last Fri. of month. Metro: Mayakovskaya.*

㊱ Moscow Art Theater (MKhAT). One of Moscow's most historically important theaters, it is renowned for its productions of the Russian classics, especially those of Chekhov. Founded in 1898 by the celebrated actor and director Konstantin Stanislavsky (1863–1938) and Vladimir Nemirovich-Danchenko (1858–1943), the theater staged the first productions of Chekhov's and Gorky's plays. It was here that Stanislavsky developed the "Stanislavsky Method," based on the realistic traditions of the Russian theater. After the successful production of Chekhov's *Seagull* (the first staging in St. Petersburg had bombed), the bird was chosen as the theater's emblem. An affiliated, more modern theater, with a seating capacity of 2,000, also confusingly called the Moscow Art Theater, was opened in 1972 on Tverskaya ulitsa, near Stanislavsky's home. ⊠ *3 Kamergersky pereulok,* ☏ *095/299–8760 or 095/290–5128. Metro: Okhotny Ryad.*

Moscow City Council (Mossoviet). This impressive structure was built at the end of the 18th century by Matvey Kazakov for the Moscow governor-general. During the reconstruction of Tverskaya ulitsa in the 1930s, the building was moved back about 45 feet in order to widen the street. The top two stories—a mirror image of the mansion's original two stories—were added at that time. ⊠ *22 Tverskaya ul. Metro: Tverskaya.*

Moscow Wax Museum. A Russian Madame Tussaud's, this place has figures of important leaders, all the way up to Yeltsin. ⊠ *14 Tverkaya ul.,* ☎ *095/229–8552.* ⊙ *Tues.–Sun. 11–7. Metro: Tverskaya.*

㊶ Pushkinskaya Ploshchad (Pushkin Square). The city's first McDonald's is at this site, where Moscow's first outer ring, the Bulvar (Boulevard), crosses Tverskaya ulitsa. If you're longing for that familiar burger, stop for lunch. There are rarely lines anymore (branches have opened throughout the city), but you'll quickly see how popular it remains. The counters are always crowded, with disorganized but swiftly moving lines. The menu hews to the original, and prices are cheaper than in the States. Russians come by the score but don't dawdle—they take the term "fast food" literally! The park on the right-hand side of the street is a popular meeting place for Muscovites. A fountain stands in the center of a terraced park, which is lined with benches. A bronze statue of Pushkin stands at the top of the park. It is the work of Alexander Opekushin and was erected by public subscription in 1880. Summer and winter, fresh flowers on the pedestal prove that the poet's admirers are still ardent and numerous. *Metro: Pushkinskaya.*

Rossiya Movie Theater. Built in 1961, the theater stands on the site of the former Strastnoi Monastery (Convent of the Lord's Passion), whose history dated back to the mid-17th century; it was destroyed in 1937. All that remains of the ancient monastery is the white-stone Church of the Nativity near the corner with ulitsa Chekhova (to the far left as you face the theater). ⊠ *Pushkinskaya Pl. Closed for repairs. Metro: Pushkinskaya.*

㊴ Russian Folk Art Museum. Founded by a wealthy merchant and patron of the arts, Savva Morozov, the museum displays a rich collection of Russian folk art dating from the 17th century to the present, including antique and modern pottery, ceramics, glassware, metalwork, wood, bone, embroideries, lace, and popular prints. Theater director Konstantin Stanislavsky, founder of the Moscow Art Theater (☞ *above*), lived for a time in the building at No. 6. ⊠ *Ul. Stanislavskovo 7,* ☎ *095/291–8718,* ⊙ *Mon., Wed., Fri.–Sun. 11–5:30; Tues., Thurs. noon–7:30. Metro: Tverskaya.*

㊸ Triumfalnaya Ploshchad. This major intersection is where the grand boulevard of Moscow, the Sadovaya (Garden) Ring, crosses Tverskaya ulitsa. Traffic here also passes through a tunnel running below Tverskaya ulitsa, and there is an underpass for pedestrians. A statue of the revolutionary poet Vladimir Mayakovsky stands in the center of the square. It is generally believed that Mayakovsky committed suicide in 1930 out of disillusionment with the revolution he had so passionately supported. *Metro: Mayakovskaya.*

Triumfalnaya Ploshchad is a center of Moscow's cultural life. The **Tchaikovsky Concert Hall** stands on the corner nearest you. It was opened in 1940 and seats 1,600. The **Satire Theater** is right next door, on the Sadovaya Ring. On the far side of the square stands the **Moskva Cinema**; the popular **Mossoviet Theater** is also located nearby, at 16 Bolshaya Sadovaya. To your far left you see the multitiered tower of the imposing **Peking Hotel.** Opened in 1956 as a mark of Sino-Soviet friendship, it houses one of the city's best Chinese restaurants. Looking to your right, you'll see the **American Bar and Grill,** popular with Russians as well as the foreign community.

While you're here, it's worth riding the escalator down for a peek at the spectacular interior of the **Mayakovskaya subway station.** Its ceiling is decorated with colorful, fluorescent mosaics depicting Soviet achievements in outer space. Like many of the early subway stations, it is deep underground (it doubled as a bomb shelter during World War II). Stalin made a famous speech here on the 24th anniversary of the Bolshevik Revolution, at the height of the Siege of Moscow.

㊲ Tserkov Voskreseniya (Church of the Resurrection). This is one of the few lucky churches to have stayed open throughout the years of Soviet rule. As a survivor, the church was the recipient of many priceless icons from less fortunate churches destroyed or closed by the Soviets. Services are still held here daily. ⊠ *Yeliseyevsky pereulok,* ☎ *095/229–6616. Metro: Tverskaya.*

㊳ Tverskaya Ploshchad. In the small park to your right stands a statue of Prince Yuri Dolgoruky, the founder of Moscow in 1147. The equestrian statue was erected in 1954, shortly after the celebrations marking Moscow's 800th anniversary. *Metro: Tverskaya.*

Tverskaya-Yamskaya ulitsa. This last section of Tverskaya ulitsa has been the object of serious reconstruction in the past few years, and there is little of historical interest along this stretch. The street ends at the Belorussky Vokzal (Belorussian Railway Station), which has two interconnecting subway stations. A statue of Maxim Gorky, erected in the 1950s, stands in a small park outside the station. It is located near the site of the former Triumphal Gates, built in the 19th century by the architect Osip Bove to commemorate the Russian victory in the war with Napoléon. The gates were demolished in a typical fit of destruction in the 1930s. Fragments can be found on the grounds of the Donskoy Monastery (☞ Side Trips from Moscow, *below*). A replica of the original gates was erected in 1968 near Poklonnaya Hill, at the end of Kutuzovsky Prospekt. *Metro: Mayakovskaya.*

NEED A BREAK?
Of all the foreign-run joint ventures in Moscow, **Pizza Hut** takes the prize for having most successfully re-created the atmosphere of a Western franchise. Step inside and in an instant you are back on the other side of the ocean. The decor is amazing, if only because it is just like that of any other Pizza Hut. The pizza is good, but the salad bar is a disappointment—lots of coleslaw but no lettuce. Service is swift and pleasant. This is the perfect place for a quick snack and a well-earned break from Russian reality. ⊠ *Ul. Tverskaya 12,* ☎ *095/229–2013. Cash or credit cards. AE, D, DC, V.*

㊵ Yeliseyevsky's. Of all the stores and boutiques on Tverskaya ulitsa, you'll find the most dazzling interior in the grocery store at No. 14, just beyond Stanislavskovo but on the right-hand side of the street. Under Communist administration, the store had the official, generic title Gastronome No. 1, but it once again carries what most people continued to call it even then—Yeliseyevsky's, after the rich merchant from St. Petersburg who owned the store before the Revolution. The interior sparkles with chandeliers, stained glass, and gilt wall decorations. Products abound. It's here that you'll find loads of good cognac and Georgian wine (including Stalin's favorite Khvanchkava—still much touted even with its unsavory stamp of approval). They also have coffee beans, and in the back room are Russian chocolate and candy of all sorts. ⊠ *14 Tverskaya ul.,* ⊙ *Mon.–Sat. 8 AM–9 PM, Sun. 8 AM–7 PM. Metro: Tverskaya.*

Yermolova Theater. The theater housed in this short building with an arched entrance was founded in 1937 and named after a famous Russian actress. ⊠ *5 Tverskaya ul.,* ☎ *095/203–7952/7628. Metro: Okhotny Ryad.*

The Old Moscow of Bolshaya Nikitskaya Ulitsa

Bolshaya Nikitskaya ulitsa (formerly ulitsa Gertsena, or "Herzen Street") is one of the many old streets radiating from the Kremlin, running more or less parallel with Tverskaya ulitsa to the northeast and Novy Arbat to the southwest. The street was laid out along the former road to Novgorod, an ancient town northwest of Moscow, and is divided into two sections. The first part is lined with 18th- and 19th-century mansions and begins at Manezhnaya Square, across from the fortification walls of the Kremlin. The second section, notable for its enchanting Art Nouveau mansions, starts at Nikitskyie Vorota (Nikolai Gates) Square, where Herzen Street intersects with the Boulevard Ring. Before the 1917 revolution, Herzen Street was named Bolshaya Nikitskaya (the name most of the street signs still carry), after the Nikolai Gates of the former white-stone fortification wall. It was renamed in 1920 in honor of the 19th-century philosopher Alexander Herzen. Although Herzen spent much of his life in self-imposed exile in London and Paris, he exerted a tremendous influence on Russian sociopolitical thought in the mid-19th century as a progressive writer and fierce advocate of liberal reform.

A Good Walk

The walk begins at **Manezhnaya Ploshchad** ㊹, which you can reach by subway, getting off at the Okhotny Ryad stop. Take the exit that leads to the National Hotel, at the corner of Manezhnaya Square and Tverskaya ulitsa. Continuing along the north side of the square, you come to the old campus of **Moscow State University** ㊺. Passing the university, you come to Herzen Street. Turn right, and one block up, at the corner of ulitsa Belinskovo, you reach the city's **Zoological Museum** ㊻. Farther up, on the left-hand side of the street at No. 13, is the **Tchaikovsky Conservatory** ㊼. Take a quick diversion off Herzen Street now, turning right onto ulitsa Stankevicha, which begins just past the conservatory, to Moscow's **Episcopal Church,** at No. 8. Continuing now up Herzen Street, you pass, on the left-hand side, the **Mayakovsky Drama Theater** ㊽. One more block brings you to the square named **Nikitskyie Vorota,** home to the TASS offices.

The busy road in front of you, intersecting Herzen Street, is the Boulevard Ring, which forms a semicircle around the city center. On the other side of the boulevard, facing the square, is the classical **Tserkov Bolshovo Vozneseniya** ㊾. Herzen Street veers sharply to the left here, so that if you continue straight ahead, keeping to the right of the square, you'll end up on ulitsa Kachalova. About half a block down, near the corner, is a marvelous example of Moscow Art Nouveau, the **Ryabushinsky Mansion** ㊿. Follow the road behind the Church of the Ascension and continue straight onto Paliashvili Street (which leads to the left off Herzen Street). As you walk down Paliashvili you pass several side streets with names like Stolovy (Dining Room), Skatertny (Tablecloth), and Khlebny (Bread). The streets are named after the servants of the czar (the waiters, the linen makers, the baker) who lived in this area. Today the district houses many foreign embassies. Walk down Paliashvili Street until you reach the busy intersection with **ulitsa Povarskaya,** where you should turn right. The mansion at No. 25 (on the left-hand side of the street) houses the **Gorky Literary Museum** ⑤. Near the end of Povarskaya ulitsa, you pass the **Central House for Writers.** Povarskaya ulitsa comes out onto Novinsky Bulvar; to the right is **Ploshchad Kudrinskaya** ㉒; down to the far left, you can see the U.S. Embassy.

TIMING

Because this walk covers quite a bit of territory and includes a number of detours down crooked streets in picturesque neighborhoods, it's best to allow a day to see everything at a leisurely pace. The tour runs from the Okhotny Ryad metro station to the Barrikadnaya station—roughly a mile and a half in a straight line—and there are no stations in between, so it's best to save this walk for a day when you're well rested.

Sights to See

Central House for Writers. The CDL (Centralny Dom Literaterov) functions as an exclusive club for members of the Writers' Union. Its dining room is now one of the city's very best restaurants, open to the public (☞ Dining, *below*). Next door (No. 52) is a large mansion, enclosed by a courtyard, that houses the administrative offices of the Writers' Union. It is commonly believed that Leo Tolstoy used this mansion as a model for his description of the Rostov home in *War and Peace.* A statue of Tolstoy stands in the courtyard. ⊠ *50 Povarskaya ul.,* ☎ *095/291–1515. Metro: Barrikadnaya.*

Chaliapin House Museum. Theodore Chaliapin, one of the world's greatest opera singers, lived in this beautifully restored manor house from 1910 to 1922. Chaliapin was stripped of his Soviet citizenship while on tour in France in 1922; he never returned to Russia again. The Soviets turned his home into an apartment building, and until restorations in the 1980s, the building contained 60 communal apartments. With help from Chaliapin's family in France, the rooms have been arranged and furnished as they were when Chaliapin lived here. The walls are covered with works of art given to Chaliapin by talented friends (such as the artists Mikhail Vrubel and Isaac Levitan). Also on display are Chaliapin's colorful costumes, which were donated to the museum by his son. When you reach the piano room, you are treated to original recordings of Chaliapin singing his favorite roles. Entrance is from inside the courtyard. English-language tours are available. ⊠ *25–27 Novinsky Bulvar,* ☎ *095/252–2530.* ☾ *Tues., weekends 10–6; Wed., Thurs. 11:30–6:30. Closed last day of month. Metro: Barrikadnaya.*

Chekhov Museum. The museum is located in the home where Chekhov lived from 1886 to 1890. The rooms are arranged as they were when he lived here, with his personal effects on display. Also on exhibit are manuscripts, letters, and photographs. ⊠ *6 Sadovaya-Kudrinskaya ul.,* ☎ *095/291–6154.* ☾ *Thurs., weekends 11–5; Wed., Fri. 2–7. Closed last day of month. Metro: Barrikadnaya.*

Episcopal Church. The attractive red sandstone church was Moscow's only Episcopalian Church. After the Revolution it was closed and turned into a recording studio, but recently the English have taken it back. ⊠ *8 Voznesensky pereulok. Metro: Okhotny Ryad.*

⑤ **Gorky Literary Museum.** For Gorky buffs only, the museum is packed with the letters, manuscripts, and pictures of the great proletarian writer. There are also, rather remarkably, portraits of him by Nesterov and Serov. Americans may be particularly riveted to read the first page (in English) of *City of the Yellow Devil,* his book about visiting New York in 1906; its opening chapter is entitled "City of Mammon." There is even a red wooden replica of his childhood home, complete with village yard and outbuildings. You won't get to leave without signing the book of the kindly but fierce matrons who protect this place. ✉ *25 Po-varskaya ul.,* ☎ *095/290–5130.* ☉ *Mon., Tues., Thurs. 10–5; Wed., Fri. noon–7. Closed 1st Thurs. of month. Metro: Barrikadnaya.*

㊹ Manezhnaya Ploshchad (Manege Square). Bordering one side of the square is the **Moskva Hotel.** Opened in 1935, it was one of the first buildings erected as part of Stalin's reconstruction plan for Moscow. If you look carefully at the facade, you'll notice that the design on the west side doesn't match the design on the east side. Legend has it that Stalin was given a preliminary draft that showed two possible versions for the hotel. He was supposed to sign under the one he liked best, but instead he signed his name right across the middle. The story goes that the architects, too timid to go back to Stalin a second time, went ahead and built the hotel with its asymmetrical facade.

The building next to the National Hotel houses the offices of **Intourist,** the travel agency that once held a monopoly over the entire tourist industry of the former Soviet Union. Until 1950 the building housed the U.S. Embassy. Older city residents still fondly recall how the Americans posted here joined in the spontaneous celebrations that erupted all over the city when the end of World War II was announced. They'll tell you how the Americans kept the party going, rolling beer kegs out these doors and onto Red Square across the way.

In the 1930s, Manezhnaya Square was renamed "50th Anniversary of the October Revolution Square." Now, with construction of an indoor shopping mall underway on its site, that cumbersome mouthful has been abandoned. The present (and prerevolutionary) name comes from the **imperial riding school** (Manege) situated on the opposite side of the square from the Moskva Hotel. Built in 1817, it has an interesting design: there are no internal columns supporting its huge roof— just the four walls. After the revolution the building was used as the Kremlin garage and then, in the late '50s, was revamped into the Central Exhibition Hall, which is used primarily for temporary art and photography exhibits. ✉ *1 Manezhnaya Pl.,* ☎ *095/202–9304. Metro: Okhotny Ryad.*

㊽ Mayakovsky Drama Theater. This three-story brick house, with the word TEATP (theater) printed in black on a sign hanging down the side, was for a time known as the Theater of Revolutionary Satire. ✉ *19 Bolshaya Nikitskaya ul.,* ☎ *095/290–2725/6241. Metro: Okhotny Ryad.*

㊺ Moscow State University. Russia's oldest university was founded in 1755 by the father of Russian science, Mikhail Lomonosov. The Classical buildings here were originally designed by Matvei Kazakov, in 1786–93. They were rebuilt and embellished in the mid-19th century, after the 1812 fire. The university's new campus is situated on Sparrow Hills (formerly Lenin Hills) in the largest of the so-called Stalin Gothic skyscrapers, though some of the law and journalism schools are still housed in the old halls. ✉ *Mokhovaya ul. Metro: Okhotny Ryad.*

Nikitskyie Vorota. This square was named after the gates (*vorota*) of the white-stone fortification walls that once stood here. To your right is a modern building with square windows; this is home to TASS, once the official news agency of the Soviet Union and the mouthpiece of the Kremlin. In the park in the center of the square stands a monument to Kliment Timiryazev, a famous botanist.

The busy road in front of you, intersecting Bolshaya Nikitskaya ulitsa, is the **Boulevard Ring,** which forms a semicircle around the city center. It begins at the banks of the Moskva River, just south of the Kremlin, running in a northeastern direction. It curves eastward, and then south, finally reaching the river bank again after several miles, near the mouth of the Yauza River, northeast of the Kremlin. Its path follows the lines of the 16th-century white-stone fortification wall that gave Moscow the name "White City." The privilege of living within its walls was reserved for the court nobility and craftsmen serving the czar. The wall was torn down in 1775, on orders from Catherine the Great, and was replaced by the present Boulevard Ring. It is divided into 10 sections, each with a different name. Running along its center is a broad strip of trees and flowers, dotted with playgrounds and benches. You may want to take a break and rest on its benches. *Metro: Arbatskaya.*

Oriental Art Museum. The museum has a large collection of art from the Central Asian republics, China, India, Japan, and Africa. ✉ *12A Nikitsky bulvar,* ☎ *095/202–4555.* ☉ *Tues.–Sun. 11–8. Metro: Arbatskaya.*

🔢 **Ploshchad Kudrinskaya** (Kudrinsky Square). To the far left of the square cars race in front of you along the busy Sadovoye Koltso (Garden Ring), the major circular road surrounding Moscow. If you approach the ring from Bolshaya Nikitskaya ulitsa or Povarskaya ulitsa, the first thing to catch your eye will be the 22-story skyscraper directly across Novinsky bulvar. One of the seven Stalin Gothics, this one is 160 meters (525 feet) high. The ground floor is taken up by shops and a movie theater, and the rest of the building contains residential apartments. This area saw heavy fighting during the uprisings of 1905 and 1917 (until recently the plaza was named Ploshchad Vosstaniya, or Insurrection Square). The Barrikadnaya (Barricade) subway station is very close by. Cross the street and bear right, through the park and down the hill; you'll see people streaming into the station to your right. *Metro: Barrikadnaya.*

Povarskaya ulitsa (Cook Street). This is where the czar's cooks lived. After the Revolution the street was renamed Vorovskovo, in honor of a Soviet diplomat who was assassinated by a Russian, but has returned to its prerevolutionary name. Povarskaya ulitsa is an important center of the Moscow artistic community, with the film actors' studio, the Russian Academy of Music (the Gnesin Institute), and the Central House of Writers all located here. Many of the old mansions have been preserved, and the street retains its prerevolutionary tranquility and charm. In the first flush days of summer, your walk is likely to be accompanied by a rousing drum set or tinkling piano sonata issuing from the open windows of the music school. *Metro: Arbatskaya.*

🔢 **Ryabushinsky Mansion.** This marvelous example of Moscow Art Nouveau was built in 1901 for a wealthy banker and designed by the architect Fyodor Shektel. (If you arrived in Moscow by train, you probably noticed the fanciful Yaroslavl Railway Station, another of his masterpieces, just opposite the Leningrad Railway Station.) Sadly, the mansion has been closed with its museum for *remont,* and it has fallen into a bit of disrepair, after having been wonderfully preserved. This was thanks in part to the fact that Maxim Gorky, the father of Soviet socialist realism, lived here from 1931 until his death in 1936. Although Gorky was a champion of the proletariat, his home was rather lavish. Gorky himself apparently hated the *style moderne.* Those who don't, however, will be charmed by this building of ecru brick and stone painted pink and mauve atop gray foundations. Step back and look up at the beautiful mosaic of irises that forms a border around the top of most of the house, and see how the strangely fanciful yet utilitarian iron fence matches the unusual design of the window frames. The spectacular interior is replete with a twisting marble staircase and stained-glass roof.

The statue in the park behind the church is of Alexey Tolstoy, a relative of Leo's and a well-known Soviet writer of historical novels. ⊠ *6/2 Malaya Nikitskaya ul., ☎ 095/290–0535 (when reopened). Closed indefinitely as the Gorky House Museum.*

㊌ **Tchaikovsky Conservatory.** You may have seen its magnificent concert hall on television; this is where the famous Tchaikovsky Piano Competition takes place. The conservatory was founded in 1866 and moved to its present location in 1870. Rachmaninoff, Scriabin, and Tchaikovsky are among the famous composers who have worked here. There is a statue of Tchaikovsky in the semicircular park outside the main entrance. It was designed by Vera Mukhina, a famous Soviet sculptor. You can buy tickets (at very reasonable prices) for excellent concerts of classical music in the lobby ticket office in the main building. ⊠ *13 Bolshaya Nikitskaya ul., ☎ 095/229–2183.*

㊾ **Tserkov Bolshovo Vozneseniya** (Church of the Great Ascension). Like Moscow University, this Classical church was designed by Matvei Kazakov and built in the 1820s. For years it stood empty and abandoned, but it has been under major repair, and though the work is not yet complete, religious services have already been resumed here. The church is most famous as the site where the Russian poet Alexander Pushkin married the younger and far less intelligent Natalya Goncharova. History has judged Natalya harshly. She was probably not guilty of adultery, although she did enjoy flirting. Pushkin died outside St. Petersburg six years after their wedding, in a duel defending her honor. ⊠ *Malaya Nikitskaya ul. Metro: Arbatskaya.*

㊈ **Zoo.** Moscow's small zoo is located near the Barrikadnaya or the Krasnopresnenskaya subway station. ⊠ *1 Bolshaya Gruzinskaya ul. ☎ 095/255–5375.☉ Summer, daily 9–8; winter, daily 9–5.*

㊈ ㊻ **Zoological Museum.** This museum is always swarming with schoolchildren, who take a special delight in its huge collection of mammals, birds, amphibians, and reptiles. The museum also has a collection of more than 1 million insects, and another collection of more than 100,000 butterflies was recently donated by a Moscow resident. ⊠ *6 Bolshaya Nikitskaya ul., ☎ 095/203–3569. ☉ Sun., Tues., Sat. 10–5; Wed., Fri. noon–5. Closed last Tues. of month.*

The Arbat, Old and New

Two of downtown Moscow's most interesting and important avenues are the **Arbat** and **Novy Arbat** (New Arbat), which run parallel to each other. Arbat Street is revered among Muscovites, who usually refer to it simply as "the Arbat." One of the oldest sections of Moscow, it dates to the 16th century, when it was the beginning of the road that led from the Kremlin to the city of Smolensk. At that time it was also the quarter where court artisans lived, and several of the surrounding streets still recall this in their names—from Plotnikov (Carpenter) to Serebryany (Silversmith) to Kalashny (Pastry Cook). Early in the 19th century it became a favorite district of the aristocracy, while a century later it became a favorite shopping street, a role it has recently reclaimed. Now under a preservation order, the area has been transformed into an attractive, cobbled pedestrian precinct with many gift shops and cafés in the restored buildings. Closed to all traffic, the Arbat attracts artists, poets, and musicians as well as enthusiastic admirers of their work.

Novy Arbat has both a different history and spirit. For almost 30 years it was named Kalinin Prospekt, in honor of Mikhail Kalinin, an old Bolshevik whose prestige plummeted after 1991. The stretch from the Kremlin to Arbat Square has been given back its prerevolutionary name of ulitsa Vozdvizhenka. The second section—which begins where Vozdvizhenka ends and runs west for about a mile to the Moscow River—is now called **Novy Arbat.** In contrast to ulitsa Vozdvizhenka, which has retained some of its prerevolutionary charm, and the Arbat, which is actively re-creating the look of its past, New Arbat is a modern thoroughfare. Once a maze of narrow streets and alleys, the avenue was widened and modernized in the 1960s, with the goal of making it the showcase of the Soviet capital. Since the entire area was rebuilt there is little of historical interest here, but the street is lined with department stores.

A Good Walk

Take the subway to either the Arbatskaya station on the dark-blue line or to **Biblioteka Imeni Lenina** (Lenin Library) on the red line. (To confuse matters, there is also an Arbatskaya station on the light-blue line, but that would leave you at the wrong end of Arbat Square.) When you come out of the the station, bear left, walking away from the Kremlin. **Ulitsa Vozdvizhenka,** like many other Moscow streets, continues to undergo massive reconstruction, and some of its prerevolutionary facades are hidden behind scaffolding. The drawings and photographs at the **Shchusev Architecture Museum** ㉝, however, can give you an idea what the area used to look like. The entrance to this museum is just a few steps down **Staravagankovsky pereulok,** the first side street to your left. Return to ulitsa Vozdvizhenka and continue west, away from the Kremlin. Using the underpass, cross to the right-hand side of the street to get a closer look at the curious **Friendship House** ㉞. Just beyond this eccentric mansion (continuing west) is the busy intersection of **Arbatskaya Ploshchad.** To your left as you emerge from the crowded underpass is the **Arbat**; to your right, **Novy Arbat.** In the distance to your far left stands a statue erected in the 1950s of the 19th-century Russian writer Nikolai Gogol. Go left to start your stroll down the Arbat, where you could easily spend a whole day browsing through the stores and stopping for a break in any of its numerous cafés.

The end of the Arbat is marked by one of the Gothic-style "Seven Sisters" skyscrapers that Stalin ordered built; this one is the Ministry of Foreign Affairs. Continuing down the Arbat, almost to the end, you'll come to the **Pushkin Apartment Museum** ㉟, on the left-hand side of the street. Once you've toured the museum and/or browsed in its gift shop (at the front), retrace your steps down the Arbat to reach the impressive building with columns at No. 26. This is the **Vakhtangov Theater** ㊱. Once you've surveyed the facade of the Vakhtangov and checked out its offerings for the season, turn off of Arbat onto narrow Bolshoi Nikolopeskovsky pereulok. Continue along the left-hand side of the street until you reach No. 7. Walk through the archway and head straight back to see **Spasso House,** the residence of the American Ambassador, and, to the playground's left, the lovely **Church of the Transfiguration on the Sands.** Retrace your path back to Bolshoi Nikolopeskovksky pereulok and turn left to continue. A few doors up, on the left-hand side of the street, you come to the **Alexander Scriabin Museum.** Go left and follow the narrow street for approximately one block to come out onto the busy Novy Arbat.

To have a look at the street's full offerings, turn right as you come out onto Novy Arbat, and make your way back toward Arbat Square, where the walk began. As you elbow your way through the crowds of shoppers and vendors, you may want to keep your eye out in particular for the country's largest bookstore, **Dom Knigi,** on the left-hand side near the street's end. Past Dom Knigi, at the corner of Povarskaya ulitsa, on a tiny grassy knoll, stands a charming 17th-century church, the

Tserkov Simeona Stolpnika ㊲. When you reach Arbat Square, turn left up Nikitsky bulvar. Inside the first courtyard to your left is a **Gogol statue** ㊳ worth seeing; this is also a peaceful spot to take a breather.

TIMING

Without stops at any of the museums, this tour should only take about two hours to complete. If you're interested in doing some souvenir shopping, however, you'll want to allot an additional few hours to browse the numerous shops and street kiosks you'll see along the way. If you want to avoid crowds, do this tour on a weekday; the pedestrian zone on the Old Arbat, in particular, draws big crowds on the weekends. The museums included on this tour are all fairly small; you'll need no more than an hour in each of them.

Sights to See

Alexander Scriabin Museum. This charming, dusty house-museum is housed in the composer's last apartment, where he died of blood poisoning in 1915. Visitors here are rare, as Muscovites long ago apparently tired of their own museums, and foreign tourist groups are not usually brought here. The rooms are arranged and furnished just as they were when Scriabin lived here. Downstairs there is a concert hall where accomplished young musicians perform his music. If you want to hear a concert, you should call ahead to find out the current schedule; they are usually held on Wednesday and Friday evenings. ☒ *11 Bolshoi Nikolopeskovsky pereulok,* ☎ *095/241–1901.* ☉ *Thurs., weekends 10–5; Wed., Fri. noon–7. Closed last Fri. of month. Metro: Arbatskaya.*

Arbatskaya Ploshchad (Arbat Square). This busy intersection is where ulitsa Vozdvizhenka crosses the Boulevard Ring. To reach the other side of the square, take the pedestrian underpass, which has become a bustling marketplace. The stairs are lined with women selling tiny kittens and puppies; their furry heads stick out from a bag or from underneath a coat, and they are nearly irresistible, so it's best not to stop and look. In the underpass itself, artists set up their easels, trying to entice passersby into having their portraits painted. And in spring and summer you'll find lots of impromptu flower vendors with the season's latest blooms (usually homegrown) for sale. When you emerge from the dizzying minimarket of the underpass, you will be in front of the Praga restaurant, a three-story Classical building whose history dates back to before the Revolution.

Dom Knigi (Book House). The country's largest bookstore has an English-language section, but you'll probably find a bigger selection at the individual vendors' stalls outside the store. ☒ *26 Novy Arbat,* ☎ *095/290–4507.* ☉ *Mon.–Sat. 10 AM–2 PM and 3–7 PM. Metro: Arbatskaya.*

NEED A BREAK?

The **New Arbat Irish Store** (which is, in fact, mainly Russian-run), located near the end of the block of buildings on the right-hand side of the street, has one of Moscow's biggest and best-stocked grocery stores. The hard-currency section is on the second floor, where the selection (and the prices) match what you might find in New York City. Also upstairs is the small **Shamrock Pub,** where you can get a reasonably priced sandwich or bowl of soup in a lively and friendly atmosphere.

㊴ **Friendship House** (Dom Druzhby). One of Moscow's most interesting buildings—it looks like a Moorish castle—was built in the late 19th century by the architect V. A. Mazyrin for the wealthy (and eccentric) industrialist Morozov (Tolstoy mentions this home in his novel *Resurrection*). The interior is a veritable anthology of decorative styles, ranging from imitation Tudor to classical Greek and Baroque. The building's name is a holdover from the Soviet days when Russians and foreigners were supposed to meet only in officially sanctioned places. Today it is the site of business functions and public forums, including international events. It's officially open to the public only by special arrangement with the administrator, but you may be able to convince the woman who guards the door to let you take a quick look around on the first floor. ⊠ *16 Vozdvizhenka ul.,* ☎ *095/290–1232. Metro: Arbatskaya.*

⑤⑧ Gogol statue. It originally stood at the start of Gogol Boulevard but was later moved and replaced by a more "upbeat" Gogol. The statue stands inside the first courtyard to your left, near the apartment building where the writer spent the last months of his life. This statue actually captures Gogol's sad disposition perfectly. He gazes downward, with his long, flowing cape draped over his shoulder, protecting him from the world. Gogol is probably best known in the West for his satirical drama *Revizor* (*The Inspector General*), about the unannounced visit of a government official to a provincial town. Characters from this and other Gogol works are engraved on the pedestal. ⊠ *7 Nikitsky bulvar. Metro: Arbatskaya.*

Khram Spasa Preobrazheniya na Peskhakh (Church of the Transfiguration on the Sands). Built in the 17th century, this elegant church was closed after the 1917 Revolution and turned into a cartoon-production studio. Like churches throughout Russia, it has been returned to its original purpose and is being restored. The church is depicted in Vasily Polenov's well-known canvas *Moskovsky Dvornik* (*Moscow Courtyard*), which now hangs in the Tretyakov Gallery (☞ Gorky Park and Environs, *below*). ⊠ *4 Spasapeskovsky pereulok,* ☎ *095/241–6203. Metro: Smolenskaya.*

Lermontov Museum. The museum is devoted to the poet Mikhail Lermontov and is located in the house where he lived from 1830 to 1832. ⊠ *2 Malaya Molchanovka ul.,* ☎ *095/291–5298.* ☉ *Thurs., weekends 11–6; Wed., Fri. 2–8:30. Metro: Arbatskaya.*

⑤⑤ Pushkin Apartment Museum. The poet Alexander Pushkin lived here with his bride, Natalya Goncharova, for several months in 1831, right after they were married. Experts have re-created the original layout of the rooms and interior decoration, and the apartment is now open as a museum. ⊠ *53 Arbat,* ☎ *095/241–3010.* ☉ *Wed.–Sun. 10–6. Closed last Fri. of month.*

⑤③ Shchusev Architecture Museum. The drawings and photographs at this museum can shed some light on what this area looked like before all of the current reconstruction. The museum's permanent home, an 18th-century classical mansion at 5 ulitsa Vozdvizhenka, is closed for reconstruction. The exhibits have been moved to a building right behind it, which can be reached via Starovagankovsky pereulok (formerly Marx and Engels Street), the first side street to your left as you approach from the Kremlin. When you enter this narrow street, the first building on the right is an old, white-brick, two-story one that was the court apothecary in the 17th century. Turn right into its courtyard; the entrance to the museum is to your immediate left. The permanent and temporary exhibits here trace the history of Russian architecture from the 11th century to the present. ⊠ *5 ul. Vozdvizhenka,* ☎ *095/290–4855.* ☉ *Tues.–Fri. 10–6, weekends 10–4. Metro: Bibliotake Imeni Lenina.*

Spasso House. The yellow mansion behind the iron gate is the residence of the American ambassador. This neoclassical mansion was built in the early 20th century for a wealthy merchant. What you first see is actually the back side of the building; it is much more impressive from the front. To get there, bear right at the small playground, which is usually filled with children from the nearby school.

⑤⑦ Tserkov Simeona Stolpnika (Church of St. Simon the Stylite). The 17th-century church stands out above in stark contrast to the modern architecture dominating the area. During the reconstruction of New Arbat in the 1960s many old churches and buildings were destroyed, but this one was purposely left standing, as a "souvenir" of the past. For years it housed a conservation museum, but now it has been returned to the Orthodox Church and is active. Nothing remains, however, of the original interiors. ⊠ *Povarskaya ul. and Novy Arbat. Metro: Arbatskaya.*

⑤⑥ Vakhtangov Theater. Named after Stanislavsky's pupil Evgeny Vakhtangov (1883–1922), this impressive structure is home to an excellent traditional theater. ⊠ *26 Arbat,* ☎ *095/241–0728,* ℻ *095/241–2625.*

From the Russian State Library to the Kropotkinsky District

This tour takes you through a picturesque old neighborhood still commonly known as the Kropotkinsky District. It takes its name from its main street, which was called Kropotkinskaya ulitsa under the Soviets but has now been returned to its 16th-century name: ulitsa Prechistenka. It is yet another ancient section of Moscow whose history dates back nearly to the foundation of the city itself. Almost none of its earliest architecture has survived, but this time the Soviets are not entirely to blame. The area suffered badly during the 1812 conflagration of Moscow, and most of its buildings date to the postwar period of reconstruction, when neoclassicism and the so-called Moscow Empire style were in vogue. Before the Revolution, the Kropotkinsky district was the favored residence of Moscow's old nobility, and it is along its thoroughfares that you'll find many of their mansions and homes, often called "nests of the gentry." It was also the heart of the literary and artistic community, and there were several famous literary salons here. Prince Kropotkin, for whom the street was named, compared it with the Saint-Germain quarter of Paris.

A Good Walk

Start at the **Russian State Library** at the bottom of ulitsa Vozdvizhenka, at the corner of Mokhovaya ulitsa (Moss Street, where moss used for wall caulking was once sold). To reach it, take the subway to the station called Biblioteki Imeni Lenina, which is directly beneath the Lenin Library. Walk south from the library along broad Mokhovaya ulitsa to reach **Borovitskaya Ploshchad** (Borovitsky Square), where several old streets converge. To your left, ulitsa Znamenka descends toward the **Borovitsky Gate** of the Kremlin and then continues across the Great Stone Bridge of the Moskva River; to your right it leads up a steep incline in the direction of the Arbat. Ulitsa Volkhonka lies straight ahead, leading into the Kropotkinsky district. On the hillock to your right, facing the Kremlin gates, is one of Moscow's most beautiful old mansions, the **Pashkov House.** Cross the square and continue straight onto **ulitsa Volkhonka,** which was first laid out sometime in the late 12th or early 13th century. It received its present name in the mid-18th century, in honor of Prince Volkhonksy, who lived in the mansion at No. 8. After a block you reach Moscow's museum of foreign paintings, the **Pushkin Museum of Fine Arts** ⑤⑨, in the middle of a small park to your right.

Just past the Pushkin Museum lies an entire block between Volkhonka and the quay of the Moskva River. This is the site of the gigantic new **Cathedral of Christ Our Savior** ⑥⓪, which is scheduled for completion in 1997. Just beyond the construction site surrounding the cathedral, ulitsa Volkhonka intersects with the Boulevard Ring. To your right, across the street, is the entrance to the Kropotkinskaya subway station. At this point ulitsa Volkhonka ends, splitting into ulitsa Prechistenka (to the right) and ulitsa Ostozhenka (to the left). A small park between the two streets holds a statue of Friedrich Engels and, behind it, a restored 17th-century boyars' chamber. Cross the square and walk up ulitsa Prechistenka. At the corner with Khrushchevsky pereulok stands the **Pushkin Memorial Museum** ⑥①. Not far from the Pushkin Museum, on the opposite side of the street, is the **Leo Tolstoy Memorial Museum** ⑥②.

If you are feeling energetic and want to see more of the area's mansions, you can continue walking straight along ulitsa Prechistenka. No. 17, on the left-hand side, belonged to the poet Denis Davidov; and a bit farther, at No. 19, you find the former mansion of Prince Dolgoruky. No. 21 now houses the Russian Academy of Arts. The mansion originally belonged to Count Potemkin and then later to the wealthy merchant Savva Morozov, whose private art collection was one of the largest in Moscow (you can see it in the Pushkin Fine Arts Museum).

To make your way back toward the Kropotkinskaya subway station, turn left after you exit the Tolstoy museum onto Lopukhinsky pereulok, and walk one block to ulitsa Ostozhenka, which runs parallel to ulitsa Prechistenka. Across the street and down to the right, you can see the remnants of the **Zachatievsky Monastery,** which is worth a closer look. Returning to ulitsa Ostozhenka, turn right, walk two blocks back in the direction of the new cathedral, and then turn right onto Vtoroi (2nd) Obydensky pereulok. Soon you come to the pretty St. Prophet Eliah Church, built in one day in 1702. Continue past the church and turn left onto Kursovoy pereulok. At the bottom of the street, to the right on Soymonovsky proyezd, is the steep-roofed Art Nouveau **Pertsov House.** From here you can either walk back up Soymonovsky proyezd to reach the Kropotkinskaya subway stop, or you can continue past the Pertsov House to reach the embankment of the Moskva River. The views from the Kropotkinskaya naberezhnaya and its extension, the Kremlyovskaya naberezhnaya, are spectacular. This river walk takes you along the southern wall of the Kremlin to the Moskvoretsky Bridge. Walk out onto the bridge for one of the best views of St. Basil's Cathedral and Red Square. From here you could either walk back to Red Square (the nearest subway stop here is Ploshchad Revolutsii), or, if this walk has worn you out, continue across the bridge and settle into the comfy Café Kranzler at the Baltschug Kempinski Hotel for some coffee and incredibly rich pastry or beer and sandwiches.

If, on the other hand, you decide you want to linger in the Kropotkinsky district, there are several interesting houses along ulitsa Ostozhenka that are worth seeing. The anarchist Bakunin was raised at No. 49. No. 38 was a governor's home in the 1700s; later it became a school, where one of its students was Ivan Goncharov, author of *Oblomov;* today it is the Institute of Foreign Languages. Next, No. 37 is a small rustic house where one of Russia's greatest writers, Ivan Turgenev, lived and worked. He set his famous story *Mu Mu* at this location. The private home of the Art Nouveau architect Kekushev, who was a contemporary of Shekhtel, stands at No. 21.

Leaving from the upper end of ulitsa Ostozhenka, you come out at the Park Kultury subway station. At the other end (back at Soymonovsky proyezd), is the Kropotkinskaya station.

TIMING

Taken at a leisurely pace, this walk could easily take three to four hours; add an extra half hour if you plan on taking the walk along the river bank at the end. With stops at any of the various museums along this route, though, your exploration could easily expand to two days (the Pushkin Museum alone is worth a day). If you are definitely interested in visiting some of the museums in this district, do *not* do this tour on a Monday, as most of the museums are closed that day.

Sights to See

60 **Cathedral of Christ Our Savior.** This site carries an amazing tale of destruction and reconstruction. Built between 1839 and 1883 as a memorial to the Russian troops who fell in the 1812 war with Napoléon, the cathedral was the largest single structure in Moscow and dominated the city's skyline. It had taken almost 50 years to build what only a few hours would destroy. On December 5, 1931, the cathedral was blown up. Under Stalin, the site had been designated for a mammoth new "Palace of Soviets," intended to replace the Kremlin as the seat of the Soviet government. Plans called for topping the 420-meter (1,378-foot) structure with a 100-meter (300-foot) statue of Lenin, who—had the plans ever materialized—would have spent more time above the clouds than in plain view. World War II delayed construction, and the entire project was scrapped when it was discovered that the land along the embankment was too damp to support such a heavy structure.

The site lay empty and abandoned until 1958, when the **Moscow Pool,** one of the world's largest outdoor swimming pools, was built. Divided into several sections, for training, competition, diving, and public swimming, it was heated and kept open all year long, even in the coldest days of winter. The pool was connected to the locker rooms by covered tunnels, and you could reach it by swimming through them. The pool was dismantled in 1994, ironically enough, a victim of the same fate engendered by it, more or less. In perhaps one of architectural history's stranger twists, therefore, everything has come full circle in the post-perestroika and -glasnost years. The area is currently humming with activity, as workmen swarm over the entire site. What are they doing? Swiftly building anew, a second and equally gigantic Cathedral of Christ Our Savior. ⊠ *Ulitsa Volkhonka. Metro: Kropotkinskaya.*

Pashkov House. Designed by Vasily Bazhenov, one of Russia's greatest architects, the mansion was erected in 1784–86 for the wealthy Pashkov family. The central building is topped by a round belvedere and flanked by two service wings. In the 19th century it housed the Rumyantsev collection of art and rare manuscripts. Following the 1917 revolution, this museum was closed; the art collection was transferred to the Hermitage and Pushkin museums of fine art, and the manuscripts were donated to the Lenin Library. The building now belongs to the Russian State Library. ⊠ *Mokhovaya ul. and ul. Znamenka. Metro: Borovitskaya.*

Pertsov House. One of the finest examples of Moscow Art Nouveau was built in 1905–07 by the architects Schnaubert and Zhukov. The facade of the steep-roofed and angled building is covered in colorful mosaics. Walk all the way to its end, coming out at the river, and straight across you'll see a large, redbrick compound. This is the **Red October candy factory.** Look to your left, where the buildings of the Kremlin line the distance, the golden cupolas of its churches all agleam. ⊠ *Soymonovsky pereulok and Kropotkinskaya nab. Metro: Kropotkinskaya.*

61 **Pushkin Memorial Museum.** Pushkin never lived here and probably never even visited this fine yellow mansion built in the 19th century by the architect Afansey Grigoriev, so it is a rather dry museum, full of manuscripts and letters. The entrance is around the corner. ⊠ *12 ul. Prechistenka, ☎ 095/202–7998. ☉ Tues. (groups tours only), Fri.–Sun. 10–6; Wed., Thurs. 11–7. Closed last Fri. of month. Closed for reconstruction.*

★ **59** **Pushkin Museum of Fine Arts.** Founded by Ivan Vladimirovich Tsvetayev (1847–1913) of Moscow University, the museum was originally established as a teaching aid for art students, which explains why many of the works are copies. The present building dates from 1895 to 1912 and was first known as the Alexander III Museum. It was renamed the Pushkin Museum in 1937, on the centennial of the Russian poet's death.

The first-floor exhibit halls contain a fine collection of ancient Egyptian art (Hall 1); Greece and Rome are well represented, though mostly by copies (Room 7). The Italian school from the 15th century (Room 5) is represented by Botticelli's *The Annunciation,* Tomaso's *The Assassination of Caesar,* Guardi's *Alexander the Great at the Body of the Persian King Darius,* and *The Beheading of John the Baptist* by Sano Di Pietro, among others. When you reach the Dutch School of the 17th Century (Hall 10), look for Rembrandt's *Portrait of an Old Woman,* who may have been the artist's sister-in-law. Flemish and Spanish art from the 17th century are also well represented, with paintings by Murillo, Rubens, and Van Dyck (Hall 11).

On the museum's second floor you are treated to a stunning collection of Impressionist art. There are many fine canvasses by Picasso (Hall 17), including several from his "blue" period. The same hall contains fascinating works by Henri Rousseau, including *Jaguar Attacking a Horse.* French Impressionism is represented by Cézanne, Gauguin, and Matisse. There are a total of 10 works by Gauguin, mainly in Hall 18, where you also find Cézanne's *Pierrot* and *Harlequin.* The museum owns several works by Matisse (Hall 21), although often they are not all on display. In the same hall you find the poignant *Landscape at Auvers After the Rain* by Vincent Van Gogh. The collection ends at Hall 23, where you find works by Degas, Renoir, and Monet, including Monet's *Rouen Cathedral at Sunset.* ⊠ *12 ul. Volkhonka, ☎ 095/203– 7998/9578. ☉ Tues.–Sun. 10–7. Metro: Kropotinskaya.*

Russian State Library. Still called Biblioteka Imeni Lenina, or the Lenin Library, it is Russia's largest, with more than 30 million books and manuscripts. The main facade is adorned with bronze busts of famous writers and scientists. The portico, supported by square black pillars, is approached by a wide ceremonial staircase. Although it's a modern building, built between 1928 and 1940, portions of the building are under reconstruction. When the subway beneath it was being expanded in the 1980s, the library suffered structural damage and a large crack appeared in its foundation. ⊠ *3 ul. Vozdvizhenka, ☎ 095/202– 5790. Metro: Biblioteki Imeni Lenina.*

62 **Tolstoy Memorial Museum.** Yet another creation by architect Afanasey Grigoriev (housing yet another literary museum), this museum opened in 1920. The mansion, a fine example of the Moscow Empire style, belonged to the minor poet Lopukhin, a distant relative of Tolstoy's. The exhibit halls contain a rich collection of manuscripts and photographs of Tolstoy and his family, as well as pictures and paintings of Tolstoy's Moscow. Even if you don't speak Russian, you can read the writer's life story through the photographs, and in each room there is a typed handout in English to help explain its holdings. If you decide to visit, look for the picture of 19th-century Moscow in the second hall (on the left-hand wall). The huge cathedral taking up more than half the photograph is the Cathedral of Christ Our Savior—the one replaced by the Moskva swimming pool. ⊠ *11 ul. Prechistenka,* ☎ *095/201–3811.* ☉ *Tues.–Sun. 11–5:30. Closed last Fri. of month. Metro: Kropotkinskaya.*

Zachatievsky Monastery (Convent of the Conception). Founded in the 16th century, this is the oldest structure in the district, although nothing remains of the original buildings. Only the 17th-century redbrick Gate Church survives, and even that is in catastrophic condition. It was built by the last surviving son of Ivan the Terrible, in what amounted to a plea to God for an heir (hence the monastery's name). He and his wife failed to have a son, however, and Boris Godunov became the next Russian leader. ⊠ *Zachatievsky pereulok. Metro: Kropotkinskaya.*

Gorky Park and Environs

Gorky Park, popularized by Martin Cruz Smith's cold war novel of the same name, is situated along the right bank of the Moskva River, just beyond **Krymsky Most** (Crimea Bridge). The highlights of this area are Moscow's famous Russian Art Museum, the Tretyakov Gallery, and the park itself and its various surrounding sites of interest.

A Good Walk

Gorky Park is between two major subway stops—the Oktyabrskaya station on the orange and circle lines and the Park Kultury station on the red and circle lines. The walk begins at the Park Kultury stop, but if your only destination is Gorky Park, the Oktyabrskaya station is closer.

Leave the Park Kultury subway station, turn right (as you face the bridge ahead) and walk along Komsomolsky Prospekt one long block. When you reach the corner with ulitsa Lva Tolstovo (Leo Tolstoy Street) you will see the striking church **Tserkov Nikoly v Khamovnikakh** ⑥; turn right here to go around to the church's entrance, which is on the side. The next stop is the **Tolstoy House Estate Museum** ⑥, the novelist's winter home. As you start your walk up the street named in his honor, look for an old white-stone building with a wood-shingled roof, on your right. Tolstoy's estate is a bit farther up the street, on the left-hand side, behind a long, red-wood fence.

Retracing your steps to the Park Kultury subway stop, go right when you reach the corner with busy Zubovsky bulvar, over the Krymsky most. The bridge spans the Moskva River, and in nice weather it offers a fine vantage point. Visitors no doubt will feel a surge of excitement looking at the flashing signs of Gorky Park and its attractions beckoning from below. If you want to save on walking, you can take either Trolleybus 10 or B (both stop on Zubovsky bulvar, right in front of the subway entrance); they will drop you off directly in front of the main entrance to **Gorky Park** ⑥. Directly across the street is the **House of Artists** ⑥, with three floors of exhibit halls. The final stop on this walk is the **Tretyakov Art Gallery** ⑥, a museum that many proudly consider the country's most important repository of Russian art. To get there, you take the subway one stop. Walk up the incline to the left of Gorky Park (as you face its entrance) to find the station. Take the orange line (not the circle line) to the Tretyakovskaya stop. Bear left at every turn as you exit the subway, and when you emerge, look for Ordynsky pereulok. Going a short distance down this street, you quickly spot the attractive grounds of the museum opening up on your right.

TIMING

This tour covers a fair amount of territory, and if you do it all on foot, it could easily take four to five hours just to see the sights. If you plan on touring the Tolstoy House Museum, add another two hours. Because there is so much to take in at both branches of the Tretyakov Gallery, it's probably best to plan those visits separately. Note that both the Tolstoy House Museum and the Tretyakov are closed on Mondays.

Sights to See

Dostoevsky Museum. This museum devoted to the great Russian novelist is located on the grounds of the hospital where he was born and where his father worked as a doctor. ⊠ *2 ul. Dostoevskovo,* ☎ *095/ 281–1085.* ☉ *Thurs., weekends 11–6; Wed., Fri. 2–7. Closed last day of month. Metro: Novoslobodskaya.*

⤿ ⑥⑤ **Gorky Park.** Muscovites usually refer to it as Park Kultury (Park of Culture); its official title is actually the Central Park of Culture and Leisure. The park was laid out in 1928 and covers an area of 110 hectares (275 acres). It is definitely the city's most popular all-around recreation center, and in summer, especially on weekends, it is crowded with children and adults enjoying its many attractions. The park's green expanse is dominated by a giant Ferris wheel; if you're brave enough to ride it, you'll be rewarded with great views of the city; for the even braver, there is also a roller coaster. Stretching along the riverside, the park includes the Neskuchny Sad (Happy Garden) and the Zelyony Theater (Green Theater), an open-air theater with seating for 10,000. The park has a boating pond, a fairground, sports grounds, a rock club, and numerous stand-up cafés. In summer, boats leave from the pier for excursions along the Moskva River, and in winter the ponds are transformed into skating rinks. ⊠ *9 Krymsky Val.* ☉ *Summer, daily 9–midnight; winter, daily 10–10.*

⑥⑥ **House of Artists.** This is a huge, modern building that also houses a branch of the Tretyakov Gallery. The entrance facing the street leads to the exhibit halls of the Artists' Union, where union members display their work, so this is a spot where you can browse for a sketch or watercolor to take home with you. The extensive exhibit halls are spread out on three floors. ⊠ *10 Krymsky Val,* ☎ *095/238–9843.* ☉ *Tues.–Sun. 11–9.*

If you're looking for the branch of the Tretyakov Art Gallery familiarly known as the **"New Tretyakov Gallery,"** or **"New Branch,"** go around to the side entrance. This annex came into being when the original Tretyakov Gallery had to be closed for restoration work (from 1986 to 1995). From this time on, it has also been the location where the museum will display its collection of art created since the 1920s, encompassing pieces, some previously outlawed, from the socialist realist, modern, and post-modern periods. ⊠ *11 Krymsky Val (side entrance, on the right),* ☎ *095/230–1116 or 095/230–7788.* ☉ *Tues.– Sun. 10–7.*

NEED A
BREAK?

Juice, coffee, and light snacks are available in the café on the ground floor of the House of Artists. It's stand-up only, but you can mingle and hear talk on the latest trends in contemporary Russian art.

⑥④ **Tolstoy House Estate Museum.** Tolstoy bought the house in 1882, at the age of 54, and spent nine winters here with his family, until 1901. In summer he preferred his country estate in Yasnaya Polyana. The years here were not particularly happy ones. By this time Tolstoy had already experienced his "religious conversion," which prompted him to disown his earlier great novels, including *War and Peace* and *Anna Karenina*. His conversion sparked a feud among his own family members, which manifested itself even at the dining table: Tolstoy's wife, Sofia Andreevna, would sit at one end with the sons, while the writer would sit with his daughters at the opposite end.

The ground floor has several of the children's bedrooms and the nursery where Tolstoy's seven-year-old son died of scarlet fever in 1895, a tragedy that haunted the writer for the rest of his life. Also here are the dining rooms and kitchen, as well as the Tolstoys' bedroom, in which you can see the small desk used by his wife to meticulously copy all of her husband's manuscripts by hand.

Upstairs, you will find the Tolstoys' receiving room, where they held small parties and entertained guests, who included most of the leading figures of their day. The grand piano in the corner was played by such greats as Rachmaninoff and Rimsky-Korsakov. When in this room, you should ask the attendant to play the enchanting recording of Tolstoy greeting a group of schoolchildren, followed by a piano composition written and played by him. Also on this floor is an Oriental den and the writer's study, where he wrote his last novel, *Resurrection*.

Although electric lighting and running water were available at the time to the lesser nobility, Tolstoy chose to forgo both, believing it better to live simply. The museum honors his desire and shows the house as it was when he lived there. Tickets to the museum are sold in the administrative building to the far back left. Inside the museum, each room has signs in English explaining its significance and contents, but you might want to consider a guided tour (which must be booked in advance). ✉ *10 ul. Lva Tolstovo,* ☎ *095/246–9444.* ☉ *Summer, Tues.–Sun. 10–6; winter, 10–4. Closed last Fri. of month.*

★ ⑥⑦ **Tretyakov Art Gallery.** The Tretyakov Gallery (often called the "Old Tretyakov"), which holds some of the world's masterpieces of Russian art, had a remarkable philanthropic and altruistic beginning. Officially opened in 1892 as a public state museum, its origins predate that by more than 35 years. In the mid-1800s, a successful young Moscow industrialist, Pavel Mikhailovich Tretyakov, was determined to amass a collection of national art that would be worthy of a museum of fine arts for the entire country. In pursuit of this high-minded goal, he began to purchase paintings, drawings, and sculpture, adjudged both on high artistic merit and on their place within the various important canons of their time. For the most part undeterred by critics' disapproval and arbiters of popular taste, he became one of the—if not *the*—era's most valued patrons of the arts, with honor and gratitude conferred upon him yet to this day.

Up until six years before his death, Tretyakov maintained his enormous collection as a private one, but allowed virtually unlimited free access to the public. In 1892, he donated it all to the Moscow city government, along with a small inheritance of other fine works collected by his brother Sergei. The holdings have been continuously increased by subsequent state acquisitions, including the nationalization of privately owned pieces after the Communist Revolution.

A visitor to the museum today will find works spanning the 11th to the 20th century, from sacred icons to stunning portrait and landscape art to the famous Russian Realists' paintings that culminated in the Wanderers' Group to the splendid creations of Russian Symbolism, Impressionism, and Art Nouveau, virtually all of them known far less intimately outside of Russia than should be the case for a collection of such critical importance.

Among the many delights to be found are icons painted by the master Andrei Rublyev, including his celebrated *The Trinity;* also featured are icons of his disciples, Daniel Chorny among them, as well as some of the earliest icons to reach ancient Kievan Rus, such as *The Virgin of Vladimir,* brought from Byzantium. The first floor, which houses the icon collection, is also where drawings and watercolors from the 18th to the 20th centuries are hung.

The second floor holds 18th-, 19th-, and 20th-century painting and sculpture and is where indefatigable Russian art lovers will find their longings satisfied several times over. A series of halls of 18th-century portraits, including particularly fine works by Dmitri Levitsky, act as a time machine into the country's noble past, followed by rooms filled with the historical painting of the next century, embodying the burgeoning movements of romanticism and naturalism in such gems of landscape painting as Silvester Shchedrin's *Aqueduct at Tivoli* and Mikhail Lebedev's *Path in Albano* and *In the Park.* Other favorite pieces to look for are Bryullov's *The Last Day of Pompeii,* Ivanov's *Appearance of Christ to the People,* and Orest Kiprensky's well-known *Portrait of the Poet Alexander Pushkin.*

It may be the rich array of works completed after 1850, however, that will please museum-goers the most, for it comprises a selection of pieces from each of the Russian masters, sometimes of their best works. Hanging in the gallery are paintings by Nikolai Ge (*Peter the Great Interrogating the Tsarevich Alexei*), Vasily Perov (*Portrait of Fyodor Dostoevsky*), Vasily Polenov (*Grandmother's Garden*), Viktor Vasnetsov (*After Prince Igor's Battle with the Polovtsy*), and many others. Several canvases of the beloved Ivan Shishkin, with their depictions of Russian fields and forests, including *Morning in the Pine Forest,* of three bear cubs cavorting, fill one room, and of course a number by the equally popular Ilya Repin (*The Volga Boatmen, Easter Procession in Kursk*) also bedeck the walls. Later works, done near the century's end, range from an entire room devoted to the Symbolist Mikhail Vrubel (*The Princess Bride, Demon Seated*) to Nestorov's glowing *Vision of the Youth Bartholomew,* the boy who would become St. Sergius, founder of the monastery Sergeyev-Posad, to the magical pieces by Valentin Serov (*Girl with Peaches, Girl in Sunlight*). Before you leave, look for the compositions, of which there are a handful, done just before the revolution by Chagall, Kandinsky, and Malevich, and the stunning *Red Horse Swimming 1912* by Kuzma Petrov-Vodkin.

When you leave the gallery, pause a moment to look back on the building itself, which is quite compelling. Tretyakov's original home, where the first collection was kept, still forms a part of the gallery. As the demands of a growing collection required additional space, the house was continuously enlarged, with finally an entire annex built to function as the gallery. In 1900, when there was no longer a family living in the house, the artist Viktor Vasnetsov undertook to create the wonderful facade the gallery now carries, and more space was later added. Closed entirely in the years 1986 to 1995 for badly needed restoration (mostly inside), new wings and full reconstruction of the main one have given the museum a fresh loveliness meant to carry it well into the next century. ⊠ *12 Lavrushinsky pereulok,* ☎ *095/230–7788 or 095/231–1362.* ☉ *Tues.–Sun. 10–7.*

63 **Tserkov Nikoly v Khamovnikakh** (Church of St. Nicholas of the Weavers). The church, which remained open throughout the years of

Communist government, is wonderfully preserved. Its elegant bell tower is particularly impressive. Built in 1679–82 and topped by five gilded domes, the saucy colorfulness of its orange and green trim against its perfectly white facade makes it look like a frosted gingerbread house. In fact, the design was actually meant to suggest a festive piece of woven cloth, for it was the weavers who settled in considerable numbers in this quarter in the 17th century who commissioned the building of this church. Morning and evening services are held daily, and the church, with its wealth of icons, is as handsome inside as out. ⊠ *Komsomolsky Prospekt and ul. Lva Tolstovo. Metro: Park Kultury.*

Novodevichy Convent and Cemetery

Novodevichy Monastyr (New Maiden's Convent) is one of Moscow's finest and best-preserved ensembles of 16th- and 17th-century Russian architecture. There is much to see here. The monastery is interesting not only for its impressive cathedral and charming churches but also for the dramatic chapters of Russian history that have been played out within its walls. It stands in a wooded section bordering a small pond, making this a particularly pleasant place for an afternoon stroll. Although it is no longer a functioning convent, one of its churches is open for services. After the Bolshevik Revolution, the convent was made part of the History Museum. Its exhibits boast rare and ancient Russian paintings, both ecclesiastical and secular, woodwork and ceramics, and fabrics and embroidery. There is also a large collection of illuminated and illustrated books, decorated with gold, silver, and jewels. Attached to the monastery is a fascinating cemetery where some of Russia's greatest literary, military, and political figures are buried.

A Good Walk

To reach the **Novodevichy Monastyr,** take the subway to the Sportivnaya station. Leave the subway via the stadium exit, and then follow ulitsa Frunzensky Val to your right. It will lead you through a small park and eventually to the southeast corner of the monastery. When you come out onto Luzhnetsky proyezd, you will see the monastery's whitewashed walls to your right. Turning right, walk up the street; the main entrance is at the other end, off Bolshaya Pirogovskaya ulitsa.

Leaving the monastery, retrace your steps, walking back down Luzhnetsky proyezd to the right. The entrance to the **cemetery** is marked by a pair of green gates. Unless you have relatives buried here, you have to buy tickets to enter; tickets are sold in the small wooden kiosk directly across the street. You can also request a tour in English from the cemetery's excursion bureau, which we highly recommend.

TIMING

It would be best to reserve an entire day for Novodevichy. It will take you about 45 minutes each way from downtown Moscow, and there's much to see.

Sights to See

Novodevichy Kladbishche (Cemetery). The Novodevichy contains a fascinating collection of memorial art, but it is difficult for non-Russian speakers to identify the graves. You may wonder how a cemetery could be controversial, but this one was. For more than a generation, the Novodevichy Cemetery was closed to the general public, in large part because the controversial Nikita Khrushchev is buried here, rather than on Red Square, like other Soviet leaders. Thanks to glasnost, the cemetery was reopened in 1987, and now anyone is welcome to visit its grounds, which are not unlike those of Père Lachaise in Paris in the scope of national luminaries from all walks of life for whom it is a final resting place.

Khrushchev's grave is near the back of the cemetery, at the end of a long tree-lined walkway. If you can't find it, any of the *babushki* will point out the way. They will usually reflect their opinion of him in the way they gesture, for they almost certainly will not speak English. The memorial consists of a stark black-and-white slab, with a curvilinear border marking the separation. The contrast of black and white symbolizes the contradictions of his reign. It caused a great furor of objection among the Soviet hierarchy when it was unveiled. The memorial was designed by the artist Ernest Neizvestny, himself a controversial figure. In the 1960s Khrushchev visited an exhibit of contemporary art that included some of Neizvestny's works. Khrushchev dismissed Neizvestny's contributions as "filth," and asked the name of their artist. When Neizvestny (which means "Unknown") answered, Khrushchev scornfully said that the USSR had no need for artists with such names. To this the artist replied, "In front of my work, I am the Premier." Considering the times, it was a brave thing to say to the leader of the Soviet Union. Neizvestny eventually joined the ranks of the great emigré artists; he is now a world-famous sculptor living in the United States.

Many of those buried in the cemetery were war casualties in 1941 and 1942. The memorials often include a lifelike portrait or a photograph of the person being remembered or convey a scene in that person's life. Flowers and photographs of the dead are at almost all the graves. Among the memorials you might want to look for are those to the composers Prokofiev and Scriabin and the writers Chekhov, Gogol, Bulgakov, and Mayakovsky. Chekhov's grave is decorated with the trademark seagull of the Moscow Art Theater, the first to successfully produce his plays. Along the right-hand wall (the southwest wall of the monastery) you will find a memorial of a crash of a huge Soviet aircraft where all the crew members are interred. The grave of Stalin's wife, Nadezhda Aliluyeva, is marked by a simple tombstone with a bust of this poor woman. She supposedly committed suicide, and many hold Stalin responsible for her death. Theodore Chaliapin, the opera singer who was stripped of his Soviet citizenship while on tour in France in the 1920s, is also buried here. His remains were transferred here in 1984. His grave is marked by a marvelous lifelike representation of him that conveys the fervor and passion that characterized his singing. ⊠ *Luzhnetsky proyezd,* ☎ *095/246–6614.* ☉ *Daily 10–5.*

★ **Novodevichy Monastyr.** Enclosed by a crenelated wall with 12 colorful battle towers, the monastery comprises several groups of buildings. Until the middle of the 20th century, when Moscow's population expanded rapidly, it effectively marked the city's southern edge. It was founded in 1524 by Czar Vasily III to commemorate Moscow's capture of Smolensk from Lithuania and was intended to serve not only as a religious institution but also as a defense fortification. Its location was strategically significant, as it stands on the road to Smolensk and Lithuania. Having been founded by the czar, it enjoyed an elevated position among the many monasteries and convents of Moscow and became a convent primarily for ladies of noble birth. Little remains of the original structure. The monastery suffered severely during the Time of Troubles, a period of internal strife and foreign intervention that began in approximately 1598 and lasted until 1613, when the first Romanov was elected to the throne. Its present appearance dates largely from the 17th century, when the monastery was significantly rebuilt and enhanced. ⊠ *1 Novodevichy proyezd,* ☎ *095/246–8526.* ☉ *Wed.–Mon. 10–5. Closed last Mon. of month.*

Among the first of the famous women to take the veil here was Irina, wife of the feebleminded Czar Fyodor and the sister of Boris Godunov. Opera fans may remember the story of Boris Godunov, the subject of a well-known work by Mussorgsky. Godunov was a powerful nobleman who exerted much influence over the czar. When Fyodor died, Godunov was the logical successor to the throne, but rather than proclaim himself czar, he followed his sister to Novodevichy. Biding his time, Godunov waited until the clergy and townspeople begged him to become czar. His election took place at the convent, inside the Cathedral of Smolensk. But his rule was ill-fated, touching off the Time of Troubles.

In the next century, Novodevichy became the residence of yet another royal: Sophia, the half-sister of Peter the Great, who ruled as his regent from 1682 through 1689, while he was still a boy. During this time there was much new construction at the monastery. The power-hungry Sophia, who did not wish to give up her position when the time came for Peter's rule, had to be deposed by him. He then kept her prisoner inside Novodevichy. Even that was not enough to restrain the ambitious sister, and from her cell at the convent she organized a revolt of the *streltsy* (Russian militia). The revolt was summarily put down, and to punish Sophia, Peter had the bodies of the dead *streltsy* hung up along the walls of the convent and outside Sophia's window. Despite his greatness, Peter had a weakness for the grotesque, especially when it came to punishing his enemies. He left the decaying bodies hanging for more than a year. Yet another of the convent's later "inmates" was Yevdokiya, Peter's first wife. Peter considered her a pest and rid himself of her by sending her to a convent in faraway Suzdal. She outlived him, though, and eventually returned to Moscow. She spent her final years at Novodevichy, where she is buried.

You enter the convent through the arched passageway topped by the **Preobrazhensky Tserkov** (Gate Church of the Transfiguration), widely considered one of the best examples of Moscow Baroque. To your left as you enter is the ticket booth, where tickets are sold to the various exhibits housed in the monastery. The building to your right is the Lophukin House, where Yevdokiya lived from 1727 to 1731. Sophia's prison, now a guardhouse, is situated to your far right, in a corner of the northern wall.

The predominant structure inside the monastery is the huge five-domed **Sobor Smolenskoy Bogomateri** (Cathedral of the Virgin of Smolensk), dedicated in 1525 and built by Alexei Fryazin. It may remind you of the Kremlin's Assumption Cathedral, after which it was closely modeled. Inside, there is a spectacular iconostasis with 84 wooden columns and icons dating from the 16th and 17th centuries. Also here are the tombs of Sofia and Yevdokiya. Simon Ushakov, a leader in 17th-century icon art, was among the outstanding Moscow artists who participated in the creation of the icons. Yet another historical tale connected to the monastery tells how the cathedral was slated for destruction during the War of 1812. Napoléon had ordered the cathedral dynamited, but a brave nun managed to extinguish the fuse just in time, and the cathedral was spared.

To the right of the cathedral is the **Uspensky Tserkov** (Church of the Assumption) and **Refectory,** originally built in 1687 and then rebuilt after a fire in 1796. It was here that the blue-blooded nuns had their meals.

If a monastery can have a symbol other than an icon, then Novodevichy's would be the ornate belfry towering above its eastern wall. It rises 71 meters (236 feet) and consists of six ornately decorated tiers. The structure is topped by a gilded dome that can be seen from miles away.

U Pirosmani, a well-known restaurant specializing in the spicy cuisine of Georgia, is situated across the pond from the monastery. On weekdays, it is almost always possible to get a table without a reservation. If you are visiting on a weekend, you may want to book ahead. ✉ *4 Novode-vichy proyezd,* ☎ *095/247–1926 or 095/246–1638. Food bill paid in rubles, alcohol in dollars. AE.*

The Monasteries of Southeast Moscow

This excursion will take you to three ancient monasteries located along the banks of the Yauza River, in the southeast section of Moscow. Their history dates back to Moscow's earliest days, when it was the center of a fledgling principality and constantly under threat of enemy attack. A series of monasteries was built across the river from the Kremlin to form a ring of defense fortifications. Two of the monasteries on this tour were once part of that fortification ring. This former suburban area did not fare well as the city grew. Beginning in the 19th century, factories were built along the banks of the river, including the famous Hammer and Sickle metallurgical plant. Today this is one of Moscow's bleaker sections, marked by busy highways, monolithic residential high rises, and factories. But in their midst you find the quaint monasteries of Moscow's past, not always in the best condition but nevertheless lasting reminders of Moscow's origins.

A Good Walk

The tour begins at **Novospassky Monastery,** which you can reach by taking the subway to the Proletarskaya station. Take only lefts to get out of the subway, and you will emerge on Sarinsky proyezd. Standing with your back to the metro, the busy street a short distance ahead is Trety (3rd) Krutitsky pereulok. This is also in the direction of the Yauza River, and as you head to where the streets intersect, the yellow belfry of the monastery gate church will appear above the construction, in the distance to your right (southwest). When you reach the intersection, use the underground passageways to cross to the other side. It is just a short walk from here up a slight incline to the monastery's entrance.

Leaving the monastery, turn right to go back to the busy Sarinsky proyezd. To do this, you will have to pick your way across the tram and trolley lines. Once on the other side, before again reaching the Trety Krutitsky pereulok, you will see on your right an older, tree-lined street leading up an incline. This is the Chetvyorty (4th) Krutitsky pereulok. Climbing to the top of the hill, where you take a quick right, you will find the **Krutitskoye Podvorye,** site of the five-domed Uspensky Cathedral.

The next monastery on the tour is best reached by subway. Return to the Proletarskaya station and take the subway one stop to the Taganskaya station. Before exiting, transfer to the connecting station on the circle line; you will come out onto Taganskaya Square. Several streets intersect at this busy square. Go left as you come out of the station and cross the short street to be on the same corner as the **Taganka Drama and Comedy Theatre,** one of Moscow's most famous theaters and quite slyly subversive when founded in 1964. From here, you should cross the whole left flank of the square in order to reach ulitsa **Bolshaya Kommunisticheskaya** (Big Communist Street), which is the third street radiating out from your left as you exit the subway. This is an old residential area; the shady street is lined with tall birch trees and two-story apartment buildings. Of late, various commercial enterprises (including Moscow's exclusive Commercial Club, for its business elite) have moved into its renovated residences. It's left to wonder when the street may be renamed, given the contradictions to it that it now displays. One block down, at No. 15, is the lovely **Church of St. Martin the Confessor.** Continue down this long street until you reach the bulging Andronevskaya Ploshchad. Carefully make your way to the opposite side of the square and turn left onto Andronevsky pereulok. On the left-hand side of the street there is a small park; you will pass through the middle of it to reach the entrance to the **Andronikov Monastery,** the last stop on this walk. The whitewashed walls of the monastery's fortification will be visible through the trees. Leave the monastery through the main gate and return to Andronevskaya Ploshchad. The nearest subway station is Ploshchad Ilyicha. To reach it, turn left from the square onto ulitsa Sergiya Radonezhskovo; the subway is just one long block away. If you want to return to the Taganskaya subway station, you can take bus 53, which stops at the corner of Tukhinskaya and will let you off where you began on ulitsa Bolshaya Kommunisticheskaya.

TIMING

This is a fairly strenuous tour, with lots of walking, so be sure to have stored up your energy and put on your athletic shoes. (You should also wear appropriate dress for visiting churches.) It's not recommended to bring younger-than-teenage children, since the street crossings are complicated and, to Westerners unskilled in Muscovite ways, slightly treacherous. Always look for the pedestrian underpasses and crossing signs as you decide your best route to get to the other side.

Sights to See

Andrey Rublyov Museum of Ancient Russian Culture and Art. Located in the Andronikov Monastery, the museum is named after the monastery's most celebrated monk, the icon painter Andrey Rublyov, who is believed to be buried here. Rublyov lived in the early 15th century, a time of much bloodshed and violence. Russia was slowly loosening the Mongol-Tatar yoke, and people lived in constant fear as the divided Russian principalities fought among themselves and against the Mongol-Tatar invaders. Rublyov's icons seem even more remarkable when viewed against the backdrop of his turbulent era. His works are amazing creations of flowing pastels conveying peace and tranquility. His most famous work, *The Holy Trinity,* is now housed in the Tretyakov Gallery (☞ Gorky Park Area, *above*). The museum in the Andronikov Monastery, strangely enough, does not contain a single Rublyov work. Its collection of ancient religious art is nevertheless a fine one and well worth a visit. Tickets to the exhibits are sold in the office located around the corner to the right as you enter the monastery grounds. The museum is divided into three sections, and you must purchase a ticket for each part that you want to see. ✉ *Andronevskaya Ploshchad 10,* ☎ *095/278–1429.* ☉ *Thurs.–Tues. 11–6. Closed last Fri. of month.*

Andronikov Monastery. The monastery underwent extensive reconstruction in the 1950s and was refurbished again in the late 1980s. It is in much better condition than the Novospassky Monastery or Krutitskoye Podvorye. A stroll inside its heavy stone fortifications is an excursion into Moscow's past. The rumble of the city is drowned out by the loud crowing of birds overhead. Even the air seems more pure here, perhaps because of the old birch trees growing on the monastery grounds and just outside its walls. The Andronikov Monastery was founded in 1360 by the metropolitan Alexei and named in honor of its first abbot, St. Andronik. The site was chosen not only for its strategic importance—on the steep banks of the Yauza River—but also because, according to legend, it was from this hill that the metropolitan Alexei got his first glimpse of the Kremlin.

The dominating structure on the monastery grounds is the **Spassky Sobor** (Cathedral of the Savior), Moscow's oldest stone structure. Erected in 1420–27 on the site of an earlier, wooden church, it rests on the mass grave of Russian soldiers who fought in the Battle of Kulikovo (1380), the decisive Russian victory that eventually led to the end of Mongol rule in Russia. Unfortunately, the original interiors, which were painted by Andrey Rublyov and another famous icon painter, Danil Chorny, were lost to a fire in 1812. Fragments of their frescoes have been restored, however. The cathedral is open for services at 5:30 PM on Saturday and 9 AM on Sunday.

The building to your immediate left as you enter the monastery is the former abbot's residence. It now houses a permanent exhibit entitled "Masterpieces of Ancient Russian Art" from the 13th through 16th centuries. The exhibit includes icons from the Novgorod, Tver, Rostov, and Moscow schools. A highlight of the collection is the early-16th-century *St. George Smiting the Dragon,* from the Novgorod School.

The next building, to the left and across the pathway from the Cathedral of the Savior, is the **Refectory.** Like the Novospassky Monastery, it was built during the reign of Ivan the Great, in 1504–06. Today it houses the museum's exhibit of new acquisitions, which consists primarily of icons from the 19th and 20th centuries. Attached to the Refectory is the Church of St. Michael the Archangel, another example of the style known as Moscow Baroque. It was commissioned by the Lopukhin family—relatives of Yevdokiya Lopukhina, the first, unloved wife of Peter the Great—as the family crypt in 1694. But there are no Lophukins buried here as Peter had Yevdokiya banished to a monastery in faraway Suzdal before the church was even finished, and her family was exiled to Siberia.

The museum's last exhibit is located in the former monks' residence, the redbrick building just beyond the Church of St. Michael. The exhibit is devoted to Nikolai the Miracle Worker and contains icons depicting his life and work.

Church of St. Martin the Confessor. This lovely church dates from the late 18th century and is in need of full restoration; its cupola is rusted and little trees are growing on its roof, but it is a working church. Farther down the street, at No. 29, you will find another building of historical importance, the apartment house where the theater director Stanislavsky was born in 1863.

Krutitskoye Podvorye (Krutitskoye Ecclesiastical Residence). This historical architectural complex is even older than the Novospassky Monastery; the first cathedral on this site was erected sometime in the 13th century. Its name comes from the word *kruta,* meaning "hill." This was originally a small monastery, a site of defense in the 14th century against the Tartar-Mongol invaders, whose prestige grew further at the end of the 16th century, when it became the suburban residence of the Moscow metropolitan. The church and grounds were completely rebuilt, and the present structures date from this period. As monasteries go, its period of flowering was short-lived; it was closed in 1788 on orders from Catherine the Great, who secularized many church buildings. In the 19th century it was used as an army barracks, and it is said that the Russians accused of setting the Moscow fire of 1812 were tortured here by Napoléon's forces. In the 20th century, the Soviets turned the barracks into a military prison. Although the buildings have now been returned to the Orthodox Church, the prison remains on the monastery grounds. There is also a police station right outside the main gate, so do not be alarmed if you are greeted by a small band of uni-formed policemen as you enter.

To your left as you enter the monastery grounds is the five-domed, red-brick **Uspensky Sobor** (Assumption Cathedral), erected at the end of the 16th century on the site of several previous churches. Stylistically medieval, more than anything else, it is a working church, undergo-ing restoration like many of its counterparts throughout the city. Still very attractive inside, it has an assemblage of icons, lovely frescoes that have been half restored, and an impressive all-white altar and icono-stasis. The cathedral is attached to a gallery leading to the **Teremok** (Gate Tower), a splendid example of Moscow Baroque. It was built in 1688–94, and its exterior decoration is the work of Osip Startsev. Ex-cept for the carved, once-white columns, the walls are completely cov-ered with colorful mosaics. The red, green, and white tiles—all of different sizes and shapes—framed in the red brick of the adjoining build-ings, give, despite the verging frenzy of the decoration, an overall ef-fect of a compositional whole. The gallery and Teremok served as the passageway for the metropolitan as he walked from his residence (to the right of the Teremok) to the cathedral. Passing through the gate tower, you will see the military prison, replete with lookout towers, located on the opposite side of the Teremok gates.

You should go through, in order to have a full walk around the tran-quil grounds. From this side, you can enter the bell tower, which dates from 1680. Taking the stairs inside, through the door off its first level, you'll have access to the gallery itself and can walk along the walls. As you go around the complex, you will encounter young artists who seem to have chosen this quiet place to sketch for their school assign-ments. ☺ *Wed.–Mon. 9–6, except first Mon. of month. For informa-tion about excursions,* ☎ *095/276–9256.*

NEED A BREAK?	Taganskaya Square is home to Moscow's most renowned drama the-ater, the Taganka, and the area is rich in restaurants catering to theater crowds. One of the best is the **Skazka** restaurant (✉ 1 Tovarishchevsky pereulok, ☎ 095/271–0998), specializing in Russian cuisine. As with most other restaurants in Moscow, you are best off making reservations.

Novospassky (New Savior) Monastery. The monastery was built in 1462, but its history dates back to the 13th century. It was originally located inside the Kremlin, and it is called the "New" Monastery because its new site on the banks of the Yauza River was a transfer ordered by Ivan III, who wanted to free up space in the Kremlin for other con-struction. Often called Ivan the Great, Ivan III was the first Russian leader to categorically (and successfully) renounce Russia's allegiance to the khan of the Golden Horde. It was during his reign that a uni-fied Russian state was formed under Moscow's rule. The Novospassky Monastery was just one of the numerous churches and monasteries built during the prosperous time of Ivan's reign. In uglier modern history, a site just outside the monastery's walls was one of the mass graves for those executed during Stalin's purges.

You enter the monastery at the near entrance to the left of the **Bell Tower Gate,** which was erected in 1786. It is now closed from the outside, though once inside the complex you can walk beneath its archway. The entire monastery is, sadly, in a state of semi-disrepair. Reconstruction *is* being done, but slowly; it has already taken more than 30 years. Since the early 1990s, however, when it was returned to the Orthodox Church, the pace has picked up. Still, except on Sunday and church holidays, the monastery grounds are often virtually deserted. A stroll among its decaying buildings will therefore feel like a very private, if not rather eerie, experience.

The first thing you see as you enter the monastery grounds is the massive white **Sobor Spasa Preobrazheniya** (Transfiguration Cathedral). You may notice a resemblance, particularly in its domes, to the Kremlin's Assumption Cathedral, which served as its model. The Transfiguration Cathedral was built in 1642–49 by the Romanov family, commissioned by the czar as the Romanov family crypt. The gallery leading to the central nave is decorated with beautiful frescoes depicting the history of Christianity in Rus. It is worth timing your visit with a church service (daily at 5 PM) to see the interior. Even if the church is closed, the doors may be unlocked. No one will stop you from taking a quick look at the gallery walls.

In front of the cathedral, on the right-hand side, is the small red **Nadmogilnaya Chasovnya** (Memorial Chapel), marking the grave of Princess Alekseyevna Tarankova, the illegitimate daughter of Empress Elizabeth and Count Razumovsky. She led most of her life as a nun in Moscow's St. John's Convent, forced to take the veil by Catherine the Great. During her lifetime her identity was concealed, and she was known only as Sister Dofiya. The chapel over her grave was added in 1900, almost a century after her death. Sister Dofiya's imposter played a more prominent role in Russian history than the real Princess Tarankova. A mysterious character of European origin, the imposter never revealed her true identity. She was imprisoned by Catherine the Great in St. Petersburg's Peter and Paul Fortress, where she died of consumption in 1775. Her death in her flooded, rat-infested cell was depicted in a famous painting by Konstantin Flavitsky in 1864.

None of the monastery's original 15th-century structures has survived. The present fortification wall and most of the churches and residential buildings on the grounds date from the 17th century. To the right as you face the cathedral stands the tiny **Pokrovsky Tserkov** (Church of the Intercession). Directly behind the cathedral is the **Tserkov Znamenia** (Church of the Sign). Painted in the dark yellow popular in its time, with a four-column facade, it was built in 1791–1808 by the wealthy Sheremetyev family and contains the Sheremetyev crypt. In the back right-hand corner, running along the fortification walls, are the former monks' residences.

DINING

Though the number of restaurants in Moscow has mushroomed in the past few years and more than a few of the city's dining rooms now offer world-class cuisine, all of this welcome culinary maturation has, of course, come at a price. If you have the cash, there are restaurants aplenty. Tourists whose wallets are fat compared with the average Russian's may even think most spots are good bargains. Those Russians with an increased discretionary income enjoy going out, but most of them are young. As a result, the boom is in restaurants that resemble those back home, as companies build similar tastes here. Travelers searching for "real" Russian food are probably not very interested in this kind of dining and may have to rough it at the low end or fork over a considerable amount of cash at the high end. Still, either way you won't go hungry.

Although impromptu appearances are increasingly acceptable in Moscow, it is usually expected that you will devote some old-fashioned planning to dining out. Even if a restaurant is half empty, you may be refused a table if you don't have a reservation. This is especially true in the evening, and sometimes it happens even during the day.

Reserve plenty of time for your meal. In Russia dining out is an occasion, and Russians often make an evening (or an afternoon) out of going out to eat. Often the meal is accompanied by a floor show or musical entertainment. Almost all the expensive hotel restaurants offer a New Orleans Jazz Brunch on Sunday, when you can enjoy their haute cuisine and decor at greatly reduced prices.

CATEGORY	COST*
$$$$	over $45
$$$	$30–$45
$$	$20–$30
$	under $20

per person for a three-course dinner, excluding drinks and service

WHAT TO WEAR

Dress at the restaurants reviewed below is casual, unless noted otherwise.

$$$$ ✕ **CDL.** You'll find one of the city's very best dining rooms—and one of the best places to sample authentic Russian cuisine—located in an elegant mansion. In the 19th century the house served as the headquarters for Moscow's Freemasons; more recently it was a meeting place for members of the Soviet Writers' Union. The name is the Russian abbreviation for "Central House of Writers." Now entirely reconstructed and renovated, with its crystal chandeliers, rich wood paneling, fireplaces, and antique balustrades, CDL is one of the warmest and most elegant eateries in the city. Though everything here is extremely well prepared, it's best to stick to the Russian items on the menu: try the borshch or *pelmeni* (or both!) for starters, and then move on to Rabbit Stroganoff, Veal Orloff, or Quail Golitsiya. It you're feeling very adventurous, cleanse your palate between courses with a glass of Russian *kvas* (bread-beer) with horseradish. ⊠ *50 Povarskaya ul.,* ☎ *095/ 291–1515. Reservations advised. AE, DC, MC, V or rubles at restaurant exchange rate. Metro: Barrikadnaya.*

$$$$ ✕ **Exchange.** This American steak house is located in the midwestern mall of the Radisson Slavyanskaya Hotel. The homesick American will enjoy the leafy salads and thick, juicy sirloins flown in from New York. The black-and-white interior decor makes for an elegant yet relaxed atmosphere, the perfect re-creation of America in Moscow. If you're not a meat lover, try the poached cod fillet or the chicken breast broiled to perfection in a tangy ginger sauce. The French onion soup or Caesar salad make good starters. Order a bottle of imported wine from the extensive wine list, and top off your meal with a piece of apple pie. True to the American way, the restaurant offers a no-smoking section. This is the ideal place to come for a well-earned break from Russian reality. ⊠ *Radisson Slavyanskaya Hotel, 2 Berezhkovskaya nab.,* ☎ *095/941–8020. Reservations advised. Hard currency only. AE, DC, MC, V.* ☺ *Daily noon–3, 6–10:30. Metro: Kievskaya.*

$$$$ ✕ **Glazur.** This Danish-Russian joint venture is one of the most upscale establishments catering to the city's foreign community. It stands
★ out from the pack for its subdued atmosphere and exquisite cuisine. Located in a renovated 19th-century mansion on the Garden Ring, the restaurant has an elegant interior, tastefully decorated in brown and gold. The Russian and European dishes are beautifully prepared; the food, much of it imported from Belgium and Denmark, is a gourmet's dream. The *russkaya zakuska,* a beef-gelatin aspic with colorful layers of finely diced ham, chicken, and tongue, makes a good starter. A specialty of the house is *baklazhany zarevshan,* a spicy Armenian mix-

ture of eggplant, carrots, onion, and garlic. For your main course, try the *svinina à la gousar,* a pork dish served with a creamy mushroom sauce. The wine list is excellent. Top off your meal with a flaming ice cream surprise, the chef's special rendition of baked Alaska. Service is swift, friendly, and professional. The musical entertainment in the evenings varies, ranging from jazz to classical to Russian folk. ✉ *12 Smolensky bulvar,* ☎ *095/248–4438. Jacket and tie. Reservations accepted. Credit cards only. AE, MC, V.* ☉ *Daily noon–5, 6–midnight. Metro: Smolenskaya.*

$$$$ ✕ **Grand Imperial.** This truly old-style restaurant serves superbly prepared and often rich dishes, such as veal Romanoff. The succulent food is well matched by the sumptuous surroundings. Every detail is fine—from the original art, to the crystal chandeliers, to the flowers, to the antique silver service personally collected by the owners. ✉ *9/5 Gagarinsky pereulok,* ☎ *095/291–6063,* FAX *095/290–0249. Reservations advised. Jacket and tie. AE, DC, MC, V. Rubles only.* ☉ *Daily 7–noon. Metro: Kropotkinskaya.*

$$$$ ✕ **Le Romanoff.** This also ranks among Moscow's finest gourmet experiences. Located on the second floor of the Baltschug Hotel, it is exquisitely managed and offers Russian/Continental cuisine that pleases both the eye and the palate. The menu is unique, the atmosphere is elegant, and the wine list is superb—the perfect spot for an important dinner. ✉ *1 ul. Balchug,* ☎ *095/230–6500. Jacket and tie. Reservations required. AE, DC, MC, V. Metro: Kitai-Gorod or Novokuznetskaya.*

$$$$ ✕ **Metropol.** The renovated interiors of the Metropol Hotel's grand dining hall are a stunning memorial to Russian Art Nouveau. The nearly three-story-high dining room, replete with stained-glass windows, marble pillars, and leaded-glass roof, recalls the splendor of prerevolutionary Russia. The beautifully laid tables and formally dressed waiters add to the elegance. In terms of its opulent atmosphere, visitors will be pleased, but they can find themselves disappointed when it comes to the food and service. The pricey menu features such Russian delicacies as smoked salmon and beef Stroganoff, but the preparation is uninspired. The highlight of the week is Sunday brunch, when the restaurant puts out an impressive spread, including an array of meat and fish dishes, home-baked French pastries, and exotic fresh fruits. ✉ *1/4 Teatralny proyezd,* ☎ *095/927–6040. Reservations advised. Jacket and tie. AE, DC, MC, V.* ☉ *Daily 7–2, 6:30–midnight. Metro: Ploshchad Revolutsii.*

$$$$ ✕ **Panda.** This American-style Chinese restaurant, virtually Moscow's first, was an overnight hit. All seafood and other hard-to-find ingredients are flown in from abroad to guarantee quality and freshness, and an award-winning Chinese cook oversees the careful preparation of each dish. The Hunan and Szechuan selections are especially good, though somehow all still retain some hint of Russian flavoring. Prices are high. Takeout orders are accepted throughout the day and evening. ✉ *3/5 Tverskoy bulvar,* ☎ *095/298–6565. Reservations advised. AE, DC, MC, V. Metro: Tverskaya.*

$$$$ ✕ **Praga.** Centrally located on Arbat Square, in a handsome prerevolutionary building, this restaurant was once one of Moscow's finest staterun dining establishments. Radical changes in the capital's restaurant scene have left the staff here nostalgic for the days when lines formed outside its doors and it took a good connection or a bribe to land a table. Although it's named for the Czech capital, the restaurant has never offered anything but standard Russian cuisine, the quality of which has fallen to new lows in recent years. If you are with a Russian who does the ordering, things might improve. The menu is huge but the actual availability of dishes listed on it is limited. Standard offerings include beef Stroganoff and chicken Tabaka (roasted spring chicken). What keeps the place in business is its striking interiors. A grand marble staircase with heavy brass

64

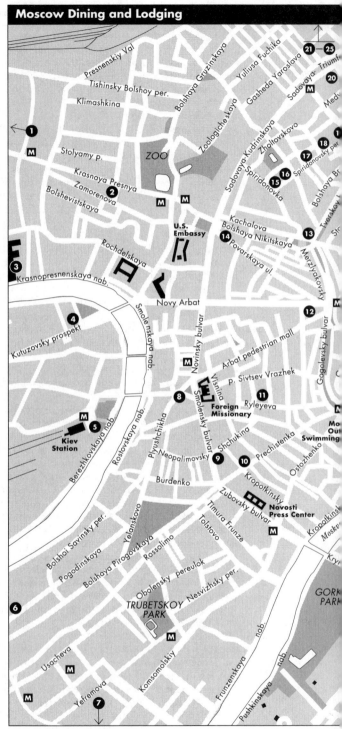

Moscow Dining and Lodging

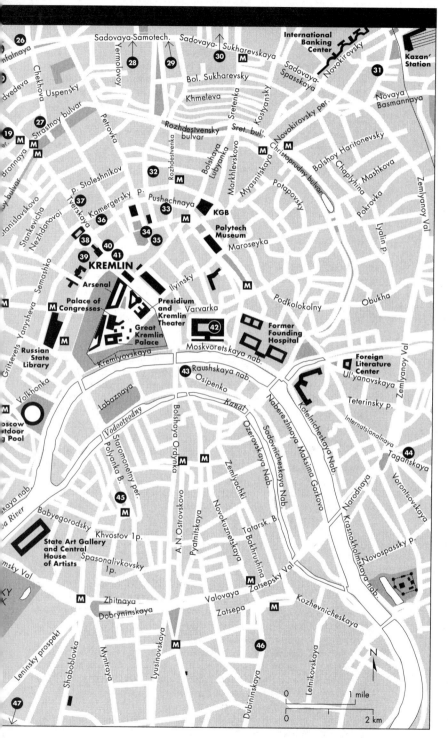

Sadovaya-Samotech.   Sadovaya-↑Sukharevskaya

International
Banking
Center

Novokirovsky

Kazan'
Station

⑳ Inalnaya

⑳ Chekhova   Uspensky

⑳

⑳ avedeva

⑳ Yermalovoy

⑳ ㉘

㉙

㉚ Ⓜ

Bol. Sukharevsky

Sadovaya-
Spasskaya

㉛

Novaya
Basmannaya

Petrovka

Khmeleva

Rozhdestvensky
bulvar

Sretenka

Sret. bul'.   Kostyansky

Novokirovsky per.

Bolshoy Haritonevsky

Zemlyanoy Val

⑲

Ⓜ Strasnoy bulvar

⑳ ⑰

Ⓜ

ronnaya

Stanislavskovo

Rozhdestvenka

Bolshaya
Lubyanka

Markhlevskovo   Myasnitskaya

Christoprudny bulvar   Ⓜ

Potapovsky

Chaplyhina   Mashkova

⑰ bulvar

P. Stoleshnikov

Tverskaya

Kamergersky p.

⑫ Ⓜ

Pushechnaya

㉝ Ⓜ

KGB

Pokrovka

Lyalin P.

Stankevicha
Nezhdanovoi

㊲
㊱

㉞
㉟

Polytech
Museum

Obukha

㊳

㊴ ㊵
㊶

Maroseyka

Semashko

Yanysheva

Ⓜ

KREMLIN

Ilyinsky

Gritsevets

Arsenal

Palace of
Congresses   Ⓜ

**Presidium
and
Kremlin
Theater**   Varvarka

Podkolokolny

**Great
Kremlin
Palace**

㊷ Ⓜ

Former
Founding
Hospital

Ul'yanovskaya

Foreign
Literature
Center

Zemlyanoy Val

Moscow
utdoor
g Pool

**Russian
State
Library**

Kremlyovskaya

Moskvoretskaya nab.

Teterinsky p.

Volkhonka

Ⓜ

Labaznaya

㊸ Ⓜ

Raushskaya nab.

Osipenko

Kanal

Nabere zhnaya Maksima Gorkovo

Kotelnicheskaya Nab.

Internatsionalnaya

kaya nab.

Babyegorodsky

Vodootvodny

Staromonetny per.

Bolshaya Ordynka

Ⓜ   Ⓜ

Ozerovskaya Nab.

Sadovnicheskaya Nab.

Narodnaya

Taganskaya

㊹

Vorontsovskaya

a River

Polyanka B.

Khvostov 1p.

㊺ Ⓜ

A.N.Ostrovskovo

Pyatnitskaya

Zemlyachki

Novokuznetskaya

Tatarsk. B.

Bakhrushina

Krasnokholmskaya nab.

Novospassky p.

emsky Val

**State Art Gallery
and Central
House
of Artists**

Spasonalivkovsky
1p.

TY

Ⓜ

Zhitnaya

Dobryninskaya

Myntraya

Shaboblovka

Lyusinovskaya

Leninsky prospekt

Valovaya

Zatsepa

Zatsepsky Val

Ⓜ

Kozhevnicheskaya

Dubininskaya

Letnikovskaya

㊻

N
↗

0   1 mile

0   2 km

㊼ ↙

railings leads you to the elegant second-floor dining halls, where gilt ceilings, parquet floors, and brass chandeliers create an Old World atmosphere. A Russian band often will play later in the evening, and things can get very boisterous as diners kick up their heels. Double-check your bill carefully. Prices are steep to begin with, and virtually every slice of bread seems to be tallied singly. The waiters here were spoiled by years of corruption and have been known to add extra items to the check. ⊠ *2 Arbat ul.,* ☎ *095/290–6171. Reservations advised. Jacket and tie. Rubles only.* ☉ *Daily noon–11:30. Metro: Arbatskaya.*

$$$$ ✕ **Savoy.** Located in the Savoy Hotel, this restaurant's fancy interior
★ and elegant menu are likely to please Russophiles and gourmands alike. The food—a mixture of Russian, Scandinavian, and French cuisine—is excellent. Ingredients are trucked in from Finland, and the Russian chef has won several international awards for his imperial creations. The restaurant features a special Czar's Menu, a re-creation of one of the 12 menus served at the coronation of Czar Nicholas II in 1896. But food aside, the real reason to come here is to see the inside. With its delicate, gilt wall coverings, long mirrors, and gilt-framed ceiling paintings, it echoes the opulence of St. Petersburg's imperial palaces. Dinner can easily run into five digits; you may prefer the more reasonable prix-fixe lunch. ⊠ *3 Rozhdestvenka ul.,* ☎ *095/929–8600. Reservations advised. Jacket and tie. Traveler's checks accepted. AE, DC, MC, V.* ☉ *Daily 7:30 AM—11 PM. Metro: Kuznetsky Most.*

$$$$ ✕ **Scandinavia.** Whereas most new restaurants in Moscow seem to have gone for glitz, the owners of Scandinavia have opted for cozy and comforting. This is one of the most serene dining rooms in the city: burnt-orange walls with blue-green trim, comfortable wooden chairs and upholstered benches, candles in wine bottles on red-and-white tablecloths, and arrangements of dried flowers on deep window ledges all combine to make you feel as if you're in a Swedish country home. This place also has one of the best kitchens in the city. As the name suggests, the menu emphasizes the cuisine of Russia's Baltic Coast neighbors to the northwest. Try fried pickled Baltic herring or Swedish cheese pie for an appetizer. Entrée selections include a variety of grilled meats and fish. And the desserts include some of the most tantalizing offerings you'll find in Moscow, such as apple strudel with a creamy, spiked vanilla custard and crêpes with sage-marinated raspberries and blackberries. ⊠ *7 Maly Palashevsky Pereulok,* ☎ *095/200–4986. Reservations advised. AE, MC, V, or rubles according to restaurant exchange rate.* ☉ *Daily noon–11:30. Metro: Pushkinskaya.*

$$$$ ✕ **Strastnoy Bulvar 7.** This is the name and address of a small but excellent restaurant located near Pushkin Square. It is a bit on the pricey side, but if tony atmosphere and intimate conversation are in order, this is the place. The suckling pig stuffed with mushrooms and the perch with crabmeat stand out as house specialties. Russian musicians play discreetly throughout the evening. ⊠ *7 Strastnoy bulvar,* ☎ *095/299– 0498. Jacket and tie. Reservations required. AE, MC, V, or rubles according to restaurant exchange rate. Metro: Chekhovskaya.*

$$$$ ✕ **Teatro.** There are actually two restaurants at this location on the lower level at the rear of the Metropol Hotel, the side opposite the Bolshoi Theater. Once you've descended the opulent marble staircase you'll be confronted with the choice of turning left to enter the Lobster Grill, which prides itself on its fresh oysters, lobster, scampi, and prawns, or turning right into the much livelier, and more popular, Teatro proper, which specializes in the foods of the Mediterranean. With its whimsical murals, bright colors, potted palms, mirrors, and salsa band, this dining room almost feels like Los Angeles (which might help explain why it's so popular with Moscow's American expat community). It's one of the few places in the city that makes good salads—even a respectable Caesar (here called a *Rimsky* (Roman) *Salat*). Though the chef has taken his inspiration from various corners of the Mediterranean, it's best to stick to the Italian entrées; the lamb and the pastas are particularly good. ⊠ *1/4 Teatralny Proezd, in the Metropol Hotel,* ☎ *095/ 927–6678. Reservations advised. AE, MC, V, or rubles according to restaurant exchange rate. Metro: Teatralnaya.*

$$$ ✕ **Artistico.** Just off Tverskaya Ulitsa and opposite the MKhAT Theater, this is the perfect spot for a pre- or post-theater dinner. The dining room, with its velvet curtains, green and creamy beige walls, Art-Deco trim, and painted ceiling, manages to be both elegant and cozy. The menu includes a large selection of soups, salads, pastas, and meats, which makes it possible to either graze or linger over a multi-course meal. Artistico's "express lunch" of two courses and dessert is one of the best deals in the city for a satisfying midday meal. ⊠ *5/6 Kamergersky Pereulok,* ☎ *095/265–7068. Reservations advised. AE, MC, V, or rubles according to restaurant exchange rate. Metro: Okhotny Ryad.*

$$$ ✕ **Kropotkinskaya 36.** This was Moscow's first cooperative, and when it opened in 1987, it was known simply by its address. Since then the street has been given back its prerevolutionary name, and the restaurant has turned private. If you're looking for a good spot to dine *à la russe,* try this. Their blinis with caviar are delicious, and you can always rely on the hearty meat-filled Siberian pelmeni. The more adventurous can order roast suckling pig, but only if they're truly hungry, for it comes on a platter. Service is decent, though not what it once was. You'll enjoy the interior, which is elegant and intimate, with mirrored walls, yellow tablecloths, and plush auburn drapes. Background music is by a tenor soloist, who does a repertoire of Russian classics and beyond ("Strangers in the Night"). A romantic setting. ⊠ *36 ul. Prechistenka,* ☎ *095/201–7500. Reservations advised. Jacket and tie. AE, D, MC, V.* ☺ *Daily noon–11. Metro: Kropotkinskaya.*

$$$ ✕ **Planet Hollywood.** You can't miss it. It's the only place for miles attracting attention to itself with neon, palm trees, and a barrage of blinking lights. Step inside and it's exactly like any other Planet Hollywood in any other world capital, so it's not the place to go if you're in the mood for balalaikas and blini, but it may be perfect if you're feeling a little homesick. The menu—in Russian and in English—offers the standard Planet Hollywood fare, everything from *krylyshki "Buffalo"* (Buffalo wings) to *rebryshki* (baby-back ribs) to thin-crust Tex-Mex pizza. The food and drinks are all very well prepared, and the service is astonishingly friendly and efficient for Moscow. ⊠ *23 B Krasnaya Presnya Ul.,* ☎ *095/252–0731. Reservations advised. AE, D, MC, V or rubles at restaurant exchange rate. Metro: Ulitsa 1905-ogo Goda.*

$$$ ✕ **Skazka.** The name, which means fairy tale, says it all. If you're tired of the industrial cuisine of state-run enterprises and the stuffy atmosphere of Moscow's private establishments, this cozy restaurant just off Taganka Square features dark-wood carvings and long narrow windows filled with pyramid-shaped frosted glass. A soft, red light filters through the heavy glass, creating a romantic yet casual atmosphere. The service is friendly and professional, and the food is excellent. The restaurant offers traditional Russian cuisine, such as Siberian pelmeni—tender, meat-filled dumplings—and mushroom noodle soup, appropriately called "Like at Home with Mama." For dessert, try the house specialty, *rizhok,* a delectable layered pastry baked on the premises. The musical entertainment runs the gamut and changes every 20 minutes, from jazz to Russian folk to classical piano and violin. Do be careful near here at night, though; traditionally, residents will tell you, it's an area favored by "bandits." ⊠ *1 Tovarishchevsky pereulok,* ☎ *095/911–0998. AE, MC, V.* ☺ *Daily noon–5, 7–11. Metro: Marksistskaya.*

$$ ✕ **Ampir.** Situated above the Garden Ring, across the street from the lively American Bar and Grill, Ampir is perfectly Russian (or at least New Russian) in atmosphere and a fine spot for an authentic dining experience in Moscow at a reasonable cost. Ignore such dishes as Turkey Arkansas and Boar à la Texas (fried boar with cranberry sauce), which are strictly for show, and head for the serious Russian cooking. The array of hot and cold *zakuski* (appetizers) is excellent, and you should join in the tradition of partaking of these heartily by ordering more than one. Baked pike-perch, roasted cheese, and crab salad are tasty choices. Soups, particularly mushroom, are well done here. For an entrée, try the *shashlik,* which fish lovers can get made of sturgeon, which is delicious. The staff is respectfully friendly and speaks English adequately, if haltingly. In further keeping with Russian ways, orders may take a while to appear, though champagne and vodka glasses always seem to be swiftly refilled. ✉ *4/10 Sadovaya-Triumfalnaya ul.,* ☏ *095/299–7974. AE, DC, MC, V. Metro: Mayakovskaya.*

$$ ✕ **Atrium.** Hidden away in one of the numerous and monolithic apartment buildings lining Leninsky Prospekt, this popular cooperative can be tricky to find. It's a journey to get here by public transportation (three stops up the hill on a crowded trolley bus from the Leninsky Prospekt subway station); the restaurant is best reached by car. Once inside, you'll wonder where you have landed. Its candlelit interiors, decorated with growling lions, armored knights, and velvet-wrapped pillars, provide a soothing change from Moscow's harried pace. Although this isn't a gourmet's paradise, the standard Russian dishes are pleasantly prepared. The appetizers and soups are excellent. Ask for *syr v testu* (garlic cheese sticks) and Staromoskovsky (Old Moscow) soup, made with a mushroom bouillon and chock-full of tender pieces of veal, chicken, and pork. For your main course, try the *zharkoye,* a veal stew served in an earthenware pot. ✉ *44 Leninsky Prospekt,* ☏ *095/137–3008. Reservations required. AE, MC, DC, V.* ☺ *Daily noon–4, 6–11. Metro: Leninsky Prospekt.*

$$ ✕ **Azteca.** One of Moscow's most popular places, this noisy watering hole offers a satisfying Mexican menu of traditional favorites for Southwestern palates. Among the nachos, guacamole, and fajitas are several chicken dishes and a few exotic ones, such as roasted duck tacos. A children's menu is also available. Pretty much any drink is served from the well-stocked bar, which makes a potent, if lemony, margarita. For a final flourish, flag down the roving *compadre* whose holster packs tequila bottles instead of six-shooters. The walls are covered in a bright Aztec motif, and the staff's mood matches the festive costumes. They have been known to break out in spontaneous dance while taking your order, inspired no doubt by the ensemble of guitar, drum, and pipe players who cheerfully rally the dinner crowd with Latin melodies all night long. ✉ *11 Novoslobodskaya ul.,* ☏ *095/956–3490. AE, MC, V.* ☺ *Daily noon–3, 7–11. Parking fee at night if you use their lot. Metro: Novoslobodskaya.*

$$ ✕ **El Rincón Español.** This Spanish restaurant and bar's central location, reasonable prices, and lively atmosphere make this a popular watering hole with European expatriates. Wash down your Galician chicken pie or chorizo (spicy fried sausage) with a refreshing glass of San Miguel beer. The nominally Spanish menu includes several European dishes, such as French onion soup and chicken cordon bleu. Although these can be tempting, you should stick to the Spanish fare, as the European dishes tend to be bland and unimaginative. Service is polite and swift. This is one of the few restaurants in Moscow where it's possible to get a table without an advance reservation, making this a good choice for a meal on the go. ✉ *13/8 Pushkinskaya ul.,* ☏ *095/*

229–7023. *Reservations accepted. AE, DC, MC, V.* ☉ *Daily noon–5 AM. Metro: Teatralnaya.*

$$ ✕ **U Pirosmani.** Named for the Georgian artist Niko Pirosmani, this
★ popular cooperative is located near the Novodevichy Monastery. Its
rustic interior, with white-washed walls and wood-paneled ceilings, re-
creates the atmosphere of an artist's studio. Ask for a table in the main
hall, which affords picturesque views of the 16th-century monastery
across the pond from the restaurant. The blackboard menu reads like
a Georgian cookbook. Instead of wrestling with the decision of which
of its tasty main courses to try, ask for a sampling of appetizers. The
spread, which includes lobio, satsivi, and *gruzinskaya kapusta* (a spicy,
marinated red cabbage), will be enough to feed the hungriest tourist.
The kitchen also serves delightful *khinkali,* Georgian meat dumplings.
Order a bottle of Georgian wine to accompany your meal, and top it
all off with a sweet Georgian pastry, baked on the premises. Although
the restaurant is very popular and often crowded, service is astonish-
ingly good by local standards. ✉ *4 Novodevichy Prospekt,* ☎ *095/247–
1926. Rubles accepted for food, dollars accepted for alcohol. AE.* ☉
Daily noon–4, 6–10:30. Metro: Sportivnaya.

$$ ✕ **U Yuzefa.** Moscow's only Jewish restaurant is strong on traditional
dishes using ingredients such as herring, cream cheeses, and matzo; they
also have gefilte fish. A jolly family atmosphere pervades, and it tends
to get crowded by the later hours. Service is no-nonsense. Yiddish folk
songs are performed throughout the evening. ✉ *11/17 Dubininskaya
ul.,* ☎ *095/238–4646. Rubles only.* ☉ *Daily 6:30–11:30. Metro:
Paveletskaya.*

$ ✕ **American Bar and Grill.** A real success story here, befitting its name,
this restaurant delivers exactly what it promises—and probably a little bit more once you throw in the atmosphere. The original is located
just off Tverskaya and is a haunt well visited by young expatriates and
locals alike, who pore over the menu of burgers, salads, appetizers, and
steaks amid animated conversation and a fair amount of smoking. A
second, near Taganskaya, has improved on the first. It's more than three
times as big, with a terrific upstairs bar and a glass-enclosed atrium
dining room downstairs. In warm weather, a café patio is open. The
menu here also expands on the first's, adding lots of barbeque dishes
(from the "Smoke Pit"), more grill items, chicken-fried steak, and
pizza. In both cases, a real attraction is the continued low cost. With
the exception of one or two of the dinner plates, everything here costs
less than $12. ✉ *32/1 Tverskaya-Yamskaya ul.,* ☎ *095/251–2847,
Metro: Mayakovskaya;* ✉ *59 Zamlyanoi Val,* ☎ *095/912–3615,
Metro: Taganskaya. AE, MC, V.* ☉ *Daily 6–2 or later.*

$ ✕ **Aragvi.** This state-run restaurant specializing in the spicy cuisine of
former Soviet Georgia has been a tourist trap for years. The kitchen
is a bit unpredictable, but the gorgeous interiors, with elaborately
painted walls and colorful mosaics, make up for the hit-or-miss food.
A safe bet is the chicken *satsivi,* served in a walnut and coriander sauce,
or the *lobio,* butter beans in a spicy sauce. The so-called Marble Hall,
with its high ceilings and wall paintings depicting ancient Georgia in
the spirit of socialist realism, features loud and lively Georgian musical entertainment. For solitude and relatively smoke-free dining, reserve
one of the private rooms on the second floor, a favorite haunt of
Lavrenti Beria, Stalin's henchman. Cognac, champagne, and a limited
selection of Georgian wines are available. ✉ *6 Tverskaya ul.,* ☎ *095/
229–2906. Reservations advised. No credit cards.* ☉ *Daily noon–1 AM.
Metro: Okhotny Ryad.*

$ ✕ **Margarita.** This café, named after the heroine of Mikhail Bulgakov's
famous novel *Master and Margarita,* is in one of Moscow's quainter
neighborhoods. Always patronized by a mixed crowd of Russians and

foreigners, Margarita combines a slightly offbeat, rustic atmosphere with a simple, inexpensive menu. The service is uncommonly fast, making it an excellent bet for a quick lunch. Try the stuffed-tomato appetizer, the soup of the day, and the Russian pot pie for a can't-miss meal. ⊠ *28 Malaya Bronnaya ul.,* ☎ *095/299–6534. Reservations advised. Rubles only. Metro: Mayakovskaya.*

$ ✕ **Moosehead Canadian Bar.** If you're looking for a comfortable, lively pub, try this loose-spirited restaurant, a 1995 newcomer to the list of places that pander to young Russian and expatriate movers and shakers. It has a warm, welcoming atmosphere, with wood paneling and local art on the walls. The lights are low; the music, at least on weekends, is not. Rove among the dining rooms—one intimate, one wide—and two barrooms, where you can grab a table, a seat at the bar, or simply stand to chat and people-watch. The menu is hearty. Breakfasts cater to healthy appetites, and you'll find a hearty portion of corned beef hash here, and certainly nowhere else. Chili, burgers, soups, salads, steak, and pasta are also available. The good-natured staff, almost all of whom are native English speakers, works hard to look after you. Alas, no Moosehead on tap—but there are Guinness, Harp, and Tuborg plus plenty of imports by the bottle. ⊠ *54 Bolshaya Polyanka ul.,* ☎ FAX *095/230–7333. AE, DC, MC, V.* ☺ *Daily noon–5 AM. Metro: Dobryninskaya.*

$ ✕ **Moskovskye Zory.** This log-cabin restaurant between Pushkin Square and Mayakovsky Square is a great place for a quick, delicious lunch. It's a tiny eatery and has just a few tables, which are decked with red tablecloths. The owner is especially friendly to Americans. The dependably tasty offerings are usually limited to two types of traditional Russian soup, salad, and a few main courses. German beer and Georgian wines are usually available. Avoid the coffee at dessert time. ⊠ *11 Maly Kozikhinsky pereulok 11,* ☎ *095/299–5725. Reservations required. Rubles only. Metro: Mayakovskaya.*

$ ✕ **Patio Pizza.** An airy place to find pizza bliss, this cheerful restaurant has a huge back room with glass ceiling and walls, so the sun pours in all day. The original is a stone's throw from the Pushkin Fine Arts Museum; a newer branch is located in the front section of the Intourist Hotel at the tip of Tverskaya ulitsa. The menu runs the gamut of pizzas, with a real salad bar and Italian entrées. The pizza has a thin and dusty crust; daily specials include such dishes as lasagna al forno and baked cannelloni. The sole near-Russian entry, Trota alla Romana, is trout with potatoes, turnips, and buttered carrots. Kids can have pint-size pizzas and kiddie cocktails. Tables are comfortably spaced, topped with checkerboard tablecloths. Pop music plays softly, and the rooms are always filled with a pleasantly bustling crowd. ⊠ *30 ul. Volkhonka,* ☎ *095/201–0050. Reservations not required. AE, DC, MC, V. Free parking and an exchange office outside. Metro: Kropotkinskaya.*

$ ✕ **Ukraina.** The main restaurant in the Ukraina Hotel has traditionally catered to tourist groups. In recent years it has become a popular night spot with young and restless Russians, who come here in the evenings for the positively tasteless erotic floor show. During the day, however, the only entertainment is an occasional Russian folk ensemble. The Stalinesque decor takes you back to the 1950s, with orange taffeta curtains, heavy chandeliers, massive marble pillars, and, for good measure, Ukrainian embroidered tapestries draping the walls. The menu, like the decor, is a reflection of the former Soviet Union. Traditional Ukrainian dishes such as chicken Kiev and borshch are featured side by side with Russian and other national dishes of the former Soviet republics. Bow-tied waiters offer polite and friendly service. Although the food is heavy and bland, the restaurant remains popular with foreigners and Russians alike thanks to its extremely reasonable prices. This is a good place to spend a rainy afternoon over a bottle of wine and a long lunch. ✉ *2/1 Kutuzovsky Prospekt,* ☎ *095/243–4732. Reservations advised. Rubles only.* ◷ *Daily noon–4:30, 6–midnight. Metro: Kievskaya.*

$ ✕ **Uzbekistan.** As its name indicates, this restaurant specializes in the spicy cuisine of the Central Asian republic of Uzbekistan. It's long been popular with tourists, but its reputation is much better than it deserves. Opened in 1949, the restaurant is a relic of the Stalinist era, when the great "friendship" of the numerous ethnic groups caught inside the borders of the Soviet Union was celebrated by opening restaurants specializing in the national cuisine of the various republics (the Aragvi and Ukraina restaurants opened under similar circumstances). The decor—high ceilings, massive pillars, ornate wood carvings, and fancy chandeliers—is a uniquely Soviet mix of Stalinism and traditional Central Asian decoration. The house specialty—*manty* (rubber dumplings filled with mystery meat and served with a thick glob of sour cream)—are just barely edible. The kitchen does a better job with the *plof* (pilaf) and *lagman* (meat and noodle soup). The restaurant makes up for the bland cuisine with its colorful atmosphere and lively entertainment. If you're looking to mingle with the locals, you can join them here for a shot or two (or three) of vodka. ✉ *29 Neglinnaya ul.,* ☎ *095/924–6053. Reservations advised. Rubles only. Metro: Teatralnaya.*

$ ✕ **Yakimanka.** A band sings Western music in heavy Russian accents as diners lounge on sunken couches before low, candlelit tables in the back room or sit at conventional tables—also lighted by candles—in the front room. This exotic bit of central Asia in Moscow is a good spot for a relaxing evening meal. Sample Yakimanka's grape leaves stuffed with meats, rice, and garlic, or try the pilaf with beef and vegetables. Don't miss the pickled-garlic appetizer. ✉ *2/10 Bolshaya Polyanka ul.,* ☎ *095/238–8888. Reservations required. Rubles only. Metro: Polyanka.*

LODGING

You might think that a world capital with a population of more than 9 million would have a large number of hotels, but this is not the case in Moscow—at least not yet. Significant improvements have occurred, but they are not comprehensive. Since 1990 several luxury hotels have opened, but the city suffers from a dearth of decent mid-range hotels, and hangovers are still evident at the old Intourist standbys. In fairness to the latter, some of them have upgraded their service (a bit), and sales and management teams are making an effort to keep afloat in a more competitive environment. However, they will probably remain in a class by themselves in terms of service, furnishings, and atmosphere—a class, unfortunately, that foreign tourists will not be entirely comfortable with. If you're not staying at one of the top hotels, be patient and ready to roll with the punches. Russia is for the intrepid traveler.

All prices are quoted in U.S. dollars.

CATEGORY	COST*
$$$$	over $350
$$$	$250–$350
$$	$125–$250
$	$60–$125
¢	under $60

All prices are for a standard double room, excluding service charge.

$$$$ 🏨 **Baltschug Kempinski.** Situated on the banks of the Moskva River, opposite the Kremlin and Red Square, this five-star hotel boasts extraordinary views—and prices, too. Long in a state of disrepair, its 19th-century building, once an aristocratic apartment house, has been completely reconstructed. The modern interiors sparkle, but they lack the distinct character of prerevolutionary Russia found in hotels such as the Metropole or the Savoy. The spacious rooms are done in stately red and cream and are equipped with all amenities. The Swiss management has thought of such niceties as bathroom slippers, perhaps to encourage guests to stay home and enjoy the picture-postcard views across the river. The location is central but not particularly convenient: the hotel is not accessible by public transportation (it's a 15-minute walk from the nearest Metro station), and the city's main attractions are on the other side of the river. You're best off having a car and driver if you stay here. Make sure you specify that you want a room with a view; otherwise you could end up staring at the factory bordering the hotel's eastern side. ⊠ *1 Balchug ul.,* ☏ *095/230–6500,* FAX *095/230–6502. From outside Russia,* ☏ *007–501–230–9500,* FAX *007–501–230–9502. 202 room with bath, 32 suites. 3 restaurants, café, nighttime bar, 24-hr room service, cable TV with CNN and BBC, complimentary minibar, fitness center with sauna and 20-meter pool, business center, hard-currency shops. Traveler's checks accepted. AE, DC, MC, V. Metro: Ploshchad Revolutsii or Novokuznetskaya.*

$$$$ **Metropol.** Originally built in 1899–1903 by William Walcott, this
★   lavish, first-class hotel reopened in 1991 after five years of extensive renovations. Now operating as a British-Russian joint venture, the Metropol is a member of the Inter-Continental Hotel groups. Its posh interiors have been the setting for many historic events. Lenin spoke frequently in the assembly hall of the building, and in 1918–19 the Central Committee of the Russian Republic met here under its first chairman, Yakov Sverdlov (for whom the square outside the hotel was named until 1991). Today this hotel is one of Moscow's most elegant, with outstanding service and amenities. The nicely appointed rooms feature hardwood floors, Oriental rugs, large closets, and modern furnishings. Antiques grace all the suites and the two presidential ones come with private saunas. The lobby, restaurants, and other common areas will transport you back a century. The location, opposite the Bolshoi Theater and a five-minute walk from the Kremlin, can't be beat. ⊠ *1/4 Teatralny proyezd,* ☏ *095/927–6000,* FAX *095/975–2355. From outside Russia,* ☏ *7501–927–1000,* FAX *7501–927–1010. 328 rooms with bath, 75 suites. 4 restaurants, 2 bars, 24-hr room service, in-room movies and cable TV television with CNN and MTV, satellite telephone, fitness center with sauna and swimming pool, travel agent, theater-ticket agency, casino, conference facilities. Traveler's checks accepted. AE, DC, MC, V. Metro: Teatralnaya.*

$$$$ **National.** When first built in 1903, the National was one of Moscow's
★   premier hotels. Reopened in 1995 after years of renovation, it is again bidding to be the city's most luxurious accommodation, a contest it probably wins. Like the Metropole, its location in the heart of Moscow is superb for travelers who want to feel at the vortex of the tornado. Across the street from Red Square, at the foot of ulitsa Tverskaya, this heavily trafficked corner would be noisy were it not for the hotel's sound-proofing. Inside, you'll find the serenity of a bygone era. All renovations in the stunning landmark building have retained the grandeur of the original Art Nouveau style. A great marble staircase spirals upward in a winding railing of pewter vine; the elevators, topped by silvered twists of ivy, echo the design. Behind the stairs, through lavender and light green stained glass, you can glimpse the atrium and tearoom below. There are four styles of suites (including ultra-deluxe corner ones), two styles of doubles, and two of singles. All rooms, except for a few doubles done in a more modern style, are elegantly plush with polished

oak furniture upholstered in silk. The white-tiled Italianate bathrooms are sparkling and modern. If price is no object—but luxury, quiet, and elite service are—this is the place to stay. Literally topping all of it is the pool in the fitness center, on the hotel's top floor, where swimmers look out, eye level, at the crenelated top of the Kremlin and the cupolas and domes of its cathedrals—a magnificent sight, particularly at night. ✉ *14/1 Okhotny Ryad,* ☎ *095/258–7000,* 🖷 *095/258–7100. 231 rooms, including 36 suites. 4 restaurants, 4 bars, tearoom, business center, 12 conference and banquet facilities, room service, fitness center, solarium, service bureau, exchange office, car service. Traveler's checks for $US (only). AE, DC, MC, V. Metro: Okhotny Ryad.*

$$$$ 🏨 **Olympic Penta Renaissance.** Opened in 1991 under German management, this was one of Moscow's first joint-venture hotels. It was built by a Finnish construction team, and everything here is imported, down to the last doorknob. The rooms are large and fully equipped with every conceivable amenity. The fitness center is one of the best in town. Service is good, although the European-trained Russian staff has been known to let its Soviet upbringing rear its ugly head. The location—near the Olympic Sports Stadium—is rather far from the city's tourist attractions, but it's convenient to all major arterial roads or the Prospekt Mira subway stop, a 10-minute walk away. ✉ *18/1 Olympysky Prospekt 18/1,* ☎ *095/931–9000 or 095/931–9833,* 🖷 *095/931–9020. 490 rooms with bath, 10 suites. Restaurant, café, beer hall, bar, 24-hour room service, minibar, cable TV, satellite telephone, fitness center with sauna and 22-meter pool, gift shops, car service, conference facilities. Traveler's checks accepted. AE, DC, MC, V. Metro: Prospekt Mira.*

$$$$ 🏨 **Palace.** With the exception of the National, the Palace is Moscow's most recently opened top-class hotel, but somehow its late 1970s decor—lots of brass, hanging plants, muted rose and evergreen textile carpets—conspires to make it look just a touch dated, at least among its rivals. Still, it is particularly popular with the European business community (Americans seem to prefer the Slavyanskaya), to which it caters with a full range of traveler's amenities. With that purpose in mind, it's heavy on double rooms for the single traveler; you'll find these offer all you need, though they are a bit crowded with furniture. The real winners are those who can afford the duplexes (double suites), which have a stunning bilevel arrangement of two upstairs bedrooms (each with full, separate bath), a dining room, and a living room below, decorated in rose-and-mint furnishings trimmed in varnished golden pine with tasteful paintings and sculpture throughout. The hotel's location, at the far upper end of Tverskaya, is excellent, but this main road isn't always easy to navigate by car. Service is pleasant, despite a hovering air of distraction. A Marco Polo Hotel. ✉ *19 Pervaya Tverskaya-Yamskaya ul.,* ☎ *095/956–3152,* 🖷 *095/956–3151; from overseas, same number plus 7 503 satellite prefix. 221 rooms, including 22 suites. 3 restaurants, café, guest bar, lobby bar, room service, minibar, satellite TV, fitness center, Jacuzzi and sauna (no pool), car and limousine service, conference and banquet facilities, 48 no-smoking rooms, 5 rooms for the disabled. Traveler's checks accepted. AE, DC, MC, V. Metro: Belorusskaya.*

$$$$ 🏨 **Savoy.** The Savoy was built in 1912 in connection with celebrations commemorating the 300th anniversary of the Romanov dynasty. Most of its working life, however, it served as an Intourist hotel (under the name Berlin). After the demise of the Soviets, it was Moscow's first joint-venture hotel (Finnish-Russian) to be completely renovated. Its somewhat frayed interiors, replete with gilded chandeliers, ceiling paintings, and polished redwood paneling, invoke the spirit of pre-revolutionary Russia. The rooms are somewhat small and dark (a legacy of Soviet remodeling), but they are nicely appointed with pretty, rose-colored wallpaper and matching upholstery. The views are mostly negligible, owing to the hotel's side-street location, but this does give the advantage of quiet. One of the gilt suites contains a piano purchased especially for Luciano Pavarotti when he stayed here while performing at the Bolshoi Theater. Popular with businesspeople who eschew busy hotel lobbies, the Savoy is centrally located, just off Theater Square and within walking distance of the Kremlin. The staff is cheerful and helpful. ⊠ *3 Rozhdestvenka ul.,* ☎ *095/929–8500,* FAX *095/230–2186. 86 rooms with bath, 29 suites. Restaurant, 2 bars, 24-hr room service, satellite telephone, cable TV with CNN, minibar, business center, casino, excursion and travel bureau. Traveler's checks accepted. AE, DC, MC, V. Metro: Kuznetsky Most.*

$$$$ 🏨 **Sofitel Iris.** Under French management, this new hotel is located in a bleak residential district on the northwest outskirts of town, adjacent to the world-famous Fyodorov Eye Institute. The hotel hoped to attract foreign patients, but their numbers are smaller than anticipated, and the hotel is operating far below capacity. Its distant location is unfortunate, because this is one of the finest of the new foreign-run hotels in Moscow. The spacious rooms are cheery and bright, with lots of closet space and large bathrooms. The views are quite dismal, though, since the hotel is surrounded by monotonous high rises. There are few shops or restaurants of any interest to the tourist in the area. The hotel's own French restaurant, however, has earned an excellent reputation among the city's foreign community. Complimentary shuttle service is provided to guests, making it easier to enjoy the city's attractions. Buses run hourly to Red Square, and five times daily to the Sovincenter. ⊠ *10 Korovinskoye Shosse,* ☎ *095/488–8000,* FAX *095/488–8888; from outside Russia, 502/220–8844. 195 rooms with bath. 2 restaurants, bar, 24-hour room service, minibar, satellite telephone, cable TV, fitness center with swimming pool, car service, complimentary shuttle service to city center, excursion bureau, gift shop. Traveler's checks accepted. AE, DC, MC, V.*

$$$ 🏨 **Aerostar.** The Aerostar, not to be confused with the rundown Aeroflot
★   Hotel next door, is a Russian-Canadian joint venture with Aeroflot and IMP Group Limited. Opened in 1992, the hotel was originally commissioned for the 1980 Olympics but never completed for that purpose. The Canadian team has worked wonders with the austere Soviet design, transforming it into a first-rate, Western-style hotel. The lobby areas are bright and cheery, and the rooms are nicely appointed, with European furnishings and redwood paneling. Unusual for Russia, the hotel has no-smoking rooms available. The rooms on the northeast side look out onto the Petrovsky Palace, a striking, crenelated redbrick palace where the czars broke their journey between St. Petersburg and Moscow. Service is excellent, and business travelers find the location—halfway between the city center and Sheremetyevo International Airport—very convenient. Tourists, though, may find the city's major attractions are too far away. Many of the city's expatriates are making the trek out here to eat at the hotel's Taiga Restaurant. The house specialty is fresh lobster flown in from Nova Scotia, and on Sunday the restaurant features a lavish champagne brunch. ⊠ *37 Leningradsky Prospekt,* ☎ *095/213–9000 or 9001, satellite* FAX *7 502/213–9001. 386 rooms with bath, 31 suites. 2 restaurants, 2 bars, 24-hour room service, international TV programming including CNN and BBC, satellite telephone, gift shop, fitness center, business center, exchange bureau, excursion bureau, car rental, conference facilities. Traveler's checks accepted. AE, DC, MC, V. Metro: Dinamo or Aeroport.*

$$$ 🏨 **Marco Polo Presnya.** Once an exclusive domain of the Communist Party, management of this modest hotel was taken over by an Austrian firm, which undertook to transform it into a Western-style hotel. So far, however, it has not entirely followed through on this. It's located in a quaint residential neighborhood in the city center not far from Patriarch's Pond, and that is its best recommendation right now. A few years ago, a handful of rooms were renovated, and they are quite attractive, but the remainder are still outfitted with the same overscale, slightly shabby Communist-era fixtures. All rooms are very clean and more than functional but do not befit a hotel in the expensive range. Service is friendly and efficient, the atmosphere quiet and composed. In the absence of full renovations, if management lowered prices this could be the mid-range hotel that Moscow currently lacks. ⊠ *9 Spiridonevsky pereulok,* ☎ *095/244–3631,* ℻ *095/926–5404; satellite* ℻ *use 7 503 prefix. 68 rooms with bath. Restaurant, lobby bar, summer terrace café, room service, minibar, cable TV, fitness center with sauna, business center, gift shop, car service, conference facilities. Traveler's checks accepted. AE, DC, MC, V. Metro: Pushkinskaya.*

$$$ 🏨 **Mezhdunarodnaya.** Its name means "international," but foreign residents have dubbed it "the Mezh." Built by the American financier Armand Hammer in 1980, this huge complex was the hub of international business in Moscow until the opening of the Radisson Slavyanskaya Hotel, when such business was first being done. Its atrium lobby and indoor mall, therefore, were once an oasis for foreign shoppers who came for the restaurants and well-stocked hard-currency stores. But when times changed for the better in Russia, they seemed to change for the worse here, and the best enterprises moved out to more exciting premises. Newly revamped management is vowing a return to its previous high standards but admits it may take two or three years. The rooms are bigger than at the Radisson, but the views are no better and the Italian furnishings have seen better days. The hotel is located within sight of the city center but far from the subway, and only one city bus stops anywhere near the hotel. You're better off elsewhere, at least until standards improve again. ⊠ *12 Krasnopresnenskaya nab.,* ☎ *095/253–1391/1392,* ℻ *095/253–2051. 530 rooms with bath. 5 restaurants, 6 bars, hard-currency shops and grocery store, service bureau, fitness center with pool and sauna, minibar. Traveler's checks accepted. AE, DC, MC, V. Metro: Krasnopresnenskaya.*

$$$ 🏨 **Radisson Slavyanskaya.** Designed with the frustrated business trav-
★ eler in mind, the hotel offers every modern amenity American-style: no-nonsense comfort in an efficient atmosphere. Its huge, two-story lobby is lined with first-class restaurants, shops, a fully equipped fitness center with Olympic pool, an independent press center, an English-language movie theater, and much more. Among the offices opened here are a full-fledged travel agency and a full-service bank. With everything you might want or need located inside the hotel, if the rest of Moscow closed down, you might never know it if you were holed up here. The location is central, but alongside the Kiev Railway Station, notorious for its pickpockets, so a walk outside the hotel will place you in a different reality altogether. Still, you needn't feel endangered. There are always lots of people around, and a protective wall and the guards posted at the hotel's main entrance keep the uninvited from wandering onto the hotel grounds. The rooms are nicely appointed but small; the views are nothing to write home about. This is a good choice for visitors who favor comfort and service over character and who don't want or need intensive contact with the real Moscow. ⊠ *2 Berezhkovskaya nab.,* ☎ *095/941–8020,* ℻ *095/941–8000, from outside Russia, 7502–224–1225. Reservations may be made through Radisson Hotels in U.S.,* ☎ *800/333–3333. 407 rooms with bath, 24 suites. 2 restaurants, café, lobby bar, fitness center with 25-meter lap pool, 24-hr room service, satellite telephone, minibar, cable TV with CNN, hard-currency shops,*

exchange bureau, car rental, excursion bureau, conference facilities. Traveler's checks accepted. AE, DC, MC, V. Metro: Kievskaya.

$$ ☎ **Belgrade II.** Built in 1975 as one of two twin towers (the other is now the Zolotoye Koltso), this former Intourist-run hotel is a typical Brezhnev-era high rise. Often, groups booked through Russian agencies get placed here. The hotel's main advantage is its central location, near the subway and the Arbat. The interior decor is unimaginative, and the hotel has the same institutional feeling as the Intourist (☞ *below*). The rooms could use some sprucing up, and renovations are underway to replace the cheap, plywood furnishings and worn industrial carpeting. When the Zolotoye Koltso across the street reopens after renovations you will be able to get similar accommodations at half the price. ✉ *8 Smolenskaya Ploshchad,* ☎ *095/248–2841 or 095/248–1676,* FAX *095/230–2129. 487 rooms with bath. 2 restaurants, 2 snack bars, 2 bars, exchange bureau, excursion bureau. AE, DC, MC, V. Metro: Smolenskaya.*

$$ ☎ **Intourist.** Centrally located at the bottom of Tverskaya ulitsa, at the back of the National Hotel, to which it once was joined, this aging skyscraper is a popular holding spot for tourist groups. Unfortunately, its super location also attracts a seedy-looking presence outside the hotel's main entrance, which makes coming and going, particularly at night, a rather unpleasant experience. Its smoke-filled lobby features the usual oversize and drab decor, although the gift and souvenir shops are better stocked than most. The hotel staff, when not busy taking personal phone calls, is receptive and relatively helpful. The interior has remained basically unchanged since the hotel opened in 1970, and the rooms are in poor condition. Although they all come with telephone and television, you also get stained furnishings, worn carpeting, and monotone polyester curtains. Despite the drawbacks, the rates here remain relatively high. This is mostly due to the hotel's prime location, which is the only reason to stay here. ✉ *3/5 Tverskaya ul.,* ☎ *095/956–8400 or 095/956–8426,* FAX *095/956–8450. 443 rooms with bath. 3 restaurants, 7 snack bars, casino, excursion bureau. DC, MC, V. Metro: Okhotny Ryad.*

$$ ☎ **Novotel.** If you need a room near the Airport, this is the place to stay. Professional European soccer teams patronize Novotel because of its few distractions. The rooms and beds are comfortable, the hallways are quiet, and at the moment, the price is still right. They are a hair's breadth from the Expensive category, though, so you may want to double-check with your travel agent before you book. In addition, the staff is eager to please, and the modern facilities are well maintained. ✉ *Sheremetyevo II Airport,* ☎ *095/926–5900,* FAX *095/926–5903/5904, from outside Russia: 7 502 220–6604. 155 rooms, 40 suites. AE, DC, MC, V.*

$$ ☎ **Ukraina.** This imposing skyscraper on the banks of the Moskva River
★ is one of the seven Stalin Gothics. The red carpeting, high ceilings, and colorful socialist-realist ceiling paintings are trademarks of the Stalinist era. The rooms are worn but relatively clean in a city where standards of cleanliness are low. Redwood and oak furnishings and fancy chandeliers create an atmosphere of faded elegance. Doors have locks and dead bolts, and supposedly soon to come are electronic strip locks. The old tradition of floor attendants has been retained here, so you'll also find a hotel staff member on every floor. The hotel is situated across the river from the Russian "White House" (where the president works). Rooms on the higher floors on this side have great views and cost 15% more. This is an almost central location, right off Kutuzovsky Prospekt at the foot of Novy Arbat. Subway travelers, however, will find their station is a good 10-minute trek away. Plusses here are the well-stocked hard-currency store and the German-run joint-venture restaurant, tucked away on the third floor. A minus is the sometimes scary-look-

ing crowd of men who seem to permanently lounge on the steps of the entryway. ⊠ *2/1 Kutuzovsky Prospekt,* ☎ *095/243–2596; reservations, 095/243–3030;* FAX *095/243–3092 or 956–2078. 1,010 rooms with bath. 2 restaurants, 6 snack bars, 3 bars, hard-currency shop, clothes boutique, casino, sauna. AE, DC, MC, V. Metro: Kievskaya.*

$ ★ 🏨 **Kosmos.** This huge, 26-story hotel was built by the French for the 1980 Olympics. It is French-equipped and furnished, but years of heavy tourist traffic have dulled its shine. Service varies wildly, with large groups getting preference over individual tourists. The slot machines and late-night bars attract unsavory types, including plenty of prostitutes, but the rooms themselves are adequate and clean. Overall, service and accommodations here are far superior to those at the Intourist Hotel, another popular destination with tourist groups. Its spacious, two-story lobby is reminiscent of a mall, full of well-stocked, hard-currency stores and shops. The hotel is across the street from the All-Russia Exhibition Center, a part of town that has interesting sites, but is far from downtown, though convenient to the subway (right across the street). ⊠ *150 Prospekt Mira,* ☎ *095/217–0785/0786 or 095/215–6791/7880,* FAX *095/215–8880. 1,777 rooms with bath. 4 restaurants, 8 bars, swimming pool, sauna, bowling alley, hard-currency grocery store. AE, MC, V. Metro: VDNKh.*

$ 🏨 **Leningradskaya.** This Soviet fortress is another of Moscow's seven Stalin Gothic skyscrapers. Its awe-inspiring, monumental interior features high ceilings, red carpets, and heavy bronze chandeliers. A faded gem of the Communist era, the hotel is often used to house Russian parliament members. The rooms are modestly furnished but surprisingly clean and well maintained. Ask for a room high up—the views from the lower floors are strictly industrial. The location is relatively central but not exactly convenient or calm. The hotel stands at a busy intersection, right across from the Leningrad, Kazan, and Yaroslav railway stations. To reach the subway you have to dash across the highway and then make your way through the rather unsavory crowds that live at the train station. There is also a major casino on the ground floor. Nevertheless, the reasonable rates here make this an okay choice for budget-minded travelers, though it's not recommended as comfortable for women traveling alone. Just be sure to pack plenty of patience; the hotel staff long ago wearied of their jobs. ⊠ *21/40 Kalanchevskaya ul.,* ☎ *095/975–3032,* FAX *975–1580. 346 rooms with bath. Restaurant, 2 snack bars, casino, hard-currency shop, exchange bureau. AE, DC, MC, V. Metro: Komsomolskaya.*

$ 🏨 **Rossiya.** Pack your compass and map if you're staying here, because negotiating the seemingly endless corridors of this huge hotel is a cartographer's nightmare. The mammoth building is one of Europe's largest hotels, able to accommodate up to 6,000 guests. Opened in 1967, it once numbered among the Soviet Union's finest hotels, but it suffered two fires and service and accommodations have rapidly sped downhill in recent years. All the rooms come with television and telephone, but there's no guarantee they'll work. Cockroaches (and worse) are also not unheard of. As with the Intourist, the main reason to stay here is the location: just off the edge of Red Square, with stupendous views of it and the Kremlin, if you have a room on the west side. Deteriorating conditions have forced the hotel to reduce its rates, making this one of the cheaper choices in downtown Moscow. ⊠ *6 Varvarka ul.,* ☎ *095/ 298–5531 or 095/232–5050,* FAX *095/232–6262. 2,800 rooms with bath. 8 restaurants, 20 snack bars, 2 bars, pool and sauna, exchange bureau. Traveler's checks accepted. AE, MC, V. Metro: Kitai-Gorod.*

$ 🏨 **Soyuz.** Yugoslav-built in 1980, this hotel on the northwestern outskirts of town has an interesting avant-garde design. Its distant location keeps its rates in the inexpensive category, though the service and atmosphere here are good. The rooms come with modern furnishings and cheery, flowery wallpaper. Some of them have views of the Moskva River, where in summer Muscovites come in droves to swim and sunbathe. The lobby area, too, is bright and cheery, with lots of windows and plants. The public areas and rooms are quite clean by local standards, but the location is a serious drawback. The surrounding area is likely to have a dispiriting effect on first-time visitors, and the hotel is convenient only to the Sheremetyevo Airport (15 minutes away). The closest subway stop—Rechnoy Vokzal, the last stop on the green line—is a 20-minute bus ride away, and it can take more than an hour to reach the city center by car. ⊠ *12 Levoberezhnaya ul.,* ☎ *095/457–2088,* FAX *095/457–2096. 154 rooms with bath. Restaurant, bar, snack bar, exchange bureau. AE, DC, V. Metro: Rechnoy Vokzal.*

¢ 🏨 **Molodyozhnaya.** Its name means "youth," and the hotel traditionally catered to groups of young people traveling under the auspices of Sputnik (the former Soviet youth tourist agency). It was built for the 1980 Olympics and features the typical drab decor of a Brezhnev-era high rise. Basically, it's for those seeking hostel accommodations. The rock-bottom prices may make you indifferent to its cement-and-steel lobby decorated with a mosaic depicting happy proletariat youth. The rooms are standard size and adequate, provided you are not a stickler for cleanliness. The decor is standard Soviet fare—heavy on the plywood and polyester. Its location on the outskirts of town is far from the city's tourist attractions, but there's a subway stop within walking distance. The three- and five-person "suites" are good for friends traveling together. ⊠ *27 Dmitrovskoye Shosse,* ☎ *095/210–4565,* FAX *095/210–4311. 600 rooms with bath. Restaurant, 4 bars. No credit cards; cash only. Metro: Timiryazevskaya.*

¢ 🏨 **Sevastopol.** This is a huge complex comprising four 16-story high rises. Although the hotel is far from the city's tourist attractions, the subway is close by. The green stucco walls give the place an institutional feeling more appropriate to a dormitory than a hotel, and you can't expect to get more than the basic plywood furnishings. But for tourists on a shoestring budget who don't mind roughing it a bit, like the Molodyozhnaya this is a bearable if far from luxurious option. During summer months be certain beforehand that they will have hot water. Citywide, section by section, it is turned off for three to four weeks for pipe *remont.* At this hotel this usually occurs in June. ⊠ *1A Pervaya Bolshaya Yushunskaya ul., reservations* ☎ *095/318–0918; Bldg. 1,* ☎ *095/119–8182; Bldg. 2,* ☎ *095/318–4972; Bldg. 3,* ☎ *095/318–6483; Bldg. 4,* ☎ *095/318–8371.* FAX *095/318–2827. 2,588 rooms with bath. 9 restaurants, 8 snack bars, bar, casino, sauna, excursion bureau. DC, MC, V. Metro: Sevastopolskaya.*

NIGHTLIFE AND THE ARTS

The Arts

Moscow is famed for its rich cultural life. The city boasts more than 60 officially registered theaters, with new ones opening all the time. Except at the most renowned theaters, such as the Bolshoi, tickets can be obtained for rubles at the theaters themselves or at theater box offices (*teatralnaya kassa*) scattered throughout the city. If you're intimidated by the language barrier, avail yourself of the EPS Theater Box Office in the main lobby of the Metropol Hotel (☎ 095/927–6982 or 6983) or the service bureau in your hotel. The prices are inflated, but they can often get tickets to sold-out performances. Another alternative is to purchase a ticket from a scalper immediately prior to the performance, but there is no guarantee that you'll get a good seat.

Every Friday the English-language newspaper *Moscow Times* publishes a schedule of cultural events for the coming week.

Art Galleries

Numerous private galleries have opened in the past few years, and you certainly will enjoy seeing, and probably purchasing, some of the excellent work done by Russian artists. The Friday edition of the *Moscow Times* carries a review of current exhibits. For opening hours, check with the galleries themselves; some are open only by appointment, and most are closed on Sunday and Monday.

A partial listing of galleries includes **Central House of Artists** (✉ 10 Krymsky Val, ☎ 095/238–9843). **Contemporary Art Center** (✉ 2/6 Bolshaya Yakimanka ul., ☎ 095/238–9666). **Fine Arts Gallery** (✉ 38 Arbat, 4th floor, ☎ 095/241–1267). **International University Gallery** (✉ 17 Leningradsky Prospekt, ☎ 095/250–3481). **M'ARS Gallery** (✉ 32 Malaya Filyovskaya ul., ☎ 095/146–2029). **Moscow Gallery Hall** (✉ 11 Kuznetsky most, ☎ 095/925–4264). **Moscow Palette Gallery** (✉ 35/28 Povarskaya ul., ☎ 095/291–1124). **NB Gallery** (✉ 6/2 Sivtsev Vrazhek (apt. 2), ☎ 095/203–4006). **Ridzhina Gallery** (✉ 36 Myasnitskaya ul., ☎ 095/921–1613). **Today Gallery** (✉ 35 Arbat, ☎ 095/248–4976). **Vostochnaya Gallery** (✉ 10 Pushkaryev pereulok, ☎ 095/208–1167).

Drama

Even if you do not speak Russian, you might want to explore the intense world of Russian dramatic theater. The partial listings below cover Moscow's major drama theaters. Take heed that evening performances here begin at 7 PM *sharp.*

Chekhov Moscow Art Theater, or MKhAT (✉ 3 Kamergersky pereulok, ☎ 095/229–8760/5370. Metro: Okhotny Ryad). Founded in 1898 by the celebrated actors and directors Konstantin Stanislavsky and Vladimir Nemirovich-Danchenko, this theater is famous for its productions of the Russian classics, especially those of Chekhov. An affiliated, modern Moscow Art Theater with a seating capacity of 2,000 is located at 22 Tverskoy bulvar.

LenKom Theater (✉ 6 Malaya Dmitrovka ul., ☎ 095/299–9668/0708. Metro: Pushkinskaya). This very popular theater presents new plays by young authors.

Maly Theater (✉ 1/6 Teatralnaya Ploshchad, ☎ 095/925–9868. Metro: Teatralnaya). Moscow's first dramatic theater is famous for its staging of Russian classics, especially those of Ostrovsky.

Mayakovsky Theater (✉ 19 Bolshaya Nikitskaya ul., ☎ 095/290–2725/6241. Metro: Arbat). Named after the great writer and poet, this theater stages serious dramas, both classic and contemporary.

Mossoviet Theater (✉ 16 Bolshaya Sadovaya ul., ☎ 095/299–2035 or 095/200–5943. Metro: Mayakovskaya). This spot is good for contemporary drama.

Taganka Theater (✉ Taganskaya Ploshchad, ☎ 095/272–6300. Metro: Taganskaya). The best-known of Moscow's avant-garde and experimental companies. Performances sell out far in advance.

Satire Theater (✉ 2 Triumfalnaya Ploshchad, ☎ 095/299–9042/6305. Metro: Mayakovskaya). This theater specializes in satirical comedies, such as Mayakovsky's *The Bathhouse* and *The Bedbug.*

Sovremmenik Theater (✉ 19A Chistoprudny bulvar, ☎ 095/921–6629/6473. Metro: Chistiye Prudy). This is one of Moscow's youngest theaters, with an experimental repertoire and company of young actors.

Vakhtangov Theater (✉ 26 Arbat, ☎ 095/241–1679. Metro: Arbatskaya). Named after Stanislavsky's pupil Evgeny Vakhtangov, this is an excellent traditional theater, good for contemporary dramas.

Yermolova International Theater Center (✉ 5 Tverskaya ul., ☎ 095/203–7952/7628. Metro: Okhotny Ryad). The repertoire here varies from the Russian classics to modern, Western plays.

Music

Moscow's musical life has always been particularly rich; the city has a number of symphony orchestras as well as song-and-dance ensembles. Moiseyev's Folk Dance Ensemble is well known in Europe and America, but the troupe is on tour so much of the year that when it performs in Moscow, tickets are very difficult to obtain. Other renowned companies include the State Symphony Orchestra and the Armed Forces Song and Dance Ensemble. Except for tickets for special performances, tickets usually are easily available and inexpensive.

Glinka Music Museum Hall (✉ 4 Fadeyeva ul., ☎ 095/972–3237. Metro: Mayakovskaya). This is one of many small concert halls scattered throughout the city.

Russian Academy of Music (✉ Ul. Paliashvili 1, ☎ 095/290–6737. Metro: Arbatskaya). The academy is highly recommended for student productions of chamber music, symphony concerts, and operas.

Russian Army House (✉ 12 Suvorovskaya Ploshchad, ☎ 095/281–5719. Metro: Novoslobodskaya). This theater is home to the Armed Forces Song and Dance Ensemble.

Scriabin Museum Hall (✉ 11 Bolshoi Nikolopeskovsky pereulok, ☎ 095/241–1901/0302. Metro: Smolenskaya). Performances are held in a small concert hall located in the apartment building where the composer Alexander Scriabin lived. Concerts are usually held on Wednesday and Friday evenings.

Tchaikovsky Concert Hall (✉ 4/31 Triumfalnaya Ploshchad, ☎ 095/299–0378/5362. Metro: Mayakovskaya). This huge concert hall with seating for more than 1,600 is home to the State Symphony Orchestra.

Tchaikovsky Conservatory (✉ 13 Bolshaya Nikitskaya ul., ☎ 095/229–7412/9436. Metro: Okhotny Ryad). The acoustics of the magnificent Great Hall are superb, and portraits of the world's great composers hang above the high balcony. Rachmaninoff, Scriabin, and Tchaikovsky are among the famous composers who have worked here. The adjacent Small Hall is usually reserved for chamber-music concerts.

Opera and Ballet

Bolshoi Opera and Ballet Theater (✉ 1 Teatralnaya Ploshchad, ☎ 095/292–9986/3319. Metro: Teatralnaya). Visitors always get a thrill out of a visit to this world-renowned theater. The current quality of its productions is erratic, however, due to management changes and the loss of many of its best performers. The gilt, 19th-century auditorium is itself a sight to behold, as is the Russian flair for set and costume design, which alone is enough to keep an audience enthralled.

Kremlin Palace of Congresses (✉ 1 ul. Vozdvizhenka, in the Kremlin, ☎ 095/929–7901/7990. Metro: Biblioteka Imeni Lenina). This modern concert hall, where Soviet Communist Party congresses were held, now has regular performances by opera and ballet troupes, including those from the Bolshoi. Of late it also has become the place for international megastars acts, including Elton John, Diana Ross, Julio Iglesias, and Tina Turner. Entrance is through the whitewashed Kutafya Gate, near the Manege.

Operetta Theater (✉ 6 Bolshaya Dmitrovka ul., ☎ 095/292–6377, Metro: Teatralnaya). Come here for classical and modern dance and music.

Pokrovsky Chamber Musical Theater (✉ 71 Leningradsky Prospekt, ☎ 095/198–7204, Metro: Belorusskaya). This experimental theater stages interesting productions of Russian classics.

Stanislavsky and Nemirovich-Danchenko Musical Theater (✉ 17 Bolshaya Dmitrovka ul., ☎ 095/229–8388, Metro: Teatralnaya). This offers classical and modern operas, ballets, and operettas.

Nightlife

Before you go out, remember that as a foreigner, you should take special precautions at night. Press reports have a way of exaggerating the situation, but, as everywhere, foreign tourists are easy crime targets, and Moscow is one of the world's biggest cities; more lawlessness than before is beseiging its streets, though this is more between local groups than aimed at individual tourists. Use common sense and make arrangements for the trip home before you leave. Keep in mind that the more you drink (and it's easy to drink a lot here), the more vulnerable you become. Do not drive under any circumstances if you drink; laws here are harsher than at home, and traffic police are entitled to stop cars at will—and they do.

Bars and Lounges

All the major hotels have their own bars and nightclubs. The lobby bars in the National, Savoy, and Metropole hotels feature glitzy, prerevolutionary decor and a soothing atmosphere. The Palace and the Slavyanskaya have more energized lobby bars, filled with businesspeople and *novy russky* types, Russian yuppies down to their beepers and cellular phones. The top-floor bar of the Baltschug Hotel offers magical views of the Kremlin. At the other end of the spectrum are the bars of the old Intourist hotels (Belgrade, Kosmos, Intourist), where the atmosphere ranges from sleazy to scary. Be forewarned that hard-currency prostitution is a thriving business in most hotels.

Some favorite Moscow bars to just relax and have fun and drinks in are the **Armadillo Tex-Mex Bar** (✉ 1 Khrustalny pereulok, ☎ 095/298–5091); the 24-hour **Piano Bar Old Square** (✉ 8 Bolshoi Cherkassky pereulok, ☎ 095/298–4688); **Rosie O'Grady's** (✉ 9 ul. Znamenka, ☎ 095/203–9087); the **Shamrock Bar,** upstairs at the **Arbat Irish House** (✉ 19 Novy Arbat, ☎ 095/291–7641); the **Sports Bar and Grill** (✉ 10 Novy Arbat, ☎ 095/290–4311); and the **TrenMos Bistro** (✉ 1/9 ul. Ostozhenka, ☎ 095/202–5722).

Moscow has a growing gay scene and a mumber of openly gay bars.

Chance. Moscow's biggest and best gay club is famous for its relatively cheap drinks, large dance floor, and late-night nude erotic synchronized swimming show (in a giant aquarium that forms the wall of one of the main rooms). ✉ *11/15 Ul. Volocharskovo,* ☎ *095/956–7102.* ◷ *Daily 11 PM–6 AM. Metro: Ploshchad Ilyicha.*

Dyke. Saturdays from 4 to 11 PM it's ladies only at Tri Obezyany (☞ *below*). ✉ *4 Trubnaya Ploshchad,* ☎ *095/163–8002.* ◷ *Sat. 4–11 PM. Metro: Tsvetnoi Bulvar.*

Tri Obezyany. The "Three Monkeys" is more mellow than Chance (☞ *above*), but's it's a fun place to hang out and has an amusing drag show. Unfortunately, entrance is by membership or invitation only, so if you're not going to be in Moscow long enough to make it worth buying membership, you'll first have to chat someone up at Chance and ask them to sponsor you. ✉ *4 Trubnaya Ploshchad,* ☎ *095/208–4637.* ☉ *Daily 6 PM–9 AM (except Sat. 4–11 PM, when it's ladies only). Metro: Tsvetnoi Bulvar.*

Casinos

Moscow has a serious case of casino fever. The number of casinos, both upscale and back-alley, that have opened in the past few years, at last unofficial count equaled the number in Las Vegas. It all makes perfect sense: people spend money in an inflationary environment, and Russia has experienced one of the world's highest inflation rates. If you feel like trying your luck, here are some of the better-known places. Don't feel so lucky that you forget where you are, though; flashing your cash is a *bad* idea. Most casinos will provide complimentary car service to and from big hotels; check with your hotel bureau. Casinos usually open late (11 or 12) and stay open until morning.

Casino Royal (✉ Begovaya ul. 22, ☎ 095/945–1963), the gem of the Moscow casinos, is located in the elegant Hippodrome, built for Nicholas I in 1834.

The **Alexander Blok** (☎ 095/255–9323) is a floating casino on a ship moored permanently near the Mezhdunarodnaya Hotel.

The **Savoy, Metropole, Mezhdunarodnaya, Leningradskaya,** and **Ukraina** hotels all have their own casinos.

Other, less flashy casinos in Moscow include the **Horseshoe Casino** (✉ 71 ul. Profsoyuznaya, ☎ 095/333–6210); the **Karo** (✉ 2 Pushkinskaya Ploshchad, ☎ 095/229–0003); and the **Metelitsa Cherry Casino** (✉ 21 Novy Arbat, ☎ 095/291–1113).

Dance Clubs and Discos

The dance scene is definitely on the up-and-up here. A few places are the expected noisy dens; others are quite mod and trendy. They open late and stay open even later. The omnipresent cover charges are frequently steep.

NightFlight (✉ 17 Tverskaya ul., ☎ 095/229–4165). This Swedish-Russian joint venture was Moscow's first authentic disco, and it seems to attract a lusty crowd, hungry for hunting.

Hermitage Club (✉ 3 Karetny Ryad, ☎ 095/299–1160) transforms its hip self from a bar on Tuesdays and Wednesdays to an energetic dance spot the rest of the time.

Manhattan Express (✉ Corner of Rossiya Hotel, ☎ 095/298–5355) is a big, flashy dance space often with performers and live bands.

Master Disco (✉ 6 Pavlovskaya Ul., ☎ 095/237–1742) is for house parties and more.

The trendy **Pilot Art Night Club** (✉ 6 Tryokhgorny Val, ☎ 095/252–2764) is loud, cavernous, and filled with large screens and hanging airplane parts.

The brazen **Red Zone** (✉ 39 Leningradsky Prospekt, ☎ 095/212–1676), located in the skating arena of the Army Central Sports Club (TsSKA) is the in spot for all-night dancing and carousing. If bared flesh makes you blush, better to go elsewhere.

Titanic (⊠ Young Pioneer's Stadium, 31 Leningradsky Prospekt, ☎ 095/213–4581) is for the college age; experimental music plays all night.

Jazz, Rock, Blues, and Beyond

Rock concerts are usually held in the city's sports stadiums; or, for big acts, the Kremlin Palace; for listings of upcoming concerts, check the Friday edition of the *Moscow Times*.

Local talent can also be found belting out rock tunes at the **Moskovsky Club** (⊠ 6 ul. Tverskaya, ☎ 095/292–1282) or at the **Stanislavsky Club** (⊠ 23 ul. Tverskaya, ☎ 095/564–8004).

Jazz has long been a favorite with the Russians and in Moscow you can hear it live at the **Arbat Blues Club** (⊠ 11 Filippovsky pereulok, ☎ 095/291–1546); **Chyortova Dyuzhina** (⊠ Baker's Dozen; 19 ul. Bolshaya Nikitskaya, ☎ 095/290–2254); or **Metro Express** (⊠ 32 ul. Baumanskaya).

Funky blues is played at the **BB King Blues Club** (⊠ 4/2 ul. Sadovaya-Samotyochnaya, ☎ 095/299–8206), a venue whose opening featured the man himself.

For Karaoke fun, try **Karaoke President** (⊠ 4 ul. Stroitely, ☎ 095/230–2337), where you can sing along in Russian, English, Korean, and presumably, Japanese.

As its name implies, the **Nostalgie Art Club** (⊠ 12a Chistoprudny bulvar, ☎ 095/916–9978) has a mix of old-time swing, Dixieland, and blues.

At the **Jerry Rubin Commune** (⊠ 62 Leninsky Prospekt, ☎ 095/246–9639) you'll find a Seattle-inspired mix of punk and grunge.

OUTDOOR ACTIVITIES AND SPORTS

Participant Sports

Access to Moscow's municipal athletic facilities is usually restricted to those holding a season pass or to club members. In addition most facilities—particularly when it comes to pools—require a special "doctor's certificate" attesting to one's good health. In principle, it is possible to obtain such a certificate by visiting a Russian clinic, but this is a time-consuming process. The listings here are therefore limited to those places that are open to short-term visitors and where it is not necessary to produce a doctor's certificate.

The **Luzhniki Sports Palace** (with Lenin Stadium) is a sports complex located at Luzhniki on the banks of the Moskva River at the foot of Lenin Hills (⊠ Lenin Hills, ☎ 095/246–5515, Metro: Sportivnaya). It is the equal of many top Western facilities. The **Olympisky Sports** compound (⊠ 16 Olympisky pereulok, ☎ 095/288–5663 or 5118, Metro: Prospekt Mira) has a number of gyms, courts, pools, and tracks. You should check which ones are available for use during your stay.

Bowling

The bowling alley at the **Kosmos Hotel** (⊠ 150 Prospekt Mira, near the VDNKh subway station, ☎ 095/215–6791) is open daily 3 PM–midnight. For tickets, inquire at the service bureau off the first-floor lobby.

Cycling

There is a cycle racetrack in the **Krylatskoye Sports Complex** (⊠ 2 Krylatskaya ul., ☎ 095/140–0347 or 095/141–2224, Metro: Krylatskoye). They also have a rowing canal.

Fitness Centers

Unfortunately, virtually all of Moscow's **gyms** are for members only. Some offer short-term memberships, so if you are in town for a while, you can explore that option. Most good hotels have their own fitness centers, but use is restricted to guests. Fees depend on what you want to use, and pool charges are always considerably higher. You can pay a fee for single visits to the gym at the **Metropol Hotel** (1/4 Teatralny proyezd, ☎ 095/927–6000, Metro: Ploshchad Revolutsii). The pool here is small but still large enough to satisfy lap swimmers. The **Palace Hotel** (✉ 19 Pervaya Tverskaya-Yamskaya, ☎ 095/956–3152, Metro: Belorusskaya) has a weight-machine room, Jacuzzi, and sauna but no pool. The **Presnya Hotel** (✉ 9 Spiridonevsky pereulok, ☎ 095/202–0381 or 095/956–3010, Metro: Pushkinskaya) has a tiny gym, massage room, and sauna.

Running

The best spots for **jogging** are along Luzhniki's riverside or through the parks at Izmailovsky or Sokolniki. You will definitely want to avoid Moscow's heavy traffic and accompanying noxious fumes. Because it is difficult to find a comfortable place and you will be in a conspicuous minority, all but utter diehards may want to give themselves a few days' break.

Skating

If you've packed your skates, head straight for **Gorky Park** (✉ 9 Krymsky Val, Metro: Oktyabrskaya), where in winter months the park's lanes are flooded to create ad hoc skating rinks. The park also has two large rinks where you can skate to piped-in Russian pop music. Be prepared for some cultural differences, however. Russians do not skate in orderly circles or clean snow off the ice regularly. The park is open 10–10; the closest subway station is the Oktyabrskaya on the orange and circle lines. You can rent skates at **Sokolniki Park** (✉ 16 Sokolnichesky Val, ☎ 095/268–8277, Metro: Sokolniki). To use the facilities, you must lease the rink, so this is not the place to come unless you're with a group; hours are daily 10–7. Luzhniki's popular **Northern Lights** (✉ Luzhnetskaya nab., ☎ 095/201–1655, Metro: Sportivnaya) rink is open to all skaters over the age of 7. There is a fee for entry and skate rental; the rink is open evenings 5–9.

Swimming

On Sunday from 4 to 8 try the **Chaika Pool** (✉ 1/2 Korobeinikov pereulok, ☎ 095/202–0474 or 095/246–0263, Metro: Park Kultury), the only time this pool is open for a fee to nonmembers. There are several pools, saunas, and a solarium at the **Olympic Health Club** (✉ Olympic Penta Hotel, 18/1 Olympiisky Prospekt, ☎ 095/971–6101, Metro: Prospekt Mira), on a fee basis.

If you have Moscow friends and/or a car, you can join in a summer tradition by heading to **Serebryanny Bor** (Silver Pine Beach) for a dip in the Moskva River, where you'll encounter lots of interestingly clad, overheated city dwellers. You can also rent rowboats there.

Tennis

Courts are in scant supply and are usually reserved in advance by residents. **Olympisky Sports** compound (✉ 16 Olympisky pereulok, ☎ 095/288–5663 or 5118, Metro: Prospekt Mira) rents courts at expensive rates. The **Olympic Health Club** (✉ Olympic Penta Hotel, 18/1 Olympisky Prospekt, ☎ 095/971–6101, Metro: Prospekt Mira) sometimes has courts availale for a fee.

Spectator Sports

Tickets for sporting events can be purchased at the sports arena immediately prior to the game or at any of the numerous theater box offices (*teatralnaya kassa*) located throughout the city. You can also ask your hotel's service bureau for assistance in obtaining tickets to sporting events, but the fee will probably far exceed the value of the ticket itself.

Horse-Racing

Races are held at the **Hippodrome** (✉ 22/1 Begovaya ul., ☎ 095/945–4516, Metro: Begovaya) on Wednesday and Friday at 6 PM and on Sunday at 1 PM. Betting is in rubles. In winter troikas are sometimes raced.

Ice Hockey

Ice hockey matches are held at the **Dinamo Stadium** (✉ 36 Leningradsky Prospekt, ☎ 095/212–7092, Metro: Dinamo), which is Moscow's second-largest stadium, accommodating 60,000. Hockey matches are also held at Luzhniki's **Lenin Stadium** (☎ 095/246–5515, Metro: Sportivnaya), its largest, seating 100,000.

Soccer

The Russian national sport is soccer (in Russian, *futbal*), and it can ignite feverish passions. The city has several first-rate soccer teams, foremost among them Spartak and Dinamo. A game between them would be considered the team event of the year. Soccer matches are also frequently played at the Central Lenin Stadium and at the stadiums belonging to individual teams.

SHOPPING

It is, at long last, time to cast away cold war images of long lines and empty shelves—it's simply no longer the case. Although the distribution of products can be uneven and unpredictable, there are nonetheless plenty of them. You should be able to locate most items you need, if in a more piecemeal way than at home. You will not go hungry or unclothed should you lose your shirt at one of Moscow's casinos. In fact, you'll find opportunities to buy something any way you turn.

The proliferation of new stores is matched only by the upward bounds in prices. Food and goods stores can be roughly divided into two categories: Western-style ("hard currency") shops and Russian stores, though this is likely not to last once more Russian stores take on characteristics of more modern standard. There is also an ever-changing array of kiosks, tabletops, and wooden stalls. Western-style stores carry familiar brands from America and Europe, often Finland, at imported-goods prices, though they are beginning to need to be more competitive as more stores open. Russian establishments stock a mix of local and imported products—the latter without any fixed schedule of purchase, so you can't count on finding specific items in these stores, though you will find a great deal of whatever stock was bought that week.

In the past, special shops called Beriozka (Birch Tree) operated exclusively for foreigners. Stock was imported, payment was in hard currency only, and it was illegal for Soviet citizens to enter—let alone shop—in one. The Beriozka effectively no longer exists, having mutated into the "hard currency" shop. Technically, this has become an inaccurate denomination, since it is illegal in Russia to accept payment in currency other than rubles. These stores, unlike their Russian counterparts, however, take credit-card payment, calculated at a ruble exchange. (Stores set their own exchange rate and, like hotels, are unlikely to offer the favorable exchange rate you'll get at banks.) You should also be able to pay in cash, in rubles. (No store takes traveler's checks.) At such shops, nationality is no longer relevant; wallet size is—anyone who can afford the higher prices is welcome.

Russian stores have had varying responses to, and degrees of success with, the new economic times. In Old World fashion, they tend to be denoted by their products (Milk, Bread, Lights, Women's Shoes) but often carry more than their name implies. For food, a Produkti (Products) carries a narrow range of goods; basically, it's a small grocery, as is a Dieta. The less-frequently encountered but larger Gastronomes might be considered the equivalent of a supermarket.

For foreigners, the main stumbling block is the arduous method of purchase; it is time-consuming and often very trying. If you do not speak Russian, you should stick to Western stores or to street purchases, where you can use the universal language of finger-pointing. If you shop in a Russian store, you choose what you want at one counter, pay a cashier at another counter (more than one cashier if you are buying different types of items), and return with a receipt to collect your goods.

Service may be testier than you are used to, also. A few words in Russian and a composed countenance may ameliorate this, but if they don't, you should not take it personally. Russians seem to have grown so inured to shoving and elbowing for position that they will display an indifference to rudeness that foreign visitors often find appalling. On the bright side, when you do encounter good manners, they are impeccable.

The following listings are intended to give a thumbnail sketch of the places you may need as a tourist; they are by no means comprehensive. On the assumption that, despite the improvements, you still don't come to Moscow to shop but may need something in a hurry, most of the stores listed are Western-style. If your schedule permits, it's always interesting to browse the shops frequented by residents and a great way to take the pulse of a place, especially one in flux.

One reminder: Before you spend a lot of money on a souvenir, think about how you will feel if you can't take it home with you. Unfortunately, customs regulations are still vague and seem to change constantly and arbitrarily, depending on who is checking your bag. Art objects, particularly if they appear old or are large, can be deemed as "of value to the Russian nation." Goods in this category can be confiscated at the border. If you are buying paintings or such art objects, it's important to consult with the seller regarding the proper documentation of sale to take with you. Keep receipts of your purchases, wherever possible.

Please also exercise caution when out shopping. You will stand out no matter what you do, and there are pickpocket and mugging rings operating, often in small bands. *Don't* be an easy target.

Shopping Districts

Historically, the main shopping districts of Moscow have been concentrated in the city center, along Tverskaya ulitsa and Novy Arbat. Extend New Arbat through Kutuzovsky Prospekt and, on the other end, add the Old Arbat, which has been particularly spruced up for the tourist trade, and these are your best bets.

The closest thing in Moscow to a mall is **GUM** (pronounced "goom"), a series of shops and boutiques inside a 19th-century shopping arcade, which was once closed to foreigners. GUM, which stands for State Department Store, is on Red Square, right across from the Kremlin. More change is coming, however, with mall fever due to hit soon enough; a major site outside the Kremlin is already under construction.

Department Stores

TsUM (✉ 2 ul. Petrovka, ⏱ Mon.–Sat. 8–9), which translates as Central Department Store, is one of two big Russian department stores (the other being GUM, ☞ *above*). **Moskva Department Store** (✉ 54 Leninsky Prospekt, ⏱ Mon.–Sat. 8–9) is a giant general store. **Petrovsky Passage** (✉ 10 ul. Petrovka), is home to a varied series of shops. Near Lubyanka Square you'll see **Detsky Mir** (✉ 2 Teatralny proyezd), the famous children's department store.

Specialty Stores

For good souvenir-hunting, you can certainly head straight to the Arbat (☞ The Arbat, Old and New, *above*). Stores here cater to tourists and Moscow's expatriate community, so you can expect good selection and service, but prices are on the high end. Its individual outdoor vendors invariably charge much more than they should, so stick to the stores.

Arts and Crafts

The **art boutiques** inside two **Varvarka ulitsa** churches—St. Maxim the Blessed (open daily 11–6) and St. George on Pskov Hill (open daily 11–7)—offer a fine selection of handicrafts, jewelry, ceramics, and other types of Russian native art. (☞ Kitai Gorod, *above*). *Metro: Kitai-Gorod.*

The **Art Salon of the Arts Industry Institute** has an excellent selection of artwork handcrafted by the institute's students and teachers, including hand-painted trays, quilts, ceramics, and leather goods. ✉ *31 Povarskaya ul., 2nd floor,* ☎ *095/290–6822. Rubles only. Metro: Arbatskaya.*

Central Art Salon. This big salon sells just about everything you might be looking for—from handcrafted nesting dolls to ceramics, *khokhloma* (lacquered wood), and jewelry, all made by members of the Russian Union of Artists. Also on sale are beautiful Dagestani rugs. ✉ *6 Ukrainsky bulvar,* ☎ *095/243–9458.* ⏱ *Sun.–Fri. 10–2, 3–7; Sat. 11–6. Rubles only. Metro: Kievskaya.*

If you are enamored of blue-and-white Gzhel ceramic ware, try their own shop, **Gzhel,** to find all manner of pieces. ✉ *22 ul. Petrovka,* ☎ *095/200–6137. Metro: Teatralnaya.*

The **Museum Shop** at the **Museum of the Revolution** is good for amber, nesting dolls, and other Soviet memorabilia such as pins, postcards, and T-shirts. ✉ *21 Tverskaya ul.,* ☎ *095/299–1695.* ⏱ *Tues.–Sun. 10–5. Rubles only. Metro: Tverskaya.*

Anyone intrigued by the beauty and variety in Russian patterns can find the full catalog at **Russkye Uzory** (Russian Patterns). ✉ *16 ul. Petrovka,* ☎ *095/923–1883. Metro: Teatralnaya.*

Russkyie Souveniry. This state-run souvenir shop is easy to find and filled with handcrafted and mass-produced folk art, *palekh* boxes, and jewelry, but its prices are very inflated. ✉ *9 Kutuzovsky Prospekt.* ⏱ *Mon.–Sat. 11–2, 3–8. Rubles only. Metro: Kievskaya.*

Salon Iskusstva has a big section of Russian items, such as samovars, dolls, and boxes. ✉ *52 Bolshaya Yakimanka ul.* ⏱ *Mon.–Sat. 10–7. Metro: Oktyabrskaya.*

You'll see occasional kiosks or counters in churches selling Russian Orthodox religious items, but for an excellent full array, try **Sofrino** (✉ 11 Nikolskaya ulitsa, ☎ 095/925–4480. Metro: Pl. Revolutsii).

Food

Arbat Irish Store offers an extremely well-stocked grocery store and small department store selling electronics, household goods, car accessories, and clothing (primarily jeans). The relatively reasonable prices here make for long lines, especially on the weekend. ⊠ *21 Novy Arbat,* ☎ *095/291–7641.* ⊙ *Daily 10–9. Rubles downstairs; credit cards only upstairs. Metro: Arbatskaya.*

Danone is a sleek shop on Tverskaya dishing out only Dannon yogurt products. Able to buy by the six-pack here, health nuts should take heart. ⊠ *4 Tverskaya ul.,* ☎ *095/292–0512. Metro: Tverskaya.*

Garden Ring Irish Supermarket. There are three of these small and expensive groceries. Each, despite the prices, is quite popular among expatriates, who seem to relish in particular the roast chickens. ⊠ *2 Bolshaya Sadovaya ul.,* ☎ *095/209–1572, Metro: Mayakovskaya; 113 Leninsky Prospekt,* ☎ *095/956–5458, Metro: Leninsky Prospekt; 2 ul. Serafimovicha,* ☎ *095/231–8187, Metro: Polyanka.* ⊙ *Daily 9– noon. Rubles, credit cards.*

Global USA. Huge (billed as an American supershop), it's where you'll find almost every brand of every product you may be looking for. ⊠ *35 ul. Usacheva,* ☎ *095/245–5657, Metro: Sportivnaya.; 78 Leningradsky Prospekt,* ☎ *095/151–3354, Metro: Belorusskaya.* ⊙ *Daily 10– 8. Rubles, credit cards.*

Kalinka-Stockmann is a major chain, with five stores offering office supplies, electronics, and clothing; its grocery shop has a broad assortment, including fresh fruits and vegetables. Like Sadko, it is not cheap. ⊠ *4/8 Zatsepsky Val,* ☎ *095/233–2602, Metro: Paveletskaya.* ⊙ *Daily 10–9. Rubles, credit cards.*

Sadko's Foodland has been on the scene forever. It has a large selection of imported grocery items, including cheese and other dairy products, alcohol, office supplies, and health and beauty products. ⊠ *16 Bolshaya Dorogomilovskaya ul.,* ☎ *095/243–7502, Metro: Kievskaya.* ⊙ *Mon.–Sat. 10–8, Sun. 10–6. Credit cards.*

Men's and Women's Clothing

The two **Benetton** shops, one on the first floor of GUM and the other on the Arbat, carry their trademark line of sweaters, skirts, pants, and jeans. ☎ *095/921–5065, Metro: Pl. Revolutsii. Credit cards only.*

Galeries Lafayette, the chic emporium from France, has clothing that runs the gamut from wool leggings to cloche hats to silk suits. ⊠ *Ground level of GUM, Metro: Pl. Revolutsii.*

Fans of **Nike** (⊠ *1 Kundrinsky pereulok*) can find their store across from Barrikadnaya subway station.

Reebok's big airy shop sells sports outfits, shoes, and equipment. ⊠ *23 Krasnaya Presnya ul.,* ☎ *095/252–6591, Metro: Barrikadnaya.*

Rifle Jeans sells Italian jeans, denim jackets and skirts, corduroys, and sweatshirts. ⊠ *10 Kuznetsky most,* ☎ *095/923–2458, Metro: Kuznetsky most.* ⊙ *Mon.–Sat. 10–7. Credit cards, rubles.*

Those looking for high-fashion items might check the **Stockmann Boutique** (⊠ 73 Leninsky Prospekt, ☎ 095/134–3546, Metro: Paveletskaya. Quality women's fashion is available at **Les Boutiques Renoir** (⊠ 15 Bolshoi Cherkassky pereulok, ☎ 095/924–6229, Metro: Lubyanka.).

Women interested in seeing the latest Russian haute couture may satisfy their curiosity at the designer house **Gallery of Fashion,** where 18 different collections can be found (⊠ 11123 Pyatnitskaya ul., ☎ 095/ 233–2508, Metro: Novokuznetskaya). A wide array of women's fashions is to be found at the **Yelena Pelyevina Salon** (⊠ 42 Komsomolsky Prospekt, ☎ 095/242–3726, Metro: Park Kultury.), where Russian folk-inspired patterns and garments are the focus.

Street Markets

For green markets, Moscow, alas, cannot compete with its European neighbors or even nearer rivals, Kiev and St. Petersburg. The best-known was the **Tsentralny Rynok** (Central Market), on Tsvetnoy bulvar, but it's been closed for *remont*. It is supposed to reopen, but it's hard to tell.

You might try the **Dorogomilovsky Market** off Mozhaiska ulitsa, near the Kievsky train station. Beyond its outdoor "Veshch Rynok" (literally, "market of things," which you'll see is certainly apt) is a large covered hall. Inside are rows of vendors hawking homemade cheese and milk products, honey, flowers, and produce of all kinds. Against one wall are sellers of pickled goods, an understandably popular form of food preparation in this part of the world; you may want to sample some of their cabbage and carrot slaws, salted cucumbers, or spiced eggplant or garlic. Tasting is free, but it's unlikely that you'll be allowed to leave without buying something. Remember to bargain. In another corner, you will also find tables of freshly cut meat, plucked chickens, and fish. The squeamish may want to avert their eyes from the whole suckling pigs and the occasional hare or goat, beheaded and proudly strung up for inspection.

You can spend a whole day at Moscow's **flea market** in Izmailovsky Park. Here you'll find hosts of reasonably priced souvenirs and handicrafts as well as Soviet memorabilia, such as army belts and gas masks, and *matryoshky* (nesting dolls), both classic and nouveau, with some bearing likenesses of recent Soviet leaders, others depicting American basketball stars. Nearby is the former royal residence of Izmailovo, situated in an old hunting preserve. The flea market is open weekends 9–6, but it's best to get there early. Many vendors close down their booths by midday. Be sure to wrangle over prices. What began as a place with reasonable prices can be a full-grown tourist trap if you're not careful. *Transportation: subway to Izmailovsky Park station on blue line (not to be confused with next stop, Izmailovskaya station), and follow crowds as you exit.*

Ptichi Rynok (Bird Market) is on Kalitnovskaya ulitsa. Open on Sunday only, this market offers a fascinating glimpse of Russians and their pets. The softhearted should be forewarned that it is very difficult to leave this place without acquiring something. The market is bustling with individuals selling adorable, furry animals—cats, dogs, and hamsters—as well as exotic birds and fish and, occasionally, a monkey. *Transportation: Metro to Taganskaya station. Exit from circle-line station, and from there take any bus or trolley from Marksistskaya ulitsa stop (across square from subway, near purple Tagansky department store). Bus line ends at pet market.*

SIDE TRIPS FROM MOSCOW

Arkhangelskoye Estate Museum

This manor-estate museum is located in the village of Arkhangelskoye, some 26 kilometers (15 miles) from Moscow, on the banks of the Moskva River. The palace, but not the grounds, have been closed for several years for restoration work, and no date has been set for its official re-opening, but excursions can still be made out there. Check first with your hotel's service bureau or the tour agency you have chosen for up-dated information.

The estate, which includes the former palace of Prince Yusupov, com-prises a striking group of 18th- and 19th-century buildings whose ar-chitecture artfully blends into the landscape. The main complex was built at the end of the 18th century for Prince Golitsyn by the French architect Chevalier de Huerne. In 1810, the family fell upon harder times and sold it to the rich landlord Yusupov, onetime director of the im-perial theaters and of St. Petersburg's Hermitage Museum. The estate became home to his extraordinary art collection.

The classical palace's holdings included paintings by Boucher, Vigée-Lebrun, Hubert Robert, Roslin, Tiepolo, Van Dyck, and many others, as well as antique statues, furniture, mirrors, chandeliers, glassware, and china. The collection also includes samples of fabrics, china, and glassware, all of which were produced on the estate.

In the French Park are allées and strolling lanes; many still hold stat-ues and monuments commemorating royal visits; there is also a mon-ument to Pushkin, whose favorite retreat was Arkhangelskoye. In the western part is an interesting small pavilion, known as the Temple to the Memory of Catherine the Great, which depicts the empress as Themis, goddess of justice. It seems that Yusupov, reportedly a Casanova, had turned the head of Russia's empress, renowned herself for having le-gions of lovers. This "temple" was built as a compliment for a paint-ing she had previously commissioned—one in which she was depicted as Venus, with Yusupov as Apollo. Overall, a definite sense of disre-pair—with the exception of the closed palace with its ongoing recon-struction—pervades. Back outside the estate grounds, the Estate (Serf) Theater, on the right side of the main road, was built in 1817 by the serf architect Ivanov; it seated 400 and was the home of the biggest and best-known company of serf-actors. The well-preserved stage dec-orations are by the Venetian artist Pietrodi Gonzaga.

Donskoy Monastery

The 16th-century **Donskoy Monastery** is a fascinating memorial to Rus-sian architecture and art. From 1934 through 1992, a branch of the Shchusev Architecture Museum, keeping architectural details of churches, monasteries, and public buildings destroyed under the So-viets, was located—more or less secretly—inside its walls. Today the monastery is once again functioning as a religious institution, and the museum is slowly removing its exhibits from inside the churches. But the bits and pieces of demolished churches and monuments remain, forming a graveyard of destroyed architecture from Russia's past.

The monastery is situated in a secluded, wooded area in the southwest section of Moscow. It is open to the public Tuesday–Friday and Sun-day 11–6 and is closed the last Thursday of the month. You can reach it by taking the subway to the Shabolovskaya station. When you exit the subway, turn right and walk one block to Donskaya ulitsa. Turn right again and follow the street until you see the copper-topped domes of the monastery's churches above the trees to your left. Follow the path along the redbrick fortification wall until you reach the main en-trance on the other side.

The monastery grounds are surrounded by a high defensive wall with 12 towers. Founded in the late 16th century, it was the last of the de-fense fortifications to be built around Moscow. It is situated on the site where, in 1591, the Russian army stood waiting for an impending at-tack from Tatar troops grouped on the opposite side of the river. According to legend, the Russians awoke one morning to find the Tatars gone. Their sudden retreat was considered a miracle, and regent Boris Godunov ordered a monastery built to commemorate the miraculous victory. Of course, it didn't happen quite like that, but historians confirm that the Tatars did retreat after only minor skirmishes, which is difficult to explain. Never again would they come so close to Moscow.

The victory was attributed to the icon of the Virgin of the Don that Prince Dmitry Donskoy had supposedly carried previously, during his campaign in 1380 (in which the Russians won their first decisive victory against the Tatars). The monastery was named in honor of the wonder-working icon.

When you enter through the western gates, an icon of the Mother of the Don looks down on you from above the entrance to the imposing **New Cathedral.** The brick cathedral was built in the late 17th century by Peter the Great's sister, Sophia. It has been under restoration for decades; services are held in the gallery surrounding the church, where the architectural exhibits were once housed. The smaller, **Old Cathedral** stands to the right of the New Cathedral. The attractive red church with white trim was built in 1591–93, during the reign of Boris Godunov. It is open for services.

One of the most fascinating sections of the monastery is its graveyard, where you find many fine examples of memorial art. After the plague swept through Moscow in 1771, Catherine the Great forbade any more burials in the city center. The Donskoy Monastery, at that time on the city's outskirts, became a fashionable burial place for the well-to-do. The small **Church of the Archangel** built against the fortification wall to your far right was the private chapel and crypt of the prominent Golitsyn family (original owners of the Arkhangelskoye estate). Many leading intellectuals, politicians, and aristocrats were buried here in the 18th, 19th, and 20th centuries. Among them are the dramatist Alexander Sumarokov, the architect Osip Bove, and the 19th-century philosopher Pyotr Chaadayev, whose modern-day followers still leave flowers at his grave.

If you walk down to the eastern wall of the monastery, you find remnants of the decorative stone facade of the original **Cathedral of Christ Our Savior** (☞ Exploring Moscow, *above*), which the Soviets blew up in 1931 and which is now being rebuilt. One of the facades shows Monk Sergei of Radonezh giving his blessing to Dmitry Donskoy before he left for the decisive battle that led to the end of Tatar rule in Russia. The northern wall is lined with portals from ancient churches destroyed or flooded along the Volga to make way for a huge reservoir. As you make your way back to the main entrance, you will notice a cast-iron pedestal in the courtyard outside the New Cathedral. This is what remains of the Triumphal Arch, which once stood at the end of Tverskaya ulitsa. That arch was destroyed in the 1930s. In the 1960s, the original was replicated and erected at the city center's end of Kutuzovsky Prospekt.

Kolomenskoye

★ If you want to spend an afternoon in the great Russian outdoors without actually leaving the city, a visit to **Kolomenskoye** is a must. Situated on a high bluff overlooking the Moskva River, this estate was once a favorite summer residence of Moscow's grand dukes and czars. Today it is a popular public park with museums, a functioning church, old Russian cottages, and other attractions. Take the subway to the Kolomenskaya station on the green line; a walk of about 10 minutes up a slight hill will bring you to the park's entrance. ⊠ *39 Prospekt Andropova,* ☎ *095/115–2384.* ⊘ *Wed.–Sun. 11–5.*

As you walk up the hill to Kolomenskoye, the first sight to greet you are the striking blue domes of the **Church of Our Lady of Kazan.** The church is open for worship. A wooden palace once stood in the park opposite the church. It was built by Czar Alexei, Peter the Great's Father, and Peter spent much time here when he was growing up. Nothing remains of this huge wooden palace (Catherine the Great ordered it destroyed in 1767), but there is a scale model at the museum. The exhibits of the museum, devoted to Russian timber architecture and folk crafts, are found in the old servants' quarters, at the end of the tree-lined path leading from the main entrance.

Most remarkable is the **Church of the Ascension,** situated on the bluff overlooking the river. The church dates from the 1530s and was restored in the late 1800s. Its skyscraping tower is an example of the tent or pyramid-type structure that was popular in Russian architecture in the 16th century. The view from the bluff is impressive in its contrasts, and there is always something happening. From your 16th-century backdrop, you can look across the river to the north, to the 20th-century concrete apartment houses that dominate the contemporary Moscow skyline. In summer you'll see Muscovites bathing in the river below the church, and in winter the area abounds in cross-country skiers.

Examples of wooden architecture from other parts of Russia have been transferred to Kolomenskoye, turning the estate into an open-air museum. In the wooded area near the site of the former wooden palace, you will find a 17th-century prison tower from Siberia, a defense tower from the White Sea, and a 17th-century mead brewery from the village of Preobrazhenskaya. One of the most attractive buildings to be seen in its original form is the wooden cottage where Peter the Great lived while supervising the building of the Russian fleet in Arkhangelsk. It was moved here from that northern city in 1934.

Kuskovo and Ceramics Palace Museum

In the 18th and 19th centuries, the country estate of **Kuskovo** was the Moscow aristocracy's favorite summer playground. It belonged to the noble Sheremetyevs, one of Russia's wealthiest and most distinguished families. Moscow's international airport, built on land once belonging to one of their many estates, takes their name. Kuskovo is located just outside the ring road marking the city boundary, but you can reach it by public transportation. Take the subway to Ryazansky Prospekt and then Bus 208 or 133 six stops to Kuskovo Park. This is obviously not as accessible as Kolomenskoye, and you may find it more convenient to book a tour that would include transportation. Whatever you do, be sure to phone ahead before making the trek out here, because the estate often closes in humid weather and when it is very cold. ⊠ *Ul. Yunosti 2,* ☎ *095/370–0160.* ⊘ *Nov.–Apr., Wed.–Sun. 10–4; May–Oct., Wed.–Fri. 11–7, weekends 10–6. Closed last Wed. of month.*

The land of Kuskovo belonged to the Sheremetyevs as far back as the early 17th century, but the estate acquired its present appearance in the late 18th century. Often called a Russian Versailles, most work on it was commissioned by Prince Peter Sheremetyev, who sought a suitable place for entertaining guests in the summer. The park was painted by Russian landscape artists who had spent much time in Europe studying their art. The French-style gardens are dotted with buildings representing the major architectural trends of Europe: the Dutch cottage, the Italian villa, the grotto, and the hermitage, where, in the fashion of the day, dinner tables were raised mechanically from the ground floor to the second-floor dining room.

The centerpiece of the estate is the **wooden palace,** built in the early Russian classical style by the serf architects Alexei Mironov and Fedor Argunov. Peter Sheremetyev owned more than 150,000 serfs, many of whom received architectural training and participated in the building of his estate. (Serfs also constituted a theater troupe that gave weekly performances, another common practice on nobles' estates.)

The palace, which is made of timber on a white-stone foundation, overlooks an artificial lake. It has been a museum since 1918, and its interior decorations, including fine parquet floors and silk wall coverings, have been well preserved. The bedroom, with its fine canopy bed, was merely for show; the Sheremetyevs used the palace exclusively for entertainment and did not live here. The marvelous White Hall, with its parquet floors, gilt wall decorations, and crystal chandeliers, served as the ballroom.

On display in the inner rooms are paintings by French, Italian, and Flemish artists, Chinese porcelain, furniture, ornaments, and other articles of everyday life from the 18th and 19th centuries. The palace also houses a collection of 18th-century Russian art and a rather celebrated ceramics museum with a rich collection of Russian, Soviet, and foreign ceramics.

New Jerusalem Monastery

The **Novoierusalimsky Monastyr** (New Jerusalem Monastery) is located near the town of Istra, some 55 kilometers (34 miles) northwest of Moscow. This is not the most visited place in Russia, and it is included in the standard offerings of tourist agencies only in the summer. In nice weather, it is a marvelous way to spend a day; its location in the picturesque Russian countryside—far from tourist crowds—only adds to its attraction. If you can't book a tour and are feeling adventurous, you could try an excursion on the commuter train. Trains leave from Rizhsky Vokzal (Riga Railroad Station) and take about an hour and a half. The best option of all would be to ask a Russian friend to guide you and make a day of it in the countryside. Be sure to pack your lunch; the best you'll find in Istra is an occasional cafeteria or outdoor café. The monastery's museums are open 10–5 and are closed Monday and the last Friday of the month.

The monastery was founded in 1652 by Nikon, patriarch of the Russian Orthodox Church. It lies on exactly the same longitude as Jerusalem; and its main cathedral, **Voskresensky Sobor** (Resurrection Cathedral) is modeled after the Church of the Holy Sepulchre in Jerusalem. Nikon's objective in re-creating the original Jerusalem in Russia was to glorify the power of the Russian Orthodox Church and at the same time elevate his own position as its head. It was Nikon who initiated the great church reforms in the 17th century that eventually led to the *raskol* (schism) resulting in the Old Believer sects of the Russian Orthodox faith. As a reformer, he was progressive and enlightened, but he lusted for power, which eventually was his undoing. In 1658, before the monastery was even finished, the patriarch quarreled with the czar over Nikon's claim that the Church was ultimately superior to the State. Eventually Nikon was defrocked and banished to faraway Ferapontov Monastery. He died in virtual exile in 1681, then was buried in the monastery that was supposed to have glorified his power. You can find his crypt in the Church of St. John the Baptist, which is actually inside the Resurrection Cathedral. Ironically, the same church commission that defrocked Patriarch Nikon later voted to institute his reforms.

The monastery also comprises the **Moscow Regional Museum,** which contains a modest collection of prerevolutionary paintings, portrait art, porcelain, and armory. One section is devoted to the history of the monastery and its reconstruction. There is also a hall for temporary exhibits of contemporary art on the monastery grounds. Besides the Resurrection Cathedral, the ensemble of buildings inside the monastery includes the Moscow Baroque Nativity Church, the Czar's Chambers, and the modest Three-Saints Church. Nikon's three-story Hermitage, where he observed his private prayer alone, is located just outside the monastery's stone walls.

If you follow the path behind the monastery leading to the river, you reach the **Architectural and Ethnographic Museum of the Moscow Region.** This open-air museum of restored Russian wooden architecture is set among the coppices on the high bank of the River Istra. Here you will find a 19th-century peasant log cabin, which is particularly interesting since dwelling houses like this are still in use. A huge stove takes up much of the living space, above which the peasants slept. Also brought to the museum grounds are a wooden inn, a 17th-century wooden church, and a windmill. Examine them closely and you will discover that they were all constructed entirely of wood, without a single nail, screw, or bolt.

Zagorsk (Sergyev Posad)

★ **Zagorsk** is some 75 kilometers (46 miles) northeast of Moscow, making it a comfortable, and popular, day trip. The city's chief attraction is the **Troitsa-Sergyeva Lavra** (Trinity Monastery of St. Sergius), which for 500 years has been the most important center of pilgrimage in Russia. Before the Revolution, the town was known as Sergyev Posad, after the monastery's founder, and in 1991 it was officially returned to its proper name. But the Soviet name of Zagorsk—in honor of a Bolshevik who was assassinated in 1919—has stuck, and you are as likely to hear the town and the monastery itself called one as the other.

The ride to Zagorsk takes you through a lovely stretch of Russian countryside, dotted with colorful wooden cottages. As you approach the town, you see the sad and monolithic apartment buildings of the modern era. Then, peeking out above the sloping hills, the monastery's golden cupolas and soft-blue **bell tower** come into view.

The city also claims fame as a center of toy making. The world's first *matryoshka* (the familiar colorful, wooden nesting doll) was designed here at the beginning of the century, and most of the matroshkas you see for sale in Moscow and St. Petersburg are made in Zagorsk. The city even has a **toy museum.** It is rarely included on organized tours, but it is located within walking distance of the monastery, at 136 Prospekt Krasnoi Armii. The museum contains a collection of toys that amused, educated, and illuminated the lives of Russian children for generations. It is well worth an hour of your time, even if your interest is only casual.

The best way to visit Zagorsk is to join an organized tour, since it is a full-day affair, out of the city. All tour services offer day trips to Zagorsk. The cost usually includes lunch in addition to a guided tour and transportation. It is also possible to visit on your own by taking the commuter train from Moscow's Yaroslavsky Vokzal (Yaroslav Railroad Station). The ride takes about two hours; tickets are purchased at the train station for rubles. This is obviously much less expensive

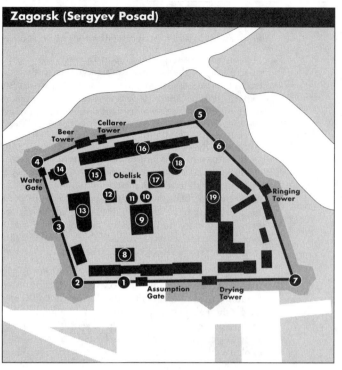

Zagorsk (Sergyev Posad)

than an organized tour, but far from hassle-free. If you choose this alternative, be sure to pack your own lunch, since Zagorsk's only full-fledged restaurant fills up fast with prebooked tourist groups, especially in the summer. You must also take care to dress appropriately for your visit to the functioning monastery, to make certain you won't go all the way there only to be turned back at the entrance. (Russia is far stricter about enforcing dress codes at religious sites than are most similar places in Europe.) Men are expected to remove their hats, and women are required to wear below knee-length skirts (*never* shorts, even walking shorts) and bring something to cover their heads. The grounds are open Tues.–Fri., 10–5.

The **Troitsa-Sergyeva Lavra** (monastery) was founded in 1340 by Sergius of Radonezh, who would later become Russia's patron saint. The site rapidly became the nucleus of a small medieval settlement, and in 1550 the imposing white walls were built to enclose the complex of buildings. The monastery was a Russian stronghold during the Time of Troubles and the Polish assault on Moscow in the early 17th century, and Peter the Great took refuge here during a bloody revolt of the *streltsy* that took the lives of some of his closest relatives and advisors. After the Bolshevik Revolution, the monastery was closed and turned into a museum. During World War II, however, in an attempt to mobilize the country and stir up patriotism, the Soviet government got the support of the Church by returning to religious purposes some of the church property that had been confiscated earlier, including the Monastery of St. Sergius. Today the churches are again open for worship, and there is a flourishing theological college here. Until the reopening in 1988 of the Danilovsky Monastery in Moscow, this monastery was the residence of the patriarch and administrative center of the Russian Orthodox Church.

You enter the monastery through the archway of the **Gate Church of St. John the Baptist.** It was erected in the late 17th century and is decorated with frescoes telling the life story of St. Sergius.

One of the most important historical events in his life occurred prior to 1380, when the decisive Russian victory in the Battle of Kulikovo led to the end of Mongol rule in Russia. Before leading his troops off to battle, Prince Dmitry Donskoy sought the blessing of the peace-loving monk Sergius, a move that is generally thought to have greatly aided the Russian victory (☞ Donskoy Monastery, *above*).

Although all of the monastery's cathedrals vie for your attention (and each visitor will have a different favorite), the dominating structure is the massive, blue-domed and gold-starred **Uspensky Sobor** (Assumption Cathedral) located in the center. Built in 1554–85 with money donated by Czar Ivan the Terrible—purportedly in an attempt to atone for murdering his own son—it was modeled after the Kremlin's Uspensky Sobor. Its interior boasts frescoes and an 18th-century iconostasis. Among the artists to work on it was Simon Ushakov, a well-known icon painter from Moscow. The cathedral is open for morning services.

The small building just outside the Uspensky Cathedral (near the northwest corner) is the **tomb of Boris Godunov** and his family. Boris Godunov died suddenly in 1605, during the Polish attack on Moscow led by the False Dmitry, the first of many impostors to claim he was the son of Czar Ivan the Terrible. The death of Boris facilitated the invaders' victory, after which his family was promptly murdered. This explains why Boris was not bestowed the honor of burial in the Kremlin normally granted to czars.

Opposite Boris Godunov's tomb is a tiny and colorful chapel built above a miracle-working fountain. It is called **Chapel-at-the-Well.** According to legend, the spring here appeared during the Polish Siege (1608–10), when the monastery bravely held out for 16 months against the foreign invaders (this time led by the second False Dmitry). You can make a wish by washing your face and hands in its charmed waters. Towering 285 feet above the monastery grounds is the five-tiered Baroque belfry. It was built in the 18th century to a design by the master of St. Petersburg Baroque, Bartolomeo Rastrelli.

Along the southern wall of the monastery, to your far left as you enter, is the 17th-century **Refectory and Church of St. Sergius.** The church is at the eastern end, topped by a single gilt dome. The long building of the Refectory, whose colorful facade adds to the vivid richness of the monastery's architecture, is where, in times past, pilgrims from near and far gathered to eat on feast days. The pink building just beyond the Refectory is the metropolitan's Residence.

A continual service in memorium to St. Sergius is held all day, every day, in the white-stone **Troitsky Sobor** (Cathedral of the Holy Trinity), situated across the path from the metropolitan's Residence. The church, which is very beautiful inside, was built in the 15th century over the tomb of St. Sergius; over the centuries it has received many precious gifts from the powerful and wealthy rulers who have made the pilgrimage to the church of Russia's patron saint. The icons inside were created by famous master Andrey Rublyov and one of his disciples, Danil Chorny. Ryublov's celebrated *Holy Trinity,* now on display at the Tretyakov Gallery, originally hung here; the work you see is a copy.

The vestry, the building behind the Church of the Holy Trinity, houses the monastery's **Museum of Ancient Russian Art.** It is often closed for no apparent reason or open only to groups, which is yet another reason to visit Zagorsk on a guided tour. The museum contains a spectacular collection of gifts presented to the monastery over the centuries. On display are precious jewels, jewel-encrusted embroideries, chalices, and censers. Next door to the vestry are two more museums, which are open to individual tourists. The first museum contains icons and icon covers, portrait art, and furniture. The other museum (on the second floor) is devoted to Russian folk art, with wooden items and toys, as well as porcelain and jewelry. There is also a gift shop where you can pick up a souvenir of your visit to ancient Zagorsk.

MOSCOW A TO Z

Arriving and Departing

By Boat

Moscow has two river ports: the Northern River Terminal (✉ Severny Rechnoy Vokzal, 51 Leningradskoye Shosse, ☎ 095/457–4050) and the Southern River Terminal (✉ Yuzhny Rechnoy Vokzal, Andropov Prospekt, ☎ 095/118–7955). International cruise lines offering tours to Russia usually disembark in St. Petersburg and continue from there by land. It is possible, however, to book a two-way cruise from Moscow along the Moscow-Volga canal, which makes for a pleasant way to see the ancient cities of the Golden Ring. Some 129 kilometers (80 miles) long, the canal links the Russian capital with the Caspian Sea, the Black Sea, the White Sea, and the Azov Sea. The Moscow port for long-distance passengers is the **Severny Rechnoy Vokzal** (northern port) on the Khimki reservoir.

By Car

You can reach Moscow from Finland and St. Petersburg by taking the Helsinki–St. Petersburg Highway (*shosse*) through Vyborg and St. Petersburg and continuing from there on the Moscow–St. Petersburg Highway. Be warned that driving in Russia is invariably more of a hassle than a pleasure. Gas shortages are frequent, repair shops are rare, and roads are very poorly maintained. In addition, you face the risk of car theft, a crime that is on the rise.

By Plane

AIRPORTS AND AIRLINES

As the single most important transportation hub in the CIS, Moscow has several airports. Most international flights arrive at **Sheremetyevo II** (☎ 095/578–5633 or 095/578–5614), which currently handles an estimated 15,000 passengers daily. One of the most modern in Russia, Sheremetyevo II was built in 1979, when there was much less international traffic; these days it is just barely coping. Expect to stand an hour or two at passport control. Disembarked passengers descend a long staircase, then collect en masse in a large, dimly lit chamber to vie for the three or four lines to the passport officials' booths. Their legendary slowness is fact, not myth. The baggage area is located directly beyond. There may or may not be luggage carts, for which you pay in rubles. There's a bank in the waiting area where you can exchange money or traveler's checks while you're waiting for your luggage. After you have collected your bags, you'll go through customs. This is frequently in a single line, so you may have another hour or so on your feet. Leaving customs, usually also in single file, you will be greeted by mobs of Russians awaiting arriving passengers and eager gypsy cab drivers shouting "*Taksi! Taksi!*" Take a deep breath and plow straight through until you find your host or group. Welcome to the capital city!

In addition to its international airport, the city has four domestic terminals. **Sheremetyevo I** (☎ 095/578–5791), some 30 kilometers (19 miles) northwest of the city center, services domestic flights to St. Petersburg and the former Baltic republics (Estonia, Latvia, and Lithuania). It has also been handling international flights of some new Russian airlines, so if you fly Transaero you may go here. **Domodedovo** (☎ 095/234–8656 or 095/234–8655), one of the largest airports in the world, is located some 48 kilometers (30 miles) southeast of Moscow; flights depart from here to the republics of Central Asia. **Vnukovo** (☎ 095/234–8656 or 095/234–8655), 29 kilometers (18 miles) southwest of the city center, services flights to Georgia, the southern republics, and Ukraine. **Bykovo** (☎ 095/155–0922), the smallest of the domestic terminals, generally handles flights within Russia and some flights to Ukraine. Be sure to find out from your travel agent which airport your flight is supposed to leave from.

If you are departing from Domodedovo or Vnukovo airport, look for the special lounges set aside for foreign tourists; they are much more comfortable than the general waiting area.

For general information on arriving international flights, call 095/578–7518 or 095/578–7816. These lines are often busy; if possible, call the airline. For information on domestic Aeroflot flights, call 095/155–0922. Calling the airports directly is usually a complete waste of time; the line is almost always busy, and even if it's not, no one answers.

Aeroflot (☎ 095/156–8019 or, for information on domestic flights, 095/155–0922) operates flights from Moscow to just about every capital of Europe, as well as to Canada and the United States. **Transaero** (☎ 095/241–4800 or 095/241–7676), another Russian carrier, now has a large network of domestic flights as well as several international routes. Among the international airlines with offices in Moscow are **Air France** (☎ 095/237–2325 or 095/237–3344), **Alitalia** (☎ 095/578–8246), **Austrian Airlines** (☎ 095/258–2020), **British Airways** (☎ 095/253–2492 or 095/578–3594), **Delta** (☎ 095/253–1288 or 095/578–2939), **Finnair** (☎ 095/292–8788 or 095/292–1762), **Japan Airlines** (☎ 095/921–6448), **KLM** (☎ 095/258–3600 or 095/578–3594), **Lufthansa** (☎ 095/975–2501 or 095/578–3151), **Malev** (☎ 095/956–2731 or 095/202–8416), **SAS** (☎ 095/925–4747 or 095/578–2727), and **Swissair** (☎ 095/258–1888).

BETWEEN THE AIRPORT AND DOWNTOWN

You would be wise to make advance arrangements for your transfer from the airport. There are plenty of gypsy cabs available, but you should *not* take them; they are notorious for swindles and much, much worse. In a pinch, use the services offered on the airport's ground floor. These private firms are somewhat costly but less risky. Most hotels will provide airport transfers (for an additional fee) upon request by prior fax (which you should make sure is confirmed). All of the airports are serviced by municipal buses operating out of the **City Airport Terminal** (*Aerovokzal*) at 37 Leningradsky Prospekt, near the airport subway station. Service is somewhat unreliable and inconvenient, especially if you have any luggage, but very inexpensive. The schedule is slightly erratic, but theoretically a bus departs from Sheremetyevo II (International) Airport every two hours or so; service to Domodedovo and Vnukovo domestic airports is more frequent. The Sheremetyevo II bus stop is 100 meters to the right as you leave, at a small shelter that has a yellow bus-route sign on it for bus 551, which is the one you take into Moscow. It *will,* inexorably, creep into the city.

By Train

Moscow is also the hub of the Russian railway system, and the city's nine railway stations handle some 400 million passengers annually. There are several trains daily to St. Petersburg, and overnight service is available to Helsinki. All the major train stations have a connecting subway stop, so they are easily reached by public transportation. The most important stations are: **Belorussky Vokzal** (Belorussia Station, ☎ 095/253–4464 or 095/266–9213, Metro: Belorusskaya), for trains to Belorussia, Lithuania, Poland, Germany, and France; **Kazansky Vokzal** (Kazan Station, ☎ 095/266–2843, Metro: Komsomolskaya), for points south, Central Asia, and Siberia; **Kievsky Vokzal** (Kiev Station, ☎ 095/240–7345, Metro: Kievskaya), for Kiev and western Ukraine, Moldova, Slovakia, the Czech Republic, and Hungary; **Kursky Vokzal** (Kursk Station, ☎ 095/240–7345, Metro: Kurskaya), for eastern Ukraine, the Crimea, and southern Russia; **Leningradsky Vokzal** (Leningrad Station, ☎ 095/266–9111 or 095/262–4281), for St. Petersburg, northern Russia, Estonia, and Finland; **Paveletsky Vokzal** (Pavelets Station, ☎ 095/233–0040, Metro: Paveletskaya), for eastern Ukraine and points south; **Rizhksy Vokzal** (Riga Station, ☎ 095/266–9535, Metro: Rizhskaya), for Latvia; **Yaroslavsky Vokzal** (Yaroslav Station, ☎ 095/266–0218, Metro: Komsomolskaya), for points east, including Mongolia and China; the Trans-Siberian Express departs every day at 2 PM.

The past few years have witnessed increased crime on the most heavily traveled routes, and as a result many travelers to St. Petersburg now prefer the high-speed, day train *Avrora,* which makes the trip in just under six hours. Of the numerous overnight trains, the most popular is the *Krasnaya Strelka* (Red Arrow), which leaves Moscow at 11:55 PM and arrives the next day in St. Petersburg at 8:25 AM. Overnight trains are considered more dangerous than day trains, and if you are traveling alone, you should take added precautions. Experienced travelers in Russia bring their own lock and buy out the entire compartment so as not to risk their luck with unknown compartment mates.

For information on train arrival and departure schedules, call 095/266–9333. For booking and ticket delivery, call 095/266–8333. Tourists must travel on a special, higher-priced ticket for foreigners. You can purchase it at the railway station on the day of departure (up to 24 hours in advance) or at the special ticket office for foreigners (✉ 6 Griboyedova ulitsa, Metro: Chistiye Prudy). Tickets may be purchased up to 10 days in advance; bring your passport.

Getting Around

If you look at a map of Moscow, you will see that the city consists of a series of distinct circles with the Kremlin and Red Square at its center. The most famous and important sites are clustered within the first circle, which was once enclosed by the fortification walls of Kitai Gorod, the city's oldest settlement outside the Kremlin. This area can be easily covered on foot. Beyond that, the sights are more spread out and are best reached by subway. To get a sense of the city's geographic layout, you might consider hiring a car for a few hours and traveling around the main roads encircling the city—the Boulevard and Garden Rings.

By Bus, Tram, and Trolley

Buses, trams, and trolleys operate on the honor system. Upon boarding, you validate your ticket by punching it in one of the machines attached to a wall of the vehicle. The buses and trolleys are almost always overcrowded, and chances are good that you won't be able to reach the canceling machine. Ask the person next to you to pass your ticket along; the canceled ticket will make its way back to you, and you should hold on to it until you get off.

You can purchase strips of tickets at subway stops and at kiosks throughout the city, or from the bus driver after you have boarded (although the driver will often be out of tickets, so it's best to buy them beforehand). The ticket is valid for one ride only; if you change buses you must pay another fare. Buses, trams, and trolleys operate from 5:30 AM to 1 AM, although service in the late-evening hours and on Sunday tends to be unreliable.

By Car

Your hotel may make arrangements for you. Otherwise, several international car rental agencies have offices in Moscow. **Avis** (✉ 12 Berezhkovskaya nab., ☎ 095/578–5646) rents Opels or Opel Astras. **Europcar** (✉ 12 Krasnopresnenskaya nab., Entr. 1, ☎ 095/298–6146 or 095/578–7534; ✉ Sheremetyevo II airport, ☎ 095/578–3878) rents Ford Sierras, Mercedes-Benzes, Volvos, and the tiny Ukrainian Zaporozhets. **Hertz** (✉ 4 Chernyakhovskogo ul., ☎ 095/151–5426) rents Toyota Corollas; for a $25 fee they will deliver the car to your location. All agencies require advance reservations (2–3 days is a good idea), and you will have to show your driver's license, an international license, and a credit card.

Each of these companies also rents cars with drivers. **Budget** (✉ 16 Verkhnaya Radishchevskaya ul., ☎ 095/915–5237 or 095/915–5590; ✉ Sheremetyevo II airport, ☎ 095/578–7344) offers this service exclusively and uses only Lincoln Town Cars. Other companies that provide cars with drivers are **InTourService** (✉ Hotel Rossiya, ☎ 095/298–5855) and **InNis** (✉ 32 Bolshaya Ordynka ul., ☎ 095/238–3077). Ask which cars they are using.

By Subway

The Moscow subway (in Russian, *metro*) ranks among the world's finest public transportation systems. Opened in 1935, the system's earliest stations—in the city center and along the circle line—were built as public palaces and are decorated with chandeliers, sculptures, stained-glass windows, and beautiful mosaics. With more than 200 kilometers (124 miles) of track, the Moscow subway carries an estimated 8 million passengers daily. Even in today's hard economic times, the system continues to run efficiently, with trains every 50 seconds during rush hour. It leaves New Yorkers green with envy.

If you're not traveling with a tour group or if you haven't hired your own chauffeur, taking the subway is the best way to get around the Russian capital. You'll be doing yourself a great favor, though, and saving yourself a lot of frustration, if you learn the Russian alphabet well enough to be able to transliterate the names of the stations. This will come in especially handy at the transfer points, where signs with long lists of the names of subway stations lead you from one of the major subway lines to another.

The subway is easy to use and amazingly inexpensive. Stations are marked with a large illuminated "M" sign and are open daily 5:30 AM–1 AM. The fare is the same regardless of distance traveled, and there are several stations where lines connect and you may transfer for free. You purchase a subway token (available at all stations) and insert it into the slot at the turnstile upon entering. Stations are built deep underground (they were built to double as bomb shelters); the escalators are steep and run fast, so watch your step. If you use the subway during rush hour (4–6 PM), be prepared for a lot of pushing and shoving.

Pocket maps of the system are available at newspaper kiosks or from individual vendors at subway stations. Plan your route beforehand and have your destination written down in Russian and its English translit-

Moscow Metro

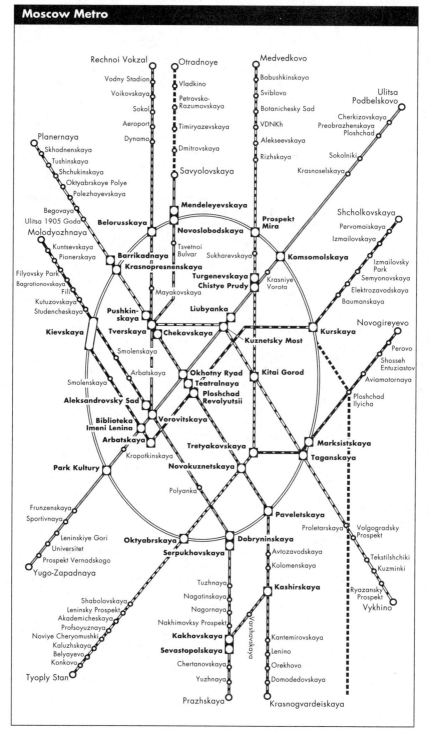

eration to help you spot the station. Each station is announced over the train's public address system as you approach it, and the name of the next one is given before the train moves off. Reminders of interchanges and transfers are also given.

If you want to avoid the lines for subway tokens, you can purchase a pass (*yediny bilyet*) that is valid for all modes of public transportation. Metro passes are on sale at the same counters as the subway tokens. They are inexpensive and well worth the added expense for the convenience. When you have a pass, you must use a far turnstile. Before entering, you show it to the watchful matron standing guard; look for the crush of other passengers doing this. You can't go through the token turnstile with a pass, and if you try, two steel bars will slam closed on you.

By Taxi

Foreign tourists should exercise caution when using taxicabs. This industry was hard hit in recent times, and most public cabs disappeared overnight. A comeback is underway, with a revamped fleet of cars ordered from Korea. For now you will sight most cabs—light-colored Russian Volgas with taxi lights on top—on major roadways. It is advised not to get into a car with more than one person in it, and you are best off ordering a cab by phone or through your hotel's service bureau. In today's strained economy, foreign tourists are crime targets. Gypsy cabs are common and often cruise the larger hotels and hard-currency restaurants in search of innocent foreigners. If you speak Russian, you can order a cab by telephone. For municipal services, call **Maryino** (☎ 095/927–0000 or 095/348–8900), a state-run firm with 24-hour service. There is sometimes a delay, but the cab usually arrives within the hour. If you order a cab in this way, you pay the official state fare in rubles (which is very reasonable when calculated in dollars), plus a fee for the reservation. Drivers will appreciate and expect a tip of at least 20%. If you hail a cab on the street, expect to negotiate and probably pay in dollars; fares for foreigners generally begin at $5. **Belmi Taxi Service** (☎ 095/318–8800) and **Moscow Taxi** (☎ 095/238–1001) provide city cabs as well as airport service in vans or buses, picking up from hotels or privately. Their prices are higher than those of city cabs.

Contacts and Resources

Dentists

Russian dental facilities are as grim as other medical ones. Of the above clinics, the **American Medical Center, European Medical Center,** and **Mediclub Moscow** also offer dental services; the **International Medical Clinic** also has access to dental facilities. **U.S. Dental Care** (✉ 8 Shabolovka ul., Corpus 3, ground floor, ☎ 095/236–8106/5471, ℻ 095/931–9909) is an independent clinic offering all types of dental treatment, with the exception of orthodontia. Laboratories and pharmacy are on-site. Optional membership, and all services are available to tourists. ☉ *Weekdays 9–6; after-hours emergency.*

The **Sofitel Dental Clinic** (✉ Sofitel Iris Hotel, 10 Korovinskoe Shosse, ☎ 095/488–8279, emergency 095/488–8000) also has a Western dental office, where Russian, English, French, and German are spoken. They offer a free shuttle service to and from the city center, since they are located outside of it. ☉ *Weekdays 10–5.*

Embassies

U. S. (✉ 19/23 Novinsky bulvar, ☎ 095/252–2451 through 095/252–2459). If there is a line of visa applicants at the entrance to the U.S. embassy, be aware that you do not need to stand in it if you are a U.S.

citizen. Just walk to the front and show the guard your passport, and he will let you by. **Canada** (✉ 23 Starokonyushenny pereulok, ☎ 095/241–5070 or 095/241–5882). **U. K.** (✉ 14 Sofiyskaya nab., ☎ 095/260–6333).

Emergencies

Ambulance (☎ 03). **Fire** (☎ 01). **Police** (☎ 02).

English-Language Bookstores

Zwemmer's is a British oasis in the shape of an English-language bookstore; it's handily located at 18 Kuznetsky most, around the corner from the metro station of the same name. ☎ 095/928–2021. ⊙ Daily 10–7.

Post International Bookstore is Moscow's newest, and its U.S. (not import) prices and mail-order service are welcome. ✉ ½ Putinkovsky Maly pereulok (behind the Rossiya Cinema), ☎ 095/209–9168. ⊙ Weekdays 9–6.

Russia's largest bookstore, **Dom Knigi** (✉ The Book House, 26 Novy Arbat, ☎ 095/290–4507), has a small foreign-literature section (inside the doors, immediately to the right), but be sure also to examine the selection outside the front door, where individual sellers spread out their wares. The bookstore on the first floor of the **Kosmos Hotel** (✉ 150 Prospekt Mira) has a good selection of maps, postcards, and English-language guidebooks to Moscow and the surrounding region, and most hotel newsshops carry a smattering of best-sellers and paperback classics.

The English-language newspapers *The Moscow Times* and *The Moscow Tribune* are published daily and carry world and local news. Pick them up in just about any Western store, restaurant, or major hotel.

Guided Tours

Every major hotel maintains a tourist bureau through which individual and group tours to Moscow's main tourist sights can be booked. In addition, there are numerous private agencies that can help with your sightseeing plans.

Apex Travel World (✉ 3 Zubovsky proyezd, ☎ 095/245–5438 or 095/247–0047), can arrange a wide range of tours, as you wish. They will also make hotel, plane, and train reservations for other CIS destinations. Call at least a day in advance to make arrangements.

Intourist (✉ 13 Mokhovaya ul., ☎ 095/292–2260 or 095/925–1300) has a special travel department to provide you with any tour you want in Moscow; they also set up trips elsewhere in the CIS and help with visa support. They work within the system of Intourist offerings, so you'll be staying at their hotels; but because the network of their services is so extensive, you should be able to have whatever excursion you want.

Sputnik (✉ 15 Kosygina ul., ☎ 095/939–8580, FAX 095/956–1067) is a company handling group and individual tours in Moscow and some day trips out of town. They can tailor plans to suit your needs.

You should call around to get competitive rates. They can vary widely, depending on the trip you want, the number of people you have, and your transportation needs.

Hospitals and Clinics

With luck, you won't have to experience the medical system. It is plagued by a lack of medicines, low hygiene standards, and shortages of disposable needles and basic medical equipment. If you are simply feeling under the weather and the situation is not urgent, you may be best off not contacting a doctor at all. If you think you are seriously ill, contact one of several Western establishments that have opened over the last two years, creating a base of clinics used by the foreign community as well as Russians who can afford the higher fees. Most of these clinics are membership organizations, but all will provide service to tourists, though perhaps not with 24-hour access; the cost of individual treatment will be higher than for members, too. Be sure to ask what payment method they accept. Usually it will be rubles, dollars, or a credit card, but it varies by clinic and without exception you will need to settle accounts up front.

In an emergency, you can also contact your country's consular section for help with the logistics of serious medical treatment. For U.S. citizens, contact *American Citizens Services* (☎ 095/956–4232 or 095/956–4295, after-hours emergency, 095/252–1898). Canadian citizens should call the embassy number, where they will be connected to a duty officer. British citizens can call 095/956–7269 or 095/956–7273, for their embassy's clinic, 24 hours.

The American Medical Center (⊠ 10 Vtoroy Tverskoy-Yamskoy pereulok, ☎ 095/956–3366) is a membership group that offers full-range family practice and emergency services, including evacuation assistance. If treatment is needed outside their clinic, they use various hospitals, but primarily Zil. The office is open 24 hours. There is a pharmacy on the premises. A tourist plan is available.

The Columbia-Presbyterian Moscow Clinic (with U.S. Global Health) (⊠ 4 Chetvorty Dobryninsky pereulok, 4th floor, ☎ 095/974–2332) is a membership facility providing comprehensive outpatient care and emergency referrals to the Kuntsevo Hospital (Kremlin VIP), plus help with evacuation. They operate their own pharmacy for their patients. They offer a tourist membership that you can join by calling in the U.S. (☎ 212/479–1950). They will also bill insurance plans directly. ☉ *Weekdays 8–8, Sat. 10–4.*

The European Medical Centre (⊠ 310 Vtoroy Tverskoy-Yamskoy pereulok 10, ☎ 095/251–6099; night emergency ☎ 095/229–6536), is not a membership group and offers a full range of services, including day and night house calls. Hospital referral is usually to the ZKB Presidential Hospital. Both English and French are spoken. The pharmacy is stocked with French medicines.

International Medical Clinic (⊠ 31 Grokholsky pereulok, 10th floor, ☎ 095/280–8388/7177/8374, pharmacy ☎ 095/280–8765) is a nonmember service that gives comprehensive care, hospitalization referral to the Kuntsevo (Kremlin VIP) Hospital, and evacuation via their in-house company (they are part of SOS International). In case overnight observation is necessary, they have on-site accommodations. English, French, and German are spoken. Pharmacy on-site.

Mediclub Moscow (⊠ 56 Michurinsky Prospekt, ☎ 095/931–5018 or 095/932–8653) is a Canadian clinic that provides full medical and ambulance service, hospital referral to Glavmosstroy Hospital, and assistance with evacuation. English and French are spoken. The pharmacy is stocked with Western and Russian medicines. Cash payment only. ☉ *Weekdays 9–6; you may call after hours, but unless you are a member, it is not guaranteed that you will reach a doctor.*

In other cases foreign tourists are usually hospitalized in the **Botkin Hospital** (⊠ 5 Vtoroy Botkinsky proyezd, ☎ 095/945–0033).

There is also a **Crisis Center** hotline in English, operating 24 hours. It is free and confidential, for adults and children. The trained counselors are native English speakers. Call 095/244–3449 and ask for the Crisis Center.

Late-Night Pharmacies

Pharmacies are generally open only until 8 or 9 PM, and though they are becoming well stocked, Western-brand medicines may not be recognizable to you in their Russian packaging. For prescription refills, you'll have the best luck contacting one of the foreign clinics' pharmacies (☞ Emergencies, *above*). You can also try **VITA** (6 Poklonnaya ul., ☎ 095/249–7818) or the more conveniently located **Farmakon** (✉ 2/4 Tverskaya ul., ☎ 095/292–0843), where you can also count on finding toothpaste, Q-tips, shaving cream, and the like, on the second floor.

Travel Agencies

There are many choices. Listed here are some Moscow travel agents, not local tour companies offering excursions. They can provide air (and sometimes train) ticketing for international travel and, as noted, travel to other points within Russia and the CIS.

American Express (✉ 21-A Sadovaya-Kudrinskaya ul., ☎ 095/755–9000/9001, FAX 755–9003/9004; open weekdays 10–1 and 2–5) handles arrangements for domestic and air tickets but not for trains. It will also help with car hire and hotel reservations. It is not necessary to be a member to receive these services. For members, it will replace your lost traveler's checks and credit cards, or issue you a cash advance against your credit card, provided you can write a personal check. The office has an ATM machine for its card holders; there is a 5% commission on its use.

Alpha-Omega Travel (✉ 5 Lubyansky proyezd, 3rd floor, ☎ 095/928–9458/9459 or 095/921–6853) can book air tickets on international charters and on Transaero and Aeroflot in the CIS. Credit cards are accepted. They deliver tickets, for which service there is a fee.

Apex Travel World (✉ 3 Zubovsky proyezd, ☎ 095/245–5438 or 095/247–0047), though primarily a tour agency, may be able to arrange train ticketing in the CIS to points out of Moscow. American Express refers its customers to them for this service.

Intourist (✉ 13 Mokhovaya ul., ☎ 095/292–2260 or 095/925–1300) runs a special travel department. They can help with domestic and international air and train tickets, accommodations throughout the CIS as well as in Moscow, and visa support.

Sac-Voyage (✉ 18 Olympiysky Prospekt, 3rd floor, ☎ 095/281–6215, FAX 095/288–9174) provides a full range of services, including airline bookings, hotel reservations, and visa support.

SVO Travel (✉ 15 Novy Arbat, ☎ 095/202–6409 or 095/202–1328) is a Canadian agency that handles ticketing on international flights. For CIS cities, it can book on Transaero, but it does not handle any Aeroflot ticketing. No trains. Free ticket delivery.

Time Travel Limited (✉ Radisson Slavyanskaya Hotel, 2 Berezhkovsky nab., ☎ 095/941–8665, FAX 095/941–8730) can arrange domestic and international tickets for both air and train travel. They'll also prepare excursion packages and make hotel reservations.

Tour Service International (✉ 5 Yana Raynisa bulvar, ☎ 095/493–2330, FAX 095/493–2330) is a service for those wanting to go from Moscow to the Ukraine. It offers visa support, including courier service (for which there is a fee) for its application, and hotel bookings. This may be your most expeditious route if you decide to visit Kiev only after you have arrived in Moscow.

For international plane tickets, you may also call the airlines directly. Ask them where you can pick up your tickets in Moscow.

Visitor Information

Moscow does not have a tourist information center *per se,* but the service bureaus of all the major hotels offer their guests (and anyone else willing to pay their fees) a wide variety of tourist services, including help in booking group or individual excursions, making a restaurant reservation, or purchasing theater or ballet tickets. You may also find help (as the hotels themselves often do) from the Intourist Service, today's reincarnation of the old Soviet tourist service (☞ Travel Agencies, *above*) or from some of the tour agencies (☞ Guided Tours, *above*). For the latest on what's happening in Moscow, check the listings in either of the two leading English-language newspapers—*The Moscow Times* or *The Moscow Tribune.* On Thursdays, the Russian newpaper *Moscow News* publishes an English-language translation of its paper, which includes a round-up of current cultural events.

Where to Change Money

All the major hotels have exchange bureaus where you can change your dollars for rubles. You can also use the Russian banks. In addition, you will find exchange bureaus all over the city, bearing the OBMEN VALUTY/EXCHANGE sign. They should have their daily rates posted in easy view. Exercise reasonable caution when using them, and don't be surprised to find a security guard, who may let only one or two people inside at a time. By law it's required that you be issued a receipt, but you may find this erratic in practice; be sure to ask for one. You can exchange traveler's checks for rubles or dollars at any of the private banks. Try the **Dialog Bank** offices in the Radisson Slavyanskaya Hotel (✉ 2 Berezhkovskaya nab., first floor, ☎ 095/941–8434) and in the Baltschug Kempinski (✉ 1 Balchug ul., first floor, ☎ 095/941–8020), or the **MOST Bank** office next door to the National Hotel on Tverskaya ulitsa. The **American Express Office** (☞ Travel Agencies, *above*) will cash American Express traveler's checks for rubles and, if it has cash available, for dollars. You can also obtain dollars by writing the office a personal check and having the exchange charged to your American Express card.

3 St. Petersburg

A powerful combination of East and West, of things Russian and European, St. Petersburg is a city born of the passion of its founder, Czar Peter the Great, to bring an unwilling Russian nation into the fold of Europe and into the mainstream of history.

By Lauri del Commune

Updated by Natalia Tolstaya

BORN IN THE HEART OF AN EMPEROR, St. Petersburg is Russia's adopted child. So unlike the Russian cities that came before it—with its strict geometric lines and perfectly planned architecture—St. Petersburg is in many ways too European to be Russian. And yet it is too Russian to be European. A powerful combination of both East and West, of things Russian and things European, St. Petersburg is, more than anything, a city born of the passion of its founder, Czar Peter the Great, to bring an unwilling Russian nation into the fold of Europe and into the mainstream of history.

It was less than 300 years ago when the grand, new capital of the budding Russian empire was built to face Europe, with its back to reactionary Moscow. Unlike some cities, it was not created by a process of gradual, graceful development but was forcibly constructed, stone by stone, under the force and direction of Peter the Great, for whose patron saint the city is named.

But if Peter's exacting plans called for his capital to be the equal of European ones, they always took into account the city's unique attributes. Peter knew that his city's source of life was water, and whether building palace, fortress, or trading post, he never failed to make his creations serve it. With most of the city nearly at sea level (there is a constant threat of flooding), it seems to rise from the sea itself. Half of the River Neva lies within the city's boundaries. When, outward bound, it reaches the Gulf of Finland, it subdivides into the Great and Little Neva and the Great and Little Nevka. Together with numerous affluents, they combine to form an intricate delta.

Water weaves its way through the city's streets as well. Covering more than 100 islands and crisscrossed by more than 60 rivers and canals, St. Petersburg can be compared to that other great maritime city, Venice, but the Russian one has a uniquely northern appeal. Even during economic hardship and political crisis, its imperial palaces sparkling on the embankments maintain the city's regal bearing, especially in the cold light of the Russian winter. In the long days of summer, the colorful facades of its riverside estates glow gently, in harmony with the dark blue of the Neva's waters. Between June and July, when the city falls under the spell of the White Nights, the fleeting twilight imbues the streets and canals with an even more delicate charm.

St. Petersburg is not just about its fairy-tale setting, however, for its history is integrally bound up in Russia's dark side too, its centuries-long procession of wars and revolutions. In the 19th century, the city witnessed the struggle against czarist oppression. Here the early fires of revolution were kindled, first in 1825 by a small band of starry-eyed aristocratic officers, the so-called Decembrists, and then by organized workers' movements in 1905. The full-scale revolutions of 1917 led to the demise of the Romanov dynasty, the foundation of the Soviet Union, and the end of the city's role as the nation's capital. But the worst ordeal by far came during World War II, when the city—then known as Leningrad—withstood a 900-day siege and blockade by Nazi forces. Nearly 650,000 people died of starvation, and more than 17,000 were killed in air raids and by indiscriminate shelling.

St. Petersburg has had its name changed three times during its brief history. With the outbreak of World War I, it became the more Russian-sounding Petrograd. After Lenin's death in 1924, it was renamed Leningrad in the Soviet leader's honor. Today, with the latest Russian revolution, its original name has been restored. A sign of the changing times is that—for the first time—the city's residents were given a choice in the matter. Many people opposed the change, primarily because memories of the siege of Leningrad and World War II had become an indelible part of the city's identity. But for all the controversy surrounding its name, many residents refer to the city simply—and affectionately—as Peter.

Pleasures and Pastimes

Dining

Dining out in St. Petersburg is an experience all visitors must have. For years the dining scene was limited for such a large, cosmopolitan city, but this is rapidly changing as a slew of top-grade, privately owned restaurants and cafés take over from their jaded state-run predecessors. Western-style bar food, such as hamburgers and pizza, are available from fast-food joints all over the city, and those in search of traditional Russian cuisine will have a wide selection to choose from. The main meal of the day is served in mid-afternoon and consists of a starter, soup, and a main course. Russian soups are excellent, including *borshch* (beet soup), *shchi* (cabbage soup), and *solyanka,* a spicy, thick stew made with vegetables and meat or fish. Delicious and filling main courses include Siberian *pelmeni* (tender meat dumplings) or beefsteak in mushroom sour-cream sauce. If you are looking for Russian delicacies, try the excellent smoked salmon, blini with caviar, or the famous Kiev cutlet, a butter-filled chicken breast covered with dried crust. Order a shot of vodka or a bottle of Georgian wine to accompany your meal. Daytime reservations are not usually necessary, but you must plan ahead for an evening meal, as restaurants are usually always full. Ask your hotel or tour guide for help and bear in mind that eating out in St. Petersburg is often an all-night affair, with a lot of drinking and dancing.

Farmers' Markets

The city's farmers' markets are a true St. Petersburg experience that should not be missed. Inside these large covered halls you'll find rows of stalls packed with dairy produce, honey, flowers, fine cuts of fresh and cured meats and fish, and fresh fruit and vegetables. Pickled goods are popular in St. Petersburg, and you will most likely be invited to taste the cabbage and salted cucumbers. Remember that you are expected to haggle.

Palaces

Many magnificent imperial residences and palaces were built in the city in the mid-18th century. Outstanding examples of Russian Baroque are the Winter Palace and the Stroganov Palace, both created by the Italian architect Rastrelli. The Classical style, which supplanted the Baroque as the favored style of the city's greatest architects, is also well represented, with such exceptional mansions as the Mikhailovsky Palace and the Taurida Palace (Tavrichesky Dvorets). Two suburban palaces, the Catherine Palace in Pushkin and the Great Palace in Petrodvorets, were the summer residences of the imperial family from the days of Peter the Great, but lay in ruins after the 900-day siege of Leningrad. Museum workers had managed to evacuate much of the art housed in the suburban palaces before the German occupation. These magnificent palaces have been restored, so you can now see them in their former splendor.

Performing Arts

St. Petersburg's reputation as Russia's cultural capital is well deserved. The city is home to countless museums, art galleries, scientific institutions, libraries, archives, and historic buildings. Its rich musical heritage is on show all over the city, with concerts, recitals, and a multitude of other musical programs given daily; the last two weeks in June are particularly rich, as the city hosts an international festival of culture. The famous Shostakovich Philharmonic, housed in a magnificent hall of the former Nobleman's Club, has superb acoustics and a history of collaborating with some of Russia's finest composers, including Anton Rubinstein and Tchaikovsky. But it is ballet that the city is most famous for: The Mariinsky Theater (formerly the Kirov) has produced some of the world's greatest dancers, among them Pavlova, Nijinski, Nureyev, and Barishnikov, all of whom are synonymous with ballet excellence. A night at the Mariinsky Theater or the Mussorgsky Theater of Ballet and Opera (formerly the Maly Theater) is sure to be one of the highlights of your stay.

EXPLORING ST. PETERSBURG

Commissioned by Peter the Great as "a window looking into Europe," St. Petersburg is a planned city whose elegance is reminiscent of Europe's most alluring capitals. Built on more than a hundred islands in the Neva Delta linked by canals and arched bridges, it is often called the "northern Venice," and its elegant embankments are reminiscent of those of Paris. The city's focal point is the Admiralty; its most-visited attraction, a stone's throw away, the Winter Palace. Three major avenues radiate outward from the Admiralty: Nevsky Prospect (St. Petersburg's main shopping street), Gorokhovaya Ulitsa, and Voznesensky Prospect. You will find neither ancient ruins nor exotic architecture in St. Petersburg, but your visit will be an unforgettable experience.

Great Itineraries

IF YOU HAVE 3 DAYS

If you have only 3 days, begin your visit of the city on **Vasilievsky Island** and the left bank. You will find most of the historical sights on the eastern edge of the island: the **Rostral Columns,** the old **Stock Exchange,** and the **Kunstkammer.** On the left bank of the Neva is **Decembrists' Square,** site of the **Bronze Horseman,** the **Admiralty,** and **St. Isaac's Cathedral.** After lunch is the right time to tackle the gargantuan **Hermitage,** one of the world's richest repositories of art. Spend the rest of the afternoon wandering through its vast galleries; you will leave feeling that your visit was incomplete, but remember that it would take at least a year to visit the museum properly! Devote the morning of your second day to visiting the **Peter and Paul Fortress** and the Petrograd Side. The main attraction of the Fortress is the Cathedral of Sts. Peter and Paul, which served as the imperial burial grounds. Near the Fortress you'll find **Peter the Great's Cottage.** Not far away the cruiser **Avrora** lies at anchor. Spend the afternoon in the **Russian Museum,** one of the country's most important art galleries with more than 300,000 works of art. On your third day, we recommend that you make an excursion to **Pushkin** (former Tsarskoye Selo), 24 kilometers (15 miles) south of St. Petersburg. Tsarskoye Selo was the summer residence of the imperial family and a popular summer resort for the Russian aristocracy. The main attraction here is the **Catherine Palace,** with its magnificent treasures and the surrounding park filled with waterfalls, boating ponds, and marble statues. Should you choose to spend the whole day here, you can have lunch and then visit the **Lyceum,** formerly a school for the Russian nobility. The most famous graduate of this school—now a museum—was Alexander Pushkin, Russia's greatest poet.

Follow the three-day itinerary described above. Devote your fourth day to St. Petersburg's inner streets, squares, and gardens. Start at the Square of the Arts. Here you can visit the **Ethnography Museum** and its unique collection of applied art, national costumes, and weapons of the various ethnic groups of the former Soviet Union. When you leave the museum, walk to the colorful **Khram Spasa na Krovi** (Church of the Saviour on the Spilled Blood). Your next stop is the **Marsovo Pole** (Field of Mars), used primarily for military exercises. After the February and October revolutions of 1917 it was turned into a burial ground for 180 people who had perished in the armed struggle against the aristocracy. Finish your walk at the **Letny Sad** (Summer Garden) with its famous railing designed by Yuri Felten in 1779. After lunch, visit the **Kazan Cathedral.** Czar Paul I commissioned this copy of St. Peter's in Rome after a visit to the Eternal City. On the fifth day, you should visit Peterhof (Petrodvorets), accessible by hydrofoil. The best time to visit is in summer, when the fountains adorned by 144 gilt statues, monumental cascades, lush parks, and the magnificent Great Palace are at their best. Devote the morning of your sixth day to a visit of the **Pushkin Apartment Museum,** where the beloved poet died. After lunch, visit the **Menshikov Palace,** the first stone building in St. Petersburg. Devote your seventh day to an excursion to **Pavlovsk,** only 5 kilometers (3 miles) from the Catherine Palace in Pushkin and 32 kilometers (20 miles) south of St. Petersburg. See the **Great Palace** with its splendid interiors featuring gilt ceilings and marble pillars. Enjoy the famous park with its numerous pavilions, waterways, and statues. After lunch, visit the **Zoology Museum,** one of the largest of its kind in the world.

Follow the itineraries described above, and on your eighth day, travel 40 kilometers (26 miles) west of St. Petersburg to reach the town of **Lomonosov.** This luxurious summer residence is the only one to have survived World War II intact. With its seaside location and splendid park it is an ideal place to spend a summer's day. On your ninth day, you may want to visit the **Yusupovsky Palace**—formerly the home of Russia's wealthiest family and now a museum with a concert hall and a theater—on the banks of the Moika River. It was in this beautiful pre-revolutionary mansion that the "mad monk," Rasputin, was killed. Devote your last day in St. Petersburg to the **Piskaryevskoye Cemetery,** a mass burial ground for more than half a million victims of the 900-day siege of Leningrad during World War II. Visit the museum and its collection of memoirs and photographs documenting that terrible time. It is perhaps fitting that you should finish your visit to this extraordinary city here, a place where memories of the past have become an indelible part of the city's identity.

Palace Square, the Winter Palace, and the Hermitage Museum

The place where you must begin to get to know St. Petersburg is the elegant Dvortsovaya Ploshchad or Palace Square. In its scale alone, it can hardly fail to impress. But there can be no better reason for coming to St. Petersburg than to visit the Hermitage. Renowned as one of the world's leading picture galleries, it is also a treasure house of ancient cultures. In addition, the Hermitage is an extension of the Winter Palace, the former residence of the Russian imperial family, and provides a setting of unparalleled opulence for its various dazzling collections.

Numbers in the text correspond to numbers in the margin and on the St. Petersburg map.

A Good Walk

Begin at **Dvortsovaya Ploshchad** ①. Extending the length of the western side of the square, with its back to the river, is the **Zimny Dvorets** (Winter Palace), part of which is the **Ermitazh** ② art gallery. In the center of the square is the **Alexander Column,** which commemorates the Russian victory over Napoléon in 1812. Dominating the eastern side is the **Glavny Shtab,** formerly the army's general staff headquarters. No matter what your plans while in St. Petersburg, make sure you set aside at least half a day for a visit to the Hermitage.

TIMING

With more than 400 exhibit halls, the Hermitage cannot possibly be seen in a single day. It has been estimated that in order to spend one minute on each object on display, a visitor would have to devote an entire year to the museum. Official guided tours tend to be rushed, and you will probably want to return on your own. If you have limited time, concentrate on the Antiquities and Italian Art rooms, which will take at least a couple of hours to view properly. Devote another couple of hours to the extraordinary collection of Impressionist and Post-Impressionist art on the third floor. There is much to keep you here in addition to the overwhelming collections, including a number of bars and restaurants. It is best to begin your tour around 11:30 AM, when the early-morning crowds have dispersed. During peak tourist season, or when there is a special exhibition, you may encounter long lines at the museum entrance. Don't forget your umbrella, no matter what the time of year or what the weather forecast. It rains at some point almost every day in St. Petersburg, and you don't need to get off to a wet start. Note that the Hermitage is closed on Mondays.

Sights to See

Aleksandrovskaya Kolonna (Alexander Column). The centerpiece of Palace Square is a memorial to Russia's victory over Napoléon. Measuring 47.25 meters (155.8 feet) from the pedestal to the top, the Alexander Column was commissioned in 1830 by Nicholas I in memory of his brother, Czar Alexander I, and was designed by August Ricard de Montferrand. The column was cut from a single piece of granite and, together with its pedestal, weighs more than 650 tons. It stands in place by the sheer force of its own weight; there are no attachments fixing it to the pedestal. When it was erected in 1832, the entire operation took only an hour and 45 minutes, but 2,000 soldiers and 400 workmen were required, using an elaborate system of pulleys and ropes. It is crowned by an angel (symbolizing peace in Europe) crushing a snake, an allegorical depiction of Russia's defeat of Napoléon.

★ ♻ ❶ **Dvortsovaya Ploshchad** (Palace Square). One of the world's most magnificent plazas, the square is a stunning ensemble of buildings and open space that manages to combine several seemingly incongruous architectural styles in perfect harmony. It is where the city's imperial past has been preserved in all its glorious splendor, but it is also resonant with the revolutionary history that followed. It was here, on Bloody Sunday in 1905, that the fate of the last Russian czar was effectively sealed after palace troops opened fire on peaceful demonstrators, killing scores of women and children. It was across Palace Square that the Bolshevik revolutionaries stormed the Winter Palace in their successful attempt to overthrow Kerensky's provisional government in October 1917, an event that led to the birth of the Soviet Union. Almost 75 years later, it was also on Palace Square that during tense days, citizens held all-night vigils to demonstrate their support for perestroika and democracy. Beautiful Palace Square is today a bustling hubbub of tourist and marketing activity, lively yet seemingly imperturbable as ever. Children will enjoy the horseback and carriage rides for hire.

★ ❷ **Ermitazh** (Hermitage Museum). The museum extends through the lavish Winter Palace as well as the various buildings later annexed to it to house the private art galleries of the czars. The museum gets its name from Catherine the Great, who used it for her private apartments, meaning them to be a place for retreat and seclusion. Between 1764 and 1775, the empress undertook, in competition with rulers whose storehouses of art greatly surpassed Russia's, to acquire some of the world's finest works of art. In doing so, sometimes acquiring entire private collections outright, she quickly filled her gallery with masterpieces from all over the world. This section of the Hermitage Museum is now known as the Maly (Little) Hermitage. It is attached to the Stari (Old) Hermitage, which was built in 1783 to house the overflow of art and also contained conference chambers for the czar's ministers. Attached to the Hermitage by an arch straddling the Winter Canal is the **Hermitage Theater** (1783–87), created for Catherine the Great by the Italian architect Giacomo Quarenghi. Yet another addition, the New Hermitage, was added between 1839 and 1852; it became Russia's first public museum, although admission was by royal invitation only. Its facade is particularly striking, with ten atlantes supporting the portico.

Today's Hermitage Museum is one of the world's richest repositories of art, continuously enlarged with czarist treasures and acquisitions, all later confiscated and nationalized, along with numerous private collections, by the Soviet government after the 1917 Bolshevik Revolution.

The entrance to the museum is on the side of the Winter Palace that faces the Neva River, not the one facing Palace Square. When you first enter the Hermitage, the *kassa* (ticket window) is ahead of you, slightly to the left. Once you have your tickets, you can check your things and then return to enter the hall that was to your left as you came in. Be forewarned that the ticket takers are strict about oversize bags and about foreigners trying to enter on Russian-rate tickets.

Through this hall you reach the second-floor galleries by way of the **Jordan Staircase,** a dazzling creation of marble, granite, and gold. The staircase was once used by the imperial family in processions down to the Neva River for christenings.

Although the museum is divided into eight sections, they are not clearly marked, and the floor plans available are not terribly useful, though they are in English as well as Russian. All of this makes it easy to get lost in the mazelike complex of the Hermitage, but do not despair. Enjoy your wander, and don't be shy about asking the special assistants placed throughout the museum to point you in the right direction.

There are three floors in the museum. In brief, the **ground floor** covers prehistoric times, showing discoveries made on former Soviet territory, including Scythian relics and artifacts; art from the Asian republics, the Caucasus, and their peoples; and Greek, Roman, and Egyptian art and antiquities.

On the **second floor** you will find many rooms that were part of the former Winter Palace. One of the first ones you pass through is the **Malachite Room,** with its displays of personal items of the imperial family. In the White Dining Room the Bolsheviks seized power from the Provisional Government in 1917. Balls were held in the small Concert Hall (which now also holds the silver coffin of the hero Alexander Nevsky) and, on grand occasions, in the Great Hall.

114

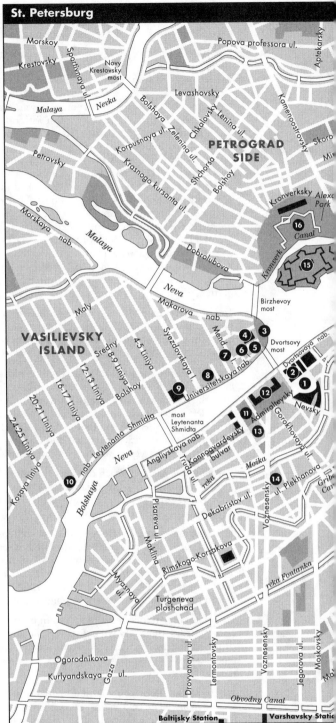
St. Petersburg

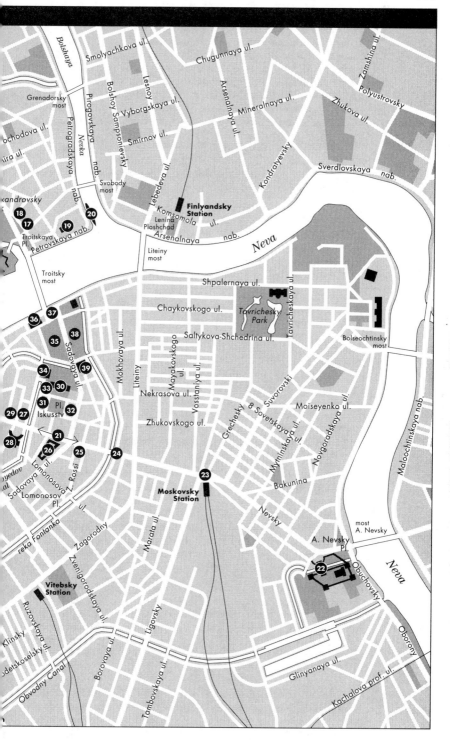

A wealth of Russian and European art is also on this floor: Florentine, Venetian, and other Italian art through the 18th century, including Leonardo's *Benois Madonna* and *Madonna Litta* (Room 214); Michelangelo's *Crouching Boy* (Room 229); two Raphaels; eight Titians; and works by Tintoretto, Lippi, Caravaggio, and Canaletto. The Hermitage also boasts a superb collection of Spanish art, of which works by El Greco, Velázquez, Murillo, and Goya are on display. Its spectacular presentation of Flemish and Dutch art includes roomfuls of Van Dycks, including portraits done in England when he was court painter to Charles I; the Hermitage has more than 40 canvases by Rubens (Room 247) and 25 Rembrandts, including *Flora, Abraham's Sacrifice,* and *The Prodigal Son* (Room 254). There is a smattering of excellent British painting, extending also to the next floor, with paintings by Joshua Reynolds, Thomas Gainsborough, and George Morland.

It is in its collection of French art, beginning on the second floor and occupying most of the third, that the Hermitage is truly extraordinary, however. The museum is second only to the Louvre in the scope of its French offerings. On this floor you will find early French art and handicrafts, including tapestries, as well as works by Lorrain, Watteau, and Poussin, including his *Tancrède et Herminie* (Room 279).

Proceeding to the **third floor,** you can start with the art of the 19th century, where you will find Delacroix, Ingres, Corot, and Courbet. You then come to a stunning array of Impressionists and Post-Impressionists, including Monet's deeply affecting *A Lady in the Garden,* Sisley, Pissarro, Renoir, and Degas' *Woman at Her Toilette* and *After the Bath.* Sculptures by Auguste Rodin and a host of pictures by Cézanne, Gauguin, and Van Gogh are followed by Picasso and a lovely room of Matisse, including one of the amazing *Joys.* Somewhat later paintings—by the Fauvist André Derain and by Cubist Fernand Léger, for example—are also here. Rounding out this floor, if your senses can absorb any more, is the museum's collection of Oriental and Middle and Near Eastern art; its (small) American collection; and two halls of medals and coins.

Possibly the most prized section of the Hermitage—and definitely the most difficult to get into—is the **Osobaya Kladovaya** (Special Collection), sometimes referred to as the Zolotaya Kladovaya (Gold Room). This spectacular collection of gold, silver, and royal jewels is well worth the hassle and expense of admission. Entry is restricted to groups of 17, which must book in advance. The easiest way to join one of these groups is through your hotel's tourist bureau, which may be able to attach you to a prebooked tour.

The collection is divided into two sections. The first section, covering prehistoric times, includes gold and silver treasures recovered from the Crimea, Ukraine, and Caucasus. The second is a dizzying display of precious stones, jewelry, and such extravagances as jewel-encrusted pillboxes, miniature clocks, and cigarette cases, from the 16th through the 20th centuries. ⊠ *36 Dvortsovaya Naberezhnaya,* ☎ *812/311–3420.* ☉ *Tues.–Sun. 10:30–6.*

NEED A BREAK?   The **Literary Café** (⊠ 18 Nevsky Prospect, ☎ 812/312-6057) is a short walk from the Hermitage Museum. The menu offers classic Russian fare, with service to match, alas, but the café stands out for its pleasant atmosphere and 19th-century decor; live chamber music further adds to the Old World atmosphere. There is also a small charge to enter, ostensibly for the musicians, but it probably subsidizes the upkeep of the elegant atmosphere. In 1837 the beloved Russian poet Alexander Pushkin was served his last meal here before setting off for his fatal duel. To reach the café, walk across Palace Square, through the arch of the General Staff Building, and then take a left onto Nevsky Prospect. It is open daily from 10 AM to 2 AM.

Glavny Shtab (General Staff Building). The eastern side of Palace Square is formed by the huge arc of this building whose form and size give Palace Square its unusual shape. During czarist rule the army headquarters and the ministries of foreign affairs and finance were here. Created by the architect Carlo Giovanni Rossi in the neoclassical style and built between 1819 and 1829, the General Staff Building is actually two structures connected by a monumental archway. Together they form the longest building in Europe. The arch itself is another commemoration of Russia's victory over Napoléon. Atop it is an impressive bronze 10 meters (33 feet) tall of Victory driving a six-horse chariot, created by the artists Vasily Demut-Malinovsky and Stepan Pimenov. The passageway created by the arch leads from Palace Square to St. Petersburg's most important boulevard, Nevsky Prospect.

Shtab Gvardeiskovo Korpusa (Headquarters of the Guard Corps). Just to the left, this structure serves as an architectural buffer between the neoclassical General Staff Building and the Baroque Winter Palace. Designed by the architect Alexander Bryullov and built between 1837 and 1843, this modest building is noteworthy for the very fact that it easily goes unnoticed. Instead of drawing attention to itself, it leads the eye to the other architectural masterpieces bordering Palace Square. Bryullov's creation was considered the ultimate architectural tribute. In his restraint he deferred to the masters who came before him; instead of disturbing the beauty they created, Bryullov used his talent to enhance it.

Zimny Dvorets (Winter Palace). This magnificent palace, the residence of Russia's rulers from Catherine the Great (1762) to Nicholas II (1917), is the focal point of Palace Square. It is built in the ornate style of Russian Baroque, adorned with rows of columns and outfitted with 2,000 heavily decorated windows. The roof balustrade is topped with statues and vases. Created by the Italian architect Bartolomeo Francesco Rastrelli, the Winter Palace stretches from Palace Square to the Neva River embankment. It was the fourth royal residence on this site, the first having been a wooden palace for Peter the Great. Oddly enough, the all-powerful czar had to observe some bureaucratic fine print himself. Since it was forbidden to grant land from this site to anyone not bearing naval rank, Peter had to obtain a shipbuilder's license before building his palace. The present palace was commissioned in 1754 by Peter's daughter Elizabeth. By the time it was completed, in 1762, Elizabeth was no longer empress and the craze for the Russian Baroque style had waned. Catherine the Great (ruled 1762—96) left the exterior unaltered but had the interiors redesigned in the neoclassical style of her day. In 1837 these were revamped once again after the palace was gutted by fire. The Winter Palace contains more than 1,000 rooms and halls, three of the most celebrated of which are the **Gallery of the 1812 War,** where portraits of Russian commanders who served against Napoléon are on display; the **Great Throne Room,** richly decorated in marble and bronze; and the **Malachite Hall,** designed by the architect Alexander Bryullov and decorated with malachite columns and pilasters. Today the only parts of the Winter Palace on view to the public are those that form a part of the Hermitage Museum. When touring the museum, you must therefore think of portions of it as the imperial residence it once was.

Vasilievsky Island and the Left Bank

Vasilievsky Ostrov, the largest island in the Neva Delta, is one of the city's oldest developed sections and is where Peter the Great wanted his city's center. His original plans for the island called for a network of canals for the transport of goods from the main sea terminal to the city's commercial center at the opposite end of the island. These plans to re-create Venice never materialized, although some of the smaller canals were actually dug (and later filled in). These would-be canals are now streets, and are called "lines" (*liniya*). Instead of names, they bear numbers, and they run parallel to the island's three main thoroughfares: the Great, Middle, and Small Avenues (Prospects). Now the island is a popular residential area, with most of its historical sites concentrated on its eastern edge. The island's western tip, facing the Gulf of Finland, houses the city's main sea terminals. Also on the island are the city's most renowned academic institutions, including the St. Petersburg branch of the Academy of Sciences, St. Petersburg University, the Repin Art Institute (formerly St. Petersburg Academy of Arts), and the city's oldest institution of higher learning, the St. Petersburg Institute of Mining Technology.

A Good Walk

Begin your tour of Vasilievsky Island at its easternmost tip, which is known colloquially as the **Strelka** ③. It is most easily reached by crossing the Dvortsovy most (Palace Bridge), the one in front of the Hermitage, or by taking Trolley 1 or 7 from any stop on Nevsky Prospect. As you stand in Birzhevaya Square, as the park on the Strelka is called, you will be between two thick, brick-red columns, known as the **Rostralnyie Kolonny.** The columns frame the most significant architectural sight on this side of the river, the **Stock Exchange** ④. Flanking the Stock Exchange are the almost identical Dokuchayev Soil Museum and, to the south, the **Zoologichesky Musey** ⑤. Farther along the embankment, just past the Soil Museum, is the former **Customs House,** also known as the Pushkin House.

Returning to the Stock Exchange, continue along the Universitetskaya naberezhnaya (University Embankment), which leads away from the Strelka (the Neva will be to your left). The next building you encounter is the **Kunstkammer** ⑥. Continue along the embankment, crossing Mendeleyevskaya liniya and passing an imposing statue of the 18th-century Russian scientist Mikhail Lomonosov. You soon come to the main campus of **St. Petersburg University** ⑦. Farther up the embankment, at the corner of Syezdovskaya liniya, stands one of St. Petersburg's grandest—and oldest—buildings, the **Menshikovsky Dvorets** ⑧. As you leave Menshikov Palace, crossing Syezdovskaya liniya, you come upon **Rumantsev Square** to your right. Another notable building farther up the embankment is the **Repin Institute of Painting, Sculpture, and Architecture** ⑨. On the landing in front of the Institute are the **Egyptian Sphinxes,** among the city's most memorable landmarks. If you have time, you should visit one last famous building on Vasilievsky Island. If you go to the end of the embankment, at the corner of 21 liniya, you find the **Gorny Institut** ⑩. It can be reached either by walking or by taking any of the trams that stop at the corner of 11 liniya and the embankment.

At this point you conclude your tour of Vasilievsky Island by crossing the bridge called **most Leytenanta Shmidta,** which will take you back across the Neva and toward the city center. Once across, you may tour the **Anglijskaya naberezhnaya,** the left bank of the Neva. Continue down the embankment with the Neva on your left. You pass the former **Senate and Synod.** Across the street from it, if you continue going straight, is **Dekabristov Ploshchad** ⑪, a large open square on your right. The golden yellow building on the other side is the **Admiralty** ⑫.

Proceed through the park in front of the Admiralty and you will come out on Admiralteysky Prospect, the eponymous avenue running parallel to it. Ahead of you is the back of massive **Isaakievsky Sobor** ⑬. Its entrance is on the other side, so go right on the prospect a bit to take a left and go around the cathedral's side. Where the prospect meets Konnogvardysky bulvar is the gracefully designed Manège. On the opposite side of the square, directly across from, is the **Mariinsky Dvorets** ⑭. To the left, past the Nicholas Statue and in front of the palace, is the short **Siniy most.** Passing over the Moika via the Blue Bridge, you will spot a stone column. Its marks show the different water levels of the many floods that have plagued the city over the years. Turn to the right and continue down the Moika embankment. The elegant yellow building is the **Yusupovsky Dvorets.** You can end your tour here, perhaps choosing to return to the Astoria for coffee or a snack. If you prefer to end up on Nevsky Prospect, follow the Moika embankment a few blocks down to where they intersect. Going this way, shortly before you reach Nevsky, on the right-hand side behind a tall fence, is the **Pedagogical Institute.** If you have time, **St. Nicholas Cathedral** is also worth a visit.

TIMING

This is a long walk, divided into two sections, though there is (literally) a bridge between them. If you have the time and want to linger in each place, you may choose to do them as two excursions. If not, do plan a lunch break midway. Note: an umbrella might come in handy. In winter be prepared for rather cold days that often alternate with warmer temperatures bringing heavy snowfalls.

Sights to See

⑫ **Admiralty.** You should walk around to the front of this lovely golden-yellow building by crossing the square diagonally. The Admiralty is considered the city's architectural center, and its flashing spire—visible at various points throughout the city—is one of St. Petersburg's most renowned emblems.

A series of important constructions, all related to the naval industry, predate the present building. The first was a shipyard of Peter's, followed by an earthen fortress that guarded the port; after these came the first Admiralty, made of stone and topped by the famous spire that has endured to grace each successive structure.

The current building was designed by Andrei Zakharov and was built between 1806 and 1823, after it was decided that the city required a much grander Admiralty to match its more impressive buildings. It is adorned with classical sculptures glorifying Russia's naval prowess, including a frieze of Neptune handing over his trident to Peter. Used as a shipbuilding center through the 1840s, it has belonged to the Higher Naval Academy since 1925 and is not open to the public.

An Admiralty Lawn once adorned its front expanse, but in Alexander's time it was turned into a small park bearing his name (to which it has been returned, after having been named for Maxim Gorky under the communists). As you walk through it, you'll see various statues, mostly of artists such as the composer Mikhail Glinka and the writer Mikhail Lermontov; the one accompanied by the delightful camel is of Nikolai Przhevalsky, a 19th-century explorer of Central Asia.

Anglijskaya naberezhnaya (English Embankment). Before the 1917 Revolution this was the center of the city's English community. Here one can find some of St. Petersburg's finest aristocratic estates. For instance, as you take a left off the bridge and follow the embankment, you come to No. 28, formerly the mansion of Grand Duke Andrei Vladimirovich Romanov. Today it is a so-called Wedding Palace, the only place under communism where marriages could be performed; the state-run, secular ceremonies, still the usual type held here, are perfunctorily recited with assembly-line efficiency.

Customs House. Constructed in the 19th century in the same style as the warehouses, it is known as the **Pushkin House** and maintained by the Academy of Sciences' Institute of Russian Literature. It holds a special place in the hearts of the Russian people. Here valuable manuscripts and original works by some of Russia's most beloved authors are stored in special archives, including effects of such Russian literary giants as Gogol and Tolstoy. ⊠ *4 nab. Makarova,* ☎ *812/218–0502.* ⊙ *Weekdays 11–5.*

⑪ Dekabristov Ploshchad (Decembrists' Square). First called Senatskaya Ploshchad (Senate Square), the square was renamed earlier this century. Officially it has returned to its original name, but it's hardly ever used. It holds one of St. Petersburg's best-known landmarks, the *Medny Vsadnik* (Bronze Horseman). The square took its new name from the dramatic events that unfolded there on December 14, 1825, when, following the death of Czar Alexander I, a group of aristocrats tried to stage a rebellion on the square in an attempt to prevent the crowning of Nicholas I as the new czar, and perhaps do away with the monarchy altogether. Their coup failed miserably, as it was bloodily suppressed by troops already loyal to Nicholas, and those rebels who were not executed were banished to Siberia. Although the Decembrists, as they came to be known, did not bring significant change to Russia in their time, their attempts at liberal reform were often cited by the Soviet regime as proof of deep-rooted revolutionary fervor in Russian society. In 1925 the square was renamed in their honor.

In the center is the grand statue called the *Bronze Horseman,* erected as a memorial from Catherine the Great to her predecessor, Peter the Great. (The simple inscription on the base reads, "To Peter the First from Catherine the Second, 1782.") Created by the French sculptor Etienne Falconet and his student Marie Collot, the statue depicts the powerful Peter, crowned with a laurel wreath, astride a rearing horse that symbolizes Russia, trampling a serpent representing the forces of evil. The enormous granite rock on which the statue is balanced comes from the Gulf of Finland. Reportedly, Peter liked to stand on it to survey his city from afar. Moving it was a herculean effort, requiring a special barge and machines and nearly a year's work. The statue was immortalized in a poem of the same name by Alexander Pushkin, who wrote that the czar "by whose fateful will the city was founded beside the sea, stands here aloft at the very brink of a precipice, having reared up Russia with his iron curb."

⑩ Gorny Institut (Mining Institute). Founded in 1773 by Catherine the Great, this is St. Petersburg's oldest technical institution of higher learning and well worth the visit if you have time. The present building in the neoclassical style was built between 1806 and 1811 by Andrei Voronikhin, architect of the Kazan Cathedral on Nevsky Prospect. The main entrance is supported by 12 Doric columns and is lined with statues designed by Demut-Malinovsky and Pimenov (creators of the bronze sculpture above the General Staff Building). The institute boasts an unusual museum of precious stones and minerals, including a piece of malachite weighing over a ton and an iron meteorite. ⊠ *21 liniya,* ☎ *812/213–7832 or 812/218–8429.* ⊙ *Weekdays. Pre-arranged visits only.*

In case you want to
be welcomed there.

We're here to see that you're always welcomed at establishments everywhere. That's why millions of people carry the American Express® Card—for peace of mind, confidence, and security, around the world or just around the corner.

do more®

In case you're running low.

We're here to help with more than 118,000 Express Cash locations around the world. In order to enroll, just call American Express before you start your vacation.

do more

AMERICAN
EXPRESS

Express
Cash

★ ⑬ **Isaakievsky Sobor** (St. Isaac's Cathedral). Entering St. Isaac's through the front portal, you buy your tickets inside. (Russians purchase lower-rate tickets at the *kassa* outside.) The guard should usher you to the proper counter; you will probably be offered a guided tour, which you can decline. Tickets are sold both to the church ("the museum") and to its outer colonnade; the latter affords a walk on the upper balustrade, where you will get an excellent view of the city. You can purchase tickets for either or both.

Of the grandest proportions, St. Isaac's is the world's third-largest domed cathedral. Its architectural distinction is a matter of taste: some consider the massive design and highly ornate interior to be excessive, while others revel in its opulence. Commissioned in 1818 by Alexander I to celebrate his victory over Napoléon, it took more than 40 years to build. The French architect August Ricard de Montferrand devoted his life to the project, and died the year the cathedral was finally consecrated, in 1858. The interior is lavishly decorated with malachite, lazulite, marble, and other precious stones and minerals. Gilding the dome required 100 kilos (220 pounds) of gold. The church can hold up to 14,000 people. After the 1917 Revolution it was closed to worshipers and in 1931 was opened as a museum. Since 1990, occasional services have been held, and talk is mounting of its eventual return to the Orthodox Church. When the city was blockaded during World War II, the gilded dome was painted black to avoid its being targeted by enemy fire. Despite efforts to protect it, the cathedral nevertheless suffered heavy damage, as bullet holes on the columns on the south side attest. To one side of the cathedral, where the prospect meets Konnogvardysky bulvar, is the gracefully designed **Manège**. Another Quarenghi creation, this former barracks of the imperial horse guards is used as an art exhibition hall. ⊠ *1 Isaakievskaya Pl.,* ☎ *812/315–9732. Admission for foreigners: $8.* ۞ *Mon., Tues., Thurs.–Sun. 11–7.*

❻ **Kunstkammer.** The Chamber of Art, also called the Chamber of Curiosities, is another fine example of the Russian Baroque. Painted bright azure with white trim, the building stands out from the surrounding classically designed architecture. Its playful character seems to reflect its beginnings; it was originally commissioned in 1718 to house Peter the Great's collection of oddities, gathered during his travels. Completed by 1734, the Kunstkammer (from the German *Kunst*="art" and *Kammer*="chamber") was destroyed by fire in 1747 and almost entirely rebuilt. Today it houses the Museum of Anthropology and Ethnography but still includes a room with Peter's original collection, a truly bizarre assortment ranging from rare precious stones to preserved human organs and fetuses. The museum is enormously popular, so purchase entrance tickets early in the day. ⊠ *3 Universitetskaya nab.,* ☎ *812/ 218–1412.* ۞ *Fri.–Wed. 11–4. Closed last Wed. of month.*

⑭ **Mariinsky Dvorets** (Maria's Palace). Completed in 1844 for the eldest and favorite daughter of Nicholas I, this palace was subsequently used as the residence of the Provisional Government (briefly) and the seat of the Leningrad Soviet's Executive Committee; today it is the home of the St. Petersburg City Council. The roof is still adorned with Soviet regalia, although the banner flying above it is the reclaimed Russian flag. Since this is a working government building, access to the public is restricted; however, group tours can be arranged by special request. ⊠ *6 Isaakievskaya Pl.,* ☎ *812/319–9443.*

❽ **Menshikovsky Dvorets** (Menshikov Palace). Alexander Menshikov, St. Petersburg's first governor, was one of Russia's more flamboyant characters. A close friend of Peter the Great's (often called his favorite), Menshikov rose from humble beginnings as a street vendor, reportedly getting his start when he sold a cabbage pie to the czar—or so the legend goes. Eventually becoming one of Russia's most powerful statesmen (he was granted the entire island outright for a while), Menshikov was famous for his corruption and political maneuvering. His palace, the first stone building in St. Petersburg, was at the time of its completion in 1720 the city's most luxurious building. Although only a portion of the original palace has survived, it easily conveys a sense of Menshikov's inflated ego and love of luxury. Particularly noteworthy is the tilework in the restored bedrooms, whose walls and ceilings are completely covered with handcrafted ceramic tiles. After Peter's death and Menshikov's subsequent exile to Siberia in 1727, his palace was turned over to a military training school and was significantly altered over the years. In June 1917 it served as the site of the First Congress of Russian Soviets. Neglected until 1967, when badly needed restoration work was launched, the Menshikov Palace is today a branch of the Hermitage Museum. In addition to the restored living quarters of the Menshikov family, there is an exhibit devoted to early 18th-century Russian culture. ⊠ *15 Universitetskaya nab.,* ☎ *812/213–1112.* ⊘ *Tues.–Sun. 10:30–4.*

Most Leytenanta Shmidta (Lieutenant Schmidt Bridge). Built in 1842–50, this was the first stationary bridge to connect Vasilievsky Island with the left bank of the Neva; it was renamed in honor of the naval officer who was a leader of the Black Sea Fleet mutiny during the 1905–07 Revolution.

Pedagogical Institute. The grounds belonged to Count Razumovsky, who had his palace here in the late 18th century. The adjacent house, dating from the early 1750s, belonged to the merchant Stegelmann, who was in charge of selling supplies to the royal court. Both houses were later taken over, linked, and made into a foundling hospital and orphanage. Today they house the Pedagogical Institute.

OFF THE
BEATEN PATH
DOSTOEVSKY LITERARY MUSEUM – This was the writer's last residence, where he wrote *The Brothers Karamazov*. Dostoevsky preferred to live in the part of the city inhabited by the ordinary people he wrote about. He always insisted that the windows of his workroom be opposite a church, as they are in this simple little house.⊠ *5/2 Kuznechny pereulok,* ☎ *812/311–4031.* ⊘ *Tues.–Sun. 11–5:30. Closed last Wed. of month.*

⑨ Repin Institute of Painting, Sculpture, and Architecture. Built between 1764 and 1788 and designed by Alexander Kokorinov and Vallin de la Mothe, this is a fine example of early Russian classicism. The sculptures above the main entrance on the embankment portray Hercules and Flora. The institute was founded as the Russian Academy of Arts in 1757 by Elizabeth I. It maintains a public museum of graduation works from the original Academy. The institute's many famous graduates include Dmitri Levitsky, Orest Kiprensky, and, of course, Ilya Repin (1844–1930), for whom it is now named. ⊠ *17 Universitetskaya nab.,* ☎ *812/213–6496.* ⊘ *Wed.–Sun. 11–6.*

On the landing in front of the Academy of Arts, leading down to the Neva, stand two of St. Petersburg's more magnificent landmarks, the famous **Egyptian Sphinxes**. These twin statues date from the 15th century BC and were discovered during an excavation at Thebes in the 1820s. They were apparently created during the era of Pharaoh Amenhotep III, whose features they supposedly bear.

NEED A
BREAK?
If you want a rest and a bite to eat at a popular local establishment, try **Lukamorye** (⊠ 19 nab. Leytenanta Shmidta, ☎ 812/218–5900). It's a

short walk (four blocks) up the embankment from the Academy of Arts and is located on the corner of the 13 liniye and the embankment. If you arrive before the lunch crowds, which begin around 1 PM, you will probably be seated without a wait. The cuisine is far from gourmet, and the café's poor lighting creates a rather dismal atmosphere. This is the real St. Petersburg, though, and despite gloomy appearances, a few items on the menu are worth trying. The *griby v smetane* (mushrooms in cream) is good and filling, as is the borshch. Since this is a state-run restaurant, whose patrons are predominantly Russian, you should expect the slow and inattentive service typical of such enterprises. ☉ *Daily noon–11. Rubles only.*

Rostralnyie Kolonny (Rostral Columns). Erected between 1805 and 1810 in honor of the Russian fleet, the name of these columns on Birzhevaya Square comes from the Latin *rostrum,* meaning "prow." Modeled on similar memorials in ancient Rome, the columns are decorated with ships' prows, with sculptures at the base depicting Russia's main waterways, the Dnieper, Volga, Volkhov, and Neva rivers. Although the columns originally served as lighthouses—until 1855 this was St. Petersburg's commercial harbor—they are now lighted only on special occasions. They were designed to frame the architectural centerpiece of this side of the embankment—the old ☞ **Stock Exchange** (Birzha), now the Naval War Museum.

Rumyantsev Square. This square was established in honor of the 18th-century general who led Russia to victory in the Russo-Turkish wars of 1768–74. Its obelisk, designed by Vikenty Brenna, originally stood in the Field of Mars (Marsovo Pole) and was moved to its present site in 1818. The new site was chosen for its proximity to the military school in the former Menshikov Palace, where Rumantsev once studied.

Russian Academy of Sciences. Next to the ☞ Kunstkammer stands the original building of the Russian Academy of Sciences. Erected on strictly Classical lines in 1783–89, it is considered Giacomo Quarenghi's grandest design, with an eight-column portico, a pediment, and a double staircase. The administrative offices of the academy, founded in 1724 by Peter the Great and known as the Russian Academy of Sciences until the 1917 Revolution, were transferred to Moscow in 1934. The building now houses the St. Petersburg branch of the Russian Academy of Sciences and is not open to the public.

St. Isaac's Square. Opening up in front of the eponymous cathedral, this is the city's most recent square, having been completed only after the cathedral was built. In its center stands a **statue of Czar Nicholas I** (1825–55). Unveiled in 1859, the Nicholas Statue was commissioned by the czar's wife and three children, whose faces are engraved (in the allegorical forms of Wisdom, Faith, Power, and Justice) on its base. It was designed, like St. Isaac's Cathedral, by Montferrand. The statue depicts Nicholas I mounted on a rearing horse. Other engravings on the base describe such events of the czar's reign as the suppression of the Decembrists' uprising and the opening ceremonies of the St. Petersburg–Moscow railway line.

St. Nicholas Cathedral (Nikolsky Sobor). This 18th-century Russian Baroque cathedral is surrounded by picturesque canals and green spaces. It's well worth a visit to hear the beautiful choir. ✉ *1/3 Nikolskaya Ploshchad.* ☎ *812/114–0862. Morning services at 7 and 10 AM.*

 St. Petersburg University. One of Russia's leading institutions of higher learning, with an enrollment of over 20,000, St. Petersburg University was founded by Alexander I in 1819. Its campuses date from the time of Peter the Great. The bright red Baroque building to your immediate right is the **Twelve Colleges Building,** named for the governmental administrative bodies established during Peter's reign. Designed by Domenico Trezzini and completed 16 years after Peter's death, in 1741, the building was transferred to the university at the time of its establishment and today houses the university library and administrative offices. It is not open to the public, but no one will stop you from looking around.

The next building in the university complex is the **Rector's Wing,** where a plaque on the outside wall attests that the great Russian poet Alexander Blok was born here in 1880. The third building along the embankment is a former palace built for Peter II, Peter the Great's grandson, who ruled only briefly. Completed in 1761, the building was later given to the University.

Senate and Synod. This long, light-yellow building, built along Classical lines, housed Russia's highest judicial and administrative body before the revolution. Designed by Carlo Rossi and erected between 1829 and 1834, it now contains state historical archives and is closed to the public.

Siniy most (Blue Bridge). The bridge, which spans the Moika River and is so called because of the paint on its underside, is so wide (116 meters, or 328 feet) and stubby that it seems not to be a bridge at all but rather a sort of quaint raised footpath on St. Isaac's Square.

❹ **Stock Exchange.** Erected in 1804–10 and, like the Rostral Columns, designed by the Swiss architect Thomas de Thomon, the neoclassical Stock Exchange was modeled on one of the Greek temples at Paestum. It was intended to symbolize St. Petersburg's financial and maritime strength. Since 1940, the building has housed the **Voenno-Morskoy Muzey** (Central Naval Museum), which was itself founded in 1805. Its collections date from Peter's reign and include, in accordance with his orders, a model of every ship built in Russian shipyards since 1709. On display are exhibits of Russia's naval history to the present. The collections also contain a 3,000-year-old dugout found on the bottom of the Bug River as well as Peter the Great's personal belongings, including his first boat and the ax he used to build it with. ⊠ *4 Birzhevaya Ploshchad, Vasilievsky Ostrov,* ☎ *812/218–2501 or 812/218–2502.* ☉ *Wed.–Sun. 10:30–4:30. Closed last Thurs. of month.*

NEED A
BREAK?   The **Astoria Hotel,** on the east side of the square, is one of St. Petersburg's best. Don't be intimidated by the regal dress of its doormen. Take the lobby elevator to the fourth floor and you will find a self-service café (☉ daily 7–4 and 5–10) that offers coffee and tea, imported beverages, and a variety of light snacks, from smoked salmon to cream-filled pastries.

❸ **Strelka.** The Strelka (arrow or spit) affords a dazzling view of both the Winter Palace and of the Peter and Paul Fortress, off to its left (☞ Peter and Paul Fortress and the Petrograd Side, *below*), and reveals the city's triumphant rise from a watery outpost to an elegant metropolis. Seen against the backdrop of the Neva, the brightly colored houses lining the embankment seem like children's toys—the building blocks of a bygone aristocracy. They stand at the water's edge, supported not by the land beneath them but almost by the panorama of the city behind them. Gazing at this architectural wonder, you start to understand the scope of Peter the Great's vision for his country. The view is also revealing because it makes clear how careful the city's founders were to build their city not despite the Neva but around and with it. The river's natural ebb and flow accords perfectly with the monumental architecture lining its course.

Yusupovsky Dvorets. Set on the bank of the Moika River, this elegant yellow palace belonged to one of Russia's wealthiest families, the Yusupovs. It was here on the cold night of December 17, 1916, that Prince Yusupov and others loyal to the czar spent several frustrating and frightening hours trying to kill the invincible Rasputin, the "mad monk" who strongly influenced the czarina during the tumultuous years leading up to the Bolshevik Revolution. When the monk did not succumb to the arsenic-laced cake given to him, the conspirators proceeded to shoot him several times (thinking him dead after the first shot, they had left the room, only to return and find he'd staggered outside—whereupon they shot him again). They then dumped him into the icy waters of an isolated section of a nearby canal. The building now serves as a cultural center for teachers but is also open for tours (by advance booking only). On display are the rooms in which Rasputin was (or began to be) killed, as well as a waxworks exhibit of Rasputin and Prince Yusupov, who was forced to flee the country when the monk's murder was uncovered. ⊠ *94 nab. Moiki,* ☏ *812/314–8893.* ⊘ *Daily noon–3. Guided tours by advance booking only.*

❺ Zoologichesky Musey. The prize of this zoological museum's unusual collection, which contains over 40,000 species, is a stuffed mammoth recovered from Siberia in 1901. ⊠ *1 Universitetskaya nab,* ☏ *812/218–0112.* ⊘ *Sat.–Thurs. 11–5. Closed holidays.*

Peter and Paul Fortress and the Petrograd Side

This walk takes you to the site where the city began, the Petropavlovskaya Krepost (Peter and Paul Fortress). The fortress is located on Zayachy Ostrov (Hare Island), almost directly across the Neva from the Winter Palace. Cut off from the north by the moatlike Kronverk Canal, Hare Island is connected by a footbridge to Troitskaya Ploshchad (Trinity Square, sometimes still referred to by its Soviet name, Revolution Square) on Petrogradsky Ostrov (Petrograd Island). This section of the city, which actually consists of a series of islands, is commonly referred to as the Petrogradskaya Storona (Petrograd Side) and is one of its earliest residential areas. Trinity Square, named for the church that once stood here (demolished in 1934), is the city's oldest square.

A Good Walk

You can reach Hare Island, site of the **Peter and Paul Fortress** ⑮, from central St. Petersburg by crossing the Troitsky most from the Palace embankment. It is also easy to reach by subway; the closest station is Gorkovskaya. After exiting the station, walk through the small park in front of you, heading in the direction of the Neva. The fortress will emerge through the trees to your right. If your visit hasn't overwhelmed you, you may want to visit one more building associated with the fortress but situated outside its walls. Across the Kronverk Canal to the north of the fortress is the horseshoe-shaped **Artileriysky Muzey** ⑯. Leaving the fort by its western end and crossing the footbridge there, bear right; leaving by the way you came in and crossing its footbridge, bear left. The large museum will soon be visible.

Return now to Trinity Square. At the northern edge of the square, at the corner of Kuybysheva ulitsa and Kamennostrovsky Prospect, stands the **Russian Political History Museum** ⑰. As you leave the museum, take a right, and then turn right again onto Kronversky Prospect. It's hard to miss the bright azure domes of St. Petersburg's only mosque—the **Mechet** ⑱—above the trees. Now head back (left) in the direction of the Neva River. When you reach the waterfront, turn left again, to walk along Petrovskaya naberezhnaya (Peter Embankment). A few minutes away, you'll find the **Domik Petra Pervovo** ⑲, Peter the Great's Cottage. Keep walking east along the embankment. When you reach the corner where the Petrovskaya and Petrogradskaya embankments meet (and the Great Nevka converges with the Neva River), you'll be in front of a blue-and-white building in the Russian Baroque style. This is the Nakhimov Academy of Naval Officers, in front of which is anchored the cruiser **Avrora** ⑳. Across the river stands the enormous **St. Petersburg Hotel.** From here you can return to your starting point by retracing your steps along the embankment. If you want to see more of the Petrograd Side's residential areas, you can take the longer route back via Kuybysheva ulitsa. Walk down to the bridge to your left (as you face the cruiser Avrora) and turn left onto Kuybysheva. This will take you back to Trinity Square. From here the Trinity Bridge is to your left and the Gorkovskaya subway stop a short walk to your right.

TIMING

Unless you plan to stop at all of the sights, devote two or three hours to simply walking the route. Don't rush through the Peter and Paul Fortress. Note that the Cathedral of Sts. Peter and Paul is closed on Wednesday. It is fun to wander through the hustle and bustle of the city on weekdays, for it is here that you will see the city's heart.

Sights to See

⑯ **Artileriysky Muzey** (Artillery Museum). This building once served as the city's arsenal and was turned over to the Artillery Museum in 1872. The museum itself dates from the days of Peter the Great, who sought to present the entire history of weaponry, with a special emphasis on Russia. Today the Artillery Museum is St. Petersburg's main army museum. ⊠ 7 Alexandrovsky Park, ☎ 812/232–0296. ☉ Wed.–Sun. 11–5. Closed last Thursday of month.

NEED A
BREAK?

If you have walked all the way over to the Artillery Museum, you may as well walk a bit farther and try out St. Petersburg's floating café, the **Petrovsky.** It is located on a ship permanently moored in the Kronverk Canal, just south of the Artillery Museum. Down below is an intimate café where you can enjoy a cup of strong coffee, pastry, or even a shot of cognac. ⊠ 3 nab. Mytninskaya, ☎ 812/232 9219. ☉ Daily noon–midnight.

 ⑳ **Avrora.** This historic cruiser is permanently moored in front of the **Nakhimov Academy of Naval Officers.** Launched in 1903, it fought in the 1904–05 Russo–Japanese War as well as in World War II, but it is best known for its role in the Bolshevik Revolution. At 9:40 PM on November 7, 1917, the cruiser fired the shot signaling the storming of the Winter Palace. A cherished relic in the Soviet era, the Avrora was carefully restored in the 1980s and opened as a museum. Although the revolution it launched brought itself under fire in the end, the cruiser is still a favorite place to bring children, and on weekends you may encounter long lines. On display are the crew's quarters and the radio room used to broadcast Lenin's victory address. ⊠ 4 Petrogradskaya nab., ☎ 812/230–8440. ☉ Tues–Thurs. and weekends 10:30–4.

Botanical Gardens. Founded as an apothecary garden for Peter the Great, the grounds display—literally—millions of different forms of plant life. ⊠ 2 ul. Professora Popova, ☎ 812/234 1764. ☉ Hothouses open Sat.–Thurs. 11-4.

⑲ **Domik Petra Pervovo** (Peter the Great's Cottage). Built in just three days in May 1703, this cottage was home to Peter the Great during construction of the Peter and Paul Fortress. It is made of wooden logs painted to resemble bricks. Inside, 18th-century furniture is on display, arranged as it might have been in Peter's day, along with a few of Peter's personal effects. The stone structure enclosing the cottage was erected in 1784 by Catherine the Great to protect the structure from the elements. The cottage consists of just three rooms, whose ceilings are surprisingly low—considering that Peter the Great was nearly 7 feet tall. In the courtyard in front of the cottage stands a bronze bust of the czar. The large stone sculptures of the Shi-Tsza (Lion-Frogs) flanking the stairwell leading down the embankment side were brought to Russia from Manchuria in 1907. ⊠ *6 Petrovskaya nab.,* ☎ *812/232–4576.* ⊘ *Wed.–Mon. 11–6. Closed last Mon. of month and in humid weather.*

Kirov Museum. This is the home of the former head of the city's Communist Party, who, it later became clear, was murdered by Stalin, marking the beginning of the infamous purges. ⊠ *26/28 Kamennostrovsky Prospect,* ☎ *812/346–0217.* ⊘ *Thurs.–Tues. 11–5. Closed last Tues of month.*

⑱ Mechet (Mosque). Built in 1910–14 to serve St. Petersburg's Muslim community, the Mosque was designed after the Gur Emir in Samarkand, where Tamerlane is buried. ⊠ *7 Kronversky Prospect,* ☎ *812/233–9819.* ⊘ *Daily 10–4. Services daily at 1:30.*

★ **⑮ Petropavlovskaya Krepost** (Peter and Paul Fortress). The fortress was erected in just a year's time, between 1703 and 1704, to defend St. Petersburg in the Great Northern War against Sweden. It was never used for its intended purpose, however, since the Russian line of defense quickly moved farther north. The war was then won before the fortress was mobilized. Indeed, Fort St. Petersburg (as it was first called), never did see the sort of warfare for which it was built. Instead, it has served mainly as a political prison, primarily under the czars.

Cross the footbridge and enter the fortress through **Ioannovskyie Vorota** (St. John's Gate), the main entrance to the outer fortifications. Once inside, you will need to stop at the ticket office, which is inside the outer fortification wall (the ticket booth to your immediate left sells only theater tickets). Although entry to the fortress grounds is free, you must buy tickets here for the exhibits or you will be sent back for them. ⊠ *3 Petropavlovskaya Krepost,* ☎ *812/238–4540.* ⊘ *Thurs.–Tues. 11–5. Closed last Tues. of month.*

Entrance to the inner fortress is through the **Petrovskyie Vorota** (St. Peter's Gate). Designed by the Swiss architect Domenico Trezzini, it was built from 1717 to 1718. Its decoration includes the double-headed eagle of the Romanovs and a wooden bas-relief depicting the apostle Peter prevailing over Simon Magus. The allegory was meant to inspire confidence in Peter the Great's impending victory over Charles XII of Sweden, which did not come until 1721.

After you pass through St. Peter's Gate, the first building to your right is the **Artillery Arsenal,** where weaponry was stored. Just to your left is the **Inzhenerny Dom** (Engineer's House), which was built from 1748 to 1749. It is now a branch of the Museum of the History of St. Petersburg (as are all exhibits in the fortress) and presents displays about the city's prerevolutionary history. The small building right after the Engineer's House is the **Gauptvakhta** (Guardhouse), built in 1743 and later reconstructed. Today it houses the museum's administrative offices and is not open to the public.

As you continue to walk down the main center lane, away from St. Peter's Gate, you soon come to the main attraction of the fortress, the **Petropavlovsky Sobor** (Cathedral of Sts. Peter and Paul). Constructed between 1712 and 1733 on the site of an earlier wooden church, it was designed by Domenico Trezzini and later embellished by Bartolomeo Rastrelli. It is highly unusual for a Russian Orthodox church. Instead of the characteristic bulbous domes, it is adorned by a single, slender gilded spire whose height (121 meters, or 400 feet) made it the city's tallest building. The spire is identical to that of the Admiralty across the river, except that it is crowned by an angel bearing a golden cross. The spire remained the city's highest structure—in accordance with Peter the Great's decree—until 1962, when the television tower was erected, greatly marring the harmony of the city's skyline.

The interior of the cathedral is also atypical. The Baroque iconostasis, designed by Ivan Zarudny and built in the 1720s, is adorned by freestanding statues. Another uncommon feature is the pulpit. According to legend, it was used only once: in 1901, to excommunicate Leo Tolstoy from the Russian Orthodox Church.

Starting with Peter the Great, the cathedral served as the burial place of the czars. You can identify Peter's tomb—a place of his own choosing, to the far right as you face the iconostasis—by the czar's bust on the railing. Nearly all of Peter's successors were buried in the cathedral as well, with a few notable exceptions: Peter II, Ivan VI, and the last czar, Nicholas II, who was executed with his family in Ekaterinburg in 1918. It is said, however, that the recently identified remains of the czar will at some point in the future be given a final resting place here. In 1992, in recognition of Russia's imperial past, the most recent Romanov pretender, Grand Duke Vladimir, was bestowed the honor of burial in the Peter and Paul Fortress, although not in the royal crypt.

You may exit the cathedral through the passageway to the left of the iconostasis. This leads to the adjoining **Usypalnitsa** (Grand Ducal Crypt), built between 1896 and 1908. It contains an exhibit on the architectural history of the fortress.

As you leave the cathedral, you will notice a small Classical structure to your right. This is the **Botny Domik** (Boathouse), built in 1762–66 to house Peter the Great's boyhood boat. The boat has since been moved to the Central Naval Museum on Vasilievsky Island (☞ Vasilievsky Island and the Left Bank, *above*), and the building is not open to the public. The wooden figurine on its roof is meant to symbolize navigation.

The long pink-and-white building to your left as you exit the cathedral is the **Komendantsky Dom** (Commandant's House). Erected between 1743 and 1746, it once housed the fortress's administration and doubled as a courtroom for political prisoners. The Decembrist revolutionaries were tried here in 1826. The room where the trial took place forms part of the ongoing exhibits, which deal with the history of St. Petersburg from its founding in 1703 to 1917.

Across the cobblestone yard, opposite the entrance to the cathedral, stands the **Monetny Dvor** (Mint), which dates from 1716. The present building was erected between 1798 and 1806. The mint is still in operation, producing coins, medals, military decorations, and *znachki,* or Russian souvenir pins. The coins that were taken on Soviet space missions were made here.

Take the pathway to the left of the Commandant's House (as you are facing it), and you will be headed right for the **Nevskyie Vorota** (Neva Gate), built in 1730 and reconstructed in 1787. As you walk through its passageway, note the plaques on the inside walls marking flood levels of the Neva. The most recent, from 1975, shows the river more than 9 feet above normal. The gate leads out to the **Komendantskaya Pristan** (Commandant's Pier). It is this side of the fortress that was meant to be viewed by would-be invaders and convince them to turn back. Up above to the right is the **Signal Cannon** fired every day at noon. From this side you get a splendid view of St. Petersburg. You may want to step down to the sandy beach, where even in winter hearty swimmers enjoy the Neva's arctic waters. In summer the beach is lined with sunbathers, standing up or leaning against the fortification wall (supposedly this allows for a more even tan).

Returning back inside the fortress, consider that it was also through the Neva Gate that prisoners were led to execution. Several of the fortress's bastions, concentrated at its far western end, were put to use over the years mainly as political prisons. One of them, **Trubetskoi Bastion,** is open to the public as a museum. If you turn left from the gate and walk the length of the fortification wall, you can identify the museum by the diagonal stripes on its door and the iron gate enclosing the entrance. Aside from a few exhibits of prison garb, the only items on display are the cells themselves, restored to their chilling, prerevolutionary appearance.

The first prisoner confined in its dungeons was Peter the Great's own son Alexei, who was tortured to death in 1718, allegedly under the czar's supervision. The prison was enlarged in 1872, when an adjacent one, Alexeivsky Bastion, which held such famous figures as the writers Fyodor Dostoevsky and Nikolai Chernyshevsky, was too small to contain the swelling numbers of dissidents of the czarist regime. A partial chronology of revolutionaries held here includes some of the People's Will terrorists, who killed Alexander II in 1881; Lenin's elder brother Alexander, who attempted to murder Alexander III (and was executed for his role in the plot); and Leon Trotsky and Maxim Gorky, after taking part in the 1905 Revolution. The Bolsheviks themselves imprisoned people here for a short period, starting with members of the Provisional Government who were arrested and "detained for their own safety" for a few days, as well as sailors who mutinied against the communist regime in Kronstadt in 1921. They were apparently the last to be held here, and in 1925 a memorial museum (to the prerevolutionary prisoners) was opened instead.

⑰ **Russian Political History Museum.** This elegant house is the former mansion of Mathilda Kshesinskaya, a famous ballerina and mistress of the last Russian czar, Nicholas II. Built in the Art Nouveau style in 1905, the mansion served as Bolshevik committee headquarters in the months leading up to the October Revolution. In 1957 it was turned into the Museum of the Great October Socialist Revolution; in 1991 it was given its current name. It offers temporary exhibits on Russian political movements, both before and after the 1917 Revolution. One hall contains an interesting collection of wax figures, showing victims and perpetrators of violence in Russian history, including Alexander II, who was assassinated by terrorists, and Stalin. The beautiful mansion itself is interesting as well, simply because it gives you a sense of prerevolutionary St. Petersburg and the lifestyle of its upper classes. ⊠ *2/4 ul. Kuybysheva.* ☎ *812/233-7052.* ☉ *Fri.–Wed. 10–5:30.*

St. Petersburg Hotel. Before 1992, this enormous hotel across the river from the ☞ *Avrora* was named the Leningrad, which was probably a more appropriate name since this Intourist offering clearly belongs to the Soviet era. Built in the monotonous style of a Brezhnev-era high rise, the concrete-and-steel structure seems horribly out of place among the prerevolutionary architecture lining the embankment.

Nevsky Prospect and the Alexander Nevsky Lavra

"There is nothing finer than Nevsky Prospect, not in St. Petersburg at any rate, for in St. Petersburg it is everything . . ." wrote the great Russian author Nikolai Gogol more than 150 years ago. Today it may not be as resplendent as it was in the 1830s, when noblemen and ladies strolled along the elegant avenue or paraded by in horse-drawn carriages. It still remains, however, the pulse of the city, unquestionably its main thoroughfare. Through the 18th century it was built up with estates and manors of the gentry, most of which still stand as testimony to the city's noble past. The next century saw a boom of mercantile growth that added sections farther south as centers for commerce, finance, and trade. Under the Communists, few new sites were planned on the Prospect. Instead, old structures found a new use, and the bulk of the Soviets' building was directed outside the city center.

A Good Walk

We turn now to the inner city and St. Petersburg's most famous avenue, **Nevsky Prospect** ㉑. Start at the relatively peaceful **Alexander Nevsky Lavra** ㉒, which is at the southeastern end of Nevsky Prospect. It can be reached by taking the subway to the Ploshchad Alexandra Nevskovo station, which comes out at the foot of the Moskva Hotel, one of Intourist's gargantuan complexes. The entrance to the Lavra is across the square from the subway exit. After visiting the monastery, return to Alexander Nevsky Square. The bridge to your right, also named for Alexander Nevsky, is the city's longest; it leads to some of St. Petersburg's main bedroom communities, where, these days, most of its residents live. You should take the subway one stop north to the Mayakovskaya station, but at that stop, follow the signs for the adjacent Vosstaniya exit, to emerge at a better location for viewing the next sights. It is at this point that the avenue's most interesting architecture begins, starting at **Ploshchad Vosstaniya** ㉓. Head west, away from the monastery and the railway station, and after three blocks you'll reach the **Fontanka River** and one of the city's most beautiful bridges, the **Anichkov most** ㉔; over the river, on the opposite corner, stands the **Anichkov Palace.** The next stop is **Ploshchad Ostrovskovo,** dominated by the city's oldest theater, the **Pushkin Drama Theater** ㉕. Before moving beyond Ostrovsky Square, step around to the back of the Pushkin Theater, where the amazing **ulitsa Zodchevo Rossi**—a street whose every proportion has been carefully detailed—begins.

Back at Ostrovsky Square, take note of the neoclassical building to your left, on the west side of the square. This is the **Russian National Library,** the nation's largest after the State Library in Moscow. You may want to cross Nevsky at this point to peek inside the **Yeliseyevsky Food Emporium.** As you pass Sadovaya ulitsa, taking up the entire block on the other side of the street is the huge **Gostinny Dvor** ㉖ department store. On its side of the street, a bit farther down, at Nos. 40–42, is the blue-and-white **Armenian Church.** You will next notice, at No. 34, another recessed church, the Catholic **Church of St. Catherine.** On the corner across, at No. 33, stands the former city hall under the czars, the **Gorodskaya Duma.** Cross the short Kazan Bridge over the Griboyedov Canal, and you'll come to the city's largest bookstore, **Dom Knigi** ㉗. Across the street is one of the city's more resplendent works of architecture, the **Kazansky Sobor** ㉘. Crossing the street and continuing one block down Nevsky, you'll reach the **Lutheran Church,** another church on a recessed lot.

Return now to the other side of the street. Before you cross the little bridge spanning the Moika Canal, you'll be at the magnificent green building overlooking the embankment. This is the former **Stroganov**

Palace ㉙. The golden building of the ☞ **Admiralty** marks the end of Nevsky Prospect. To return to the subway, take trolleybus 1, 5, 7, or 22 one stop to Nevsky Prospect Station. Since trolleybuses on Nevsky are notoriously overcrowded, you might prefer to walk. Palace Square and the Winter Palace, if you somehow haven't noticed, are nearby, across from the street flanking the Admiralty's right side. If you have the time and are interested in farmers' markets, you can easily include **Kuznechny Rynok** in your walk, one of St. Petersburg's most popular markets. Get on the subway at Mayakovskaya metro and get off at Kuznechny pereulok, only ten minutes away. Other worthwhile sites in the area include **Smolny,** on the left bank and the **Taurida Palace,** on Shpalernaya.

TIMING

Your best bet to avoid the crowds that pack the trolleybuses and the trains is to visit in the morning. However, if you take the subway or the trolleybus rather than walk from one sight to the next you will save at least a couple of hours, hours that you can then devote to a little shopping; most of the souvenir shops are on and around Nevsky Prospekt.

Sights to See

★ ㉒ **Alexander Nevsky Lavra.** The monastery complex includes the Church of the Annunciation—converted under the Soviets into the Museum of City Sculpture—the Holy Trinity Church, a theological seminary, and several cemeteries. Entrance to the monastery grounds is free, but you must purchase a ticket for the two most interesting cemeteries and the museum. The ticket office is outside the monastery, to the right of the main gate. ✉ *1 Pl. Alexandra Nevskovo,* ☎ *812/274–1612.* ☺ *Fri.–Wed. 11–6.*

The word *lavra* in Russian is reserved for a monastery of the highest order, of which there are just four in all of Russia and Ukraine. Named in honor of St. Alexander Nevsky, this monastery was founded in 1710 by Peter the Great and given *lavra* status in 1797. Prince Alexander of Novgorod (1220–63), the great military commander, became a beloved national hero because he halted the relentless eastward drive for Russian territory by the Germans and the Swedes. Peter chose this site for the monastery, thinking that it was the same place where the prince had fought the battle in 1240 that earned him the title Alexander of the Neva (Nevsky), though the famous battle actually took place some 20 kilometers (12 miles) away. Alexander Nevsky had been buried in Vladimir, but in 1724, on Peter's orders, his remains were transferred to the monastery that was founded in his honor.

Entrance to the monastery is through the archway of the elegant **Gate Church,** built by Ivan Starov in 1783–85. The walled pathway is flanked by two cemeteries, whose entrances are located a short walk down the path. To the left lies the older Lazarus Cemetery. The list of famous people buried here reads like a catalogue of St. Petersburg architecture and includes Quarenghi, Rossi, Voronikhin, and Thomas de Thomon. The cemetery also contains the tombstone of the father of Russian science, Mikhail Lomonsov. The **Tikhvin Cemetery,** on the opposite side, is the final resting place of a number of St. Petersburg's great literary and musical figures. The grave of Fyodor Dostoevsky, located in the northwestern corner, is easily identified by the tombstone's sculpture, which portrays the writer with his flowing beard. Continuing along the path you'll soon reach the composers' corner, where Rimsky-Korsakov, Mussorgsky, Borodin, and Tchaikovsky are buried.

Having pondered St. Petersburg's cultural legacy, return to the path and cross the bridge spanning the quaint **Monastyrka Canal.** As you enter the monastery grounds, the **Church of the Annunciation** greets you on your left. The red-and-white rectangular church was designed by Domenico Trezzini and built between 1717 and 1722. The Museum of City Sculpture inside contains models of St. Petersburg's architectural masterpieces as well as gravestones and other fine examples of memorial sculpture. Also in the church are several graves of 18th-century statesmen. The great soldier, Generalissimo Alexander Suvorov, who led the Russian army to numerous victories during the Russo-Turkish War (1768–74), is buried here under a simple marble slab that he purportedly designed himself. It reads simply: "Here lies Suvorov."

Continuing along the same path, you'll reach the monastery's main cathedral, the **Troitsky Sobor** (Trinity Cathedral), which was one of the city's few churches left functioning during the Soviet era. Designed by Ivan Starov and completed at the end of the 18th century, it stands out among the monastery's predominantly Baroque architecture for its monumental Classical design. Services are held here daily, and the church is open to the public, although it closes between 2 and 5 in the afternoon for housekeeping. The magnificent interior, with its stunning gilded iconostasis, is worth a visit. The large central dome, adorned by frescoes designed by the great architect Quarenghi, seems to soar toward the heavens. It is in this church that the main relics of Alexander Nevsky are kept.

OFF THE
BEATEN PATH

CHESMENSKAYA TSERKOV – Surrounded by dreary Soviet high rises in a remote residential area, this bright red, white-striped church is a delightful surprise. A rare example of pseudo-Gothic Russian architecture, the church was built to accompany the Chesma Palace (across the street), which served as a staging post for the imperial court en route to the summer palaces of Tsarskoye Selo (now Pushkin) and Pavlovsk. Commissioned by Catherine the Great, the palace was built to commemorate the Russian naval victory at Chesma in the Aegean in 1770. Both buildings were constructed by Yuri Felten, designer of the famous Summer Gardens fence. Before the Bolshevik Revolution, the palace became a home for the elderly and was not open to the public. Today it is a training school for aircraft designers. The church, in turn, was made into a branch of the city's Naval Museum, dedicated to the battle at Chesma. In recent years, baptisms and weddings have occasionally been performed here. Now the Church is open to the public and has regular services. Not far from the Pulkhovskaya Hotel, the Chesma Church is within walking distance of the Moskovskaya subway stop and the Alexander Nevsky Lavra. ✉ *12 ul. Lensoveta,* ☎ *812/293-6114 (church).* ☉ *Services daily 10 and 6.*

❷❹ **Anichkov most.** Each corner of this beautiful bridge spanning the **Fontanka River** (the name means "Fountain") bears one from a quartet of exquisite equestrian statues. Designed by Peter Klodt and erected in 1841, the bronze sculptures depict phases of horse-taming. Taken down and buried during World War II, the beautiful monuments were restored to their positions in 1945. The bridge was named for Colonel Mikhail Anichkov, whose regiment had built the first, wooden drawbridge here. At that time, early in the 18th century, the bridge marked the city limits, and the job of its night guards was much the same as that of today's border guards, to carefully screen those entering the city. As you cross the bridge, pause for a moment to look back at No. 41, the colorful Baroque building on the corner of Nevsky and the Fontanka. The highly ornate, deep rose mansion belonged to Prince Beloselsky-

Belozersky. Finished in 1848, by Stackenschneider, who wanted to replicate Rastrelli's Stroganov Palace, this lavish building, once opulent inside and out, housed the local Communist Party headquarters during the Soviet era. Today it is the setting for classical music concerts. The interiors have unfortunately been largely destroyed and are no longer nearly as magnificent as the facades.

OFF THE BEATEN PATH **BOAT RIDES –** A float down the Neva or through the city's twisting canals is always a pleasant way to spend a summer afternoon. For trips through the canals, take one of the boats at the pier near Anichkov Bridge on Nevsky Prospect. Boats cruising the Neva leave from the pier outside the Hermitage Museum. Both boat trips have departures early morning–late afternoon from mid-May through mid-September.

Anichkov Palace. This palace was named for the colonel whose regiment built the ☞ **Anchikov most.** It was built by Empress Elizabeth for her lover Alexei Razumovsky between 1741 and 1750. As if to continue the tradition, Catherine the Great later gave it to one of her many favorites, Grigory Potemkin. An able statesman and army officer, Potemkin is famous for his attempts to fool Catherine about conditions in the Russian south. He had fake villages put up for her to view as she passed by during her 1787 tour of the area. The term "Potemkin village" has come to mean any impressive facade that hides an ugly interior—a phrase put to good use during the Soviet era.

The Anichkov Palace was originally designed by Mikhail Zemtsov and completed by Bartolomeo Francesco Rastrelli. The building has undergone a number of changes, and little remains of the elaborate Baroque facade. This was once a suburban area, which explains why its main entrance faces the Fontanka rather than Nevsky, where there is only a side entrance. Today it houses the Youth Palace (once the Pioneer Palace), which offers activities for young people.

Armenian Church. This blue-and-white church was built by Velten between 1771 and 1780 and set back from the street. A fine example of the early Classical style, the church fell into disrepair and is under full restoration, but it is holding some services and is open to the public. At the corner of Mikhailovskaya ulitsa is the **Grand Hotel Europe** (☞ From the Square of the Arts to the Field of Mars, *below*).

Church of St. Catherine. Built between 1762 and 1783 by Vallin de la Mothe and Antonio Rinaldi, it is done in a mixture of Baroque and Classical, styles that were then converging in Russia. The grave of the last king of Poland (and yet another lover of Catherine the Great), Stanislaw Poniatowski, is here. ⊠ *34 Nevsky Prospect.*

㉗ Dom Knigi (House of Books). The city's largest bookstore still goes by its generic Soviet name. Before the revolution, it was the offices of the Singer Sewing Machine Company, whose distinctive globe trademark still adorns the roof. Here one finds Russians in a favorite pursuit, buying and perusing books. The store contains a wonderful collection of books and maps.

Gorodskaya Duma (City Duma). This building with a notable red-and-white tower was the city hall under the czars. Its clock tower, meant to resemble those in European cities, was erected by Ferrari between 1799 and 1804. It was equipped with signaling devices that sent messages between the Winter Palace and the royal summer residences.⊠ *1 ul. Dumskaya.*

㉖ Gostinny Dvor. Taking up an entire city block, this is St. Petersburg's answer to the GUM department store in Moscow. Started by Rastrelli in 1757, it was not completed until 1785, by Vallin de la Mothe, who was responsible for the facade with its two tiers of arches. When it was erected, traveling merchants were routinely put up in guest houses (called *gostinny dvor*), which, like this one, doubled as places for doing business. This arcade was completely rebuilt in the last century, by which time it housed some 200 general-purpose shops that were far less elegant than those in other parts of the Nevsky. It remained a functional bazaar until alterations in the 1950s and 1960s connected most of its separate shops into St. Petersburg's largest department store. Many sections of the store are operating, but a large portion of Gostinny Dvor has been gutted, undergoing what Russians call "capital" repairs. Virtually across the street is the city's other major "department store," also an arcade, called **Passazh** (Passage) and built in 1848.

NEED A BREAK? The **Konditorei** on the other side of Nevsky Prospect, at No. 40, offers a soothing place to take a break. The wood-paneled interior and parquet ceilings have been restored to their original, prerevolutionary appearance. Coffee, ice cream, and scrumptious cakes are available in a no-smoking environment. If you're looking for something more substantial, try the German restaurant and bar next door.

OFF THE BEATEN PATH **KIROVSKY PARK ON YELAGIN OSTROV –** Yelagin Ostrov (island) is named after its 18th-century aristocratic owner. The park covers most of the island and has an open-air theater, boating stations, a beach, and the Yelagin Palace, designed by Carlo Rossi for Alexander I, who then presented it to his mother, Catherine the Great. The palace contains a number of fine rooms, including the Porcelain Room, beautifully decorated with painted stucco by Antonio Vighi, and the Oval Hall. If you walk along Primorsky Prospekt for about half a mile to the *strelka* (spit), you can catch a view of the sunset over the Gulf of Finland. To reach the park, take the subway from Gostinny Dvor to the Chyornaya Rechka station and then take Tram 2 or 31. ✉ 4 Yelagin Ostrov, ☎ 812/239–1411. ☉ Wed.–Sun. 10–6.

RAILWAY MUSEUM – Farther down Sadovaya, this family museum displays Russia's railroad history—complete with moving model trains—this museum is a hit with kids and parents alike. ✉ 50 ul.Sadovaya, ☎ 812/315-1476. ☉ Sun.–Thurs. 11–5:30. Closed last Thurs. of month.

㉘ Kazansky Sobor (Kazan Cathedral). Czar Paul I commissioned this magnificent cathedral after a visit to Rome, wishing to copy—and perhaps present the Orthodox rival to—St. Peter's. Erected between 1801 and 1811 to a design by Andrei Voronikhin, the huge cathedral is approached through a monumental, semicircular colonnade. Inside and out, the church abounds with sculpture and decoration. On the prospect side the frontage holds statues of St. John the Baptist and the apostle Andrew as well as such sanctified Russian heroes as Vladimir and Alexander Nevsky. Take note of the enormous bronze front doors. They are exact copies of Ghiberti's Gates of Heaven at Florence's Baptistery.

In 1932 the cathedral, which was closed right after the Revolution, was turned into the Museum of Religion and Atheism, with emphasis on the latter. The history of religion was presented from the Marxist point of view, essentially as an ossified archaeological artifact. The museum still operates here but has dropped the "Atheism" from its name and reorganized its displays. Simultaneously, it is again open as a place of worship, with services resumed in the cathedral.

Back outside the church, have a look at the square that forms its front lawn. At each end are statues of a military leader, one of Mikhail Barclay de Tolly, the other of Mikhail Kutuzov. Both reflect the importance in the 19th century of the cathedral as a place of military tribute, specifically after Napoléon's invasion in 1812. Kutuzov is buried in the cathedral's northern chapel, where he is supposed to have prayed before taking command of the Russian forces. ⊠ *2 Kazanskaya Pl.,* ☎ *812/311–0495 or 812/312–3586.* ⊙ *Mon., Tues., Thurs., Fri. 11– 5; weekends noon–5. Church services weekdays at 9* AM *and 6* PM, *weekends and holidays at 10* AM.

Lutheran Church. Designed by Alexander Briyullov, the rounded arches and simple towers of this church follow the Romanesque tradition. This church can no longer be used at all. It suffered the same fate as the giant Cathedral of Christ Our Savior in Moscow: during the years when religion was repressed, it was turned into a municipal swimming pool. When you enter, go up the staircase to the third floor. From the upper bleachers, you can look down at the remnants of the pool, which are slowly being ripped out so that the structure can be turned back into a church. Farther down, at No. 20, is the **Dutch Church** (now a library), yet another reminder of the many denominations that once peacefully coexisted in old St. Petersburg.

★ ㉑ **Nevsky Prospect.** St. Petersburg's most famous avenue was laid out in 1710, making it one of the city's first streets. Just short of 5 km (3 mi) long, beginning and ending at different bends of the Neva River, it starts at the foot of the Admiralty building and runs in a perfectly straight line to the Moscow Railway Station, where it curves slightly before ending a short distance farther at the Alexander Nevsky Lavra, or monastery. Because St. Petersburg was once part of the larger lands of Novgorod, the road linking them was known as Great Novgorod Road, and trade and transport traveled over it. By the time Peter the Great built the first Admiralty, however, another major road clearly was needed to connect the Admiralty directly to the shipping hub. It was decided to begin the new avenue at the Admiralty. Originally the new street was called the Great Perspective Road, and after that, the Nevsky Perspektiv, and finally Nevsky Prospect.

On the last few blocks of Nevsky Prospect are a few buildings of historical importance. No. 18, on the right-hand side, is the **Literary Café.** Originally a private dwelling, Kotomin's house, it subsequently held a café called Wulf and Beranger. Reportedly, it was here that Pushkin ate his last meal before setting off for his fatal duel (☞ Dining, *below*). Called **Chicherin's House,** No. 15 was one of Empress Elizabeth's palaces before becoming the Nobles' Assembly and, in 1919, the House of Arts. Farther down, at No. 14, is one of the rare buildings on Nevsky Prospect built *after* the Bolshevik Revolution. The blue sign on the facade dates from World War II and the siege of Leningrad. It warns pedestrians that during air raids the other side of the street is safer. The city was once covered with similar warnings; this one was left in place as a memorial.

Nevsky Prospect boasts the city's finest hotels and shops, but it also attracts all the problems of its difficult economy. It is the favorite gathering place of homeless children, whose dirty faces and pitiful looks evoke sympathy but whose tricks may easily catch you off guard and without a wallet. The street is also roamed by bands of colorfully dressed Gypsy women and children, who can smell a tourist miles away. Unfortunately, a stroll down today's Nevsky Prospect requires some caution. As in any large city, you need to use common sense.

OFF THE
BEATEN PATH
PUSHKIN APARTMENT MUSEUM – This former palace of Prince Volkhonsky is where, on January 27, 1837, the beloved Russian poet Alexander

Pushkin died after participating in a duel to defend his wife's honor. Although he lived there less than a year, the apartment/museum has been restored to its appearance at that time. Although few of the furnishings are authentic, his personal effects (including the waistcoat he wore at the duel) and those of his wife are on display. The library, where Pushkin died, has been rebuilt according to sketches made in his last hours by his friend and fellow poet, Vasily Zhukovsky, who was holding vigil. A moving account leads you through the apartment and retells the events leading up to the poet's death. The museum is a short walk from the corner of Nevsky Prospect and the Moika embankment. ⊠ *Nab. Moiki, 12,* ☎ *812/311–8001.* ⊙ *Wed.–Mon. 11–5. Closed last Fri. of month.*

㉓ Ploshchad Vosstaniya (Insurrection Square). Originally called Znamenskaya Ploshchad (Square of the Sign) after a church of the same name that stood on it, the plaza was the site of many revolutionary speeches and armed clashes with military and police forces—hence its second name. Like Decembrists' Square, it's now officially back to its first name, but it's unusual to hear it called that—yet at least. (The subway station of the same name hasn't changed.) The busy Moscow Railroad Station is here, and from this point, the street is lined with almost every imaginable shop, from fruit markets to art salons to bookstores. A stroll here is not a casual affair, for Nevsky is almost always teeming with bustling crowds of shoppers and street artists. Budding entrepreneurs, who sell their wares on the sidewalk on folding tables, further obstruct pedestrian traffic. Here you will also see an increasingly rare sight, the old men of the Great Patriotic War (the Russian name for World War II) still proudly wearing their medals.

OFF THE
BEATEN PATH

PISKARYEVSKOYE KLADBISHCHE – The vast extent of this city's suffering during the 900-day siege between 1941 and 1944 becomes clear after a visit to the sobering Piskaryevskoye Cemetery. Located on the northeastern outskirts of the city, the field here was used, out of necessity, as a mass burial ground for the hundreds of thousands of World War II victims, some of whom died from the shelling, but mostly from cold and starvation. The numbingly endless rows of common graves carry simple slabs indicating the year in which those below them died. In all, nearly 500,000 people are buried here, and individual graves were impossible. The cemetery, with its memorial monuments and an eternal flame, has been made into a moving historical marker. Inscribed on the granite wall at the far end of the cemetery is the famous poem by radio personality Olga Bergholts, which ends with the oft-repeated phrase, "No one is forgotten, nothing is forgotten." The granite pavilions at the entrance house a small museum with photographs and memoirs documenting the siege. On display is Tanya Savicheva's diary, scraps of paper on which the young schoolgirl recorded the death of every member of her family. The last entry reads, "May 13. Mother died. Everyone is dead. Only I am left." (Later, she too died as a result of the war.) To get there, board the metro at the Mayakovskaya stop in Ploshchad Vosstaniya and ride north, getting off at Ploshchad Muzhevstva; then take Bus 123 to the cemetery. ⊠ *74 Nepokorennykh,* ☎ *812/247–5716.* ⊙ *Daily 10–5 (museum).*

RIMSKY-KORSAKOV MUSEUM – From Insurrection Square go south and west to Zagorodny where you'll find this small museum. Classical concerts are occasionally held in the small concert hall of the composer's former home. ⊠ *28 Zagorodny Prospect, Apt. 39.* ☎ *812/113–3208.* ⊙ *Wed.–Sun. 11–6, closed last Fri. of month.*

㉕ Pushkin Drama Theater. The most imposing building on **Ploshchad Ostrovskovo** (Ostrovsky Square, although you may hear it referred to as

Ploshchad Alexandrinskaya) was originally named the Alexandrinsky Theater (for the wife of Nicholas I) and built in Classical style between 1828 and 1832. Six Corinthian columns adorn the Nevsky facade. Apollo's chariot dominates the building, with statues of the muses Terpischore and Melpomene to keep him company. In the small garden in front of the theater stands the **Catherine Monument,** which shows the empress towering above the principal personalities of her famous reign. Depicted on the pedestal are Grigory Potemkin, Generalissimo Suvorov, the poet Gavril Derzhavin, and others. Among the bronze figures is the Princess Dashkova, who conspired against her own sister's lover—who just happened to be Catherine's husband, Peter III—to help the empress assume the throne.

Russian National Library. Opened in 1814 as the Imperial Public Library, it was Russia's first built for that purpose and today is known fondly as the "Publichka." It has over 20 million books and claims to have a copy of every book ever printed in Russia. Among its treasures are Voltaire's personal library and the only copy of *Chasovnik* (1565), the second book printed in Russia. The building comprises three sections. The main section, on the corner of Nevsky Prospect and Sadovaya ulitsa, was designed by Yegor Sakolov and built between 1796 and 1801. The wing nearest you, built between 1828 and 1832, was designed by Carlo Rossi as an integral part of Ostrovsky Square. True to the building's purpose, the facade is adorned with statues of philosophers and poets, including Homer and Virgil, and the Roman goddess of wisdom, Minerva.

Smolny. Confusion abounds when you mention the Smolny, for you can mean either a beautiful Baroque church or a classically designed institute that went down in history as the Bolshevik headquarters in the 1917 Revolution. It doesn't help matters much that the two architectural complexes are right next door to each other, on the Neva's left bank. Construction of the Smolny Convent and Cathedral began under Elizabeth I and continued during the reign of Catherine the Great, who established a school for the daughters of the nobility within its walls. The centerpiece of the convent is the magnificent five-domed **Cathedral of the Resurrection,** which was designed by Bartolomeo Rastrelli. Some say it is his greatest creation. At first glance, the highly ornate blue-and-white cathedral seems to have leaped off the pages of a fairy tale. Its five white onion domes, crowned with gilded globes supporting crosses of gold, convey a sense of magic and power. Begun by Rastrelli in 1748, the cathedral was not completed until the 1830s, by the architect Vasily Stasov. It is now open to the public, but few traces of the original interior have survived. ⊠ *3/1 Pl. Rastrelli.* ☎ *812/311–3560.* ☉ *Daily 11–5, 11–4 if there is a concert.*

The **Smolny Institute,** just south of the cathedral, is a far different structure. Designed by Giacomo Quarenghi in 1806–08, the Classical building was done in the style of an imposing country manor. The Smolny Institute will long be remembered by the Russian people as the site where Lenin and his associates planned the overthrow of the Kerensky government in October 1917. Lenin lived at the Smolny for 124 days. The rooms in which he resided and worked are now a memorial museum. Today the building houses the offices of the mayor of St. Petersburg and can be visited only by a special request. ⊠ *1 Proletarskoy Diktatury,* ☎ *812/276–1461.* ☉ *Lenin memorial museum daily 9.30–5.*

㉙ Stroganov Palace. This palace, completed in 1754, is an outstanding example of the Russian Baroque and one of Rastrelli's finest achievements. Its entrance is unique, in that it faces Nevsky Prospect. Above the archway you still see the family coat of arms: two sables holding a shield with a bear's head above. It symbolizes the Stroganovs' source of wealth—vast holdings of land, with all its resources, including furs—in Siberia. You can go into the courtyard and even peek inside, for there is a small branch of the applied arts section of the Russian Museum operating here; the renovation is extensive but far from complete. Unfortunately, most of the palace's interior was ravaged by fire at the end of the 18th century, though the outside remained intact. Before you leave, you may find it amusing to remember that this was the birthplace of beef Stroganoff.

Taurida Palace (Tavrichesky Dvorets). Built in 1783–89 on the orders of Catherine the Great for her favorite, Count Grigori Potyomkin, the palace is one of St. Petersburg's most magnificent buildings. Potyomkin had been given the title of the Prince of Taurida for his annexation of the Crimea (ancient Taurida) to Russia. The Taurida Palace is a splendid example of Classicism, the main trend in Russian architecture in the late 18th century. The luxurious interior decor contrasts with its modest exterior. For a long period after Potyomkin's death the palace remained inhabited. Later on in 1906 it was partially rebuilt for the State Duma, the Russian parliament. During the February Revolution of 1917 the Taurida Palace became a center of revolutionary events. Today the palace is used for international conferences and meetings. ⊠ 47 *Shpalernaya.*

Ulitsa Zodchevo Rossi. The proportions of this extraordinary street are perfect. It is bounded by two buildings of exactly the same height, its width (22 meters, or 72 feet) equals the height of the buildings, and its length is exactly 10 times its width. A complete view unfolds only at the end of the street, where it meets Lomonosov Square. The perfect symmetry is reinforced by the identical facades of the two buildings, which are painted the same subdued yellow and decorated with impressive white pillars. One of the buildings is the famous **Vaganova Ballet School** (founded in 1738), whose pupils included Karsavina as well as Pavlova, Nijinsky, and Ulanova.

Yeliseyevsky Food Emporium. The name has finally been returned to this famous store, after having been officially called Gastronome No. 1 under the Communists. It is located directly across the street from the Catherine Monument. Built at the turn of the century for the immensely successful grocer Yeliseyev, it is decorated in the style of early Art Nouveau, with colorful stained-glass windows, gilded ceilings, and brass chandeliers. Before the revolution it specialized in imported delicacies, and after several lean decades, goods again overflow its shelves. (The Moscow branch is on Tverskaya ulitsa.) ⊠ *Ul. Nevsky 56.*

OFF THE
BEATEN PATH
ANNA AKHMATOVA LITERARY MUSEUM – Opened in 1989, the museum is located in the former palace of the Count Sheremetyev, which was home to the famous St. Petersburg poet for many years. ⊠ *34 Nab. Fontanki,* ☎ *812/272-2211 or 812/272-5895.* ⊙ *Tues.–Sun. 10.30– 5:30. Closed last Wed. of month.*

From the Square of the Arts to the Field of Mars

This walk takes you to some of St. Petersburg's prettiest inner streets, squares, and gardens, starting at Ploshchad Iskusstv (Square of the Arts). Along the route are several squares and buildings of historical interest: it was in this area of the city that several extremely important events in Russian history took place, including the murder of czars Paul I, who was assassinated in the Mikhailovsky Dvorets by nobles opposed to his rule, and Alexander II, killed when a handmade bomb was lobbed at him by revolutionary terrorists as he was riding by the Griboyedov Canal in a carriage.

A Good Walk

Go down Nevsky Prospect to ulitsa Mikhailovskaya (you can take the subway to the stop of the same name). Walking up this short street will take you past the handsome Grand Hotel Europe, built in the 1870s. Given its Art Nouveau facade in 1910, it remains one of St. Petersburg's most elegant lodging places. Straight up this street is **Mikhailovsky Dvorets** ㉚, at the far end of Ploshchad Iskusstv. The building to the right of the palace appears to be an extension of its right wing but is a different building entirely; it is the **Ethnography Museum.**

If you stand in front of the palace and turn to survey the entire square, the first building on your right, with old-fashioned lanterns adorning its doorways, is the **Maly Theater** ㉛. The next one, No. 3, is the **Isaac Brodsky Museum.** Bordering the square's south side, on Mikhailovskaya ulitsa's east corner, is the former **Nobles' Club** ㉜, now home to the St. Petersburg Philharmonic. The buildings on the square's remaining side are former residences and school buildings, including a special school, funded and staffed since perestrojka by the **Russian Museum** ㉝, for pupils interested in history and culture. The museum's entrance is around the corner. Leave the Square of the Arts and go down ulitsa Inzhenernaya toward the Griboyedev (Ekaterininsky) Canal. Take a right and you find the entrance a few steps away. Go right when you leave the museum, and straight ahead is the almost outrageously colorful **Khram Spasa na Krovi** ㉞.

To the right as you walk past the church is a small park behind a lovely wrought-iron fence. Known as Mikhailovsky Sad (Mikhail Gardens), it forms the back of Grand Duke Mikhail's former estate. On the other side of this pleasant park runs Sadovaya ulitsa. You should follow the street you're on, however, as it curves around gently to the right. Opposite the gardens, across the street, spreads **Marsovo Pole** ㉟.

The long line of buildings flanking the left side of Marsovo Pole are the former Barracks of the Pavlovsky Guards Regiment. They were completed in 1819, in homage to the regiment's victories in the war against Napoléon. Go down this side of the street, and you will reach Millionaya ulitsa (Millionaire's Street), which, as the name implies, was once one of St. Petersburg's swankest.

On this street, in front of you, is the **Mramorny Dvorets** ㊱. Take a right and walk down Millionaya ulitsa the length of the Field of Mars. On the left you pass **Suvorovskaya Ploshchad** ㊲. Walk up to the river and continue going east (right). Very soon you will find yourself in front of the marvelous grille that marks the entrance to **Letny Sad** ㊳, the Yuri Felten-designed summer gardens. You enter at the far left end of the railing. Exiting at the south end of the park will bring you out in front of the former castle of Czar Paul I, across the street, the **Inzhenerny Zamok** ㊴. The tour ends here. From the castle, you can walk down ulitsa Sadovaya until it intersects with Nevsky Prospect. If you take the first right off of it, you will return to the Square of the Arts. If you like, you can stop in the Mikhail Gardens now; there is an entrance on this side, to the right.

TIMING

Including stops, this walk should take between two and three hours. Letny Sad, Mikhailovsky Sad, and Marsovo Pole are worth visiting at any time of the year. Note that the Neva is very close here and it is windy year-round.

Sights to See

Ethnography Museum. This museum contains a fascinating collection of applied art and many sociological displays about peoples of the 19th and 20th centuries, including the various ethnic groups of the former Soviet Union. ⊠ *4/1 Inzhenernaya ul.,* ☎ *812/219–1174 or 812/219–1676.* ☉ *Tues.–Sun. 11–6. Closed last Fri. of month.*

㊴　Inzhenerny Zamok (Engineer's Castle). This orange-hued building belonged to one of Russia's stranger and more pitiful leaders. Paul I grew up in the shadow of his powerful mother, Catherine the Great, whom he despised; no doubt correctly, he held her responsible for his father's death. By the time Paul became czar, he lived in terror that he, too, would be murdered. He claimed that, shortly after ascending the throne, the Archangel Michael appeared to him in a dream and instructed him to build a church on the site of his birthplace. Paul then proceeded to erect not just a church but a castle, which he tried to make into an impenetrable fortress. Out of spite toward his mother, he took stones and other materials from castles that she had built. The Fontanka and Moika rivers cut off access from the north and east; and for protection everywhere else, he installed secret passages, moats with drawbridges, and earthen ramparts. All of Paul's intricate planning, however, came to naught. On March 24, 1801, a month after he began living there, he was murdered—suffocated with a pillow in his bed. Historians speculate that his own son, Alexander I, knew such a plot was underway and may even have participated. After Paul's death, the castle stood empty for 20 years, then was turned over to the Military Engineering Academy. One of the school's pupils was Fyodor Dostoevsky, who as a novelist was absorbed with themes of murder and greed. The building now belongs to the Russian Museum (☞ *below*).

NEED A BREAK?	The **Grand Hotel Europe** has a lovely mezzanine café, where you can relax and enjoy a pot of tea or a glass of champagne, served with bowls of strawberries. While there, take a peek at the beautifully renovated Art Nouveau lobby, replete with stained-glass windows and antique furnishings.

Isaac Brodsky Museum. This structure was built in the 1820s for the Golenishchev-Kutuzovs, a high-ranking military family. The painter Isaac Brodsky lived here from 1924 to 1939, and it is now a memorial museum to him. On view are some of his works as well as some from his private collection, which included pieces by Ilya Repin and Valentin Serov. ⊠ *3 Pl. Iskusstv,* ☎ *812/314–3658.* ☉ *Wed.–Sun., 11–7. Provisionally closed for repairs.*

OFF THE BEATEN PATH	**JACQUOT'S HOUSE –** No. 5 Ploshchad Iskusstv had a famous café *cum* art salon in its basement from 1911 to 1915, called the Stray Dog. A diverse range of painters, writers, and musicians, including Anna Akhmatova, Nikolai Gumilev, and Osip Mandelstam used it as a creative meeting point.

㉞　Khram Spasa na Krovi (Church of the Saviour on the Spilled Blood). The highly ornate, old Russian style seems more befitting to Moscow than St. Petersburg, where the architecture is generally more subdued and subtle; and indeed, the architect Alfred Parland was consciously aiming to copy Moscow's St. Basil's. The drama of the church's inception more than matches the frenzy of its design, however. It was commissioned by Alexander III to memorialize the shocking death of his father, Alexander II, who was killed on the site in 1881 by a terrorist's bomb.

The church opened in 1907 but was closed by Stalin in the 1930s. It suffered damage throughout the years, especially during World War II. Under meticulous reconstruction for decades (painstaking attempts have been made to replace all original components with identically matched materials), it is due to reopen by 1996. The interiors reportedly are as extravagant as the exterior, with glittering stretches of mosaic from floor to ceiling. Scenes of martyrdom include one that draws a parallel between the czar's death and the crucifixion of Christ. Stone carvings and gold leaf adorn the walls, the floors are all of pink Italian marble, and the remarkable altar is made entirely of semiprecious gems and supported by four jasper columns.

★ ㉘ **Letny Sad** (Summer Gardens). The Summer Gardens were another of Peter the Great's passions, inspired by Versailles. When first laid out in 1704, they were given a regular, geometric style and decorated with statues and sculptures as well as with imported trees and plants. Grottoes, pavilions, ponds, fountains, and intricate walkways were placed throughout, and the grounds are bordered on all sides by rivers and canals. In 1777, however, disastrous floods did so much damage (entirely destroying the system of fountains) that the imperial family stopped using the gardens for entertaining. When they decamped for environs farther afield, they left the Summer Gardens for use by the upper classes. Today they remain a popular park, accessible to everyone, but you will have to imagine the first formal gardens, for they are no longer there. The graceful wrought-iron fence that marks the entrance to the gardens was designed in 1779 by Yuri Felten, and is supported by pink granite pillars decorated with vases and urns.

Just inside this southeastern corner is Peter's original Summer Palace, **Letny Dvorets.** Designed by Domenico Trezzini and completed in 1714, the two-story building is quite simple in design, as most of Peter's dwellings were. The walls are of stucco-covered brick, painted primrose yellow. Open since 1934 as a museum, it has survived without major alteration. Two other attractive buildings nearby are the **Coffee House** (built by Rossi in 1826) and the **Tea House** (by L. I. Charlemagne in 1827), neither of which, alas, serves the beverages for which it was named.

As you walk through the park, have a look at some of its statues, of which more than 80 still remain. You can see *Peace and Abundance,* sculpted by Pietro Baratta in 1722, an allegorical depiction of Russia's victory in the war with Sweden. Another statue, just off the main alley, is of Ivan Krylov, "Russia's La Fontaine." It is by Peter Klodt (who also did the Anichkov Bridge horse statues) and was unveiled in 1855. Scenes from Krylov's fables, including his version of "The Fox and the Grapes," appear on the pedestal. As in many other parks and public places, the sculptures are protected from the harsh weather by wooden covers from early fall to late spring.

㉛ **Maly Theater** (Little Theater). This historic theater is better known as the Maly, the name given it during the Communist era. Before the Revolution it was the Mikhailovsky Theater, but French companies performed here so often that it was more commonly referred to as the French Theater. Since 1991 it is officially the **Mussorgsky Theater of Opera and Ballet,** St. Petersburg's second most important theater, after the Mariinsky (Kirov).

★ ㉟ **Marsovo Pole** (Field of Mars). The site was once a marsh, from which both the Mya and the Krikusha rivers began. Peter the Great had it drained (and the rivers linked by a canal), and the space was subsequently used for parades and public occasions. The field acquired its present name around 1800, when it began to be used primarily for military exercises. Shortly after 1917 it was turned into a burial ground for Red Army victims of the Revolution and ensuing civil war. The massive granite **Monument to Revolutionary Fighters** was unveiled there on November 7, 1919, with an eternal flame lit 40 years later, also on the Revolution's anniversary.

30　Mikhailovsky Dvorets. The plaza in front of the palace was originally named Mikhailovsky Ploshchad for Grand Duke Mikhail Pavlovich (1798–1849), the younger brother of Alexander I and Nicholas I and resident of the palace. The square's appearance is the work of Carlo Rossi, who designed the facade of each building encircling it as well as the palace. Each structure, as well as the plaza itself, was made to complement Mikhail's residence on its north side. Built between 1819 and 1825, it comprises a principal house and two service wings. The central portico with eight Corinthian columns faces a large courtyard now enclosed by a fine Art Nouveau railing, a late (1903) addition. The statue of Alexander Pushkin in the center of the plaza was designed by Mikhail Anikushin and erected in 1957.

36　Mramorny Dvorets (Marble Palace). Designed by Arnoldo Rinaldi and built between 1768 and 1785 for Grigori Orlov, this building was not completed until after Orlov's death. It was one of Catherine the Great's favorite palaces. Its name derives from its pale pink-purple marble facing. From 1937 to 1991, it housed the Lenin Museum; in the courtyard was the armored automobile from which he made his revolutionary speech at the Finland Station. Today, instead of Lenin's automobile you can see an equestrian statue of Czar Alexander III. The statue survived under the Soviets hidden in the Russian Museum's courtyard. The palace now belongs to the Museum.

32　Nobles' Club. This former private club is now home to the **St. Petersburg Philharmonic.** Its main concert hall, with its impressive marble columns, has been the site of many famous performances, including the first presentation of Tchaikovsky's Sixth (*Pathetique*) Symphony, his final masterpiece, with the composer conduction. (He died 9 days later.) More recently, in 1942, when Leningrad was completely blockaded, Dmitri Shostakovich's Seventh (*Leningrad*) Symphony was premiered here, an event broadcast in the same spirit of defiance against the Germans in which it was written. Later the concert hall was officially named for Shostakovich.

★　**33　Russian Museum.** One of the country's most important art galleries has been housed in the Mikhailovsky Palace since 1896, when Nicholas II turned it into a museum. He did so in tribute to his father, Alexander III, who had a special regard for Russian art and regretted, after seeing Moscow's Tretyakov Gallery, that St. Petersburg had nothing like it.

Officially named the **Gosudarstvenny Muzey Russkovo Iskusstva** (State Museum of Russian Art), its collection is now the equal—or more important, the complement—of the Tretyakov's, with scores of masterpieces on display. Outstanding icons include the 14th-century *Boris and Gleb* and the 15th-century *Angel Miracle of St. George*. Seventeenth- and 18th-century paintings are also well represented, especially with portraiture. One of the most famous 18th-century works here is Ivan Nikitin's *The Field Hetman*. By far the most important cache, however, comprises 19th-century works—huge canvases by Repin, many fine portraits by Serov (his beautiful *Countess Orlova* and the equally beautiful, utterly different portrait of the dancer Ida Rubinstein), and Mikhail Vrubel's strange, disturbing *Demon Cast Down*. Since so little of this work was well known in the West, it is fascinating to see stylistic parallels and the incorporation of outside influences into a Russian framework. Painters of the World of Art movement—Bakst, Benois, and Somov—are also here. There are several examples of 20th-century art, with works by Kandinsky and Kazimir Malevich. Natan Altman's striking portrait of the poet Anna Akhmatova is in Room 77. The museum usually has at least one excellent special exhibit going on. ✉ *4/2 Inzhenernaya ul.,* ☏ *812/314–3448,* 𝔽𝔸𝕏 *812/314–4153.* ☉ *Mon. and Wed.–Sun. 10–6.*

③⑦ Suvorovskaya Ploshchad (Suvorov Square). In the middle of this square there is a statue of the military commander Alexander Suvorov, cast as Mars, god of war. Appropriately enough, when first unveiled in 1801, the statue stood in Marsovo Pole, but in 1818 it was moved to its present location.

OFF THE
BEATEN PATH

ST. PETERSBURG CIRCUS – Though perhaps not as famous as the Moscow Circus, the St. Petersburg Circus dates from 1867 and remains a popular treat for children. Avid young circus fans may get a kick out of its adjacent **Circus Art Museum** (☏ 812/210–4413), as well, with displays about the world of the circus. ✉ *3 nab. Fontanki,* ☏ *812/210–4198.* ☉ *Performances daily 7 PM; matinees on weekends. Closed Thurs.* ☉ *Museum, weekdays noon–6).*

MONUMENT TO THE HEROES OF THE DEFENSE OF LENINGRAD DURING WORLD WAR II – You are likely to see this on the way from the airport or if you visit the Park Pobedy region. Financed and built by city residents, it faces the southern part of St. Petersburg, which saw the fiercest fighting. The center obelisk inside a broken ring symbolizes the breaking of the enemy blockade. Surrounding it are groups involved in the battles—sailors, partisans, soldiers, and people's volunteers. Underneath is a memorial hall museum. ✉ *Pl. Pobedy,* ☏ *812/293–6563.* ☉ *Thurs.–Tues. 11-5. Closed last Tues. of month.*

DINING

In the age-old rivalry between Moscow and St. Petersburg, the capital wins when it comes to the sheer breadth of offerings for the tourist dining out. For such a large city, St. Petersburg's restaurant scene still seems more limited than it should. Of course if you look back into the not-so-distant past, when the best you could do was a large and rowdy state enterprise in one of the city's foreign hotels, you realize how good things really are. There is still plenty of that type of dining, but there's also a fair crop of smaller, more relaxed establishments. Like the city itself, restaurants here seem less "foreign" than those in Moscow or Kiev; the accent is on warm atmosphere, friendly service, tasty food, and a decidedly more European ambience. You won't have that "either/or" feeling—that either you're at a rowdy expatriate establishment and still aware that you're from elsewhere, or that you're adrift in a strange brew of strictly Russian places, where heavy atmosphere, unpredictable food, and tacky decor make you feel equally alien.

Remember that landing a table in a good restaurant is still not done on a whim: You must plan ahead. Reservations are almost always essential, especially in the evening, partly because there just aren't *that* many places. You're likely to have better luck if you ask your hotel or tour guide for help—the best meals are often still had through connections. Keep in mind that at large establishments with live entertainment dining out will be an all-night affair, for at restaurants featuring floor shows, eating out means not only a meal but drinking and dancing the night away as well. Although you may find it in poor taste, the entertainment usually entails exceptionally loud music (with some perennial favorites played over and over again), colored disco light shows, and scantily clad dancers. Few restaurants offer no-smoking sections. Remember that most restaurants stop serving food between 11 and midnight, although some cater to all-night dancing.

As with the shopping scene, St. Petersburg's restaurants can be divided roughly into categories based on the type of payment accepted and the anticipated clientele. Prices, in general, are lower than Moscow's and higher than Kiev's. Private and (the remaining) cooperative restaurants, which often accept both credit cards and rubles, are far more expensive—and usually of much better quality—than the state-run restaurants operating exclusively in rubles.

CATEGORY	COST*
$$$$	over $40
$$$	$25–$40
$$	$10–$25
$	under $10

per person, excluding drinks and service

WHAT TO WEAR

Dress at the restaurants reviewed below is casual, unless noted otherwise.

$$$$ ✕ **Europe.** This elegant restaurant in the Grand Hotel Europe is in a
★ category all of its own. It offers luxury and fine dining of a kind that St. Petersburg has not seen since the 1917 Revolution. Like the grand dining room at the Metropole in Moscow, this has a breathtaking interior, complete with stained-glass roof and private balconies, and seems fit for a czar. But then, so do the prices. The menu, which features European and Russian cuisines, is exotic by local standards. For starters, try the fresh goose liver, served with a honey-and-wine sauce. The main dishes vary, but a highlight is the fillet of salmon, filled with cream cheese and served with a wine-and-herb sauce. If you're not up for an opulent dinner, you may enjoy the popular Sunday morning jazz brunch. Don't think about it too long, though, because tables book up fast, especially in the summer. ✉ *1/7 Mikhailovskaya ul., in Grand Hotel Europe,* ☎ *812/329-6000. Reservations essential. Jacket and tie. AE, MC, V. Rubles only. Breakfast every day 7–10:30, dinner every day except Sun. 7–11. Sun. brunch noon–3.*

$$$$ ✕ **Imperial.** This is the Nevsky Palace Hotel's swank restaurant, and whereas the Europe (☞ *above*) emphasizes Old World grandeur, it settles for sleek comfort. It, too, is a top-class spot, nicely nestled above Nevsky Prospect, so at some tables you can watch the Russian world go by. The changing dishes are strong on good Continental fare, with meat the house specialty: beef, pork, lamb, and chicken, all grilled with vegetables. In the evening there's a buffet, which includes an assortment of all the meats on the menu. There's usually a jazz trio livening things up in the background. ✉ *57 Nevsky Prospect,* ☎ *812/ 275–2001. Reservations advised. Jacket and tie. AE, MC, V. Rubles only.* ☼ *Daily 7–11, noon–3, 7–11.*

$$$$ ✕ **Nevski Melody.** This Russo-Swedish venture ranks among St. Petersburg's finest gourmet experiences. The menu is exquisite, the atmosphere is elegant, and the wine list is superb. The restaurant offers beautifully prepared Russo-European and Mexican dishes. The restaurant opens at 12, but stays open until 6 AM. ✉ *62 Sverdlovskaya nab.,* ☎ *812/227–1596. Jacket and tie. AE, DC, MC, V. Rubles only.*

$$$$ ✕ **Senat Bar.** Housed in the famous Senate building, this delightful restaurant serves exquisite European cuisine in an elegant atmosphere highlighted by a stylized interior with crystal chandeliers and old-fashioned

chairs. The menu, a mix of Russian and Continental dishes, offers up such appetizers as black and red caviar, crab, and spicy chicken in a walnut sauce. For your main course try the exellent *Kievskaya kotleta* (chicken Kiev). The staff cultivate a high level of service and foreign visitors are always welcomed. Excellent wines from France, Spain, Germany, and Argentina stock the extensive cellar, and there is a large choice of beer from Holland and Belgium. The kitchen is open daily from 11 to 5. ⊠ *1 ul. Galernaya.* ☏ *812/314–9253 or 812/314–4920. Reservation required. Jacket and tie. AE, MC, V. Rubles only.*

$$$$ ✕ **Venice.** Situated among the gloomy high rises of Vasilievsky Island, this Russo–Italian venture is easy to spot: It's the only building in the area that isn't dominated by the color gray. Its distant location makes it truly convenient only for those already staying at the Pribaltiskaya Hotel, for whom the immaculate and snazzy interior is a welcome change of pace. There's often a singer performing, but it's not the standard over-the-top floor show by any means, and because the dining room is spacious, you won't be acoustically overwhelmed. The service, provided by formally dressed waiters, is rather pretentious but not too stiff, and the food is a delight. With an Italian chef and imported ingredients (right down to the flour and salt), the kitchen produces authentic pasta and Italian meat dishes. The menu changes weekly depending on shipments, but standard offerings include a tangy pasta *arrabbiata* (with hot peppers, tomatoes, garlic, and oil) and a succulent lasagna. The wide selection of Italian and other imported wines is unusual for St. Petersburg. Attached to the restaurant is an inexpensive pizzeria, which operates for rubles and has takeout, very popular with foreign students staying in the university dormitory across the street. ⊠ *21 ul. Korablestroitelei,* ☏ *812/352–1432. Reservations advised. Jacket and tie. No credit cards. Rubles only.*

$$$ ✕ **Angleterre.** This pretty restaurant off the main lobby of the Astoria Hotel offers average food at above-average prices. Though it advertises European cuisine, the unimaginative menu is dominated by standard Russian dishes, such as borshch, herring, and beefsteak in mushroom–sour cream sauce. The food, once it actually makes it to your table, is quite good, if unsurprising. What the restaurant lacks in speed and innovation, however, it does make up for in atmosphere. The lovely all-white room is lit by crystal chandeliers and light from the exquisite lobby outside also filters through its discreetly curtained glass walls. The quiet piano music tinkling in the background is reminiscent of the hotel's better days at the turn of the century. The restaurant also offers a popular buffet breakfast, which comes with all the blini you can eat and at a more reasonable prix fixe than the prices found on the lunch and dinner menus. The kitchen closes at 11 PM. ⊠ *39 Bolshaya Morskaya ul.,* ☏ *812/210–5906. Reservations advised. AE, MC, V. Rubles only.*

$$$ ✕ **Aphrodite.** This Russo-Finnish restaurant has a decidedly Scandinavian slant, serving lots of fish and seafood along with its equally interesting Russian dishes. Its two white rooms, graced with archways and filled with soft, filtered light, provide a soothing place to unwind after a long day of touring. Talk is quiet (it's a good choice for dinner *à deux*), background music is light (Sinatra classics are a favorite), and service is attentive—even deferential. The eccentrically amusing array of appetizers includes smoked reindeer salad, oysters on the half shell, and warm frogs' legs. The excellent selection of fish dishes features salmon, sturgeon, turbot, and perch. You may want to try the red perch in paper with ginger and bacon or the wolffish in spices with vegetables. Other appetites can have a beefsteak but may be more interested by the rabbit stew or elk steak. The wine list is small but decent. ⊠

146

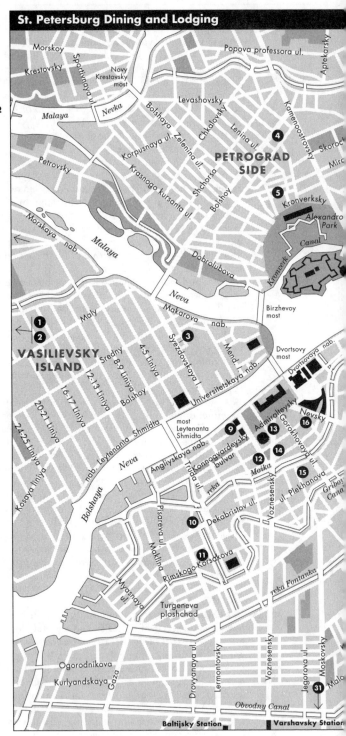

St. Petersburg Dining and Lodging

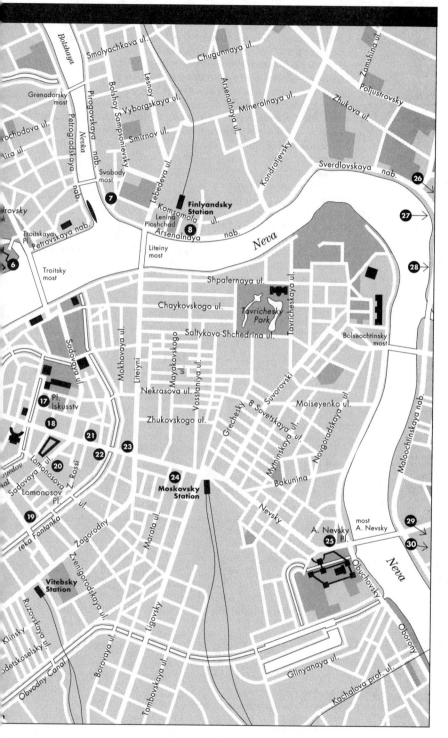

86 Nevsky Prospect, ☎ *812/275–7620. Reservations accepted. AE, MC, V. Rubles only.*

$$$ ✕ **Brasserie.** This restaurant off a ground-floor wing of the Grand Hotel Europe is the perfect place for a refreshing Caesar salad or a well-prepared steak. The menu has some nice Russian standbys but aims toward bistro exotic—try the garlicky snails with tomato bread. There is always a satisfying plat du jour as well. The relaxed atmosphere is enhanced by the efficient and excellent service: come to the Brasserie if the outside has been getting you down. ⊠ *1/7 Mikhailovskaya ul.,* ☎ *812/329–6000. Reservations accepted. AE, MC, V. Rubles only.*

$$$ ✕ **Dvoryanskoye Gnezdo** (Noblemans' Nest). Tucked away in the ★   garden pavilion of the amazing Yusupov Palace, this very chic spot is particularly attractive to the after-theater crowd (the Mariinsky is not far away). Formal attire matches its service, decor, and food, which is mainly of the European, French-influenced variety. You may be able to close your eyes and imagine the carriages waiting outside the door. ⊠ *21 ul. Dekabristov,* ☎ *812/312–3205. Jacket and tie. AE, MC, V. Rubles only. Reservations required.*

$$$ ✕ **Kalinka.** In this restaurant on Vasilyevsky Island you can enjoy a combination of Russian cuisine with European service. Kalinka's excellent soups include solyanka, a spicy thick stew made with vegetables and meat or fish, and borshch. Kalinka recommends the *griby v smetane* (mushrooms baked in sour cream sauce) and blinis served with black or red caviar. ⊠ *9 Syezdovskaia linya,* ☎ *812/218–2866.*

$$ ✕ **Cat.** A popular café with the young and trendy, on a side street off Nevsky Prospect, it has Russian food all the same, solid and predictable. You may be better off dropping in for lunch, when it's a convenient place to unwind and recharge, and just order rounds of appetizers. ⊠ *24 ul. Karavannaya,* ☎ *812/315–3800. Rubles only.*

$$ ✕ **Chaika.** This lively, smoke-filled restaurant and bar is popular with young locals and expatriates alike. A German-Russian venture, it offers good, hearty North German food and great German beer (which you can enjoy until 3 AM). The dark wood interior, with lots of booths, long tables, and paneling, is right out of Germany, and the food, except for such Russian delicacies as caviar, is dominated by dishes like frankfurters with sauerkraut. It's a great place to come on a rainy day for a piping hot bowl of French onion soup or Hungarian goulash. The system of taking orders is a bit odd: you're handed a punch card on entering, on which your waiter records your choices. When you leave you present it, not a bill, to the cashier. The staff seems studiously blasé but gets the job done. ⊠ *14 Kanal Griboyedova,* ☎ *812/312–4631. Reservations not accepted. AE, MC, V. Rubles only.*

$$ ✕ **Chopsticks.** It doesn't seem quite fair that the Grand Hotel Europe, among its other excellent offerings, also has the best Chinese food in town. With Chinese chefs and authentic ingredients (most supplies are imported), Chopsticks is in a league of its own. Its emphasis is on the sweet-and-sour dishes from the north, tangy but not too hot. If you crave American-style Chinese food, this is a gold mine. One word of advice: Don't count on nabbing one of its few tables if you just drop by; the cozy restaurant is always full. ⊠ *1/7 Mikhailovskaya ul.,* ☎ *812/329–6000. Reservations essential. AE, MC, V. Rubles only.*

$$ ✕ **John Bull Pub.** As easy to get to as it is on the nerves, this English pub serves Russian food in its dining hall and standard snacks at the bar. For a bowl of borshch, or just a foamy mug of beer and refuge from architectural overload, try this cozy inn. ⊠ *79 Nevsky Prospect,* ☎ *812/164–9877. Rubles only.*

$$ ✕ **Literary Café.** You may have encountered this slice of history on one of your walks. Famous as the site of Pushkin's last meal (it was a confectionery then), it's imbued with a melancholy air of the past. The old-fashioned dining rooms, adorned with white linen and old silver, draw a cultured crowd. You'll find only Russian food, but there's a lot to choose from. Service is the sore point: waiters are frequently testy but still can't spoil the pleasantly hushed ambience. There's usually a small entrance fee, for the attendant classical musicians. The kitchen stays open until 2 AM. ⊠ *18 Nevsky Prospect,* ☎ *812/312–6057. AE, MC, V. Rubles only.*

$$ ✕ **Na Fontanke.** This restaurant's reputation rests on its status as St. Petersburg's first cooperative. When it opened in 1988, it met with immediate and resounding success, in large part because it faced little competition. Even though Na Fontanke is no longer the only private restaurant in town, reservations are still essential. Although the restaurant is right on the bank of the Fontanka (hence its name), there are no tables with a view of the city's canals: As in most Russian restaurants, all the windows are heavily draped. The one small dining room is elegantly decorated in blue and gold. The food is uninspired, but what it lacks in originality it does make up for in presentation. The menu is a mix of Russian and Continental dishes, emphasizing the former. The prix fixe dinner includes an array of Russian appetizers (cold cuts, herring, mushrooms in cream sauce in a pastry shell), a main course, ice cream, and coffee. The nightly entertainment is a fascinating—but loud—extravaganza of Gypsy music and dance. This is not the place for intimate dining and conversation, but it's not a bad choice for an authentic Russian meal. ⊠ *77 nab. Fontanki,* ☎ *812/310–2547. Reservations essential. No credit cards. Rubles only.* ☉ *Daily 1–5 and 7–11. Closed for repairs at press time.*

$$ ✕ **Sadko.** This lively and comfortable restaurant-bar is another pleasant eating establishment of the Grand Hotel Europe, without any of its pomp and circumstance. Check your tie at the door and sit down for a refreshing (imported) draft beer and pizza. The blackboard menu, which changes daily, offers satisfying Western-style bar food, such as hamburgers, spare ribs, and pasta. The good food, fun atmosphere, and nightly entertainment (the place closes at 1 AM), which usually features popular local performers and up-and-coming new bands, make this a good choice if you just want to kick back and settle in. You can also get a good view of life on the Nevsky Prospect. ⊠ *1/7 Mikhailovskaya ul. (separate entrance from Grand Hotel Europe),* ☎ *812/329–6000. AE, MC, V. Rubles only.*

$$ ✕ **Shvabsky Domik.** You can tell the food here is authentic by the crowds of German expatriates who keep coming back for the schnitzel and wurst. The simple decor, with heavy wood paneling and long wooden benches, makes for a relaxed and pleasant atmosphere. The waitresses, all in German national dress, aim to please and offer a pleasant change of pace from the usual harried service. Unlike most restaurants in St. Petersburg, advance reservations aren't necessary. Combine that with the quick service and location—right outside the Krasnogvardeiskaya subway station—and this becomes a good stop for a quick meal on those days when you haven't planned ahead. A German-Russian joint venture, the restaurant specializes almost exclusively in German cuisine, with a few Russian appetizers like blini with caviar or cabbage soup thrown in for variety. The kitchen produces its own homemade pretzels, the *Shvabski Brezel.* Wash down your sausage and sauerkraut with a cold mug of refreshing German draft beer, while you listen to the balalaika-strumming folk trio. ⊠ *28/19 Krasnogvardeisky Prospect,* ☎ *812/528–2211. Reservations accepted. AE, DC, MC, V. Rubles only.*

$$ ✕ **Tandoor.** This restaurant, specializing in the cuisine of Northwest India, gets high marks across the board and is a good find for vegetarians. Among the many tandooris and excellent fish and meat dishes (try the lamb kurma or chicken tikka masala), you'll find plenty of paneer, lentil, and vegetable-only dishes. The friendly atmosphere is inviting, the service solicitous. Its location is good, too—at the foot of Voznesensky Prospect, which converges with Nevsky and Moskovsky prospects at the Admiralty. After touring St. Isaac's or the nearby Palace Square, you may want to drop by here. ⊠ *2 Voznesensky Prospect,* ☎ *812/312–3886. AE, MC, V. Rubles only.*

$ ✕ **Austeria.** This state-run restaurant inside the Peter and Paul Fortress dates from the reign of Peter the Great. Formerly an officer's club (hosteria), the restaurant offers Russian cuisine in an 18th-century setting. Handcrafted, cast-iron chandeliers provide the lighting, while the thick stone walls and fully draped windows create the somber atmosphere appropriate to a fortress. The cooking isn't exactly gourmet, but the appetizers and soups are consistently good, and prices are very reasonable. For starters, try the *Petrovsky shchi* (cabbage soup), served in a crock topped by a pastry shell. The kitchen does a good job with the St. Petersburg fillet, a local favorite served with a creamy mushroom sauce. Since this restaurant is still state-run, many items on the menu may not be available when you visit. The restaurant is rarely crowded, but since it closes for private parties or tourist groups, it's best to call ahead. It's located inside the fortress's outer fortification wall, a short walk to your left after entering through the Ivan Gate. The cast-iron sign above the entrance can be easily missed. ⊠ *St. John's Ravelin, Peter and Paul Fortress,* ☎ *812/238–4262. No credit cards. Rubles only.*

$ ✕ **Dom Arkhitektorov.** Previously open only to members of the Ar-
★ chitecture Union, this little-known restaurant is in a beautiful 18th-century mansion just off St. Isaac's Square. The dazzling interior features carved oak paneling, ceiling paintings, brass chandeliers, and gilt window frames. Its astounding beauty has somehow remained a secret, and unlike other elegant dining establishments, the place is not swarming with tourists. The cuisine, unfortunately, is far less appealing than the decor. The kitchen offers simply prepared meat and fish appetizers, as well as standard Russian dishes. The house specialty, *myaso po Arkhitektorsky,* is a beef dish baked in a mayonnaise sauce and topped with thinly sliced potatoes. This is obviously not gourmet food, but with interiors like these it doesn't matter. If you're nice to the friendly waitresses, they may let you take a peek upstairs at the oak-paneled library and gilt ballroom. ⊠ *52 ul. Bolshaya Morskaya,* ☎ *812/311–1402. Reservations essential. AE, MC, V. Rubles only.* ⊘ *Closed Sun.*

$ ✕ **Metropole.** Centrally located near Gostinny Dvor and just off Nevsky Prospect, this faded, state-run restaurant was once one of St. Petersburg's finest. Today it faces stiff competition, and the kitchen is having trouble keeping up with the city's better-run and -funded ventures. The menu offers standard Russian fare, such as chicken Kiev and fried perch. The selection of *zakuski* (hors d'oeuvres) is good, but the main courses tend to be heavy on the sauces and fried potatoes. Where the Metropole has the city's shiny cafés beat is in atmosphere. Opened in 1898, it's the city's oldest restaurant, and its atmosphere can't be reproduced with modern decor—no matter how tasteful. Although it has clearly seen better days, the marble pillars, ceiling moldings, and crystal chandeliers still exude a sense of elegance. For a price, you can reserve one of the private balcony rooms (which accommodate up to 30 people) overlooking the main dining hall. Russian pop bands provide nightly entertainment. If you want to mingle and dance with the locals, ask for a table in the main hall. There is a limited selection of wine—but plenty of Russian vodka and champagne. Except for the unpleasant reception you might get from the grouchy man guarding the front door, service here is pleasant, although typically slow. ⊠ *22 ul. Sadovaya,* ☎ *812/310–1845. No credit cards. Rubles only.*

$ ✗ Saigon Neva. Don't be fooled by the name—you'll find nothing but Russian cooking at this pleasant restaurant just a block off St. Isaac's Square. And don't be fooled by the finely remodeled interior. The Vietnamese partners in this newly opened private restaurant pulled out at the last minute, but the Saigon Neva opened anyway. It's a lovely, quiet place in which to take a break from the hustle and bustle of downtown St. Petersburg. The varying selection of Russian main dishes, although pleasantly prepared, is heavily laden with french fries and oily vegetables. The appetizers and soups are better. Try the house specialty, *griby po Domashnemy* (homestyle mushrooms), served with a heavy sauce inside light pastry shells. If you like squid, you'll enjoy the *stolichnyi Salat,* garnished with onions and radishes in a mayonnaise base. The chicken soup comes with a tasty open-faced grilled cheese sandwich. Where the Saigon Neva is ahead of the competition is in its soothing atmosphere, complete with background music that's quiet enough to allow conversation. ⊠ *33 ul. Kazanskaya,* ☎ *812/315–8772. Reservations accepted. No credit cards. Rubles only.* ⊗ *Mon.–Sat. noon–11, Sun. 2–11.*

$ ✗ Tbilisi. One of St. Petersburg's first cooperatives, the Tbilisi was immediately besieged by hungry crowds eager for a decent restaurant, and it made it into just about every guidebook on the city. Today it is definitely the worse for wear. In addition to the thick clouds of smoke, its sometimes shady clientele makes for a seedy atmosphere, especially in the evening. During the day, however, it's a great place to try some Georgian food (it's named after the capital of the former Soviet republic), provided loud music doesn't curb your appetite. Despite the rowdy crowds, the service is friendly. The food is much better than the atmosphere and is reasonably priced. The *lobio* (butter beans in a spicy sauce), *satsivy,* and *kharcho* (a spicy meat soup) are the best in town. Lobio, served warm, is also available as a main course and is highly recommended. Don't forget to order *lavash* (Georgian bread) and *khachapuri* (cheese-filled fried dough). Georgian wine, German beer, cognac, and Soviet champagne (when available) are sold. Located near the Gorkovskaya subway station. ⊠ *10 Sytninskaya ul.* ☎ *812/232–9391. No credit cards. Rubles only.*

$ ✗ Tête-à-Tête. As its name suggests, this exclusive private restaurant,
★ which has just one small dining room, specializes in French cuisine. Tables are available only by advance booking, and the front door is bolted shut to keep unwanted customers from entering "off the streets." (If you have a reservation, ring the bell.) Although the chef is clearly not from Paris, the kitchen does a creditable job of producing French dishes with locally procured ingredients. For starters, try the rich and creamy onion soup, or the *julienne s gribami,* served in a cream sauce with mushrooms and onions. The French menu also features *myaso po Milanski,* grilled beef wrapped inside a cheese omelet and served with a heavy mushroom cream sauce. The classically designed interior suits the restaurant's exclusive image well. In the evenings, the grand piano tucked away in the corner provides light background music. The fully draped windows and dim lighting further add to the intimate atmosphere. Just don't go in groups larger than four. ⊠ *65 Bolshoi Prospect, near Petrogradskaya metro station,* ☎ *812/232–7548. Reservations essential. Jacket and tie. No credit cards.* ⊗ *Daily 1–11. Rubles only.*

LODGING

St. Petersburg's hotel industry has undergone changes in recent years. Until the late 1980s, all of the city's hotels were controlled by Intourist, the Soviet tourist agency that enjoyed a monopoly over the tourist trade. Rates for foreign tourists were standardized, and there were few distinctions in service and facilities from one hotel to the next. Perestroika—and St. Petersburg's sudden rise in popularity as a tourist destination—changed this. The influx of tourists prompted foreign contractors to launch a number of renovation projects, with the result that two of the city's most prestigious hotels, the Grand Hotel Europe and the Astoria Hotel, reopened to luxury-class status after major reconstruction; a third, the Nevsky Palace Hotel, joined their ranks as a brand-new contender.

The choices are still limited, however. As in Moscow, but with fewer offerings, hotels fall into two groups, with a wide gulf in between. Since the least expensive way to come to Russia is on an organized tour, you are likely to land in one of the old Intourist standbys, whose quality has hardly improved. Most U.S. and British tour operators take advantage of the deeply discounted rates available to them at these hotels and usually place groups at the Moskva, the Pribaltiskaya, the Pulkhovskaya, or the St. Petersburg (formerly Leningrad). These hotels were built in the late 1970s and early '80s, though they look at least 30 years older. Their facilities are all much the same. They would be considered inferior by Western standards. The service, though mildly unpredictable, is perfectly acceptable, however, provided you are not expecting royal treatment. The main reason to choose them is their vastly lower rates. You probably should opt for those with the best location for you, for in addition to their other inconveniences, only one or two are close to the major attractions.

If your surroundings don't affect you, and especially if you plan to have a car or easy access to group transport, you'll probably want to save on hotel rates and make do with one of the less expensive hotels. If you want insulation from the uglier sides of life here, however, plan to pay up in order to stay at accommodations where you can have it.

CATEGORY	COST*
$$$$	over $200
$$$	$140–$200
$$	$65–$140
$	under $65

All prices are for a standard double room for two, excluding service charge.

$$$$ **Astoria.** Reopened in 1991 after major reconstruction, the Astoria is actually two hotels: it interconnects with the old Angleterre, a hotel with enduring "fame" because it's where the much-loved poet Sergei Yesenin committed suicide in 1925. Originally built in the *style moderne* in 1910–12, the Astoria was one of St. Petersburg's most renowned hotels before the 1917 Revolution. Its renovation by Finnish contractors was bitterly opposed by many residents, as plans to merge the two hotels called for the complete destruction of the original building where Yesenin died. The contractors won out, and their renovations produced a fine hotel: not a trace of St. Petersburg's dusty streets can be found. The splendid interiors have been decorated using antiques retrieved from various museums. Adding to the hotel's attraction is its convenient location in the heart of downtown St. Petersburg, directly across the street from St. Isaac's Cathedral and a 10-minute walk from the Hermitage. The somewhat lackluster service, however, is disappointing, and standards of efficiency need polishing. Among the top three hotels here, however, this one is considerably (about $100) less expensive. ✉ *39 Bolshaya Morskaya ul.,* ☎ *812/210–5757,* FAX *812/210–5059. 436 rooms with bath. 3 restaurants, 2 cafés, bar, pool, exercise room, sauna, nightclub, business services, travel services. AE, MC, V.*

$$$$ **Grand Hotel Europe.** This five-star hotel is without question the
★   finest in town. Reopened in 1991 after extensive renovations, it offers the elegance of prerevolutionary St. Petersburg along with every mod-

ern amenity. Its stunning Baroque facade has been carefully restored, and the Art Nouveau interior, with its stained-glass windows and authentic antique furniture, brings back its past glory. The stylish and comfortable rooms, done in pleasing tones of mauve, cream, and gold, verge on luxurious. The hotel is operated as a Russo-Swedish venture and is managed by Reso Hotels of Sweden. The Russian staff has been carefully trained in European standards of excellence, and the service shines. The Swedish management has thought of everything: 24-hour room service, direct-dial international telephone, mail service via courier to Helsinki, and satellite TV and radio, with CNN and MTV programming. The central location can't be beat: Nevsky Prospect, the Hermitage, and the Square of the Arts are all within walking distance. If money is no object, this is the place to stay. ⊠ *1/7 Mikhailovskaya ul.,* ☎ *812/329–6000,* FAX *812/329–6001 or 812/329–6002. 211 rooms with bath, 17 junior suites, 18 terrace rooms, 23 penthouse suites, 26 2-room suites, 4 executive suites, 2 deluxe suites. 4 restaurants, café, bar, sauna, health club, nightclub, meeting rooms. AE, MC, V.*

$$$$ 🏨 **Nevsky Palace Hotel.** Sister to the Palace Hotel in Moscow, this modern and spacious five-star establishment was refashioned on the site of an old building but is completely new. The top-notch service caters to the business elite who are looking for no fuss and serious comfort. Well situated not far from the Moscow Rail Station, it's accessible to everything you're likely to want to see. ⊠ *57 Nevsky Prospect,* ☎ *812/275–2001,* FAX *812/301–7323. 287 rooms with bath. 3 restaurants, coffee shop, 2 bars, business center, shopping arcade, conference rooms, sauna with dipping pool, service bureau. AE, DC, MC, V.*

$$$ 🏨 **Deson-Ladoga.** Only five minutes from the Novocherkasskaya metro station and within walking distance of St. Petersburg's most famous historical sites, this Russo–Hong Kong joint venture was opened after reconstruction in September 1994. The rooms (of which 10 are designated for non-smokers) are furnished with direct-dial satellite telephone and television. The decor is modest but very fresh. ⊠ *26 Shaumiana Prospect,* ☎ *812/528–5393,* FAX *812/528–5448. 95 rooms with bath. Nightclub, sauna, beauty salon. MC, V.*

$$$ 🏨 **Pribaltiskaya.** Swedish-built but Soviet-designed, this huge 16-story skyscraper is frequently used for placing tourist groups. Opened in 1978, it was once considered the city's top hotel. The rooms are clean and all come with cable television (including CNN and MTV). The modest furnishings are adequate, although slightly worn. Its first major drawback is the location: far out on the western tip of Vasilievsky Island, the hotel is a good 20-minute drive from downtown St. Petersburg, and the closest subway station is several bus stops away. The predominantly residential area offers rows and rows of benumbing Soviet-era high rises—but very few shops and restaurants. If you can stand the isolation, the views of the Gulf of Finland are phenomenal, especially at sunset (ask for a room on the western side of the hotel). Another disadvantage is its increasing appeal to unsavory crowds, which may particularly bother single travelers. One plus is the hotel's well-stocked "Baltic Store," where you can pick up bottled water, imported snack foods, and a fairly recent copy of the *International Herald-Tribune* or *USA Today.* ⊠ *14 ul. Korablestroiteley,* ☎ *812/356–0263 or 812/356–0001,* FAX *812/356–4496 or 812/356–0094. 11 restaurants, 10 snack bars, 5 bars, bowling alley, sauna with dipping pool, banquet and convention center, parking (fee), gift shop, travel bureau. AE, V, MC.*

$$$ 🏨 **Pulkhovskaya.** Opened in 1981, this Finnish-built hotel has with-
★ stood heavy tourist traffic, and its attractive Scandinavian-designed interior is still surprisingly well maintained. Accommodations are on the same level as the Pribaltiskaya (*above*), although the rooms are slightly cleaner and more attractive. Service is friendly and efficient by local

standards. Unusual for a Russian hotel, the curtains and bedspreads actually match the upholstery; and the bathrooms, complete with Finnish plumbing, are relatively large. Again, the disadvantage here is location. The hotel is not near the city center and is convenient only to the airport; the subway is a 10-minute walk away, and the ride into town takes at least 20 minutes. But in contrast to the Pribaltiskaya's surroundings, the area around the Pulkhovskaya is much easier on the nerves. Mainly residential, it has plenty of shops and even a restaurant or two. The views from the rooms, though, can depress you: you have a choice between gloomy high rises and smokestacks or the severe, very Soviet, Victory Square monument outside the hotel's main entrance. ⊠ *1 Pl. Pobedy,* ☎ *812/123–5022 or 812/123–5122,* ℻ *812/264–6396 or 812/264–5845. 850 rooms with bath, telephone, TV, refrigerator. 2 restaurants, 6 snack bars, 6 bars, beauty salon, 2 saunas and dipping pool, shops, business center, travel bureau, car rental. AE, DC, MC, V.*

$$ ☷ **Moskva.** The unimaginative and depressing decor at this enormous, visibly aging hotel is yet another prime example of Brezhnev-era design. Store up on patience before checking in, because the lackluster service can make even paying your bill a frustrating experience; the desk clerks spend more time at lunch and on the phone than they do serving guests. The dreary rooms and public areas show obvious signs of neglect, but the hotel management keeps making stabs at renovations. The hotel's reputation for seedy mobs hanging out at the main entrance seems to have improved. Perhaps because this is the best-located of the Intourist hotels, many groups stay here, and while they may sometimes remind you of the crowds at Disneyland, you feel safe. Location is good here: it is literally on top of the subway and faces the entrance to the 18th-century Alexander Nevsky Monastery. This is at one end of Nevsky Prospect, which is still the center of town. Another plus is that rates are on the low end of the $$ category. ⊠ *2 Pl. Alexandra Nevskovo,* ☎ *812/274–3001 or 812/274–4001,* ℻ *812/274–2130. 770 rooms with bath. Restaurant, 7 snack bars, 5 bars, shops, business services, travel services. AE, DC, MC, V.*

$$ ☷ **Okhtinskaya.** The location, directly across the river from the Baroque
★ Smolny Sobor, is great for views but terribly inconvenient if you ever plan on going anywhere by public transportation. St. Petersburg's museums and tourist attractions are all on the other side of the river, and the subway is several bus stops away. Canadian-built and opened in 1991, the hotel is now run as a French-Russian venture. Service is unusually friendly, and the rates are extremely reasonable. Although the interior features the usual marble-and-chrome decor, the public areas are cheery and bright and, most important, devoid of the ubiquitous slot machines. The rooms are clean and well appointed, with imported furnishings and pretty flowered wallpaper. While almost all the rooms come with balconies, only the suites have full baths. Unfortunately only one room on every floor faces the cathedral, but the views of the urban landscape on this side of town are more refreshing than most. ⊠ *4 Bolsheokhtinsky Prospect,* ☎ *812/227–4438 or 812/227–3767,* ℻ *812/227–2618. 204 rooms with bath or shower. 2 restaurants, snack bar, 2 bars, sauna, shops, conference rooms. AE, DC, MC, V.*

$$ ☷ **St. Petersburg.** Formerly called the Leningrad, this aging hotel of-
★ fers both the best and worst views of contemporary St. Petersburg. Although the rooms overlooking the Neva have magnificent vistas of the city's waterfront architecture, the other half face the depressing other side of the building. Although this is definitely not the luxury hotel it once was, if you can land a waterfront room, it is the only place to stay during the White Nights. The Finnish-decorated interior is faded and the furnishings are a bit worn, but the rooms and public areas are

clean, and overall, not nearly as shabby as the Moskva's. The vast lobby holds a host of stores, including souvenir and gift shops. The location, however, is good only for the views. The Finland Train Station and subway are within walking distance, but the route is unpleasant and takes you along a busy highway. ⌧ *5/2 Vyborskaya nab.,* ☎ *812/542–9411* FAX *812/248–8002. 410 rooms with bath. 2 restaurants, 3 snack bars, 3 bars, sauna with dipping pool, shops, business center, meeting rooms, travel services. DC, MC, V.*

$$ ⊞ **Sovietskaya.** The name says it all: this is a Soviet hotel with the typically slow and disgruntled service of a state-run enterprise. Yet another concrete-and-steel monstrosity, the hotel is in an attractive section of downtown St. Petersburg. Although the location allows for some good views of St. Petersburg's canals, it's still a long walk to just about anywhere, including the subway. There are two buildings, both built in the late 1960s, but the "newer wing" (the part called Fontanka) was recently remodeled. All rooms in both wings are relatively clean and have decent views. But accommodations in the "new" wing are generally in better shape and come with Finnish furnishings (and higher rates). ⌧ *43/1 Lermontovsky Prospect,* ☎ *812/329–0186 or 812/329–0182,* FAX *812/329–0188. 1,099 rooms with bath. 3 restaurants, café, 4 snack bars, 3 bars, sauna, business services, travel services. No credit cards.*

$ ⊞ **Holiday.** The International Hostel "Holiday," opened in 1993 in the center of St. Petersburg, on the Neva embankment, is a five-minute walk from Finland Station (Ploshchad Lenina metro station). There is a pier in front of the building where you can arrange a sightseeing tour through rivers and canals of the city. The hostel can accommodate from 70 people in winter to 100 in summer. Two- to 6-bed rooms have the Neva river view. Showers and toilets are in the corridor on each floor. The hostel is open 24 hours and there is a bar on the 4th floor in summer. This is a good choice for budget-minded tourists who want to get closer to real life in Russia. ⌧ *1 Mikhailova ul.,* ☎ *812/542–7364,* FAX *812/325–8559. MC, AE, V.*

$ ⊞ **Karelia.** Situated in a gloomy residential area dominated by monotonous and crumbling high rises, this former Intourist hotel is a prime example of Brezhnev-era architecture. Built for the 1980 Olympics, it looks years older than it is. The lobby, decorated with gaudy, socialist-realist paintings depicting an outdated Leningrad, is dismal and smoky. Service, however, is surprisingly friendly, and the rates are the best in town. The double and triple rooms (no singles available) are adequate and relatively clean, and the friendly floor attendants willingly address complaints. While the decor is less than attractive (bedspreads, curtains, and carpets are all different colors), the furnishings have been imported from Finland, and the beds are more comfortable than most. Some rooms come with television, and all come with telephone and balcony (and dreary views). The hotel's business center is equipped with satellite telephones and a fax. For tourists on a budget who don't mind long excursions on the city's unreliable trolleybuses, the hotel offers bearable if far from luxurious accommodations. But if you're not counting your rubles, stay elsewhere. ⌧ *27/2 ul. Tukhachevskovo,* ☎ *812/226–3515,* FAX *812/226–3511. 430 rooms with bath or shower. Restaurant, 5 snack bars, 3 bars, sauna, casino, nightclub, business services, travel services. No credit cards.*

NIGHTLIFE AND THE ARTS

The Arts

St. Petersburg's cultural life is one of its top attractions. Except for the most renowned theaters, tickets are easily available and ridiculously inexpensive. You can buy them at the box offices of the theaters themselves and at theater kiosks (*teatralnaya kassa*) located throughout the city. Central Box Office No. 1 is at 42 Nevsky Prospect (☎ 812/311–3183) and is open daily from 11 to 7. For performances at the Mariinsky Theater (better known in the West by its Soviet name, Kirov) and the Mussorgsky Theater of Ballet and Opera (also known as the Maly) you have two choices: pay the inflated rates charged by hotel excursion bureaus, or buy a ticket from a scalper outside the theater just before the performance. The second route is invariably cheaper, although there's no guarantee that your seat will have a view of the stage.

Even if you're not staying at the Astoria Hotel, you're welcome to use its service bureau (☎ 812/210–5045) for booking theater tickets. Most hotels post performance listings in their main lobby. The two English-language newspapers, *Neva News* and *St. Petersburg Press,* have theater and concert listings as do the quarterly English-language magazine *St. Petersburg Premier* and the monthly *St. Petersburg News.*

All sorts of special arts performances are organized for the White Nights' Festival, held in the last two weeks of June. After that, most major theaters close down for the summer and start up again in mid-September.

Concerts

Classical music can be enjoyed all over the city. The famous **St. Petersburg Shostakovich Bolshoi Philharmonic** (✉ 2 ul. Mikhailovskaya, ☎ 812/311–7333) offers excellent performances in its concert hall on the Square of the Arts, located in the former Nobleman's Club. Concerts are also given in the Philharmonic's **Maly Zal imeni Glinki** (Little Glinka Hall; ✉ 30 Nevsky Prospect, ☎ 812/311–1531), around the corner. One of St. Petersburg's best-kept secrets is the lovely **Glinka Kapella Choral Hall** (✉ 20 nab. Moiki, ☎ 812/314–1159), which presents not only choral events but also symphonic, instrumental, and vocal concerts. The concert hall dates from the 1780s, and many famous musicians, including Glinka and Rimsky-Korsakov, have performed here.

For a relaxing evening of classical music in a prerevolutionary setting, try the concert halls in some of St. Petersburg's mansions and palaces. Performances are held regularly at: the **Anichkov Palace Concert Hall** (✉ 39 Nevsky Prospect, ☎ 812/310–4822); **Beloselsky-Belozersky Palace** (✉ 41 Nevsky Prospect, ☎ 812/315–4076); **Bosse Mansion** (✉ 15, 4 liniya, ☎ 812/213–3488); the **Smolny Cathedral and Convent** (✉ 3/1 Pl. Rastrelli, ☎ 812/271–9182); the **Oktyabrski Bolshoi Concert Hall** (✉ 6 Ligovsky Prospect, ☎ 812/275–1273); and the **St. Petersburg Music Hall** (4 Alexandrovsky Park, ☎ 812/232–9201 or 812/233–0243).

Opera and Ballet

The world-renowned **Mariinsky Theater of Opera and Ballet** (✉ 1/2 Teatralnaya Pl., ☎ 812/114–1211) should not be missed. Its elegant blue-and-gold auditorium has been the main home of the Russian ballet—the Kirov—since the 1880s. The lesser-known **Mussorgsky Theater of Opera and Ballet** (✉ 1 Pl. Iskusstv, ☎ 812/219–1949), also known as the Maly, offers outstanding performances but at much lower prices than the Kirov. Operas are usually sung in Russian, and the repertoire is dominated by Russian composers.

Theater

St. Petersburg also offers some excellent dramatic theaters, with performances almost exclusively in Russian. Even if you can't understand the dialogue, you may want to visit the famous **Bolshoi Drama Theater** (✉ 65 nab. Fontanki, ☎ 812/310–0401). Russia's oldest theater is the elegant **Pushkin Drama Theater** (✉ 2 Pl. Ostrovskovo, ☎ 812/ 312–1545), where the repertoire is dominated by the classics.

CHILDREN'S THEATER
St. Petersburg's puppet theaters all perform regularly for children: **Bolshoi Puppet Theater** (✉ 10 ul. Nekrasova, ☎ 812/273–6672); **Puppet-Marionette Theater** (✉ 52 Nevsky Prospect, ☎ 812/311–1900).

Talented skaters perform at the **Improvisionational Children's Theater on Ice** (✉ 148 Ligovsky Prospect, ☎ 812/112–8625), whose office is open weekdays 11–5). Children may enjoy a show at the **Through the Looking-Glass Children's Theater** (✉ 13 ul. Rubinsteina, ☎ 812/ 164–1895), one of the city's best, open Fri.–Sun.

Nightlife

Compared with Moscow, which is bursting at the seams with hot new night spots, St. Petersburg borders on tame. Yet it can still outdo its rival in trendiness. Maybe it's simply that St. Petersburg looks so arty, but it's always been considered the style capital and is also inarguably the home of Russian rock 'n' roll. So when you're stepping out for the latest music, you will have a good time here. And do step out of an Intourist monolith if you're staying there. The floor shows that their clubs traditionally arrange are a deafening assault on the senses, so if you want something else, you'd better look well outside their doors for entertainment.

A note about security: Though media reports on increased crime in Russia exaggerate the situation, foreigners in this economically strapped country are easy prey for robbery and muggings. Use common sense and stay away from the sleazy bars and clubs where prostitution thrives and the main goal of guests seems to be to to reach a drunken bliss. If you plan to spend the evening outside your hotel, you'll be glad if you make arrangements for the trip home before setting out. Although there are virtually no after-dark hours during the White Nights, a too late evening stroll down Nevsky Prospect may be an invitation to trouble.

Bars and Lounges
All the major hotels have bars and nightclubs, but except for the Astoria and Grand Hotel Europe, the local clientele is often of questionable intention and the atmosphere tends to get sleazy as the night wears on.

One of the better spots in town is **Sadko** (✉ Grand Hotel Europe, 1/7 ul. Mikhailovskaya, ☎ 812/329–6000). Nightly entertainment often features top local performers, such as a Russian reggae band. The crowds are mostly foreign tourists and Russian students, with a few *novye russkye,* or new Russians (BMW-owning, free-spending locals) mixed in. In the summer **The Beer Garden** (✉ 86 Nevsky Prospect, ☎ 812/ 275–7620) is a good spot for a big mug of beer.

Casinos
Casino fever is lower in St. Petersburg than in Moscow and Kiev, but high rollers can still have fun. Some restaurants have their own casinos, as do the Hotels Astoria and Pribaltiskaya and the restaurant Nevsky Melody. **Conti** (✉ 44 Kondratievsky, ☎ 812/540–8130 is a full-out casino. **Fortuna** (✉ 71 Nevsky Prospect☎ 812/ 164–2087), in the city center, is the most popular casino in the city.

Dance Clubs
For performance art, live rock, and the very trendy, there's **Art Clinic** (✉ Pushkinskaya 10 commune); **Fish Fabrique,** at the same address, has a funky bohemian air. You can hear pop, techno, or reggae—or most likely, a concoction of all three—at **Domenico's** (✉ 70 Nevsky

Prospect, ☎ 812/272–5717). That it takes its artiness seriously is reflected in its steep cover charge. Home to the Russian rave, **The Tunnel** used to be a fallout shelter, but it's definitely not for the already shell-shocked—but only the rough and tough. The noisy and lively **Wild Side** (✉ 12 nab. Bumazhnovo Kanala, ☎ 812/186–3466) accompanies its blasting music with lots of lights.

The Russo-Swedish venture **Nevsky Melody** (✉ 62 nab. Sverdlovskaya, ☎ 812/227–1596) has a hopping dance floor and an erotic floor show that is definitely a matter of taste. This night spot is extremely popular with St. Petersburg's nouveaux riches.

Jazz, Rock, and Blues
To hear Russia's top jazz musicians, head for the St. Petersburg **Jazz Philharmonic Hall** (✉ 27 Zagorodny Prospect, near the Dostoevskaya metro station, ☎ 812/164–8565). Regular performances by the likes of the world-renowned Leningrad Dixieland Band and David Goloshchyokin's Ensemble make this a favorite night spot. Serious jazz lovers will enjoy the fantastic atmosphere in this turn-of-the-century building. It makes for a classy night out. The **New Jazz Club** (✉ 33 ul. Shpalernaya, ☎ 812/272–9850)—which also hosts a Sunday blues night—is a less emphatically highbrow jazz venue.

The **Gora Club** (✉ 153 Ligovsky Prospect) showcases local rock bands. For heavy rock, try the small **Archwall Club** (10 ul. Pravdy). Rockabilly fans will find their fellows at the **Money Honey Saloon** (✉ Dom 14, Apraksin Dvor), but pay heed: Although the music may be good, the neighborhood is not.

OUTDOOR ACTIVITIES AND SPORTS

Participant Sports

Unfortunately, athletic facilities available to tourists in St. Petersburg are rather limited. As in Moscow, access to the municipal facilities is restricted and requires a special "doctor's certificate" attesting to the user's health. They are possible to get, but you'd have to spend at least a few hours at a Russian clinic to do so. Most hotels have their own athletic facilities, however, and sometimes they are open to nonguests also; these spots do not require a doctor's certificate.

Cycling
You may enjoy biking through St. Petersburg's parks and along its picturesque canals and river embankments. You can rent bikes from the **Burevestnik Cycling Club** (✉ 81 Prospect Engelsa, ☎ 812/554–1741), which can also arrange tours.

Fitness Centers and Sports Complexes
The **Army Sports Club** (✉ 13 ul. Inzhenernaya, ☎ 812/219–2967) has a pool and both volleyball and basketball courts. The **Dinamo Sports Center** (✉ 44 Dinamo Prospect, ☎ 812/235–0170) has a range of facilities, including volleyball courts and running tracks. Weight lifters can try the **Olympia Shaping Center** (✉ 14 ul. 6 Krasnoarmeiskaya, ☎ 812/110–1887); a one-month package here is very reasonable, so you may simply want to purchase one, even if your stay is shorter.

If your own hotel doesn't have a place to work out, the fitness center at the **Astoria Hotel** is open to nonguests. Its pool (10 meters) is by far the largest in the city's hotels. ☎ *812/210–5757.* ⊙ *Daily 9 AM–10PM, weekends 9–9. Fee for use of gym, pool, and sauna for 2 hours, $20.*

The **Hotel Rossiya** (⊠ 11 Chernyshevskovo Pl., ☎ 812/296–3144), has a gym, pool, and sauna.

Running

Runners, like cyclists, can find some lovely spots to exercise. You might stick to the Neva embankments or head for gardens like Letny Sad or the Field of Mars. It's easier here than in Moscow to avoid huge clumps of traffic and the attendant congestion. And though you'll still be in a minority, you probably won't feel as conspicuous if you just put on those track shoes and go.

Skating

You can skate at the following rinks: **Moskovsky Park Pobedy** (⊠ 25 ul. Kuznetsovskaya, ☎ 812/298–4521), open daily 2–9 in winter; **Yubileyny Palace of Sports** (⊠ 18 ul. Dobrolyubova, ☎ 812/119–5609), by advance booking only.

Swimming

The fitness centers listed above have pools. The **World Class Fitness Center** also offers a 25-meter, 6-lane pool. Onetime use is an option, but at twice the members' price.

Tennis Courts

Tennis players should be able to find an open court. Public indoor courts are located at **Dinamo Stadium** (⊠ 44 ul. Dinamo. ☎ 812/235–0055). The stadium can be reached by Tram 21 or 34. There are also **municipal courts** (37 ul. Kazanskaya, ☎ 812/315–6220). Outdoor public courts are across the street from the Field of Mars at 16 Aptekarsky pereulok. The World Class Fitness Center (☞ *above*) has tennis courts available for rental if they aren't previously reserved. If these options don't pan out, check with the **Lawn Tennis Sports Center** (⊠ 116 Metallistov Prospect, ☎ 812/540–1886).

Spectator Sports

Tickets for sporting events can be purchased at the sports arena immediately prior to the game or at one of the many theater box offices (*teatralnaya kassa*) located throughout the city: 22–24 Nevsky Prospect, 33 Nevsky Prospect, 42 Nevsky Prospect, 74 Nevsky Prospect, and 27 Sredny Prospect (Vasilievsky Island).

Basketball and Volleyball

Basketball and volleyball matches are held at **Yubilieny Sports Palace** (⊠ 19 Prospect Dobroluybova, ☎ 812/119–5612). **Zimny Stadium** (⊠ 2 Manezhnaya Pl., ☎ 812/315–5710) hosts matches.

Hockey

Besides the Yubilieny Sports Palace, hockey can be found at the **Sports and Concert Complex** (⊠ 8 Yuri Gagarin Prospect, ☎ 812/298–2164).

Soccer

International matches are held at the **Petrovsky Stadium** (⊠ 2-g Petrovsky Ostrov, ☎ 812/233–1752). **Kirov Stadium** (⊠ 1 Morskoi Prospect, Krestovsky Ostrov, ☎ 812/235–5452) also hosts soccer matches.

SHOPPING

If you have come to St. Petersburg to shop, you will be disappointed. Although there have been improvements, they consist mostly of at last bringing in a solid array of products that are considered "normal"— whether juice, cosmetics, or socks—elsewhere. In other words, apart from certain arts and crafts, there is nothing to whet your appetite for the unusual or exquisite; you'll have to let your experience of St. Petersburg alone fulfill that. The good news, of course, is that basic items are no longer scarce.

The same sense of a two-tiered system of stores exists in St. Petersburg as in Moscow and Kiev. The "Western style" shops taking credit-card payment have effectively replaced the old Beriozkas, which were stocked only for foreigners. With increased competition, some of their prices have gone down, and they are open to anyone who can afford them.

State-run shops are much better stocked than ever, and you might as well look into some of these groceries and department stores if you don't want anything too fancy. Only rubles will be accepted here, however, and you'll have a tough time maneuvering through the cashiers if you don't speak some Russian.

Kiosks, tables on the street, and impromptu markets offer a colorful jumble of junk most of the time. But this mini-industry of individual entrepreneurs, which mushroomed wildly in the first years of glasnost, is on the wane. Everything's being tidied up and taken back inside.

Shopping Districts

Historically, St. Petersburg's main shopping districts are two: Nevsky Prospect and Gostinny Dvor. Located smack in the center of town, at 35 Nevsky Prospect, Gostinny Dvor is easily reached by subway; a station right outside its doors is named in its honor. Some sections of Gostinny Dvor are currently closed due to ongoing restoration.

Department Stores

The patient shopper may chance upon some tremendous bargains at **DLT** (*Dom Leningradskoi Torgovly*), just off Nevsky Prospect, at 21/23 Bolshaya Konyushennaya ulitsa. **Passage,** at 48 Nevsky Prospect, caters primarily to the local population. The souvenir sections, however, are often a shopper's paradise as prices, in rubles, are significantly lower here than in the souvenir shops around hotels and in other areas usually frequented by tourists.

Outside the large department stores of Nevsky Prospect, you will find some boutiques and lots of "variety shops," which can be a bit bewildering. Part souvenir-oriented, part practical, look in them if you have time; you never know what you may find.

Specialty Stores

Art Galleries
Although they cater primarily to the lucrative tourist market, art shops in St. Petersburg offer items of much higher quality than what you will find on the streets. Nevsky Prospect is lined with such shops, where local artists sell their wares on commission. Before making a major purchase at these stores, be sure to ask if they will take care of the paperwork necessary to allow you to take the item out of the country. It's also a good idea to clarify whether they charge an additional fee for this service. Some of the best art shops are: **Borey** (⊠ 58 Liteyny, ☎ 812/273–3693), with both avant-garde and academic artists, painting, graphics, and applied art; **Diaghilev Art Center** (⊠ 20 Nevsky Prospect, ☎ 812/311–5620), selling the work of the best artists of St. Petersburg; **Guild of Masters** (⊠ 82 Nevsky Prospect, ☎ 812/279-0979), which offers paintings, graphics, applied art, and items of jewelry; **Lavka Khudozhnikov** (⊠ 8 Nevsky Prospect, ☎ 812/312–6193), whose stock includes paintings, graphics, ceramics, and textiles; and **Palitra** (⊠

166 Nevsky Prospect, ☎ 812/277–1216), which carries primarily the work of young Russian artists.

Clothing Stores

You aren't here to find clothes, presumably, but if you are, try the department stores listed above. Chic boutiques in the better hotels have some designer pieces, usually at higher-than-designer prices. If you're looking for handmade traditional Russian garments, check out **Aquilon Salon** (✉ 6 Kamennostrovsky Prospect, ☎ 812/232–6783).

Craft and Souvenir Shops

Besides the counters in hotel lobby shops, where prices are often wildly inflated, you can find tasteful gifts in **Art Boutique** (✉ 51 Nevsky Prospect, ☎ 812/113–1495), including hand-knitted scarves and mittens, hand-painted trays, Khohloma, and ceramics; **Guild of Masters** (✉ 82 Nevsky Prospect, ☎ 812/279–0979) sells jewelry, ceramics, and other types of Russian native art, all made by members of the Russian Union of Artists; **Khudozhestvenny Salon** (✉ 8 Nevsky Prospect, ☎ 812/312–6193) stocks ceramics, boxes, jewelry, painting, dolls, and a fine selection of handicrafts; and **Nasledie** (✉ 116 Nevsky Prospect, ☎ 812/279–5067) carries *palekh* and *khokhloma* (different types of hand-painted lacquered wood), samovars, nesting dolls, amber, and hand-painted trays.

Farmers' Markets

The farmers' markets in St. Petersburg are lively places where a colorful array of goods and foods are sold by individual farmers, often from out of town and sometimes from outside the Russian republic. In recent years the variety of goods available at the market (in Russian, *rynok*) has increased tremendously. Because markets are much cleaner and better lit than in Moscow, it's also fun to visit and browse. In addition to the fine cuts of fresh and cured meat, dairy products, and homemade jams and jellies, piles of fruits and vegetables can be found, even in winter. Try some homemade pickles or pickled garlic, a tasty local favorite. You can also find many welcome surprises like hand-knitted scarves, hats, and mittens. You are expected to bargain, and—as in any crowded area—watch out for pickpockets. Farmers' markets are generally open daily from 8 AM to 7 PM and usually close at 5 PM on Sunday.

St. Petersburg's most popular markets are: **Kuznechny Rynok** (✉ 3 Kuznechny pereulok), just outside the Vladimirskaya metro station; **Sytny Rynok** (✉ 3/5 Sytninskaya Pl.), in the Petrograd Side district, not far from the Gorkovskaya subway station; and the huge, sprawling flea market known as **Sennoi Rynok** (✉ Sennaya Pl.), at the exit from the subway station of the same name.

Grocery Stores

For those looking for a big Western supermarket that takes credit cards, try **Kalinka-Stockmann** (✉ 1 Finlandsky Prospect, ☎ 812/542–2297), open daily 9–10. **Super Babylon** (✉ 54/56 Maly Prospect, ☎ 812/230–8096), is a superstore open daily 24 hours. For imported cheese and excellent fruit and vegetables, try **Supermarket** (✉ 48 Nevsky Prospect, ☎ 812/219–1732), open Monday–Saturday 10–9 and Sunday 11–9. Another option is the **Gin** supermarket (✉ 61 Sredniy Prospect, ☎ 812/218–0469), open daily 10–10). Otherwise, have a go at the local dietas, gastronoms, and produkti.

SIDE TRIPS FROM ST. PETERSBURG

Several extraordinary palaces are located in the suburbs of St. Petersburg. Following the 1917 Revolution, these former summer residences of the czars were nationalized and turned into museums.

Of all the palaces you will see in Russia, one that will make a distinct and lasting impression is Petrodvorets, on the shore of the Baltic Sea, some 29 kilometers (18 miles) from St. Petersburg. Petrodvorets, originally called Peterhof, is more than just a summer palace: It is an imperial playground replete with lush parks, monumental cascades, and gilt fountains. In czarist times, Tsarskoye Selo, now renamed Pushkin, was a fashionable haunt of the aristocracy, who were anxious to be near the imperial family and to escape the noxious air and oppressive climate of the capital. After the Revolution of 1905 Nicholas II and his family lived here more or less permanently. Pavlovsk, the imperial estate of Paul I (in Russian Pavel, hence Pavlovsk) is some 30 kilometers (18 miles) south of St. Petersburg and only 5 kilometers (3 miles) from Pushkin and the Catherine Palace. Because of the proximity of the two towns, it's often suggested that tours to them be combined. If you decide to do this, make sure to give yourself enough time to do justice to both. The estate of Lomonosov, on the Gulf of Finland, some 40 kilometers (25 miles) west of St. Petersburg and about 9 km (5½ miles) northwest of Petrodvorets, is perhaps the least commanding of the suburban imperial palaces. It is, however, the only one to have survived World War II intact.

All of the destinations in this section can be reached by commuter trains (*elektrichka*), but the simplest way to see the palaces is to book an excursion (available through any tour company). The cost is reasonable and covers transportation, guided tour, and admission fee. An organized excursion to any of the suburban palaces will take at least four hours. If you travel on your own, it's likely to take up the entire day. Although you'll find some cafeterias and cafés, they're nothing special, so you may prefer to pack a lunch or bring a snack with you.

Petrodvorets (Peterhof)

During World War II and the siege of Leningrad, most of the suburban palaces were occupied by enemy forces and used as army headquarters, barracks, or stables. At the end of the war, what little remained of the former palaces was burned and looted by the retreating German troops. Museum workers had managed to evacuate much of the art housed in the palaces before the German occupation, but for the most part the original interiors were lost forever. Painstaking restoration using pieces of fabric, photographs, and written descriptions has returned the palaces to their former splendor, although some renovation work is still ongoing.

○ **Petrodvorets** is best visited in summer; a winter visit can be quite disappointing. From late September to early June the fountains and cascades are closed down, and take on the depressing look of a drained pool. You can reach the palace by commuter train from St. Petersburg, but, minimal fog permitting, the best way to go is by hydrofoil, from which your first view is the panorama of the grand palace overlooking the sea. Be aware that the lines to get into the palace can be excruciatingly long in summer. Sometimes guided tours get preferential treatment. ⊠ *2 ul. Razvodnaya, town of Petrodvorets,* ☎ *812/427–9527.* ☉ *Great Palace Tues.–Sun. 10:30–6. Closed last Tues. of month. Transportation: commuter train from Baltisky Vokzal (Baltic Station) to Novy Peterhof station, approximately 40 min from St. Petersburg.*

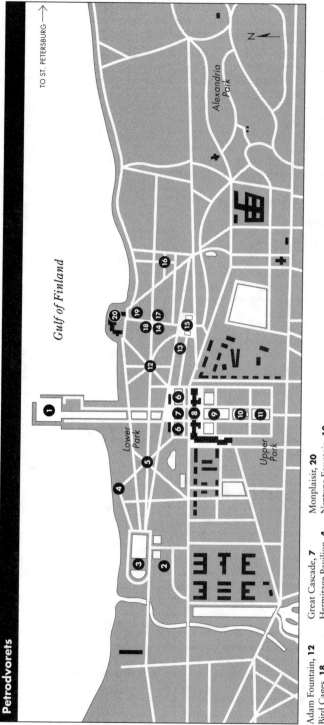

Petrodvorets

Gulf of Finland

TO ST. PETERSBURG →

Lower Park

Upper Park

Alexandria Park

Adam Fountain, **12**
Bird Cages, **18**
Bolshoi Dvorets, **8**
Chess Hill, **15**
Cup Fountains, **6**
Eve Fountain, **5**
Golden Hill Cascade, **2**

Great Cascade, **7**
Hermitage Pavilion, **4**
Hydrofoil Pier, **1**
Little Oak Fountain, **14**
Marly Palace, **3**
Mezheumny Fountain, **11**

Monplaisir, **20**
Neptune Fountain, **10**
Oak Fountain, **9**
Pyramid Fountain, **16**
Sun Fountain, **19**
Triton Fountain, **13**
Umbrella Fountain, **17**

From station take Bus 351 to Dvorets. In summer, hydrofoils to Petrod-vorets leave from pier outside the Hermitage Museum approximately every 30 min. Ride takes about ½ hr.

The myriad complex of gardens and residences at Petrodvorets was masterminded by Peter the Great, who personally drew up the first plans, starting around 1720. His motivation was twofold. First, he was proud of the capital city that he was building and wanted its newmade imperial grandeur showcased with a proper summer palace. Second, he became attached to this spot while erecting the naval fortress of Kronstadt on a nearby island across the Gulf of Finland; because it lay in easy view, he often stayed here during the fort's construction. When it was finished, at a time when he had had a series of naval victories (including the Northern War against the Swedes), he threw himself into establishing many parts of the grounds that would be called Peterhof (Peter's Court), a German name changed to Petrodvorets after World War II.

If you travel by hydrofoil, you will arrive at the pier of the Lower Park, from where you work your way up to the Grand Palace. If you arrive by land, you'll simply go through the process in reverse. Either way, the perspective always emphasizes the mightiness of water. Half-encircled by the sea, filled with fountains and other water monuments, with the Marine Canal running straight from the foot of the palace into the bay—Peter's place was also his loving tribute to the role of water in the life, and strength, of his city. The Lower Park was a formal Baroque garden in the French style adorned with statues, fountains, and cascades. Peter's playful spirit is still very much in evidence here. The fun-loving czar installed "trick fountains"—hidden water sprays built into trees and tiny plazas and brought to life by stepping on a certain stone or moving a lever, much to the surprise of the unsuspecting visitor and the delight of the squealing children who love to race through the showers on hot summer days.

Located in the eastern half of Lower Park is the oldest building at Petrodvorets, **Monplaisir** (literally "My Pleasure"). This is where Peter the Great lived while overseeing construction of the main imperial residence, and as was often the case with Peter, he greatly preferred this modest Dutch-style villa to his later, more extravagant living quarters. The house is open to the public and makes a pleasant tour. Some of its most interesting rooms are the **Lacquered Study**, decorated with replicas of panels (the originals were destroyed during World War II) painted in Chinese style; **Peter's Naval Study**; and his bedroom, where personal effects, such as his nightcap and a quilt made by his wife, are on display. Attached to Peter's villa is the so-called **Catherine Wing**, built by Rastrelli in the mid-18th century, in an utterly different style. The future Catherine the Great was staying here at the time of the coup that overthrew her husband and placed her on the throne; it was later used mainly for balls.

In the western section of the Lower Park, you can find another famous structure, the **Hermitage.** This two-story pavilion gives new meaning to the concept of a movable feast. The building, which was used primarily as a banqueting hall (for special guests), was at one time equipped with a device that would lift the dining table—diners and all—from the ground floor to the private dining room above. A slightly different system was put in place after Czar Paul I's chair broke while doing this. The center part of the table could be lifted out, and guests would write down their dinner preferences and then signal for their notes to be lifted away. Shortly thereafter, the missing piece would be lowered, complete with the meals everyone had ordered. The only way to the Hermitage was over a drawbridge, so privacy was ensured.

A walk up the path through the center of the Lower Park (along the Marine Canal) leads you to the famous **Great Cascade.** Running down the steep ridge separating the Lower Park and the Grand Palace towering above, the cascade comprises three waterfalls, 64 fountains, and 37 gilt statues. The system of waterworks has remained virtually unchanged since 1721. The ducts and pipes, which convey water over a distance of some 20 kilometers (12 miles), work without pumping stations: the water flows downhill, while the fountains operate on the principle of communicating vessels. The centerpiece of the waterfalls is a gilt Samson rending the jaws of a lion from which a jet of water spurts into the air. The statue represents the Russian victory over the Swedes at Poltava on St. Samson's day. The present figure is a meticulous replica of the original, which was carried away by the Germans.

Crowning the ridge above the cascade is the magnificent **Bolshoi Dvorets** (Great Palace). Little remains of Peter's original two-story house, built between 1714 and 1725 under the architects Leblond, Braunstein, and Machetti. The building was altered considerably and enlarged by Peter's daughter Elizabeth. She entrusted the reconstruction to her favorite architect, the Italian Bartolomeo Rastrelli, who transformed the modest residence into a sumptuous blend of medieval architecture and Russian Baroque. Before you begin your tour of the palace interiors, pause for a moment to enjoy the breathtaking view from the marble terrace. From here a full view of the grounds below unfolds, stretching from the cascades to the Gulf of Finland to the city horizon on the shore beyond.

An integral part of visiting any museum-palace in Russia is encountering the autocratic *babushki* who now control them. In this, Petrodvorets is no exception. No matter how annoying, they deserve respect, for they have survived the 900-day siege of Leningrad, witnessed the palaces' destruction, and seen them rise again, nearly miraculously, from the ashes. As you enter the palace, you will be given tattered shoe covers to protect the highly polished floors as you walk through the splendid halls. One cautionary note: on most occasions flash photography is not allowed, although for a fee, fast film and videotaping are. Sometimes the babushki aren't aware of the difference. So hang on tight to your equipment to avoid having it confiscated by an overzealous custodian of Peter's treasures.

The palace's lavish interiors are primarily the work of Rastrelli, although several of the rooms were redesigned during the reign of Catherine the Great in accordance with the architectural style of her day, Classicism. Of Peter's original design, only his **Dubovy Kabinet** (Oak Cabinet) survived the numerous reconstructions. The fine oak panels (some are originals) lining the walls were designed by the French sculptor Pineau. The entire room and all its furnishings are made of wood, with the exception of the white marble fireplace, above which hangs a long mirror framed in carved oak.

One of the largest rooms in the palace is the **Tronny Zal** (Throne Room), which takes up the entire width of the building. Classically designed, this majestic room—once the scene of great receptions and official ceremonies—features exquisite parquet floors, fine stucco ceiling moldings, and dazzling chandeliers. The pale green and dark red decor is bathed in light, which pours in through the two tiers of windows (28 in all) taking up the long sides of the room. Behind Peter the Great's throne at the eastern end of the room hangs a huge portrait of Catherine the Great. The empress, a picture of confidence after her successful coup, is shown riding a horse, dressed in the uniform of the guards regiment that supported her bid for power.

Next to the Throne Room is the **Chesmensky Zal** (Chesma Hall), whose interior is dedicated entirely to the Russian naval victory over the Turks in 1770. The walls are covered with 12 huge canvases depicting the battles, which were created by the German painter P. Hackert at Empress Catherine's behest. According to legend, the artist complained that he could not paint a burning ship since he had never seen one. Catherine arranged to have ships blown up for him to use as models. Such were the days of divine right. Arguably the most dazzling of the palace's rooms is the **Audients Zal** (Audience Hall). Rastrelli created the definitive Baroque interior with this glittering room of white, red, and gold. Gilt Baroque bas-reliefs adorn the stark white walls, along which tall mirrors are hung, further accentuating the richness of the decor.

Other notable rooms include the **Kitaiskye Kabinety** (the Chinese Study Rooms), designed by Vallin de la Mothe in the 1760s. As was the fashion in Europe at the time, the rooms are ornately decorated with Chinese motifs. Finely carved black-lacquered panels depict various Chinese scenes. Between the two rooms is the **Kartinny Zal** (Picture Hall), whose walls are paneled with 368 oil paintings by the Italian artist Rotari. The artist used just eight models for these paintings, which depict young women in national dress.

After a tour of the palace interiors, a stroll through the **Upper Park** is in order. Lying on the south side of the palace, this formal garden with its symmetrical design is far less imaginative than the Lower Park, with its playful fountains and cascading waterfalls. Its focal point is the Neptune Fountain, originally made in Germany in the 17th century and bought by Paul I in 1782. During the war the three-tiered group of bronze sculptures was carried away by the Germans. It was eventually recovered and reinstalled in 1956.

Pushkin (Tsarskoye Selo)

The town of **Pushkin,** 24 kilometers (15 miles) south of St. Petersburg, was the summer residence of the imperial family from the days of Peter the Great right up to the last years of the Romanov dynasty. Formerly known as **Tsarskoye Selo** (czar's village), its name was changed after the 1917 Revolution, first to Detskoye (Children's) Selo and then to Pushkin, in honor of the great Russian poet who studied at the lyceum here. During the 18th and 19th centuries, Tsarskoye Selo was a popular summer resort for St. Petersburg's aristocracy and well-to-do. Not only was the royal family close by, but it was here, in 1837, that Russia's first railroad line was opened, running between Tsarskoye Selo and Pavlosk, followed three years later by a line between here and St. Petersburg.

★ Pushkin's main attraction is the dazzling **Yekaterininsky Dvorets** (Catherine Palace), a perfect example of Russian Baroque. The exterior is painted bright turquoise and features row after row of white columns and pilasters with gold Baroque moldings alternating the entire length (985 feet) of the facade. Although much of the palace's history and its inner architectural design bears Catherine the Great's stamp, it is for Catherine I, Peter the Great's second wife, that the palace is named. Under Empress Elizabeth, their daughter, the original modest stone palace was completely rebuilt. The project was initially entrusted to the Russian architects Kvasov and Chevakinsky, but in 1752 Elizabeth brought in the Italian architect Bartolomeo Rastrelli (who went on to build the Winter Palace in St. Petersburg). Although Catherine the Great had the interiors remodeled in the Classical style, she left Rastrelli's stunning facade untouched. ⊠ *7 ul. Sadovaya, town of Pushkin,* ☎ *812/465–5308.* ⊙ *Wed.–Mon. 10–5. Closed last Mon.*

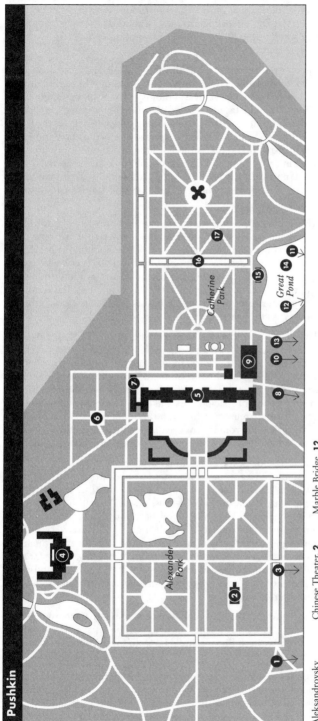

Pushkin

Alexander Park

Catherine Park

Great Pond

Aleksandrovsky
Dvorets, **4**
Cameron Gallery, **9**
Cameron's
Pyramid, **10**
Canal, **16**
Chapel, **1**
Chesma Column, **11**

Chinese Theater, **2**
Chinese Village, **3**
Concert Hall, **8**
English Garden, **17**
Great Pond, **14**
Grotto, **15**
Lyceum, **7**

Marble Bridge, **12**
Pushkin
Monument, **6**
Ruined Tower, **13**
Yekaterininsky
Dvorets (Catherine
Palace), **5**

of month. Park open daily. Transportation: commuter train from Vitebsky Vokzal (Vitebsk Station) to Pushkin–Detskoe Selo, approximately 30 min from St. Petersburg. From station take Bus 371 or 382 to Dvorets (palace).

You'll enter the palace grounds through the gilt and black iron gates designed by Rastrelli. The *E* atop is for Catherine (Ekaterina in Russian). To your right, a visual feast unfolds as you walk the length of the long blue-and-gold facade toward the museum entrance. Sparkling above the palace at the northern end are the golden cupolas of the Palace Church. Inside, the palace is just as spectacular; many of the rooms are famous in their own right. Although little of Rastrelli's original interior remains, the many additions and alterations made between 1760 and 1790 under Catherine the Great do; these were carried out by top architects, the Scottish Charles Cameron and the Italian Giacomo Quarenghi.

Entering the palace by the main staircase, which was not added until 1861, you will see displays showing the extent of the wartime damage and the subsequent restoration work. Like Peterhof, the palace was almost completely destroyed during World War II. It was used by the occupying Nazi forces as an army barracks, and as the Germans retreated, they blew up what remained of the former imperial residence. Today the exterior of the palace again stands in all its glory, although the interior is still being restored.

The largest and arguably most impressive room is the **Bolshoi Zal** (Great Hall), which was used for receptions and balls. The longer sides are taken up by two tiers of gilt-framed windows. Tall, elaborately carved and gilt mirrors have been placed between them. The light pouring in through the windows bounces off the mirrors and sparkles on the gilt, amplifying the impression of spaciousness and light. The huge ceiling painting, depicting Russian military victories and accomplishments in the sciences and arts, makes the room seem even larger. Here it is easy to imagine the extravagant lifestyle of St. Petersburg's prerevolutionary elite.

On the north side of the State Staircase is one of the palace's most famous rooms, the **Yantarnaya Komnata** (Amber Room), so named for the engraved amber panels that once lined its walls. A treaty gift to Peter the Great from the king of Prussia in 1716, all the panels were stolen by the Nazis. They have never been found, and although speculation continues to circulate about their eventual rediscovery, in 1979 the Soviet government finally gave up hope of ever retrieving them and began the costly work of restoring the room. The restoration is far from complete, but the few restored panels—and a prewar black-and-white photograph of the room—give you some idea of how marvelous the original interior was.

Leaving the Amber Room, you will come to the large **Kartinny Zal** (Picture Gallery), which runs the full width of the palace. The paintings are all from Western Europe and date from the 17th to the early 18th century.

Highlights among the other splendid rooms on the north side include the Blue Drawing Room, the Blue Chinese Room, and the Choir Anteroom, all of which face the courtyard. Each has pure silk wall coverings. The Blue Chinese Room, originally designed by Cameron, has been restored on the basis of the architect's drawings. Despite its name, it is a purely Classical interior, and the only thing even remotely Chinese is the Oriental motif on the blue silk covering the wall. The fine golden-yellow silk of the Choir Anteroom is from the same bolt used to decorate the room in the 18th century. When the postwar restoration began, an extra supply of the original silk was discovered tucked away in a storage room of the Hermitage.

Having savored the treasures inside the palace, you can now begin exploring the beautiful **Yekaterininsky Park** outside, with its marble statues, waterfalls, garden alleys, and boating ponds, pavilions, bridges, and quays. The park is split into two sections. The inner, formal section, known as the French Garden, runs down the terraces in front of the palace's eastern facade. The outer section centers around the Great Pond and is in the less rigid style of an English garden. If you follow the main path through the French Garden and down the terrace, you will eventually reach Rastrelli's Hermitage, which he completed just before turning his attention to the palace itself. Other highlights of the French Garden include the Upper and Lower Bath pavilions (1777–79) and Rastrelli's elaborate blue-domed Grotto.

There is much to be seen in the English Garden, too. A good starting point is the **Cameron Gallery,** which actually forms a continuation of the palace's parkside frontage. It is over to the right (with your back to the palace). Open only in the summer, it contains a museum of 18th- and 19th-century costumes. From its portico you get the best views of the park and its lakes—which is exactly what Cameron had in mind when he designed it for Catherine the Great in the 1780s. The double-sided staircase leading majestically down to the Great Pond is flanked by two bronze sculptures of Hercules and Flora.

From here, go down and begin your exploration of the park. Just beyond the island in the middle of the Great Pond, which is actually an artificial lake, stands the **Chesma Column,** commemorating the Russian naval victory in the Aegean in 1770. At the far end of the pond is **Cameron's Pyramid,** where Catherine the Great reportedly buried her favorite dogs.

If you follow around the pond's right side, you will come to the pretty, blue-and-white **Marble Bridge,** which connects the Great Pond with a series of other ponds and small canals. At this end, you can rent rowboats. Farther along, up to the right, you come to the "**Ruined Tower.**" It's not authentic or old, just built to enhance the romantic ambience of these grounds.

Outside the park, just north of the Catherine Palace, stands yet another palace, the **Alexandrovsky Dvorets,** a present from Catherine to her favorite grandson, the future Czar Alexander I, on the occasion of his marriage. Built by Quarenghi between 1792 and 1796, the serene and restrained Classical structure was the favorite residence of Russia's last czar, Nicholas II. The building is not open to the public.

Built in 1791 and originally intended for the education of Catherine the Great's grandchildren, the **Lyceum** later became a school for the nobility. Its most famous student, enrolled the first year it opened, was the adored Alexander Pushkin. The building is now open as a museum; and the classroom, library, and Pushkin's bedroom have been restored to their appearance at the time he studied there. In the school's garden is a statue of the poet as a young man, sitting on a bench, presumably deep in creative meditation. The building is attached to the Catherine Palace.

Pavlovsk

The estate grounds of **Pavlovsk** had always been the royal hunting grounds, but in 1777 Catherine the Great awarded them to her son

Paul I, upon the birth of his first son (future czar Alexander I). Construction of the first wooden buildings started immediately, and in 1782 Catherine's Scottish architect Charles Cameron began work on the Great Palace and the landscaped park. In contrast to the dramatically Baroque palaces of Pushkin and Peterhof, Pavlovsk is a tribute to the reserved beauty of Classicism. Paul's intense dislike of his mother apparently manifested itself in determinedly doing exactly what she would *not*— and here, visitors may be grateful, to excellent result. The place is popular with St. Petersburg residents, who come here to stroll through the 600-hectare (1,500-acre) park, with its woods, ponds, alleys, and pavilions. ✉ *20 ul. Revolutsiy, town of Pavlovsk,* ☏ *812/470–2156.* ⊙ *Sat.–Thurs. 10–5. Closed 1st Mon. of month. Transportation: commuter train from Vitebsky Vokzal (Vitebsk Station) to Pavlovsk, approximately 25–35 min from St. Petersburg. From station walk to palace, or take Bus 370 or 383.*

A tour of Pavlovsk begins with the **Bolshoi Dvorets** (Great Palace), which stands on a high bluff overlooking the river and dominates the surrounding park. The building is painted golden yellow and crowned with a flat, green dome supported by 64 small white columns. Built in 1782–86 as the summer residence of Paul and his wife, Maria Fyodorovna, the stone palace was designed in imitation of a Roman villa. It was enlarged by Vincenzo Brenna in 1796–99, when a second story was added to the galleries and side pavilions. Despite a devastating fire in 1803 and further reconstruction by Voronikhin in the early 19th century, Cameron's basic design survived.

In front of the palace stands a statue of the snub-nosed Paul I, a copy of the statue at Gatchina, Paul's other summer residence. When you enter, you'll find many rooms on view, and you may start on either the ground or the second floor. The splendid interiors, with their parquet floors, marble pillars, and gilt ceilings, were created by some of Russia's most outstanding architects. Besides Cameron, Brenna, and Voronikhin, the roll call includes Quarenghi, who designed the interior of five rooms on the first floor, and Carlo Rossi, who was responsible for the library, built in 1824. The state apartments on the ground floor include the pink-and-blue **Ballroom;** the formal **Dining Hall,** where the full dinner service for special occasions is set out; and the lovely **Corner Room,** with walls of lilac marble and doors of Karelian birch. Among the lavishly decorated state rooms on the second floor is the famous **Greek Hall,** whose layout is that of an ancient temple. Its rich green Corinthian columns stand out starkly against the white of the faux marble walls. The hall, which also served as a small ballroom, linked the state rooms of Paul I to those of his wife, Maria. The last room on his side, leading here, was the **Hall of War.** Her first private suite, called the **Hall of Peace,** was designed to correspond to it. The gilt stucco wall moldings are decorated with flowers, baskets of fruit, musical instruments, and other symbols of peace.

Beyond the empress's apartments, you come to the light-filled **Picture Gallery,** with its floor-length windows and eclectic array of paintings. From it, via a small, pink marble waiting room, you reach the palace's largest chamber, **Throne Hall.** Once it held Paul I's throne, but for a victory party after Napoléon's defeat it was removed and somehow never returned.

Leave the palace to explore its grounds. Covering over 1,500 acres, Pavlovsk's splendid park boasts numerous pavilions, tree-lined alleys, waterways, and statues. Like the palace, the park was designed by the leading architects of the day—Brenna, Cameron, Voronikhin, and Carlo Rossi. Once again, the Pavlovsk park differs greatly from the blueprint ones of the other imperial palaces. They applied strict rules of geometrical design, whereas at Pavlosk nature was left unfettered, with simple beauty, instead of precisely determined effect, the result.

The combined length of the park's paths and lanes is said to equal the distance between St. Petersburg and Moscow (656 kilometers [410 miles]). Since you can't possibly cover the entire territory in one day anyway, you might just want to follow your whim and see where it leads you. If you walk down the slope just behind the palace to the **Czar's Little Garden** (Sobstvenny Sadik), you can see the Three Graces Pavilion. Created by Cameron, the 16-columned pavilion encloses a statue of Joy, Flowering, and Brilliance. A stone staircase, decorated with lions, is directly behind the palace and will take you to the Slavyanka Canal. On the canal's other side, down to the left is the graceful **Apollo Colonnade**, whose air of ruin was not entirely man-made; built in 1783, it was struck by lightning in 1817 and never restored. If you bear right at the end of the stairs, you come to the **Temple of Friendship**, meant to betoken the friendship between Empress Maria and Catherine the Great, her mother-in-law. Beyond it is a monument from the empress to her own parents; the center urn's medallion bears their likenesses. Of the other noteworthy pavilions and memorials dotting the park, the farthest one up the bank is the **Mausoleum of Paul I.** Set alone on a remote and overgrown hillside toward the center of the park, it was built by Maria for her husband after he was murdered in a palace coup. Paul was never interred here, however, and lest it sound too heartrending for his widow (portrayed as inconsolable in a statue here), evidence indicates that she was well aware of the plot to kill her husband.

Lomonosov

Renamed for the 18th-century scientist Mikhail Lomonsov, **Lomonosov** was originally named Oranienbaum for the orangery attached to its palace. It was the property of Alexander Menshikov, Peter the Great's favorite, who followed Peter's lead and in 1710 began building his own luxurious summer residence on the shores of the Baltic Sea. Before his plans could be realized, however, Peter died and Menshikov was stripped of his formidable political power and exiled, leaving his summer estate only half finished. The palace reverted to the crown and was given to Peter III, the ill-fated husband of Catherine the Great. Most of the buildings on the grounds were erected during his six-month reign, in 1762, or completed later by Catherine. ⊠ *48 ul. Yunovo Lenintsa, town of Lomonosov,* ☎ *812/422–4796.* ☉ *Wed.–Mon. 11–5. Closed last Mon. of month. Transportation: commuter train from Baltisky Vokzal (Baltic Station) to Oranienbaum-1 (not II), approximately 1 hr from St. Petersburg.*

Menshikov's Great Palace, the original one here, is also its biggest. It is situated on a terrace overlooking the sea. Built between 1710 and 1725, it was designed by the same architects who built Menshikov's grand mansion on Vasilievsky Island, Giovanni Fontana and Gottfried Schaedel. The Great Palace has been under reconstruction for some time and is currently not open to the public.

Nearby is **Peterstadt Dvorets,** the modest palace that Peter III used, a two-story stone mansion built between 1762 and 1785 by Arnoldo Rinaldi. Its interior is decorated with handsome lacquered wood paintings. That it seems small, gloomy, and isolated is perhaps appropriate since it was here, in 1762, that the czar was murdered in the wake of the coup that put his wife, Catherine the Great, on the throne.

The building that most proclaims the estate's imperial beginnings, however, is unquestionably Catherine's **Kitaisky Dvorets** (Chinese

Palace), also designed by Rinaldi. Intended as one of her private summer residences, it is quite an affair—Rococo inside, Baroque without. Lavishly decorated, it has ceiling paintings created by Venetian artists, inlaid-wood floors, and elaborate stucco walls. The small house outside served as the kitchen.

Down the slope to the east of the Great Palace is the curious **Katalnaya Gorka** (Sledding Hill). All that remains of the slide, which was several stories high, is the pavilion that served as the starting point of the ride, where guests of the empress could catch their breath before tobogganing down again. Painted soft blue with white trim, the fanciful pavilion looks like a blue-frosted birthday cake. Also on the premises, near the pond, is a small amusement park offering carnival rides.

ST. PETERSBURG A TO Z

Arriving and Departing

By Boat

Cruise ships of the Baltic Line call at St. Petersburg. Cruises are available from Kiel, Germany. The sea passenger terminal is on Vasilevsky Island at Morskoi Slavy Ploshchad (☎ 812/355–1310). The river passenger terminal is at 195 Obukhovskoi Oborony Prospect (☎ 812/262–1318).

By Bus

The Russian firm **Sovavto St. Petersburg** (☎ 812/298–1352, FAX 812/298–7760) offers daily departures to Helsinki from the following hotels: Astoria, Grand Hotel Europe, Pulkhovskaya, and St. Petersburg. The Finnish bus company **Finnord** (☎ 812/314–8951, FAX 812/314–7058) offers daily service to Vyborg and Helsinki, leaving from 37 ul. Italyanskaya.

By Car

You can reach St. Petersburg from Finland via the Helsinki–St. Petersburg Highway through the border town of Vyborg. To reach Moscow, take the Moscow–St. Petersburg Highway, which leaves the city near the Varshavsky (Warsaw) Railroad Station, close to Izmailovsky Cathedral.

Again, a word of warning about driving: be aware of lines at fueling stations, the risk of car theft, and the lack of repair shops and replacement parts, added to the poor road conditions and maintenance. It's advisable not to drive.

By Plane

AIRPORTS AND AIRLINES

St. Petersburg is served by two airports, **Pulkhovo I** (domestic) and **Pulkhovo II** (international), located just 5 kilometers (3 miles) apart and 12 kilometers (7 miles) south of downtown St. Petersburg. The runways of the two Pulkhovos interconnect, so it's possible you could land at Pulkhovo I and taxi over to Pulkhovo II.

Compared to Moscow's Sheremetyevo II, Pulkhovo II is a breeze. It's small and well lit, with signs in Russian and English. Remember that on departure you will need to fill out a final customs declaration (available at all the long tables) before proceeding through the first checkpoint.

For domestic flight information, call 812/104–3822. For international information, call 812/104–3444.

Aeroflot (☎ 812/104–3444) offers direct flights to more than 20 countries out of Pulkhovo II. Other international airlines maintaining offices in St. Petersburg include: **Balkan** (☎ 812/315–5030) **Delta** (☎ 812/311–5819); **Finnair** (☎ 812/315–9736); **Air France** (☎ 812/325–8252); **KLM** (☎ 812/325–3440); **Lufthansa** (☎ 812/314–4979); **Malev** (☎ 812/317–6380); and **Swissair** (☎ 812/314–5086).

BETWEEN THE AIRPORT AND DOWNTOWN
From Pulkhovo I, Municipal Bus 13 will take you to the Moskovskaya subway stop at the end of Nevsky Prospect; the stop at the airport is right outside the terminal. Tickets are sold on the bus, which runs every 40 minutes during the day and every 90 minutes at night. From Pulkhovo II, the service is less reliable and more inconvenient. If you have any luggage, the only realistic way to reach downtown St. Petersburg is by car. If you are traveling with a tour package, all transfers will have been arranged. Independent tourists are advised to make advance arrangements with their hotels for transfers from the airport. There are plenty of taxis available, but for safety reasons non-Russian speakers should not pick up a cab on their own. Foreign tourists, especially arriving passengers at train stations and airports, are prime crime targets. Cab fare from the airport will depend entirely on your negotiating skills; the range is $10 to $50. The airport is about a 40-minute ride from the city center.

By Train

Train travel is by far the most convenient and comfortable mode of travel in Russia. St. Petersburg has several train stations, the most important of which are **Finlandsky Vokzal** (Finland Station), for trains to Finland; **Moskovsky Vokzal** (Moscow Station), at Ploshchad Vostania, off Nevsky Prospect, for trains to Moscow and points east; **Varshavsky Vokzal** (Warsaw Station) for trains to the Baltic countries; and **Vitebsky Vokzal** (Vitebsk Station) for trains to Ukraine and points south. All the major train stations have a connecting subway stop, so they are easily reached by public transportation.

There are several trains daily from Moscow to St. Petersburg, the most popular of which is the **Red Arrow,** a night train that departs Moscow at 11:55 PM and arrives in St. Petersburg at 8:25 AM the next day. During the day travelers prefer the high-speed **Avrora,** which makes the trip in less than six hours. There are two trains daily to and from Helsinki; the trip takes 6½ hours.

For information on train arrival and departure schedules, call 812/168–0111. Train tickets may be purchased through the tourist bureau in your hotel or at the Central Railway Agency Office at 24 Kanal Griboyedova (off Nevsky Prospect, adjacent to the Kazan Cathedral; ☎ 812/201, an unusual three-digit number). Tickets for anything other than same-day departures are *not* for sale at the train stations.

A reminder about train travel: You must travel on an Intourist train ticket or risk being fined by the railway. As a foreigner you pay the special higher price for train travel and, in return, usually get above-average service (the best trains are still reserved for foreign tourists).

Very long-distance travelers should be aware that trains can often lack heat and hot water, a result of feuds between rail administrations in different republics. To avoid discomfort, be sure to bring along some drinking water whenever traveling by train. You are also advised to have your own supply of toilet paper.

Getting Around

Although St. Petersburg is spread out over 650 square kilometers (150 square miles), most of its historic sites are concentrated in the downtown section and are best explored on foot. Most of the historic sites are not well served by the extensive public transportation system, so be prepared to do a lot of walking.

By Bus, Tram, and Trolley

Surface transportation operates on the honor system: Upon entering, you validate your ticket by punching it in one of the machines on the wall of the vehicle. You can purchase strips of tickets at subway stops and kiosks throughout the city or, sometimes, from the driver after you have boarded. The ticket is valid for one ride only; if you change buses you must pay another fare. Buses, trams, and trolleys operate from 5:30 AM to midnight, although service in the late evening hours and on Sundays tends to be unreliable.

St. Petersburg has an elaborate surface transportation system, but in contrast to the subway, service has greatly deteriorated in recent years. Vehicles tend to be dilapidated and extremely overcrowded during rush hours. People with claustrophobia should avoid them. In the last years of the Soviet regime, Russia depended on Hungary for buses, but in today's economic order, they are no longer forthcoming. It is not uncommon to ride a bus with holes in the ceiling and doors that will not close due to constant overcrowding, or that keels to the side when turning corners like a sailboat on rough seas.

By Subway

Although St. Petersburg's metro does not boast the elaborate design and decoration of the Moscow subway, its beauty and convenience are still great. And despite economic hardships, St. Petersburg has managed to maintain efficient service. The only drawback to the system, which is simple to use and inexpensive as well, is that the stops tend to be far apart.

To use the subway, you must purchase a token (available at stations) and insert it upon entering into the slot at the turnstile. The fare is the same regardless of distance. Alternatively, you may purchase a pass valid for the entire month and good for transport on all modes of city transportation. The cost is insignificant and well worth the convenience if you plan to use the subway a lot. The subway operates from 5:30 AM to midnight and is best avoided during rush hours. Stations are deep underground with long escalator rides. Some of them have encased landings so that entry is possible only after the train has pulled in and the secondary doors are opened. Note that a section between Lesnaya Station and Ploshchad Muzhestva Station is out of service due to an accident. The repair works can take a year or two.

By Taxi

Although taxis roam the city quite frequently, it is far easier—and certainly safer—to order a cab through your hotel. Fares vary according to the driver's whim; you are expected to negotiate. Foreigners are always charged much more than Russians, and tourists tend to be gouged. If you speak Russian, you can order a cab by dialing 812/312–00–22. There is sometimes a delay, but usually the cab arrives within 20–30 minutes. If you order a cab this way, you pay the official state fare, which turns out to be very reasonable in dollars, plus a fee for the reservation. Drivers will appreciate and expect a tip of at least 20%. If you hail a cab on the street, expect to pay the ruble equivalent of at least $5.

Tourists should take the same precautions when using taxicabs in St. Petersburg as in Moscow.

St. Petersburg Metro

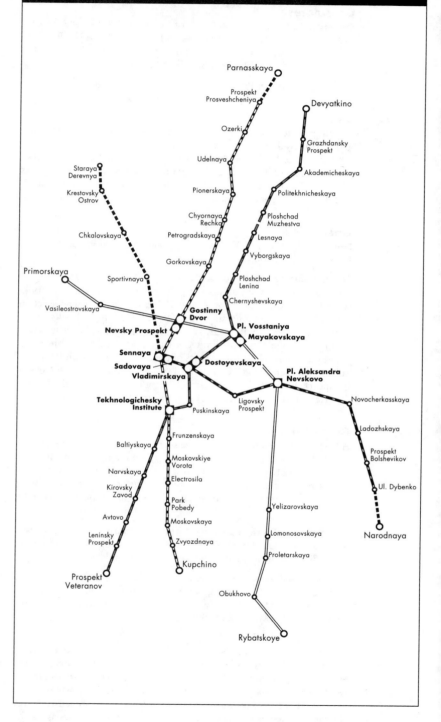

Contacts and Resources

Consulates

Canada (⊠ 32 Malodetskoselsky Prospect, ☎ 812/325–8448, ℻ 812/325–8393). **U. K.** (⊠ 5 Pl. Proletarskoi Diktatury, ☎ 812/119–6036, ℻ 812/325–6037). **U. S.** (⊠ 15 Furstadtskaya, ☎ 812/275–1701, 812/274–8568, or 812/274–8689, ℻ 812/110–7022).

A word of warning: Phone lines to the U.S. Consulate are constantly busy. It may take hours of persistent dialing to get through.

Dentists

Several private dental practices operate in St. Petersburg. In an emergency, you could ask your hotel for a referral, or try one of the following private clinics: **St. Petersburg Polyclinic No. 2** (22 Moskovsky Prospect, ☎ 812/316–6272); **Dental Polyclinic No. 3** (12, 21 liniya, ☎ 812/213–7551 or 812/213–5550); **Dental Center** (10 Sovetskaya, ☎ 812/274–6480); or **Nordmed** (12/15 ul. Tverskaya, ☎ 812/110–0654 or 812/110–0401).

Emergencies

Fire (☎ 01). **Police** (☎ 02, Russian speakers only). **Ambulance** (☎ 03, Russian speakers only).

English-Language Bookstores

For English-language publications, try St. Petersburg's largest bookstore, **Dom Knigi** (House of Books), at 28 Nevsky Prospect. The selection is nothing to write home about, but it's still the biggest bookstore in town and fun to see. **Planeta,** at 30 Liteiny Prospect, has a selection of imported books, too. A limited selection of outdated English-language guidebooks on various parts of the former Soviet Union is available at **Akademkniga** (57 Liteiny Prospect). **Iskusstvo** (52 Nevsky Prospect), like Akademkniga, stocks English-language guidebooks. American and British paperbacks, newspapers, and magazines are on sale in hotel gift shops.

Guided Tours

A host of private tour agencies have surfaced in the past few years, primarily because tourism is seen as an easy source of foreign currency. Keep in mind that whatever the price quoted for a tour, it may very well be negotiable. In addition to the private agencies, every major hotel has a tourist bureau through which individual and group tours can be booked.

St. Petersburg Tourist Company, formerly Intourist (60, nab. Moiky, ☎ 812/315–5129, ℻ 812/312–2558) offers group or individual excursions to all of the major sites and suburban palaces.

The **St. Petersburg City Excursion Bureau** (⊠ 56 nab. Krasnovo Flota, ☎ ℻ 812/311–4019) arranges sightseeing trips throughout the city. Specially tailored tours can be made by **Staraya Derevnya** (⊠ 72 ul. Savushkina, ☎ ℻ 812/239–0000).

Hospitals and Clinics

Medical facilities in St. Petersburg still are poorly equipped and short on supplies. As in the other cities, it is recommended that tourists seek emergency medical help at Western-style clinics. The **American Medical Center** (⊠ 77 nab. Fontanky, ☎ 812/325–6101; ℻ 812/325–6120) is open weekdays 8:30 to 6, and offers 24-hour comprehensive care. **The Medical Centre for Foreigners** has been around for years as the St. Petersburg Polyclinic No. 2 (⊠ 22 Moskovsky Prospect, ☎ 812/316–6272, ℻ 812/316–5939); it is open weekdays 9–9, Saturday 9–3. Although care is still below Western standards, the facilities are clean and foreign medicines are available. A doctor is on call 24 hours a day. If you are unfortunate enough to be hospitalized while in St. Petersburg, you will probably be placed in **Hospital No. 20** (⊠ 21 ul. Gastello, ☎ 812/108–4808 or 812/108–4066).

Pharmacies

Most pharmacies in St. Petersburg close by 8 or 9 PM. **PetroFarm** (22 Nevsky Prospect, ☎ 812/164–4410) has a pharmacist on call daily 9–3.

Pharmacies that regularly stock imported and Western medicines are: **Pharmacy Damian** (⊠ 22 Moskovsky Prospect, ☎ 812/110–1240); **PetroFarm** (also at 83 Nevsky Prospect, ☎ 812/277–7966); and **Pharmadon** (⊠ 5 Nevsky Prospect, ☎ 812/312–7078).

Travel Agencies

For international travel help, **American Express** operates an office in the Grand Hotel Europe. Besides ticketing, the office replaces lost traveler's checks and credit cards or take out a cash advance (in traveler's checks only). The office does not have an automated teller machine, and due to limited availability of cash, it is not always possible to cash your traveler's checks for dollars. ⊠ *1/7 ul. Mikhailovskaya, just off Nevsky Prospect,* ☎ *812/329–6060.* ☉ *Weekdays 9–5.*

Avista Tours (⊠ 7 ul. Millionaya, ☎ 812/275–6635, ℻ 275–3488) arranges international bookings.

Visitor Information

You may consult the **St. Petersburg Council for Tourism.** ⊠ *3 ul. Italianskaya,* ☎ *812/314–8786, office, or 812/110–6739, foreign section;* ℻ *812/110–6824 or 812/311–9381.*

Your most expeditious route is your hotel, for virtually all of them have established tourist offices for their guests. These offices, which provide a wide variety of services, will help you book individual and group tours, make restaurant reservations, or purchase theater tickets. Even if you are not a hotel guest, you are usually welcome to use these facilities, provided you are willing to pay the hefty fees (charged in foreign currency only) for their services.

Where to Change Money

Inkombank (⊠ 41 ul. Komsomola, ☎ 812/542–3611); **St. Petersburg Bank** (⊠ 8 Admiralteyskaya nab., ☎ 812/314–6095); **Industry and Construction Bank** (⊠ 38 Nevsky Prospect, ☎ 812/110–4958).

Again, your hotel is more convenient; all of them also have exchange bureaus, which are generally open from 9 AM to 6 PM, with an hour's break for lunch in the afternoon.

4 Kiev

The political and industrial center of modern Ukraine, Kiev displays both the tranquillity of its ancient past and the agitation of a newly independent nation grappling with the political and economic problems of moving ahead as an autonomous nation.

THINK OF YOUR TRIP TO KIEV as a journey by time machine that will transport you back to the earliest moments of Ukrainian-Russian history. Kiev (in Ukrainian, *Kyiv*) is known as the mother of Russia, for it was here, around the end of the 9th century, that the Eastern Slav lands collectively called Rus were first unified. The city of Kiev itself was reportedly founded near the end of the 5th century by a family for whose eldest brother, Kii, it was named. For the next 1,500 years it was a center of unceasing activity in trade, religion, and politics. Today it is a bustling modern metropolis—the capital of independent Ukraine—beginning a new chapter in its identity but still closely tied to its ancient past and founding role in the development of Russian culture.

By Lauri del Commune

Between the 10th and 12th centuries Kiev flourished as the capital of Rus. After Christianity became the official religion in 988, Kiev became one of the most significant points of religious exchange and learning in the ancient empire. A gradual decline began in the late 1100s, ending abruptly in 1240, when the city was razed to the ground by Mongol invaders. Thereafter, until 1991, Kiev was the capital of an independent nation for only brief periods. Freed from the Mongol yoke in the 14th century, it fell under the rule of the Lithuanians and then the Poles. In 1654, choosing the lesser of two evils, Ukraine joined the Russian empire.

Much of what is known of Kiev's early history comes from the *Primary Chronicle*, written in the 11th–12th centuries by monks at Kiev's Monastery of the Caves. It was there that Nestor first wrote of the "three brothers . . . Kii lived upon the hill where the Borich trail now is; and Shchek dwelled upon the hill now named Shchekovitza; while on the third resided Khoriv, after whom this hill is named Khorevitsa. They built a town and named it Kiev after their oldest brother." (The founding family also had a sister named Lybid, but her legacy today seems to be an eponymous hotel, not a city.) Archaeological findings confirm that there was indeed a settlement called Kii around the end of the 6th century, and the hills still exist. You will see them and the golden domes of Kiev's ancient churches rising above the green expanses that carpet the hilly terrain and vast plains.

The city has always had its full share of violence and bloodshed, which, along with its ancient glory, is an essential key to understanding today's Kiev. In the aftermath of the Bolshevik Revolution and the ensuing civil war, Kiev saw bitter fighting that pitted brother against brother. The city suffered heavy losses and was nearly destroyed again during World War II, when it was captured and held by German forces for almost 800 days. Liberated by the Soviet army, Kiev again suffered terribly under Red recapture, when many Ukrainians were perceived as Nazi collaborators—sometimes merely because the city had been occupied by the Germans. Postwar punishment escalated as Stalin's notorious purges, intense in the Ukraine starting in the 1930s, were translated into famines, camp deportations, land collectivizations, and executions. After Stalin's death in 1953, three decades of enforced Russification took hold, with Ukrainian educational, governmental, and social institutions being made to fit the Soviet mold. In 1986, the Ukraine suffered the tragedy of Chernobyl when one of its nuclear power reactors, just 104 kilometers (65 miles) north of the city, exploded, spewing radioactive materials into the air and into the city's water supply. Scientists affirm that Kiev is now safe for visitors, but residents will feel the effects of the accident for decades to come. As the former USSR began to founder in the late 1980s, so did much of its authority over the Ukrainian state. In 1991, the Ukrainian parliament rejected Soviet Russian hegemony altogether, by declaring itself a fully independent nation and electing its own president.

Pleasures and Pastimes

Parks
Kiev has miles and miles of beautiful parkland, and exploring these green oases is one of the joys of a visit to the Ukrainian capital, especially in spring and summer. The right bank of the Dnieper is lined with a series of adjoining parks, collectively called **Central Park.** The first is the **Volodymyrska Girka** (☞ The Khreshchatik and Kiev's Art Museums, *below*), which then becomes **Khreshchaty Park;** that in turn runs into the **Park of Askold's Grave,** which later becomes the **Vechnoi Slavy (Eternal Memory) Park.** The entrance to Khreshchaty Park is at Lenkomosol Square; Eternal Memory Park can be reached by taking the subway to Arsenalna Station. From there it is one stop south on any trolleybus.

EXPLORING KIEV

The Ukrainian capital straddles the wide Dnieper River. To the east lie the steep hills of Old Kiev, and to the west you will find the newly developed regions of the low-lying left bank.

Great Itineraries
You need three days in Kiev to see the essential center and its main sights. A week would allow you to do a more thorough job of exploring the city's museums and to travel to see the historical monasteries and monuments on the outskirts of Kiev. A stay of 10 days would allow one or two more trips out of the city and give you time to wander at leisure through the parklands and lesser known museums.

IF YOU HAVE 3 DAYS
Start with a **Slavutich** or **Sputnik** guided tour to get a quick overview of the main sights and to orient yourself to the city's layout (☞ Guided Tours *in* Kiev A to Z, *below*). Then spend the first afternoon stretching your legs on our tour of the **Khreshchatik and Kiev's Art Museums.** Try to devote at least the first half of the second day to exploring the 21 halls of the **Museum of Ukrainian Art.** Then move back outdoors and follow the route suggested in our tour of **St. Sophia's and the Upper Town.** On the third day spend the morning at the **Russian Art Museum** and then spend the balance of the day browsing and shopping on the **Khreshchatik** and surrounding streets.

IF YOU HAVE 7 DAYS
Follow the three-day itinerary above, and then take our **St. Andrew's Cathedral and the Podol** tour. If you spend some time in the museums along the way, this should take most of the day. Spend the fifth day familiarizing yourself with the holdings of the **Taras Shevchenko State Museum** and strolling through either the **Volodymyrska Girka** or **Khreshchaty Park.** On day six head out to the **Monastery of the Caves** and the **World War II Museum.** Save your last day for visits to some of Kiev's lesser museums and/or last-minute souvenir shopping.

IF YOU HAVE 10 DAYS
On this amount of time it is possible to see most of the above, then take some day trips out of the city, either using public transportation or joining an organized tour. With three extra days you should easily be able to visit the memorial site at **Babi Yar,** the open-air **Folk Architecture Museum** in the village of Pirogova, and **Askold's Grave.**

The Khreshchatik and Kiev's Art Museums

This walk takes you along Kiev's main thoroughfare—the **Khreshchatik**—and to the city's most important art museums. It might be tempting to begin your exploration with the city's many monuments to ancient history, but the Khreshchatik is the best place to gain a sense of today's Kiev. The avenue's role as the city's cultural center and main shopping district invites comparison with St. Petersburg's Nevsky Prospect. Kievans themselves like to think of it as a Ukrainian Champs-Elysées.

Numbers in the text correspond to points of interest in the margin and on the Kiev map.

A Good Walk

Begin your walk at **Evropeyska Ploshcha** ①, at the eastern end of the Khreshchatik. You can reach it by taking the subway to Maidan Nezalezhnosti. Take a right as you exit the stop, and go all the way to the end of the Khreshchatik (you will already be on it when you emerge). Evropeyska Ploshcha marks the end of the Khreshchatik, and other main streets radiate from it. Take the underpass that goes beneath the square to cross to the opposite side. The yellow building here is the **Hall of Columns** ②. As you enjoy the view, look across the ravine to your immediate left. There you will see **Volodymyrska Girka** ③ and the Monument to the Baptism of Russia.

Return now to Evropeyska Ploshcha and turn left to go up Vulytsya Mikhaila Grushevskoho. The attractive mauve stone building on the corner is the National Parliamentary Library. The street just beyond it leads to the Central Park of Culture and Rest, where Kiev's Dynamo Stadium is located. Keep to the right of this street and, going up another block farther, you'll find the **Museum of Ukrainian Art** ④. Leaving the museum, return again to Evropeyska Ploshcha to begin a tour of the Khreshchatik itself. Most of the architecture here dates from the 1950s and '60s, with a few exceptions at the beginning of the street. On the right-hand side stand the former St. Petersburg Bank (No. 8) and the former Volzhsko-Kamsky Bank (No. 10), both built at the turn of the century. One block from Evropeyska Ploshcha, the Khreshchatik meets **Maidan Nezalezhnosti** ⑤, to which you came by subway. If you're feeling energetic, climb up Vulytsya Instituska, which runs alongside the hotel. Crowning the hill, at No. 5, the **Palace of Culture** ⑥, one of the city's largest concert halls.

The building below and to the right as you face the hotel is the Tchaikovsky Conservatory, a restored version of the 1899 original. Look across the street at the large and elaborate building on the opposite corner. It is Kiev's main **post office.** If you turn left onto the street that skirts the conservatory's right side, you will be on Gorodetskoho Vulytsya, a lovely side street with a cinema, small park, and shops. Not far away, it is bisected on the right by Zamkovetskaya Vulytsya. Take a right onto it.

This area, with its many boutiques and cooperatives, is a pleasant place to browse and shop. To get back to the Khreschatik, go through one of the "passages," unmarked lanes that lead through the large arches linking sections of the long, connected buildings that front this part of the Khreshchatik.

Back on this main street, heading away from Maidan Nezalezhnosti, the next block contains several large department stores and administrative buildings, including the imposing Office of the President of Ukraine. Cross to the right-hand side via one of the underground crossings. At the very end of the Khreshchatik, one of the city's few sur-

182

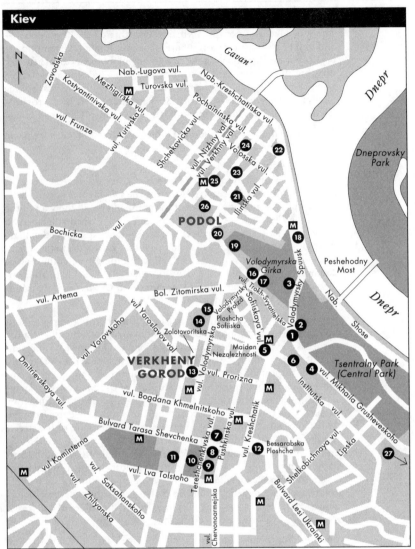

Kiev

viving statues of Lenin marks the beginning of Bulvar Tarasa Shevchenka, named in honor of the 19th-century Ukrainian poet and artist. Walk two blocks up the boulevard, and on your right, at the corner with Tereshchenkivska Vulytsya, is the **Taras Shevchenko State Museum** ⑦. Turning left onto Tereshchenkivska Vulytsya, you'll come to the impressive **Russian Art Museum** ⑧. Just a few doors down the street is yet another important art museum, the **Museum of Western and Oriental Art** ⑨.

Bordering Tereshchenkivska Vulytsya to the north is **Taras Shevchenko Park** ⑩. On the opposite side of the park, on Vulytsya Volodymrska, stands the bright red building of **Kiev University** ⑪. To the south (to your left as you face the university) Vulytsya Volodymrska intersects **Vulytsya Lva Tolstoho** (Leo Tolstoy Street). Turn left at the corner and walk to the end of the street. The street ends at **Ploshcha Lva Tolstoho** (Leo Tolstoy Square), where it intersects Vulytsya Chervonoarmiiska.

If you continue down Vulytsya Chervonoarmiiska, you will come out at the western end of the Khreshchatik. Here, on Bessarabska Ploshcha, you will find Kiev's first indoor market, the **Kriti Rynok** ⑫. Your tour of the Khreshchatik area ends here; to reach the subway you can either walk down the street to Maidan Nezalezhnosti or return to Vulytsya Lva Tolstoho, where there is a subway station of the same name.

TIMING
Taken at a leisurely pace, and without stops at the museums, this walk should take about one–and–a–half to two hours. Each of the museums along the route is worth at least a half day on its own, though, so a thorough exploration of this area and its sights could easily expand to two or three days. This will all depend on how carefully you want to view the exhibits in Kiev's major museums.

Sights to See

❶ **Evropeyska Ploshcha.** This square at the eastern end of the Khreshchatik recently got its pre–revolutionary name back. For the last thirty years of the Soviet era it was known as Lenkomsomol Square, before that as Stalin Square. Several of Kiev's main streets radiate from the square: from the left side of the rectangular, all-white Ukrayinsky Dim (the Ukrainian House, formerly the Lenin Museum (☞ St. Sophia's and the Upper Town, *below*) **Vulytsya Trokh-Svyatitelska** (Three Saints Street) leads up a steep incline to the famous St. Andrew's Church (☞ St. Andrew's and the Podol, *below*). **Vulytsya Mikhaila Grushevskoho** to the right leads to the Pechersk district and the ancient Monastery of the Caves (☞ Monastery of the Caves and World War II Museum, *below*). Volodymyrsky Spusk, diagonal from the Hotel Dnipro, leads down to the riverbank. *Metro: Maidan Nezalezhnosti.*

Fomin Botanical Garden. This park in the center of town was laid out in 1841. It is named after Alexander Fomin, a botanist and director here in the 1920s. The entrance is near the Universitet subway station.

Gidro Park. This pretty park on an island near the left bank is a popular spot in summer for boating and bathing. To reach it, take the subway to the Gidro Park station.

❷ **Hall of Columns.** Built in 1882, the former meeting place of the pre-revolutionary Merchants' Assembly is now home to Kiev's Philharmonic Society. A broad stairway next to this yellow building winds its way up alongside a park. Climb to the top and head toward the back of the park. You will soon be greeted by a huge steel rainbow, which is the Monument Commemorating the 325th Anniversary of the Reunion of Russia and Ukraine. The union is over now, of course, but the monument remains. Erected in 1982, the gigantic arch has five sections representing the Earth's continents, and the proletarian figures with a bas-relief depict Russo-Ukrainian brotherhood. You may prefer to concentrate on the splendid view behind it of the wide Dnieper, the long bridges that span its islands, and the vast plains of the left bank. ⊠ *Volodymyrsky Uzviz,* ☎ *44/229–6251. Metro: Maidan Nezalezhnosti.*

★ **Khreshchatik.** Kiev's main thoroughfare is lined with monumental high rises, many in the Stalinist architectural style, interspersed with broad strips of green lanes and parks. As thoroughfares go, the Khreshchatik is quite short—just 1.6 kilometers (less than a mile) long. It is located in a valley and runs along the lines of a deep ditch that once occupied the site. Hills rise steeply along both sides, especially to the south. The Khreshchatik was almost completely destroyed during World War II and was rebuilt at twice its original width. The street's name may come from the dried-up riverbed that once ran through the valley. The river was called Khreschata (meaning criss-crossed), for the valley was crossed by numerous ravines. Other possibilities are that the name derives from the word *khreshchennya,* meaning "baptism," or from *khrest,* which means "cross." The street leads to the site in the Dnieper River where, according to legend, the people of Kiev were baptized en masse in 988. *Metro: Khreshchatik.*

NEED A
BREAK?
The **Konditerska** (⊠ 5 Khreshchatik) has a stand-up café where you can have coffee or tea and pastry. Kiev has always been known for its delicious cakes, and you will find Kievans lining up here to buy them. If you're looking for a place to sit down, you can stop by the **Dnipro Hotel,** back at the corner with Evropeyska Ploshcha, where you can have a cup of coffee or a draft beer at the lobby bar.

⓫ **Kiev University.** Also known as Shevchenko University, this is Ukraine's most prestigious institution of higher education. Built in 1837–43, this is another Classical structure created by Vikenty Beretti. The long central facade is adorned by an eight-columned portico in the Ionic style. Completely destroyed during World War II, the building has been restored to its original appearance. According to legend, the building acquired its unusual color in 1901, when Czar Nicholas II ordered it doused in bright red in retaliation against rebellious students who refused to comply with the draft. The color was supposed to embarrass them and intimidate others. ⊠ *60 Volodymyrska Vul. Metro: Universitet.*

☾ **Kiev Zoo.** A favorite with kids, the Kiev Zoo is easy to reach by subway from downtown. ⊠ *32 Prospect Peremogi,* ☎ *44/274–6054.* ☉ *Apr.–Nov. daily 9–6, Dec.–Mar. 9–4. Metro: Politekhnicheski Institut.*

☾ **Kievsky Circus.** The circus has been a favorite outing for children since 1959. Further details and tickets are available at all hotel information desks. ⊠ *1 Ploshcha Peremogi,* ☎ *44/216–3856. Metro: Universitet.*

⓬ **Kriti Rynok.** Designed by Heinrich Gay and completed in 1912, Kiev's first indoor market was established in Art Nouveau style on this site for Bessarabian (Moldovan) merchants who came to trade in Kiev. Today it is Kiev's most important market, and inside the domed building you'll find rows of private farmers selling fruit, meat, and vegetables, as well as an occasional Ukrainian souvenir. In a separate section on the market's far side, you'll find the glass-enclosed dairy section. Ukrainian matrons, bedecked in neat caps or kerchiefs and smocks, dole out generous samples of their freshly made cheeses, including the sweet *tvorog,* and sour cream. Once you venture in, each vendor will try to persuade you that only her product is worthy of you. *2 Bessarabska Ploshcha. Metro: Khreshchatik.*

Magdeburg Law Column. Designed by the Ukrainian architect Andrei Melensky, this monument was completed in 1808 and honors Kiev's right to self-government. ⊠ *In Khreshchaty Park, at bottom of Volodymyrska Girka. Metro: Maidan Nezalezhnosti.*

⑤ Maidan Nezalezhnosti (Independence Square). In Yaroslav's day the southeastern gates of the high defensive wall surrounding the city stood near here, at the bottom of Vulytsya Zhitomirska (to your right, beyond the fountains). During the communist regime, this broad, sprawling square was named in honor of the October Revolution, and a huge, red granite statue of Lenin once stood on the terrace (to your left) across the street. Towering above the square on the left, fronted by a series of broad steps, is the **Moskva Hotel,** built in the early 1960s and designed after the Moscow original. *Maidan Nezalezhnosti.*

OFF THE
BEATEN PATH

BABI YAR – There was a time when Babi Yar was just another pretty ravine on the outskirts of town. World War II changed that. In September 1941, the German occupying forces ordered Kiev's 33,700 Jewish residents to gather their belongings and march to Babi Yar. Thinking they would be transported to another location, the men, women, and children did as they were told and lined up along the edge of the ravine. Nazi firing squads proceeded to execute them, and their bodies toppled into the ravine below. Throughout the Nazi occupation Babi Yar was used for mass killings. In all, over 100,000 people were killed here, including partisans and members of the Soviet underground. In 1976 a monument was erected on the site, with the official, cumbersome title of **Monument to Soviet Citizens, Soldiers, and Officers, Prisoners of War, Who Were Tortured and Killed by the Nazi Invaders in 1941–43.** Although Soviet officials denied for decades that Jews had been a specific target of the Nazis, the dramatic monument—crowned by the figure of a young mother—is a moving testament to their suffering. To reach Babi Yar, take Trolleybus 16 or 18 from Maidan Nezalezhnosti (No. 16 stops across the street, at the bottom of Vulytsya Zhitomirska; No. 18 stops at the bottom of Vulytsya Sofiska). The trip takes 30–40 minutes; Babi Yar is located just past the tall television tower.

KIRILOVSKA TSERKVA – Even if you are sated with church architecture, the trip to the magnificent 12th-century St. Cyril's Church, at the northwestern end of the Podol, is well worth it. Inside, more than 800 square meters (8,600 square feet) of medieval frescoes have been preserved. The church was once attached to the St. Cyril Monastery, founded in 1140 by Vsevolod II, prince of Chernigov, a pretender to the Kievan throne. Sviatoslav Vsevolovich, a hero in the ancient Russian epic, *The Lay of Igor's Campaign,* was buried here in 1194. Badly damaged during the Mongol invasion, the church has been rebuilt several times. Its present Baroque exterior dates from the 18th century, when it was reconstructed by Alexander Beretti. Restoration of the frescoes was entrusted to the art historian Adrian Prakhov. Among his apprentices was Mikhailo Vrubel, at that time an unknown artist from St. Petersburg. Vrubel's distinctive Symbolist brush is evident in the paintings on the marble altar screen and in the figures of the Holy Virgin and St. Cyril on the iconostasis. Like many churches in the Soviet Union, St. Cyril's was closed after the Bolshevik Revolution and opened as a museum in 1929. To reach the church, take Trolleybus 18 from Maidan Nezalezhnosti (the trolleybus stops across the street, at the bottom of Vulytsya Sofiskaya) to the stop Stadion Spartak. The ride takes about 40 minutes. ⊠ *12 Oleni Teligi,* ☎ *44/435–1126.* ۩ *Mon.–Thurs., weekends 10–5:30.*

Museum of the History of Kiev. Situated in the Klovsky Mansion, this museum was designed in the 1750s by the serf-architect Stepan Kovnir.

✉ *8 Vul. Pilila Orlika,* ☏ *044/293–6071.* ☯ *Mon.–Thurs., Sat., Sun. 10–5. Closed last Thurs. of month. Metro: Khreshchatik.*

❹ **Museum of Ukrainian Art.** Opened in 1899, this museum with huge granite steps flanked by a pair of lions originally housed Kiev's Museum of Antiquities and Art. In 1936 the exhibits were moved to another location, and the present museum, devoted to Ukrainian art from the 12th to early 20th centuries, was opened.

The museum's 21 halls house a wonderful collection of Ukrainian paintings, sculptures, and drawings as well as religious art. The rich collection of icons, located on the first floor, includes the 12th-century St. George with scenes from his life and the 14th-century Virgin Hodegetria, brought here from the town of Lutsk. The 18th-century Intercession is interesting for its portrait of Bogdan Khmelnitsky, the hetman who led the revolt that liberated Ukraine from Polish rule. The first-floor exhibits also contain fine examples of Ukrainian portrait and landscape paintings from the 17th to the 19th centuries, including Vasily Tropinin's *Girl from Podolia* and Taras Shevchenko's *Self-Portrait.* Several well-known works by Nikolai Pimonenko, including his *Wedding in Kiev* and *Victim of Fanaticism,* are also on display. The second-floor exhibits are devoted to modern Ukrainian art. Strongly influenced by Soviet propaganda and the demands of socialist realism, the works here are interesting primarily as a sociopolitical statement. ✉ *6 Vul. Mikhaila Grushevskoho,* ☏ *44/228–6482.* ☯ *Mar.–Nov., Mon.–Thurs., weekends 10–6.; Dec.–Feb., 10–5. Metro: Maidan Nezalezhnosti.*

❾ **Museum of Western and Oriental Art.** Like the ☞ Russian Museum, this museum was founded after the Bolshevik Revolution on the basis of a private collection. It is housed in the former mansion of the well-known archaeologist Bogdan Khanenko, who started the collection in the 1870s. The holdings include a rich collection of Corinthian and Attic painted vases from the 3rd to 4th centuries, found in digs in the Black Sea area, as well as terra-cotta statuettes (400 BC) and Roman sculptural portraits of the 2nd century. There are also several Byzantine icons dating from the 6th and 7th centuries. The section devoted to Western European art includes Italian Renaissance and Baroque art and works from the golden age of Spanish Art. Velázquez's *Portrait of the Infanta Margarita,* a highlight of the collection, was a study for a large formal portrait now housed in Madrid's Prado. Flemish and Dutch schools of the 15th–18th centuries are also represented. Unfortunately, the museum was closed in 1993 for major restoration work and is not scheduled to reopen until at least 1998. Its holdings may be moved to other locations; for information, call the museum. ✉ *15 Tereshchenkivska Vul.,* ☏ *44/224–6162 or 44/225–0206.*

Natural Science Museum. This is four museums in one: the Archaeological Museum, the Botanical Museum, the Geological Museum, and the Zoological Museum. ✉ *15 Vul. Bogdana Khmelnitskoho,* ☏ *044/224–9383.* ☯ *Fri.–Tues. 10–4:30. Metro: Universitet.*

❻ **Palace of Culture.** This prerevolutionary building with a Classical colonnade was built by the architect Vikenty Beretti in the early 1840s as a finishing school for young ladies of the nobility. Today it is one of the city's largest concert halls. ✉ *5 Institutska Vul.,* ☏ *44/228–7491. Metro: Maidan Nezalezhnosti.*

❽ **Russian Art Museum.** This is one of the largest repositories of Russian art outside Moscow and St. Petersburg. The building was built in the 1880s and belonged to the wealthy Tereshchenko family. The museum was founded in 1922 on the basis of the Tereshchenko collection and other private collections confiscated and nationalized by the Soviet government. The splendid interiors were designed by Robert Friedrich Meltzer, known for his work in the Winter Palace in St. Petersburg. The fine collection includes masterpieces from the 12th to the 20th centuries.

The permanent exhibits are on the second floor; the gallery on the first floor is reserved for temporary exhibits. Tickets for the two sections are sold separately. The outstanding collection of religious art is contained in the first two galleries on the second floor. Here you'll find icons from the Novgorod, Rostov-Suzdal, and Moscow schools, including a 12th-century icon from Novgorod of the Russian saints Boris and Gleb. Russian 18th-century portrait art is also represented by Vasily Borovikovsky's *Portrait of Vera Arsenyeva* as well as by Dmitry Levitsky's *Unknown Woman in Blue* and his portrait of Catherine the Great. Most important is the museum's extensive collection of works from the 19th century, such as Vasily Tropinin's *The Gamblers,* Vasily Perov's *God's Fool,* and Victor Vasnetsov's *Three Tsarevnas of the Underground Kingdom.* There are also many fine landscapes by Isaac Levitan and the seascape painter Ivan Aivazovsky. The World of Art Movement (*Mir Isskustva*) is represented by works of Serov, Korovin, and Benois. The last exhibit hall contains an interesting display of 18th–20th century china, porcelain, and glass, including plates produced in St. Petersburg in the early 1920s. ⊠ *9 Tereshchenkivska Vul.,* ☎ *44/224–6218.* ◷ *Mon.–Wed. and Sat.–Sun. 10 AM–5 PM, Fri. noon–5 PM. Closed last Wed. of month.*

Taras Shevchenko Memorial House Museum. The personal effects and literary manuscripts of Taras Shevchenko (☞ Taras Shevchenko State Museum, *below*) are on display in the house where the Ukrainian writer lived in 1846. ⊠ *8a Pereulok Shevchenko,* ☎ *44/228–3511.* ◷ *Sat.–Thurs. 10–5. Metro: Maidan Nezalezhnosti.*

⑩ Taras Shevchenko Park. In the center of this park stands a statue of the Ukrainian classical writer and national hero, erected in 1939 on the 125th anniversary of his birth. It replaced an earlier statue of the deposed Russian czar, Nicholas II. *Metro: Ploshcha Lva Tolstoho.*

❼ Taras Shevchenko State Museum. If you have spent any time in Ukraine, you have probably heard about this beloved national hero. Born into serfdom in 1814, he became one of the nation's greatest artists and poets, as well as a leader in the fight against serfdom. A member of the secret Society of Sts. Cyril and Methodius, which opposed serfdom, he was arrested in 1847 and spent more than 10 years in internal exile. In failing health when he returned, he died four years later, at the age of 47. At the age of 16 he had gone to St. Petersburg, where he quickly gained recognition for his artistic abilities, despite his lack of formal training. Art critics encouraged him to enter the St. Petersburg Academy of Arts, but first he had to purchase his freedom from his owner. The artist Karl Bryullov came to his aid, auctioning his portrait of the Russian poet Vasily Zhukovsky and donating the proceeds to Shevchenko. The portrait is now one of the museum's 4,000 exhibits. Also on display are more than 800 literary and artistic works by Shevchenko, as well as many of his personal effects. ⊠ *12 Bulvar Tarasa Shevchenka,* ☎ *44/224–2556.* ◷ *Tues.–Sun. 10–5.*

NEED A BREAK? **Arlechino Pizzeria** (⊠ 2 Bulvar Tarasa Shevchenka, ☎ 44 225–0271). Take a break here before you head into the heart of Kiev's museum district. It's a cheery spot, and their array of pizzas and drinks will refresh you. They have take-out service, too.

Volodomirsky Sobor. Commissioned in 1862, this elaborate neo-Byzantine cathedral was supposed to have been finished in time for the

900th anniversary of Russia's conversion to Christianity. A series of construction problems delayed its completion, and the celebrations (in 1888) came and went before the cathedral was finally consecrated in 1896. Construction was begun by Ivan Strom and finished by Alexander Beretti, with several other architects working on the cathedral in the meantime. Frequent changes in design resulted in a diversity of styles. The highly ornate exterior is a strange and not particularly attractive mix of Baroque and Byzantine; the interiors, however, are splendid, with frescoes, icons, and murals created by some of Russia's most prominent artists, including Nesterov. The work was supervised by the art historian Professor Adrian Prakhov, who was also in charge of the restoration of St. Cyril's Church (☞ *above*). Among the historical figures depicted are Prince Vladimir (the pagan ruler who brought Christianity to Russia), Princess Olga, Alexander Nevsky, and Monk Nestor (co-author of the *Primary Chronicles*). ✉ *20 Bulvar Tarasa Shevchenka,* ☎ *44/225–0362). Services daily Mon.–Sat. 9 AM, 6 PM. Metro: Universitet.*

➌ **Volodymyrska Girka** (Vladimir Hill). Atop this hill is the **Monument to the Baptism of Russia,** a 20-meter (66-foot) statue showing Prince Vladimir—the pagan ruler who brought Christianity to Russia—dressed as a Russian warrior and holding a cross in his right hand. The pedestal, shaped like a Russian chapel, is engraved with the ancient seal of Old Kiev. Erected in 1853, the bronze statue was designed by Vasily Demut-Malinovsky, a St. Petersburg sculptor, and was cast by Peter Klodt, creator of the famous horse statues adorning St. Petersburg's Anichkov Bridge. *Metro: Maidan Nezalezhnosti.*

St. Sophia's and the Upper Town

This tour takes you through the hilly section of the **Verkhny Gorod** (Upper Town), also known as Old Kiev, where you will find the surviving monuments of Kiev's ancient past.

A Good Walk

The tour begins at the **Zoloti Vorota** ⑬, or Golden Gate, located just outside the subway station of the same name. When you exit the subway, you'll find yourself at the back side of the Golden Gate. We will follow the path of Yaroslav and his contemporaries, down the road leading to the city's oldest church, **Sofiisky Sobor** ⑭. Walk down Vulytsya Zolotovoristska, which begins directly across the street from the entrance to the Golden Gate. Bear right at the end of this short street, onto Vulytsya Reitarska, which will soon come out onto Vulytsya Volodymyrska. The entrance to St. Sophia's is just a few steps down to your left.

As you leave the St. Sophia complex, turn left onto Volodymyrska Vulytsya. The street opens onto **Sofiiska Ploshcha** ⑮. Follow the street running down the right-hand side of the square, with the statue to your left and a small strip of park to your right. Before you leave the square, pause for a moment for another look at St. Sophia's, whose massive bell tower and helmet-shaped cupolas dominate the square. You are now on Volodymyrsky Proizd; the strip of park bordering the street to your right is dotted with sculptures of pagan gods. Walk the length of the street, approximately three blocks, and you will come to **Mikhailivska Ploshcha** ⑯. Turn right off the square, onto Vulytsya Trokh-Svyatitelska (Three Saints' Street). At the left-hand corner (with your back to the square) stands the 18th-century **Refectory** ⑰. Continue on Three Saints' Street, walking away from St. Michael's Square. The street soon turns down a steep incline, which ends at Evropeyska Ploshcha. To your right as you head down the steep hill is the Catholic

Church of St. Alexander. To your left, at the bottom of the hill, is the **Ukrayinsky Dim.** The square marks the beginning of Kiev's main thoroughfare, the tree-lined Khreshchatik (☞ The Khreshchatik and Kiev's Art Museums, *above*). The subway is just one block away, to your right as you enter the square from Three Saints' Street.

TIMING

The sights on this tour, which basically runs south to north along Volodymyrska Vulytsya, are all fairly close to each other, and simply following the route from beginning to end without stopping should only take about an hour. The tour includes some of the most important cultural sights in Kiev, however, and to really do them justice, you should plan on spending the better part of a day inside the various churches and museums. Don't set out on a Thursday, though, because two of the most important sights—the museum of Russian architecture at Zoloti Vorota and the Sofiisky Sobor—are closed.

Sights to See

Historical Museum. The museum's extensive exhibits cover the history of Kiev from prehistoric times to the present. The section on Kievan Rus is particularly interesting. Also on display are examples of Ukrainian folk art from the 17th to the 20th centuries. ⊠ *2 Volodymyrska Vul.,* ☏ *44/228–4864 or 44/228–2924.* ◷ *Mon., Tues., Thurs.–Sun. 10–6. Metro: Zoloti Vorota.*

⑯ Mikhailivska Ploshcha (St. Michael's Square). This square takes its name from the Mikhailovsky-Zlatoverkhy Monastery (St. Mikhail Monastery of the Golden Roof) that was founded on this site in 1051; its cathedral, built by Prince Sviatopolk in 1108, was the city's second most important house of worship after Sofiisky Sobor. It survived the brutal Mongol invasions and the years of Polish and Lithuanian rule—but not the Soviets. In 1936 it was destroyed to make way for the massive and severe Central Committee headquarters of the Ukrainian Communist Party, on the western edge of the park; the building now houses the Ukrainian Ministry of Foreign Affairs. Because St. Mikhail was considered the city's patron saint, many Kievans find a connection between the monastery's destruction and subsequent disasters that have struck the city such as Germany's World War II occupation and the Chernobyl nuclear accident. Now that the monastery has been restored, it is hoped that Kiev's patron saint will spare the city any further misfortune. A monument dedicated to three other saints revered by the Ukrainians—Kievan princess Olha and Slavic missionaries Cyril and Methodius—was recently erected in the center of the square. *Metro: Zoloti Vorota.*

⑰ Refectory. This 18th-century building is the only one of the 11th-century monastery to have been spared destruction in World War II. The stone church, with its single wooden cupola, was built in 1712. Like many churches in the former Soviet Union, it was turned into a museum after the Bolshevik Revolution. Little remains of its original interior, and, like the rest of the monastery, the building had to be restored. With the recent religious revival, the museum was closed and the refectory now belongs to the Ukrainian Orthodox Church. Services are held daily at 7 AM and 5 PM. ⊠ *Vul. Trokh-Svyatitelska. Metro: Maidan Nezalezhnosti.*

⑮ Sofiiska Ploshcha (St. Sophia Square). Until recently St. Sophia Square was named in honor of Bogdan Khmelnitsky, whose equestrian statue stands in the square's center. Khmelnitsky (1595–1657) led the Ukrainian people in the war of liberation against Poland and later pushed for reunification with Russia. The statue stands on this site where the residents of Kiev gave their hero a triumphant welcome. Paid for primarily by public conscription, it was designed by a well-known St. Petersburg sculptor, Mikhail Mikeshin, and was erected in 1888. The hetman bestrides a rearing horse that towers above a red-granite pedestal. In the distance above the trees, to your far left, is St. Andrew's Church (☞ St. Andrew's and the Podol, *below*). *Metro: Maidan Nezalezhnosti or Zoloti Vorota.*

★ ⑭ **Sofiisky Sobor** (St. Sophia's Cathedral). Today the complex of buildings and churches that make up St. Sophia's is a museum. In addition to the cathedral itself, on display are models of ancient Ukrainian and Russian towns, as well as local archaeological discoveries. You'll enter the complex through the Southern Gate Tower, following the path directly in front of you to reach the cathedral entrance. Tickets are sold at the kiosk to your right, just before you reach the cathedral. ⊠ *24 Volodymyrska Vul.,* ☎ *44/228–6152.* ⊙ *Mon.–Wed., Fri.–Sun. 10– 5. Metro: Zoloti Vorota.*

Dedicated in 1037, St. Sophia's (also known as the Cathedral of Holy Wisdom) was built by Prince Yaroslav the Wise in gratitude for winning a battle against the Pechenegs, an invading tribe from the east. Prince Yaroslav, the Peter the Great of Kievan Rus, looked not west but south for inspiration, basing his cathedral on the Hagia Sophia of Constantinople. Over the centuries, the Cathedral of St. Sophia acquired an importance far exceeding its religious role: It was not only the seat of the metropolitan but also the center of political and social life in Kievan Rus. It housed the nation's first library, whose rich collection included manuscripts from Europe and Greece. It was the site of cultural events, and it was here that princes were crowned and foreign ambassadors received.

At first glance you may wonder how the cathedral's helmetlike cupolas could possibly adorn the city's oldest church. The church was reconstructed on several occasions, and its present exterior owes much to the era of Ukrainian Baroque. The original design, strongly influenced by Byzantine architecture, also contained elements of Ukrainian wooden architecture. The huge, five-aisled church originally had 13 cupolas and was built in the shape of a Greek cross. The main cupola in the center represented Christ; the surrounding cupolas depicted the 12 Apostles. After the death of Yaroslav (who is buried inside) in 1054, the northwestern tower was added and a vault was built for his tomb. Badly damaged during the Mongol invasion and further destroyed by the Poles and Lithuanians, the cathedral lay in ruins until after the reunification of Ukraine and Russia in 1654, when restoration began. In the early 18th century, on orders from Peter the Great, the cathedral was reconstructed and the six additional domes (for a total of 19) were added.

In contrast to the exterior, much of the 11th-century interior has been preserved. It is richly decorated with mosaics and frescoes, many of which date from the 11th and 12th centuries. One curious feature of the fresco work is the use of secular subjects. Frescoes depicting hunting scenes, wild animals, court jesters, and musicians afford a glimpse of everyday life in Kievan Rus. The spiral staircase of the towers, whose entrance was once located outside the cathedral, led to the choir loft, where Yaroslav and his family sat during services.

Continue now to the central nave, whose walls, ceilings, and pillars are decorated with colorful mosaics and frescoes. You will be immediately struck by the golden glow of the central dome. Peering down at you is an 11th-century mosaic of Christ as the Pantokrator; his portrayal as Father, Son, and Holy Ghost was influenced by Byzantine traditions. The vault of the main apse is adorned by a beautiful mosaic of the Orant Virgin. Because this mosaic has survived intact after centuries of abuse and reconstruction, it has become known as the Indestructible Virgin. The magnificent gilded iconostasis in front of the altar was erected in 1747; it was partially dismantled in the 19th century, and only the lowest of the three original tiers remains.

In addition to religious themes, the frescoes include portraits of Yaroslav and his family. Considering that Yaroslav was alive when they were painted, the portraits are highly unusual for church decoration. A portrait of his four daughters, including Anna, the future queen of Henry I of France, are on the southern wall, while four of his sons are depicted on the northern wall. Fragments of portraits of Yaroslav himself and his wife, Irina, their eldest daughter, Elizabeth (later queen of Norway), and their eldest son, Vladimir, are on the western wall.

Yaroslav's marble sarcophagus is in the northeast chapel, to the left of the central nave as you face the iconostasis. The tomb, which weighs six tons, dates from the 5th or 6th century. It was brought from Greece, and its carved decoration includes such early Christian symbols as palms, cypresses, fishes, and grapevines.

Behind the cathedral stands a four-story, stone **bell tower,** painted azure with white trim. This is a fine example of Ukrainian Baroque; the lush ornamentation includes the double-headed eagle of the Romanov dynasty. Measuring 76 meters (249 feet), the bell tower was erected between 1744 and 1752; the fourth story and gilded cupola were added in 1852.

Head back in the direction of the main entrance to the cathedral grounds. To your left, just before you reach the ticket booth, is the 18th-century **refectory,** which houses archaeological and architectural displays. Its finds include the sarcophagus of Princess Olga, which once stood in the 10th-century Tithe Church (☞ St. Andrew's and the Podol, *below*) destroyed by the Mongols. The model panoramas of Kiev in the 10th–12th centuries will give you an idea of what the city looked like before it was razed to the ground by Mongol invaders.

NEED A
BREAK?

Kulinaria. If you're not disturbed by the obligatory cats on the windowsills, you can sit down and have a coffee or hot cocoa at this café on the corner of Volodymyrska Vulytsya and Reitarska Vulytsya (to your right as you exit the cathedral through the southern gate). The coffee is very sweet and heavily diluted with milk. Pastries and cakes are sometimes available, as well as sausages and champagne.

Ukrayinsky Dim. Kiev's obligatory but short-lived Lenin Museum (it was erected in 1982) was closed and converted into the **Ukrainian House of Culture** in 1991. It contains temporary displays on Ukrainian culture, from food to dress. Up the steep hill that leads to the museum is the Catholic **Church of St. Alexander** (1817–42), renovated in 1994 by Polish contractors.⊠ *2 Khreshchatik.* ☉ *Tues.–Sun. 11–6:30. Metro: Khreshchatik.*

❸ **Zoloti Vorota** (Golden Gate). In Yaroslav's day it served as the main entrance into the city, which was surrounded by a high defensive wall. Walk around to the front. Of the original gates, only the two parallel walls supporting the main entrance remain. The reconstructed version before you was completed in 1982, to coincide with celebrations of the city's 1,500th anniversary. Today the pavilion houses a museum of ancient Russian architecture, which is open only in summer. ⊠ *48A*

Yaroslavov Val, ☎ *44/224–7068.* ☼ *Mar.–Nov., Mon.–Wed. and Fri.–Sun. 10–6. Metro: Zoloti Vorota.*

Built in 1037 by Yaroslav the Wise, the original Golden Gate, inspired by the gates of Constantinople, was famous throughout Europe. Covered by beaten gold and other precious metals, it was topped by a tiny Church of the Annunciation. According to legend, it was through the Golden Gate that Batu Khan entered the city after the Mongols captured Kiev in 1240. Four centuries later, in 1648, Bogdan Khmelnitsky (the Cossack hetman who led the Ukrainian liberation movement), rode triumphantly through these gates after freeing the city from its Polish captors.

St. Andrew's and the Podol

This tour takes you to the magnificent ★**Andriyivska Tserkva** (St. Andrew's Church), on a high bluff overlooking the Dnieper, and then down the steep incline to the **Podol,** the old trading quarter, on the lower right bank. Although settlement of the Podol dates from Kiev's earliest days, none of the original architecture survives; the Mongol invasion obliterated the original wooden settlement. Rebuilt in the 17th and 18th centuries, the Podol burned to the ground in 1811 after a three-day fire. Its charm today lies in the rectangular pattern of its streets, lined with 19th-century apartment buildings and trading arcades, and the glorious views of St. Andrew's Church towering above.

A Good Walk

Begin your tour at the **Ploshcha Poshtova** ⑱ subway stop. To reach the bluff on which St. Andrew's sits, take the funicular (cable car), built in 1905. Its entrance is at the bottom of the hill, just outside the subway. When you reach the top, walk straight to the square ahead of you and take a right onto Desyatinna Vulytsya, which will lead you directly to St. Andrew's. On your right, you will pass again the monolithic Ukrainian Ministry of Foreign Affairs building, formerly the seat of the Central Committee of the Ukrainian Communist Party (☞ St. Sophia's and the Upper Town, *above*). To your right as you reach the end of Desyatinna Vulytsya stands **Andriyivska Tserkva** ⑲. When you are done basking in the glories of St. Andrew's, begin your walk down the cobblestone incline of Andriivski Uzviz. At No. 13 Andriivski Uzviz, on the right, readers of Bulgakov will be thrilled to find the seven-room **Bulgakov Museum** ⑳.

When you reach the bottom of the hill, turn right onto Borichiv Tik and then, not too much farther, left onto Vulytsya Andriivska. At the end of this short street is busy Vulytsya Petra Sagaidachnoho; at this point you can turn right to return to the subway at Poshtova Ploshcha, just a few blocks away. To continue your excursion on through the Podol, however, turn left. This busy shopping district is very different from the Khreshchatik, which is dominated by the monumental architecture of the Stalinist era. Before the revolution, the Podol was inhabited by merchants and craftsmen. A stroll through its quaint, narrow streets gives you a sense of Old Kiev.

After one long block, you will enter the broad **Kontraktova Ploshcha** ㉑, site of the **Gostinny Dvir** shopping arcade and the **Kontraktovy Dom.** Cross Vulytsya Sagaidachnoho (the large street that runs in front of the square), backtracking slightly to the north end of Contract Square. Turn left onto Vulytsya Illinska, heading in the direction of the river. Three blocks down the street, at the corner of Vulytsya Pochaininska (just before you reach the harbor), stands the 17th-century **Illinska Tserkva** ㉒. Now return to Contract Square and turn right again onto

Sagaidachnoho. The rectangular building on the right is the former **Kievo-Mogilianksa Academy** ㉓. Take a right onto Vulytsya Spaska, which begins across from the Contract House. On the first side street on the left, you'll see a 19th-century yellow-brick building with a rectangular tower. Formerly a fire station, the building is now the **Chernobyl Museum** ㉔. Return again to Vulytsya Petra Sagaidachnoho (the continuation of which is called Mezhigirska Vulytsya). A short walk down this block of decaying buildings brings you to Vulytsya Khoreva. Turn left and walk one block. At the corner of Kostyantinivska Vulytsya stands **Peter the Great's headquarters** ㉕ for his 1706 war against the Swedes. Continuing up Vulytsya Khoreva, you will reach the oldest surviving building in the Podol, the **Nikolai Pritiska Tserkva.** Turn left onto Vulytsya Pritisko-Mikilska, and a few steps will bring you to the **Florivski Monastir** ㉖. The area may be swarming with uniformed soldiers, because directly across the street is the headquarters of the Ukrainian National Guard. Look up to the bluff as you leave, and you'll see soaring St. Andrew's, dominant against the sky. To reach the subway again, retrace your steps to Peter the Great's house. Turn right onto Vulytsya Kostyantinivska. The entrance to the subway station Kontraktova Ploshcha is just a few steps away, on the left-hand side of the street.

TIMING

Taken at a leisurely pace, this walk takes about two hours without stops at the museums. If you want to see the museums and do some shopping along the way, the time could easily expand to a full day. Note that the Florivski Monastery is closed on Monday, the Bulgakov Museum is closed on Wednesday, and the Chernobyl Museum is closed on Sunday.

Sights to See

Andriivski Uzviz. This picturesque street, lined by cafés, art galleries, and small museums, is home to many artists; you'll see them offering their work for sale. In look and spirit, the area evokes the fin de siècle Montmartre. As you descend the hill, you'll come to sets of twisting iron steps. They will take you to lookout platforms affording fantastic views of Kiev old and new, with its rows of Soviet-made apartment buildings, the ubiquitous heavy cranes idle alongside them, the colored, older buildings of the Podol merchant district, and the bright tops of small churches glistening like drops of gold throughout, with the lovely Dnieper benignly winding its way down the middle. The first sloping hill to your left is **Zamkova Gora,** also known as Kiselyovka Mount. It is believed that this is the hill mentioned in the ancient chronicles in connection with Kii, who with his two brothers founded the city of Kiev around the end of the 6th century. At No. 22, on the left-hand side of the street, is the Podol Museum (☞ *below*). *Metro: Ploshcha Poshtova.*

NEED A BREAK?

Andriivski Uzviz, with its cafés and art salons, is the heart of Kiev's artist community. **Svitilitsa,** at No. 13A, is a popular hangout for writers and artists. Join them for some Turkish coffee or a shot of vodka. Pastries and small sandwiches are also available. The interior is reminiscent of a peasant cottage, with Ukrainian embroidery, a tile stove, and wooden picnic tables.

⑲ Andriyivska Tserkva (St. Andrew's Church). A fine example of Ukrainian Baroque, St. Andrew's green, blue, and gold cupolas light up the skies above Kiev's sweeping hills and the gently flowing Dnieper. Designed by the Italian architect Bartolomeo Rastrelli, who built so many of St. Petersburg's masterpieces, this church was erected at the behest of Peter the Great's pious daughter Elizabeth, who visited Kiev in 1744. The site, the highest point of Old Kiev, was allegedly chosen because it was here that the Apostle Andrew, who first preached the Gospel in Kievan Rus, erected a cross. Construction of the monumental cathedral proved a complicated task due to the hilly terrain—the foundation is 15 meters (50 feet) deep—and was completed in 1752. The church was not consecrated until 1767.

St. Andrew's stands on a platform above a broad flight of steps. The proportions are perfect, and the elegant interior is monumental and striking. Its three-tiered iconostasis, whose red-velvet background accentuates the gilded wooden carvings and sculptures, is the work of the Russian painter Alexei Antropov and the Ukrainian artist Grigory Levitsky. Unfortunately, the church has been closed for interior renovation since 1991 and will not reopen until at least 1996. Although you cannot go inside, don't be dissuaded from visiting the site, however, for a view of its elaborate exterior alone is worthwhile, and you can see the church quite close up. ⊠ *33 Andriivsky Uzviz,* ☎ *44/228–5861.* ☉ *Mon., Tues., Thurs.–Sun. 10–6; May–Sept., also Wed. noon–8.*

⑳ Bulgakov Museum. This seven-room mansion was the family home of Mikhail Bulgakov, the renowned Russian writer whose satirical works were long suppressed by the Soviet regime. He lived here from 1906 to 1916 and again in 1918 and 1919, and it provides the setting of his first major work, the novel *The White Guard.* For years the house stood unmarked, but today it has been lovingly redone. On exhibit are rooms that are either made to look as they did when he lived there (with the effect heightened by displays of personal items, such as his familiar spectacles) or as he described them in his writings. A pleasingly ghostly air pervades, too, for the rooms are virtually all white, in homage to the novel's theme. A terrific blend of the imaginative and the factual, the museum will be most appreciated by those who have read Bulgakov's work. All visitors are shown through with their own guide; you should ask for one who speaks English though there may not be one every day. ⊠ *13 Andriivskii Uzviz,* ☎ *44/416–5254.* ☉ *Mon., Tues., Thurs.–Sun. 10–6. Metro: Ploshcha Poshtova.*

㉔ Chernobyl Museum. Opened on April 25, 1992, the sixth anniversary of the Chernobyl disaster, the museum houses a somber exhibit depicting the accident and its horrifying aftermath. On display are the personal effects of the young soldiers who died as a result of their heroic efforts to put out the fire. Above the exhibit hangs a clock, permanently set at 1:23 AM, the time the explosion occurred. A reminder of the secrecy that shrouded the event is found in the display case containing newspaper clippings from around the time of the accident. The first official announcement by Soviet authorities, not issued until April 29, consists of just three short lines: "An accident occurred at the Chernobyl Atomic Power Plant. Measures are being taken to rectify the damage. The injured are being cared for." Other exhibits contain photos of Kiev's May Day celebrations and parade, after which residents were instructed to stay indoors and keep their windows tightly closed. Another display contains graphic photos of the dying, as well as mutilated animals and children born after the accident. The displays are supplemented with videos and documentary films. Entrance and guided tours (in Russian or Ukrainian) are free. ⊠ *1 Provulok Khorevii,* ☎ *44/417–5422.* ☉ *Weekdays 10–6, Sat. 10–5. Closed last Mon. of month. Metro: Kontraktova Ploshcha.*

Desyatinna Tserkva. Desyatinna Vulytsya is named for this church—whose name translates as Tithe Church—that once stood at the end of the street. Founded in 989 as the Church of the Holy Virgin, it became known as the Tithe Church because Prince Vladimir the Great, father of Yaroslavl the Wise, gave one-tenth of his income toward its maintenance. During the Mongol invasion, women and children took refuge inside its massive stone walls. But the roof collapsed under the weight of the fiery blows, killing everyone inside. If you turn left at the end of the street and walk a few hundred feet up Vulytsya Volodymyrska, you will find the outline of its foundation, which has been reconstructed with red quartz. Desyatinna itself is a very attractive street, now home to the British embassy and the first (and former) president of independent Ukraine. ⊠ *Desyatinna Vulytsya. Metro: Ploshcha Poshtova.*

㉖ Florivski Monastir (St. Flor's Convent). The convent, whose history dates from the 16th century, miraculously survived the antireligious campaigns of the Stalin era and remained open under Soviet rule. Enter the convent through the bell-tower gates, designed by Andrei Melensky (who also built the shopping arcade on Contract Square) in the 1830s. To your right stands the **Voznesenska Tserkva** (Church of the Ascension), the convent's main cathedral and the only functioning church left on its territory. Built in 1732, it suffered severely in the Podol fire of 1811, when the original iconostasis was destroyed. Tourists are not overly appreciated here, so to avoid a bitter scolding from the elderly women at prayer, leave your camera in your bag and your hands outside your pockets. To the right of the cathedral is a well at which you will see people lining up with glass jars. The water, which comes from an underground spring, is thought to have medicinal powers.

Just outside the convent walls, to your left as you exit through the bell tower, stands Kiev's very first **apothecary**, which dates from 1728. Restored to its original appearance, the building contains a functionary pharmacy, as well as a museum devoted to the history of medicine. The unusual exhibits, obviously compiled during the Soviet era, include a room decorated with authentic church icons and devoted to the "Christian Era" of medicine. The museum is open only for group excursions, which can be arranged by calling in advance (you'll have to provide your own interpreter). ⊠ *7 Pritisko-Mikilska Vul.,* ☎ *44/416–2437.* ⊙ *Tues.–Sun. 9–4. Metro: Kontraktova Ploshcha.*

㉒ Illinska Tserkva (St. Elias Church). Although the actual church dates from the 17th century, its history actually dates from Kiev's earliest days. According to legend, the first wooden church built on this site was erected by Askold (Rurik), the Kievan prince who was murdered by his rival from Novgorod, Prince Oleg, in 882. The present white-stone church, which holds services daily at 5 PM, was built in 1692. ⊠ *2 Pochaininska Vulytsya. Metro: Kontraktova Ploshcha.*

㉓ Kievo-Mogilianksa Academy. This institute was founded in the late 17th century inside the walls of the now destroyed Bratsky Monastery. In 1701 Peter the Great turned it into the Kiev Academy, which became one of the largest and most prestigious institutions of higher learning in all of Russia and Ukraine. Many famous scholars worked here, including the Russian scientist Mikhail Lomonsov, the composer Dmitry Bortnyansky, and the Ukrainian philosopher Grigory Skovoroda. Today the building houses a branch of the central library of the Ukrainian Academy of Sciences. *Vul. Sagaidachnoho. Metro: Kontraktova Ploshcha.*

NEED A BREAK?   If you're up for some hearty Ukrainian cooking, stop by the **Spadshchina** (⊠ 8 Spaska Vul., ☎ 44/417–0358), just one block off Kontraktova Ploshcha. Ask for a table in the back room, where you can rest in a comfy private booth. The specialty is *Kotleta Spadshchina,* fried chicken rolled in bread crumbs. The *vareniki,* filled with meat, potatoes or cabbage, are also homemade. ☺ *Daily noon–11.*

❷❶ **Kontraktova Ploshcha** (Contract Square). The long, white **Gostinny Dvir** shopping arcade splits the square down the middle. Originally built in 1809, it was destroyed in the 1811 fire and rebuilt in 1833 by the prominent Ukrainian architect Andrei Melensky. The arcade is similar to Moscow's GUM and St. Petersburg's Gostiny Dvor, but much smaller. Walk beyond it and you will be on the second side of the square. The statue in the center is of the 18th-century Ukrainian poet and philosopher Grigory Skovoroda. At the far corner of the square stands the **Kontraktovy Dom** (Contract House), for which the square is named. An interesting example of the Classical style, it was built in 1817 expressly as a headquarters for negotiating and signing agreements with foreigners. In dire need of reconstruction, which seems to have been abandoned, it still provides a hint of its past grandeur. *Metro: Kontraktova Ploshcha.*

Lesya Ukrainka Museum. This is a memorial museum to the well-known Ukrainian poetess Lesya Ukrainka. ✉ *97 Vul. Saksahanskoho,* ☏ *044/220–1651.* ☺ *Mar.–Nov., Mon.–Sat. 10–5; Dec.–Feb., Mon.–Sat. 10–4. Metro: Kontraktova Ploshcha.*

Nikolai Pritiska Tserkva (Pritisko-St. Nicholas Church). The modest, white-stone church, which bears just two cupolas, was built in 1631 (it is the oldest building in the Podol) and is similar in design to Ukrainian wooden cathedrals. Closed during the Soviet era, it was recently returned to the Ukrainian Orthodox Church and is open for services on Saturdays at 9 and 5, and Sundays at 10. ✉ *Vul. Georgiya Livera. Metro: Kontraktova Ploshcha.*

❷❺ **Peter the Great's Headquarters.** This 18th-century, white-stone building was occupied by the czar and his staff in 1706, when he prepared his attack on the Swedes, who had advanced to within 40 kilometers (25 miles) of Kiev. The building is not open to the public. ✉ *6 Konstyantinovska Vulytsya. Metro: Kontraktova Ploshcha.*

☾ ❶❽ **Ploshcha Poshtova.** In order to reach the bluff on which St. Andrew's sits, you will have to come to this subway station to take the funicular, which was built in 1905. Its entrance is at the bottom of the hill, just outside the subway. The ride up, which takes only a few minutes, gives you an excellent view of the city.

OFF THE
BEATEN PATH

RIVER CRUISE – There is no better way to spend a hot summer day than cruising the Dnieper. Excursion boats ply the river from late spring to early fall, leaving from pier No. 3 at the River Passenger Terminal (subway Ploshcha Poshtova). Check for excursions with your travel bureau.

PODOL MUSEUM – Opened in 1994, this museum offers an overview of the history and architecture of the district, using documents, photographs, and reconstructions. Signs on the displays are in Ukrainian and Russian. ✉ *22 Andriivski Uzviz,* ☏ *44/416-0398.* ☺ *Mar.–Nov., daily noon-8; Dec.–Feb., daily noon-6.*

TRUKHANOV ISLAND – There are several parks with outdoor recreational facilities on this island in the Dnieper. The beach is crowded with sunbathers in summer. You can reach the island via the pedestrian footbridge, south of the main river terminal. *Metro: Ploshcha Poshtova.*

Monastery of the Caves and World War II Museum

The fascinating **Kievo-Pecherska Lavra** (Monastery of the Caves) is not only a functioning monastery, with miles of mazelike underground tunnels containing numerous churches and ancient crypts, but also houses some of Kiev's richest museums. Among them are the Museum of Historical Treasures (the Ukrainian equivalent of Moscow's Armory or the Gold Rooms in the Hermitage), the Museum of Ukrainian Decorative and Applied Art, and the Museum of Ukrainian Books and Printing. You should also try to make time for the **Museum of the Great Patriotic War.**

A Good Walk

To reach the **Kievo-Pecherska Lavra** ㉗, take the subway to Arsenalna. When you exit, cross the street and take Trolleybus 20 two stops. You will see the whitewashed walls of the fortification across the street. Walking south, follow the wall until you reach the entrance, a few hundred feet down the street. Before you begin your excursion of the monastery, you may want to stop by the **Tserkva Spas-na-Berestove** located just outside its walls. Follow the road directly across the street from the trolleybus stop, running along the northern edge of the fortification walls. The road will lead you directly to the church. Continuing to the monastery, you will enter the grounds of the Upper Lavra through the archway of the **Trinity Gate Church.** The ticket office is in the kiosk to your left before you enter; here you will buy tickets for all the exhibits and museums on the monastery's territory, except for the Museum of Historical Treasures, the Bell Tower, and the Caves, where you will purchase a candle in lieu of a ticket. To your right, as you first come in, is a long white building, the former **Monks' Dormitories.** Going forward, past these exhibits, you reach the **Velika Lavskra Dzvinitsa;** in the square in front are the ruins of the **Uspensky Sobor.** Follow the pathway as it curves around the ruins, and it leads to the five-domed **Vsikhsvyatska Tserkva.** Before you reach it, you get to the **"Economic Wing"**; at the window to your left, just beyond the entrance to the building, tickets are sold to the **Museum of Historical Treasures.** Next door, in an adjoining building (to your left as you exit), is the **Museum of Ukrainian Books and Printing.** Exit left from the museum's courtyard and walk straight down the short path to the *vidovaya* (lookout) platform. It offers a spectacular view.

As you leave the platform, turn left, back in the direction of the Great Bell Tower. On your left is the large **Refectory Church.** The former Metropolitan's House now contains the **State Museum of Ukrainian Folk Art.** The entrance is to your left, a few steps up the path from the Refectory Church. The last stop on the tour of Upper Lavra museums is the fascinating exhibit of **"microminiatures"**; the entrance to the exhibit is across the pathway from the Metropolitan's House, to your left as you exit the museum.

Leave the Upper Lavra and its museums to begin your visit of the cave sites by returning to the pathway, keeping the Great Bell Tower to your left, and starting down the hill. Just past the viewing platform, the road twists and curves down a steep incline. Follow it as it goes to the right, through the iron gates marking the boundary of the Upper Lavra, and soon the road shoots off to your left, leading down, again steeply, to the **Blizhnyie Pechery,** or Near Caves, which are also sometimes called St. Anthony's Caves. Instead of a ticket, you'll purchase a candle outside the entrance.

After you buy a candle, you'll enter a courtyard of green-and-white church buildings, abutted by a botanical park on the right. Walk

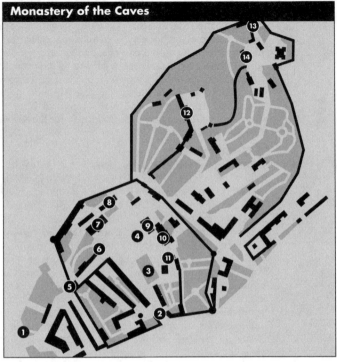

Monastery of the Caves

toward the far end, where you will see a clock and short bell tower, and past which you can look over the parapet for more breathtaking views of Kiev. To your left, next to the **Khrestovozdvizhenska Church** (Church of the Exaltation of the Cross) is the entrance to the Near Caves. Join the line for the next small group that will be ushered in, and buy a candle inside, if you were unable to do so before. To reach the **Dalnyie Pechery,** or Distant Caves, follow the covered gallery, which begins across the courtyard from the Church of the Exaltation of the Cross. It is a very long passageway. If it is closed you can take the longer route, walking back up the hill to the path along the Upper Monastery fortification wall. Turn left, and keep walking until you reach the second road branching off to the left. It will lead you to the territory of the Distant Caves, also known as St. Theodosius' Caves. Here the entrance is actually through the **Annozachatievska Church** (Church of the Conception of St. Anne). Again, you will purchase a candle from the monk before you start. Unless you are an expert in early Russian church history, you don't need to be particular about which set of caves you see.

To leave, walk back up the hill to the road along the fortification wall of the Upper Lavra. Continue climbing the incline as it leads up the hill to your left; at the top you will find the stop for Trolleybus 20, which will take you back to the subway (three stops). You'll find snack booths outside the monastery walls, if you want a coffee or soda before going on your way. You may want to stop by the **Museum of the Great Patriotic War** (World War II), located on the hillside to the south of the monastery (to your left).

TIMING

You'll need to set aside an entire day to visit the Lavra and the shops and museums on this walk. The monastery is on two hills divided by a shallow valley; it has two distinct sections. The Verkhnya Lavra

(Upper Lavra) is on the highest hill and is surrounded by its own fortification wall. On the lower hill lies the Territory of the Dalnyie Pechery (Distant Caves). The Blizhnyie Pechery (Near Caves) are in the gully between them. Unless you're specifically interested in attending a church service it's best to avoid the monastery and grounds on Sunday, which is when the crowds are heaviest. Note also that most of the public areas and buildings of the monastery are closed on Tuesday.

Sights to See

Academy of Sciences Botanical Garden. This park is situated on the banks of the Dnieper River and covers 180 hectares (445 acres). It can be reached by tram from the Arsenalna and Dnieper subway stations.

Blizhnyie Pechery (Near Caves). The passageways of the caves run about ½ kilometer (⅓ mile), but the visitors' route does not take you into every nook and cranny. Inside there are 73 tombs and three underground churches. Icons and fragments of 18th-century frescoes cover the walls. Many important historical figures are buried here, including Antony, the monastery's founder; Nikon and Nestor, the monks who authored the *Primary Chronicle;* Alimpy, thought to be Kievan Rus's first icon painter; and other revered monks. The caves are open every day, with a break from 11:30 to 1, but close when it rains, due to flooding. Sometimes they reopen after just a few hours, so it may be worth waiting around.

The experience of visiting can be rather spooky. You'll follow a twisting path through the cool interiors of the underground labyrinth. Often the only light comes from your candle and threatens to go out in the damp drafts that waft below. Of the two, the Distant Caves are on the sharpest incline, but it is not advisable for people with serious conditions of the heart, lungs, or legs, or pregnant women, to go into either one. Women will be asked to cover their head, and short skirts, pants, or all-black clothing (except for the monks, it seems!) may bar you from entry. ⊠ *Kievo–Pecherska Lavra. Metro: Arsenalna.*

Dalnyie Pechery (Distant Caves). These caves are older than the ☞ **Blizhnyie Pechery**; they contain 47 tombs and another three churches, all of which date from the 12th century. As you make your way, along the walls you'll see the covered remains of the mummified monks, buried in or near the cells where they prayed during their lifetime. ⊠ *Kievo–Pecherska Lavra.*

★ ㉗ **Kievo-Pecherska Lavra.** A *lavra* is a monastery of the highest order. The Monastery of the Caves received this honored title in 1598, but its history goes back much farther. It was founded in 1051 by a monk named Antony and his follower, Theodosius. They chose this hilly site, on the banks of the Dnieper, for its natural caves (in Ukrainian, *pechery,* hence the name). The monks lived in underground cells and were also buried in them. The cool temperatures and humid atmosphere of the caves allowed their bodies to mummify; even today their bodies allegedly remain almost perfectly preserved. At the time of the monastery's foundation, this appeared to be a miracle, enhancing the monastery's prestige in a land where Christianity had been adopted less than a century earlier.

From the 11th to the early 13th centuries, the Pechersky Monastery was the ecclesiastical center of the Orthodox Church in Kievan Rus. Like the city of Kiev, its demise came with the Mongol invasion of 1240. Its religious life revived in the 15th century, but it wasn't until the 18th century that the monastery began to prosper again. It became the site of imperial pilgrimages, and Peter the Great financed much new construction. Many of its churches as well as the surrounding fortification wall, date from this time. By the mid-18th century the monastery was so wealthy that it owned several villages, 80,000 serfs, and three glassworks. It suffered the same fate as many churches after the Bolshevik Revolution; in 1927 it was closed and converted into a museum. With the advent of perestroika and the religious revival in Russia and Ukraine, the monastery was returned to the church in 1987, on the anniversary of 1,000 years of Christianity in Rus. Parts of the grounds are still functioning as a museum, but the two sets of caves and their many churches are once again open for worship. ⊠ *21 Vul. Sichnevoho Povstannya*, ☎ *44/290–6646.* ☉ *Mar.–Nov., Wed.–Mon. 9:30–6; Dec.–Feb., Wed.–Mon. 9:30–5.*

OFF THE
BEATEN PATH

ASKOLD'S GRAVE – This memorial to Kiev's ancient past is in a picturesque park not far from the Park of Glory and World War II Tomb of the Unknown Soldier (☞ *below*). Askold (also known as Rurik) was the legendary Varangian (Viking) prince who ruled Kiev during the second half of the 9th century. According to the ancient chronicles, he was murdered by the Novgorodian Prince Oleg, who seized Kiev in 882. Legend has it that Askold was buried on this hillside site overlooking the Dnieper River. A wooden church, dedicated to St. Nicholas, was built above his tomb but was later moved to the Monastery of the Caves. In 1810 a small Classical rotunda church was built on the gravesite to a design by the architect Andrei Melensky, and in 1936 a colonnade was added to protect it. You can reach Askold's grave by taking the subway to Arsenalna Station and walking south (left as you exit the subway) until you reach Dneprovskii Spusk, which slopes off to your left. Follow the road down the incline, and the rotunda will appear in the distance to your left.

MARIINSKY DVORETS – If you have visited St. Petersburg, this lovely blue-and-cream palace will probably bring back memories of the imperial summer estates, and with good reason. Like St. Andrew's Church (☞ St. Andrew's and the Podol, *above*), this palace was commissioned by Empress Elizabeth during her 1744 visit to Kiev. It was designed by her favorite architect, Bartolomeo Rastrelli, and was built between 1750 and 1755 under the direction of the Moscow architect Ivan Michurin. Styled after Rastrelli's Razumovsky Palace in Perovo (near Moscow), it is a lovely mixture of Ukrainian and Russian Baroque. The main building faces an open courtyard surrounded by an elaborate wrought-iron fence. Corinthian columns and sculptures adorn the main entrance. The park facade is even more impressive: Balustrades decorated with vases and sculptures of lions lead majestically down to the formally landscaped park, also designed by Rastrelli. Unfortunately, only the main facade is open for viewing; the building now houses offices of the Ukrainian government and is closed to the public. Before the 1917 Revolution, the palace was used as the residence for visiting members of the imperial family. It has undergone many reconstructions. In 1819 the upper, wooden floor of the main building burned. It was rebuilt in the 1870s, in preparation for an impending visit from Czar Alexander II and his wife, Maria, for whom the palace is now named. Severely damaged during World War II, it has been faithfully restored to its original appearance. To reach the palace, take the subway to Arsenalna Station. When you exit, do not cross the street. Take Trolleybus 20 one stop. The palace is a short walk to your left through a small park.

"Microminiatures" Exhibit. Not surprisingly, the subject here is art so tiny that it can be seen only with a microscope. This is a strange place for an exhibit of art that clearly belongs to the modern age of technology (its establishment here was probably the decision of a Soviet bureaucrat), but it is interesting all the same. The creator of the work is Nikolai Syadristy, a contemporary artist who has received many awards for his unusual medium. The works on display include a portrait of Ernest Hemingway engraved on a pear seed; a glass portrait of the Russian balalaika virtuoso Vasily Andreyev (complete with balalaika and case), which is set inside a poppy seed; and the world's tiniest book (0.6 sq. mm.), which is engraved with Taras Shevchenko's portrait. ☒ *Kievo–Pecherska Lavra.* ☉ *Wed.–Mon. 10–6. Metro: Arsenalna.*

Monks' Dormitories. This building houses small exhibits of Ukrainian icon painting (17th–19th centuries), portraits from the Kiev Monastery (18th–19th centuries), and religious manuscripts. They are interesting, but if you are short on time, pass them by, for there is much to see. The passageway to your left, through the archway, leads to the St. Nicholas Church, which houses an exhibit of 17th-century Western European graphic art. *Exhibits open Wed.–Mon. 9:30–6, with 30-min lunch break between 12:30 and 2.*

Museum of the Great Patriotic War. This museum is topped by a gigantic steel statue called *Mother Russia.* It is 72 meters (236 feet) high, and it dwarfs the monastery domes on the riverbank. Its construction was controversial; it is a gaudy, oversize structure typical of the wasteful spending of the Brezhnev era. It looks very strange and inappropriate after an excursion through the ancient monastery, but it, too, is representative of Kiev's past—albeit more recent.

The museum contains several sections, the most recent of which is devoted to the Afghan War (in the building to your right as you walk down the terrace leading to the *Mother Russia* statue). The building is surrounded by an open-air museum of Soviet artillery, planes, helicopters, and military jeeps. The somber exhibits display the uniforms and medals of the war dead, as well as their letters home and the death notifications sent to their families. Soviet propaganda photographs of smiling Afghan children hang on the walls. Russian pop songs written about the war in Afghanistan add to the emotional effect.

The exhibit to World War II located in the base of the statue has also recently been updated. The theme of the museum is the devastating effect of war on children. The main exhibit shows how children suffered during World War II, with photos and letters from Ukrainian children deported to Germany, as well as the concentration-camp garb of babies. The central dome of the statue is inlaid with a huge mosaic, which is eerily reminiscent of a religious icon. The mosaic is in the shape of a five-pointed red star with the words USSR–VICTORY. ☒ *44 Vul. Sichnevoho Povstannya, on the hillside to the south of the Kievo–Pecherska Lavra,* ☎ *44/295–9452.* ☉ *Tues.–Sun. 10–6. Metro: Arsenalna.*

Museum of Historical Treasures. This museum is not open to groups, but if you are patient, after a short wait enough people will gather to form a group tour. If you call ahead, you can request a tour in English. The tour begins on the second floor, with the museum's collection of Scythian gold found in archaeological digs along the coast of the Black Sea. The highlight of the collection is a massive gold chest ornament, decorated with scenes from everyday Scythian life in the 4th century BC. One of the rooms contains the tomb of a Scythian princess and her baby, found in an ancient settlement in the Black Sea area. The skeletons of the princess and her child are arranged as they were buried, surrounded by gold and priceless jewelry. The museum's coin collection includes the first metal coins produced in Kievan Rus, which were introduced in the 10th century. ☒ *Kievo–Pecherska Lavra.* ☎ *44/290–1396.* ☉ *Wed.–Mon. 10–5 (lunch break 1–1:45). Metro: Arsenalna.*

Museum of Ukrainian Books and Printing. This museum is housed in the Kievo–Pecherska monastery's former printing shop, where Russia's first printing press was established. The collection includes manuscripts dating from the 12th century and features ornately designed, jewel-encrusted volumes. ⊠ *Kievo–Pecherska Lavra,* ☎ *44/290–1396.* ⊙ *Wed.–Mon. 10–6. Metro: Arsenalna.*

Refectory Church. This church was built at the end of the 18th century and attached to the Metropolitan's House (☞ State Museum of Ukrainian Folk Art, *below*). The church is open for viewing as a museum, but it is also a functioning church (services at 7 AM and 5 PM). It's worth a quick look inside; the gilded interiors were designed by the Russian architect Alexei Schusev. Outside the church are the graves of the Cossack leaders Ivan Iskra and Vasily Kochubei, who were executed by Ivan Mazepa in 1708.

State Museum of Ukrainian Folk Art. The extensive exhibits of this museum are housed on two floors and date from the 16th to the 20th centuries. An entire room is devoted to folk dress and another to bedspreads. Also on display are embroidered linens, handicrafts, pottery, wood carvings, and ceramics. A highlight of the collection is the *krashanki,* delicately painted Easter Eggs. ⊠ *Kievo–Pecherska Lavra,* ☎ *44/293–9442.* ⊙ *Wed.–Mon. 10–5:45. Metro: Arsenalna.*

Tomb of the Unknown Soldier of World War II. An eternal flame burns in memory of soldiers lost during the war. ⊠ *In Vechnoi Slavy (Eternal Memory) Park, 1 trolleybus stop s. of Arsenalna subway station.*

Trinity Gate Church. You enter the grounds of the Upper Lavra through the archway of this church, which is crowned by a gilded cupola. Built in 1108, it once doubled as a watchtower. The majestic blue-and-gold exterior dates from the 18th century. The interior is decorated with colorful frescoes and a beautiful wooden iconostasis.

Tserkva Spas-na-Berestove (Church of the Redeemer in the Birchwood). This church was built in the early 12th century by Prince Vladimir Monomakh as a burial place for the princes of Kiev. The founder of Moscow (and Monomakh's son) Yuri Dolgoruky was buried here in 1157. The church is built in the characteristic style of the time: a cross dome with six pillars. Its eastern wing, which faces the Dnieper, was added in 1640–44. In 1947, on the 800th anniversary of the founding of Moscow, a marble sarcophagus was installed here in memory of Yury Dolgoruky. It was recently returned to the Ukrainian Orthodox Church; it is open for viewing daily 9:30–1:30 and 2–6. *Kievo–Pecherska Lavra. Metro: Arsenalna.*

Uspensky Sobor (Assumption Church). Built in the 11th century, the huge stone cathedral was, like St. Sophia's (☞ St. Sophia's and the Upper Town, *above*), influenced by Byzantine architecture. It became a center of ecclesiastical learning and was the monastery's most important cathedral between the 11th and the 13th centuries. Like the rest of the monastery, it was destroyed during the Mongol invasion and rebuilt in 1470. The restored church, which burned in the same fire of 1718 that took the Bell Tower, was rebuilt again in the 1720s. The church was destroyed for the last time during World War II, when it was blown up by the Nazis.

Velika Lavskra Dzvinitsa (Great Belfry). Great is the right name for it; in its day the belfry was Russia's tallest structure. The present belfry, which reaches a height of 96.5 meters (317 feet), was built in the 18th century to replace a wooden version that had burned down in 1718. It was designed by the German architect Gottfried Schädel, who was dispatched from St. Petersburg. Each of the four tiers is of a different design, with Doric columns on the second level, Ionic on the third, and Corinthian on the fourth. It is under reconstruction, but the belfry is open to visitors. You buy a ticket at the foot of it. From the top you'll get a marvelous view of the monastery, the rolling hills, and the Dnieper. But the wooden stairs are somewhat rickety, and every once in a while you see a piece of sky shining through the holes.

Vsikhsvyatska Tserkva (All Saints' Church). This five-domed church was built over the northern gate at the end of the 17th century. Its ornate design is considered a pure example of Ukrainian Baroque. Like the Trinity Gate Church, it also served as a watchtower on the fortification wall.

OFF THE **Vydubetsky Monastery.** Founded in 1070 by Prince Vsevolod, son of
BEATEN PATH Yaroslavl the Wise, this monastery was largely destroyed by a landslide in the 15th century. A section of St. Michael's Cathedral (1077–88) remains, including a fragment of a 12th-century fresco of the Last Judgment. Also on the monastery grounds is St. George's Church (1696–1791), a five-domed masterpiece of Ukrainian architecture. You can reach the monastery, which is in botanical gardens, by tram from the Arsenalnaya or Dneiper subway stations. ✉ 5 km (3 mi) s. of Monastery of the Caves, on bank of Dnieper.

DINING

Compared with St. Petersburg and Moscow, dining in Kiev is, simply put, provincial, and before Ukraine's declaration of independence in 1991 the situation was downright bleak. Although Ukraine was always considered the breadbasket of the Soviet Union, its capital had only a handful of decent restaurants, located primarily in hotels catering to foreign tourists. The cuisine here differs little from the bland, meat-laden dishes offered in the state-run hotels of Moscow and St. Petersburg. The overall situation in Kiev is slowly improving, however. The establishment of several foreign embassies and the influx of Western businesspeople have spurred the opening of more sophisticated establishments, though unfortunately, if you're looking for traditional Ukrainian cuisine, you're not likely to find it in these places. The menus tend to cater to the city's growing expatriate community, which long ago had its fill of chicken Kiev. Prices, too, are high, not only because there are more foreigners than restaurants but also because many of the supplies are often imported.

As in Moscow and St. Petersburg, dining out requires planning. Reservations are almost always essential in the evenings and are advised even during the day. Most restaurants close in the afternoon for a "dinner break," and some are open only in the evenings. You are unlikely to meet "typical" Kiev residents by dining out. The current inflation rate makes a restaurant meal a luxury that few Kievans can afford.

Like their languages, the cuisines of Russia and Ukraine differ only slightly; both concentrate on meat-and-potato dishes, usually served with heavy sauces. Mushrooms, served in a variety of forms, are a favorite in both countries. Both Russians and Ukrainians love to smother their dumplings and potatoes with *smetana*, a rich sour cream. Despite these similarities, Ukrainian cuisine does have its specialties. One, of course, is the famous *Kievskaya kotleta* (chicken Kiev), which is very tricky to make. If prepared correctly, a fountain of butter spurts out of the fried chicken breast when pierced with a fork. Another Ukrainian specialty is *vareniki*, boiled dumplings filled with *tvorog* (a sweet cottage cheese), potatoes, mushrooms, cabbage, or meat. Ukrainian *borscht,* beet soup served with a huge dollop of *smetana,* is usually accompanied by *pampushki,* hot rolls dripping in garlic butter.

CATEGORY	COST*
$$$$	over $50
$$$	$35–$50
$$	$15–$35
$	under $15

per person for a three-couse dinner, excluding drinks and service

WHAT TO WEAR

Dress at the restaurants listed below is casual, unless noted otherwise.

$$$$ ✕ **El Dorado.** If you'd rather be anywhere but in Kiev, seek out this ritzy restaurant and bar, tucked away in a cellar off Bessarabska Square. Its modern decor features a high-tech lighting system that re-creates a starlit night through the restaurant's crystal-studded ceiling. The Ukrainian owner caters to Kiev's foreign business community and its fat expense accounts. The menu features traditional European cuisine, such as smoked duck breast and roasted lamb. The prix fixe dinner changes weekly and includes appetizer, soup, main course, and dessert. Although the business-oriented clientele can make for a rather stuffy atmosphere, things turn lively after the kitchen closes. Unlike most establishments in Kiev, the bar stays open until the last patron leaves. ⊠ *13 Chervonoarmiiska Vul.,* ☏ *44/244–2921. Jacket and tie. AE, V. Lunch daily noon–3, dinner daily 7–10:30, bar open daily until 2 AM. No Sun. lunch. Metro: Ploshcha Lva Tolstoho.*

$$$$ ✕ **Napoleon.** This extravagantly ornate restaurant must be Kiev's challenge to Paris. If you can cope with its overly opulent interior (ivory-hued and wood-inlaid walls, marble floors, an abundance of crystal and silver) you'll find attentive and serious service and very good food. Dressed in full Empire regalia, the waiters proffer a heavy, 14-page menu (with English translation) and are happy to walk you through it. A melange of cold dishes like aspics, poached fish, and various kinds of caviar is followed by salads, hot appetizers, and a series of wonderful soups. You may want to try the Marseilles fish soup or the consommé with apples. Then there are more than 25 meat courses, from beef in burgundy sauce to chicken fricassee to beef tongue with nuts. You may prefer one of the fish dishes, however, all of which are excellently prepared. Lighter appetites can opt for omelets, but make up for it by ordering mousse or cake with fruit for dessert. The string quartet tends to overwhelm the room but plays beautifully nonetheless. Lest it all sound too serious, the well-laid table also includes a pack of mints and pieces of bubble gum! ⊠ *16 Shota Rustaveli,* ☏ *44/221–5597. Reservations advised. Jacket and tie. AE, D, MC, V.* ☽ *Daily 10 AM–midnight. Metro: Ploshcha Lva Tolstoho.*

$$$ ✕ **Apollo.** One of the main restaurants catering to the city's foreign
★   community, this Swiss-Ukrainian joint venture has set a standard for fine dining in Kiev. The beautifully restored interior, with ceiling paintings from the 19th century, Greek statues, and high-back wooden chairs, creates an elegant atmosphere far removed from the hustle and bustle of the nearby Khreshchatik. The service, like the interior, is elegant, and the formally dressed waiters have clearly been trained to meet European standards of excellence. Thanks to its Swiss partners, the restaurant imports 80 percent of its supplies, allowing it to offer truly European cuisine. For starters, try the quiche Lorraine, prepared in a light cream sauce and served in a delicate pastry shell, or the creamy broccoli soup. The light mushroom omelet makes for a nice break from meat-laden Ukrainian cuisine. But if you're a meat lover, you won't be

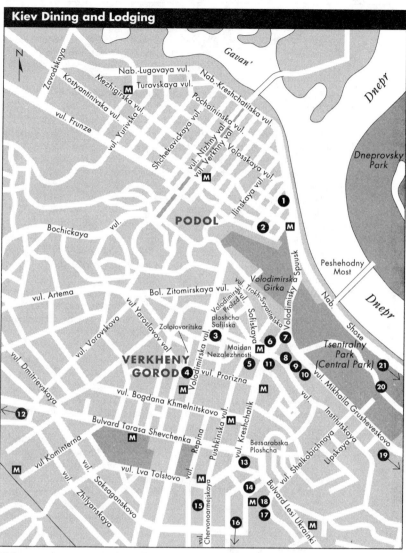

Kiev Dining and Lodging

Dining
Apollo, **6**
Arizona Barbeque, **1**
Dnipro, **7**
El Dorado, **13**
Gostinny Dvir, **2**
Italia, **5**
Kureny, **20**
Layala Odessa, **9**
Napoleon, **14**
Pantagruel, **4**
Skhodi, **3**
Slavuta, **15**
Studio, **10**

Lodging
Bratislava, **21**
Dnipro, **7**
Khreshchatik, **11**
Kyivska, **18**
Libid, **12**
Mir, **16**
Moskva, **8**
Rus, **17**
Salyut, **19**

disappointed by the steak fillet, served with melted cheese and mushrooms and accompanied by Italian green noodles. The dessert menu features fruit salad—a rare find in this city—made of mango, kiwi, pineapple, and bananas. On Sundays the restaurant offers a popular champagne brunch. Good wine list. ⊠ *15 Khreshchatik, passage,* ☎ *44/229–0437. Jacket and tie. AE, DC, MC, V.* ☉ *Daily noon–3, 5–11; bar open until 1* AM. *Metro: Maidan Nezalezhnosti.*

$$$ ✕ **Italia.** If you prefer spaghetti Bolognese to chicken Kiev, come to this centrally located spot for anything but Ukrainian cuisine. The restaurant offers a taste of Western Europe in a post-Soviet setting. With the no-frills atmosphere still a bit haunted by the state-run "dietetic cafeteria" that once occupied the space (watercolors of faraway Italy decorate the walls, but the modest decor, disco lighting, and simple furnishings place you firmly in the former Soviet Union), it's comfortable nonetheless. The extensive menu offers several kinds of pizza, a wide variety of traditional meat dishes, as well as spaghetti, lasagna, and other pasta. For the full effect, order a bottle of imported Chianti from the extensive wine list, and top off your meal with a strong espresso and Italian ice. ⊠ *8 Prorizna Vul.,* ☎ *44/224–2054. No credit cards. No traveler's checks.* ☉ *Daily 1* PM*–2* AM. *Metro: Maidan Nezalezhnosti.*

$$ ✕ **Arizona Barbeque.** This Southwestern bar and grill will make you feel as if you're back in Tucson, *almost.* What it lacks in authenticity, this restaurant makes up for with its service and warm and welcoming ambience—the place is always lively. Go for the chili—it's true tex/mex style. If that's too spicy for you, you can opt for great steaks, ribs, and nachos. The bar serves up a number of mixed drinks alongside the beer and wine. ⊠ *25 Naberezhno-Kreschatitska Vul.,* ☎ *44/416–2438.* ☉ *Daily 7* AM*–11* PM. *Metro: Ploshcha Poshtova.*

$$ ✕ **Dnipro.** Centrally located at the eastern end of the Khreshchatik, on the second floor of the Dnipro Hotel, this used to be the best restaurant in town. With the recent opening of cooperatives and Western-run joint ventures, it now faces some stiff competition, but it's still the best of the hotel restaurants. Heavy chandeliers, high ceilings, and the view onto Evropeyska Ploshcha make for a relatively pleasant atmosphere. You can opt for the buffet dining room if you want a slightly lower bill and a sample of various decent dishes. In the main dining room, the service is polite and formal although a bit slow. The kitchen offers a wide selection of standard Ukrainian and Russian dishes, but only half the items listed are ever available at any time. The food is not particularly imaginative, and the main courses come loaded with greasy fried potatoes. Therefore, it might be best to stick to staples like beef Stroganoff. As is often the case, the appetizers and soups fare much better than entrées and the restaurant serves an excellent Ukrainian borscht, chock-full of fresh vegetables. ⊠ *1/2 Khreshchatik,* ☎ *44/229–8179. AE, E, MC, V.* ☉ *Daily 8–noon, 1–5, 6–11. Metro: Maidan Nezalezhnosti.*

$$ ✕ **Layala Odessa.** Just across from the Palats Ukrayina, this Lebanese restaurant serves excellent hummus, tabuleh, and other Middle Eastern specialties. Its consistently well-prepared food is outdone only by the service—Layala Odessa may have the best waiters in Kiev! ⊠ *114 Chervonoarmiiska Vul.,* ☎ *44/269—7707. No credit cards. Metro: Ploshcha Lva Tolstoho.*

$$ ✕ **Pantagruel.** This charming café-bar right next to the Golden Gates (Zoloti Vorota) serves authentic and tasty Italian food (prepared by a real Italian chef). There are also a few Ukrainian dishes on the menu, but you'd do better having your *pampushki* and chicken Kiev elsewhere.

✉ *1 Vul. Lysenka,* ☎ *44/228–8142. No credit cards.* ☉ *Sun.—Thurs. 11—11, Fri. and Sat. 11 AM–2 AM. Metro: Zoloti Vorota.*

$$ ✗ **Slavuta.** This low-key, casual place is another favorite of Kiev's expatriate community. The modest menu features mainly chicken and fish dishes, including several of Finnish origin. The dark interior, with imitation stained-glass windows and trompe l'oeil brick walls, seems right out of a latter-day Monastery of the Caves. Compared to the city's other hard-currency establishments, the prices are reasonable, and the restaurant's central location keeps the crowds coming back. ✉ *14 Vul. Gorkoho,* ☎ *44/227–6484. AE, DC, MC, V.* ☉ *Daily noon–midnight. Metro: Ploshcha Lva Tolstoho.*

$$ ✗ **Studio.** This glitzy hot spot offers a wide selection of wonderfully prepared European and international cuisine. In general, it's best to stick to steaks, chops, and veal, though they also do a respectable job with fresh salmon. There's a bar for pre-dinner cocktails and live jazz every evening. ✉ *4 Muzeiny Pereulok,* ☎ *44/228—7208. AE, D, DC, MC, V.* ☉ *Daily 11:30 AM—11:30 PM. Metro: Maidan Nezalezhnosti.*

$ ✗ **Gostinny Dvir.** Located in the heart of the Podol, in the 19th-cen-
★ tury merchant's arcade, this lively restaurant specializing in traditional Ukrainian cooking is the perfect place to top off a day of sightseeing. The interior is warm and inviting, with high arched ceilings decorated with Roman motifs and brass chandeliers. The friendly waitresses, dressed in colorful Ukrainian costumes, will insist that you eat every bite—which shouldn't be too hard, because the food is excellent. Start off with a spicy bowl of Ukrainian borscht, which comes with *pampushki,* piping hot rolls topped with finely diced garlic and dripping with garlic butter. The *Gribi v Smetanoi Sousi,* the local version of mushrooms in cream sauce, is a tasty appetizer. For your main course, try the house specialty, *Vareniki z Kartopleyu,* boiled dumplings filled with potatoes and topped with crisp, butter-fried onions. The slightly sweet *Varenki z Sirom* come filled with tvorog. Great food and atmosphere make this restaurant attractive as well to local residents, so chances are you won't be completely surrounded by foreigners. ✉ *4 Kontraktova Ploshcha,* ☎ *44/416–2271. No credit cards.* ☉ *Daily noon–5, 7–11. No Mon. dinner. Metro: Kontraktova Ploshcha.*

$ ✗ **Kureny.** If you are a summertime visitor to Kiev, you may find this enjoyable as an excursion as well. It is an open-air restaurant near the river, and it's laid out like a tiny Ukrainian village. The staff is in folk costume, and both the decor and food are traditional. ✉ *4 Parkova Aleya,* ☎ *44/293–4062.* ☉ *Noon–midnight. Metro: Maidan Nezalezhnosti.*

$ ✗ **Skhodi.** Better known by its Russian translation, *Lesnitsa,* this popular restaurant gets its name from the long stairway leading down into its dark premises, formerly used as an all-purpose storage room by the Ukrainian Architecture Union. Although a modest attempt has been made to pretty it up with wall mirrors and fake flowers, the dust still hasn't settled. But what the restaurant lacks in modern decor, it makes up for in lively atmosphere and excellent food. The dishes are all prepared from products purchased daily at the local markets. The menu features traditional Ukrainian fare, such as *Kievskii Bitok,* fried pork rolled in flour and served with a plate of vegetables and french fries. For starters, try the *Salat Kashtan,* a mayonnaise-based salad made of finely diced roast beef, pickles, hard-boiled egg, peas, and carrots. The borscht is always tasty. To add to the pleasure, the service shines. For local color and wholesome Ukrainian food, this is just the place. ✉ *7 Vul. Borisa Grichenka,* ☎ *44/229–8629. No credit cards.* ☉ *Daily noon–4, 7–11, except Sundays. Metro: Maidan Nezalezhnosti.*

LODGING

The building boom that has taken Moscow and St. Petersburg by storm has so far bypassed the Ukrainian capital. Even at the height of perestroika, when the Soviet Union suddenly became a hot new destination, Kiev was never besieged with tourists. As a result, accommodations are pretty much limited to the old Intourist standbys, which are primarily of modern construction, heavy on chrome and cement, and light on character. There are no grand, prerevolutionary hotels or new luxury ones—even though you'll feel that you are paying near-luxury prices. And although you'll find that staff members exude hospitality, the service in general is still redolent of Soviet inefficiency. But thanks to the growing demands of foreign businesspeople, improvements are slowly being made.

Tourist groups are usually placed at one of Intourist's three-star hotels: the **Libid, Rus,** or **Kyivska.** Although standards here fluctuate greatly, all provide adequate, if not exactly sightly, accommodations. Bring your patience and be prepared for a few unexpected touches. Shower curtains and sink stoppers are not standard issue. Not all rooms come with telephone and television, but most of them have refrigerators.

All prices are quoted in U.S. dollars; with only rare exceptions, hotels require payment in foreign currency or by credit card and do not accept Russian rubles or Ukrainian coupons.

CATEGORY	COST*
$$$$	over $250
$$$	$175–$250
$$	$100–$175
$	under $100

*All prices are for a standard double room for two, excluding service charge.

$$$$ **Dnipro.** Conveniently located at the eastern end of the Khreshchatik,
★   this hotel is one of the city's most popular, particularly for business travelers and groups. It's an organizing site for conferences and quite user-friendly for those with business needs. All the major tourist sites are easily accessible by public transportation, and the Philharmonic Concert Hall is just across the street. The interior is typically unimaginative for a Soviet-built hotel, but the friendly staff does its best to brighten up the place with flowers and plants. The rooms are clean and pleasant, and all have television and telephone. The double rooms have nice views onto the square below, but the singles all face the back alley. Newly renovated deluxe-quality rooms on the 11th and 12th floors cost between $200 and $400 and generally need to be reserved at least three weeks in advance. The second-floor restaurant is the best of the city's hotel restaurants. ✉ 1/2 *Khreshchatik,* ☎ 44/229–8287, FAX 44/229–8213. *180 rooms with bath. Restaurant, 3 banquet halls, 3 bars, excursion bureau, exchange bureau. AE, DC, V. Metro: Maidan Nezalezhnosti.*

$$$$ **Kyivska.** Built by Polish contractors, this huge complex overlooking
★   the gigantic sport stadium is Kiev's newest hotel. Although the dark lobby features the usual marble decor, the rooms are pleasant and nicely appointed. All of them come with refrigerator, television, and telephone, and the higher floors feature balconies with superb views of the city. Popular with businesspeople, all of the suites have been leased as offices. The business center on the first floor offers satellite communications with direct dialing abroad. The only major drawback is the hilltop location: You'll have to put on your hiking shoes to reach the subway, since the closest stop is a 10-minute trek down the steep hill. ✉ *12 Gospitalna Vul.,* ☎ 44/220–4144, FAX 44/220–4568. *350 rooms with bath. Restaurant,*

snack bar, sauna, casino, souvenir shop, excursion bureau, exchange bureau. AE, DC, MC, V. Metro: Ploshcha Lva Tolstoho.

$$$$ 🖭 **Rus.** Situated next door to the Kyivska Hotel, this high rise has smaller rooms and a less appealing interior. The walls with their dark floral paper don't match the faded orange curtains, and the chairs are upholstered with the same carpeting material as the floors, and neither is particularly clean. All rooms come with telephone, television (local stations only), and refrigerator. The staff is professional and courteous. Thanks to good relations with the Intourist, guests can use the sauna next door. The views here are just as good, and the walk to the subway just as exhausting. ✉ *4 Gospitalna Vul.,* ☎ *44/227–8594 or 44/220–4255,* 🖷 *44/220–4396. 477 rooms with bath. 3 restaurants, 2 bars, 3 snack bars, exchange bureau. AE, DC, MC, V. Metro: Ploshcha Lva Tolstoho.*

$$ 🖭 **Khreshchatik.** Another hotel with a good location, this one is named after Kiev's main street. Less than 10 years old, it has comfortable and spacious rooms, including suites. Located amid various international airline offices, it is popular with tourists. ✉ *14 Khreshchatik,* ☎ *44/229–7339 or 44/229–7193,* 🖷 *44/229–8544. 2 restaurants, bar, sauna. Credit cards. Metro: Maidan Nezalezhnosti.*

$$ 🖭 **Libid.** If you're on a tour arranged through any of Intourist's retooled groups, you may very well land in this cement block. Although it advertises a central location, the walk to the subway is a 20-minute climb up a steep hill. Opened in the early 1970s, the hotel offers the cement-and-steel decor of Brezhnev-era architecture, with plywood furnishings and green stucco walls. Only half the rooms come with television, but they all come with industrial carpeting stained from years of overuse and undercleaning. You may also find the mob of taxi drivers hanging around the main entrance a bit unpleasant. The service doesn't exactly shine, but it certainly beats the decor and atmosphere. ✉ *Ploshcha Peremogi,* ☎ *44/274–0063,* 🖷 *44/224–0578. 280 rooms with bath. 14 suites. Restaurant, bar, exchange bureau, excursion bureau. AE, MC, V. Metro: Vokzalna.*

$$ 🖭 **Moskva.** Located just off the Khreshchatik, this 16-story high rise towers on the steep hill above Kiev's main thoroughfare. Its monumental design reeks of Stalinism, though the hotel was built in the early 1960s. The rooms are spacious, with high ceilings and thick walls, but the place could use some sprucing up. Nevertheless, standards of cleanliness are higher than at the Libid, and the overly friendly floor attendants will be more than willing to respond to any complaints. Some rooms come with balconies offering grand views of the city. A telephone and television in every room just about exhausts the list of modern amenities. The main lobby is lined with souvenir kiosks selling such imported goods as Polish cosmetics and American bubble gum. Slot machines in a back room off the main entrance attract a seedy crowd that fills the lobby with cigarette smoke. This is obviously not the place for luxury accommodations, but it does offer local color and a good location. ✉ *4 Institutska Vul.,* ☎ *44/229–0347,* 🖷 *44/229–1353. 360 rooms with bath. Restaurant, 3 snack bars, sauna with dipping pool, excursion bureau. No traveler's checks or credit cards. Metro: Maidan Nezalezhnosti.*

$$ 🖭 **Salyut.** Yet another Soviet concrete monstrosity, this circular high rise looks like a spaceship fuselage but is really one of Kiev's finest hotels. It, too, is popular with businesspeople. For the tourist, it is within walking distance of the Monastery of the Caves. The rooms are relatively large, and some offer glorious views of the Dnieper and the golden cupolas of the monastery's churches. The furniture is slightly worn, but the overall atmosphere is light and cheerful. Throw rugs cover the industrial carpeting, and flowered wallpaper and framed dried flowers replace the usual stucco green walls. All rooms come with direct-dial telephone, cable television (including CNN), refrigerator, and balcony. Service is excellent by local standards. ⊠ *11a Vul. Sichnevoho Povstannya,* ☎ *44/290–6130,* FAX *44/290–7270. 110 rooms with bath. Restaurant, snack bar. AE, MC, V. Metro: Arsenalna.*

$ ★ ⊞ **Bratislava.** This low-budget hotel is a good choice if you don't mind roughing it and being far from the city center. It's located on the left bank 11 kilometers (7 miles) from downtown Kiev, with the metro about 10 minutes away, though the ride (aboveground) takes you through pretty Gidro Park. The modest rooms have telephones and small balconies, but no television. The hotel's official rating is lower than the Libid's, but the rooms are cleaner and the atmosphere is far more pleasant. Missionary groups like to stay here. Single accommodations are not available. ⊠ *1 Vul. Andreya Malyshka,* ☎ *44/559–7570,* FAX *44/559–7788. 347 rooms with bath. Restaurant, 2 bars, snack bar, excursion bureau. AE, E, MC, V.*

$ ⊞ **Mir.** Formerly owned by Sputnik, the Soviet youth tourist agency, this very basic hotel is essentially a youth hostel and far from the city center and accessible public transportation. Considering its super low rates, though, the accommodations are quite decent, and all rooms come with television and telephone. However, water-pressure problems make a hot shower next to impossible. The lobby's slot machines and all-night bar attract large numbers of the city's youth. ⊠ *70 Prospekt Sorokorichcha Zhovotnya,* ☎ *44/264–9646. 216 rooms with bath. Restaurant (for groups only), 3 snack bars, casino, sauna with dipping pool. No credit cards.*

NIGHTLIFE AND THE ARTS

The Arts

Kiev's cultural life is as rich as its ancient past, and the city boasts numerous theaters and concert halls. Except for popular ballet performances at the elegant Opera House, tickets are easy to come by and not expensive. The excursion bureau at your hotel will obtain tickets for you, but if you want to avoid their fee, which is often 10 times as much as the ticket itself, go directly to the theater's ticket office or to one of the ticket kiosks scattered throughout the city. They post available tickets in the window, together with a full schedule of upcoming events.

Concerts

The **House of Organ and Chamber Music** (⊠ 77 Chervonoarmiiska Vul., ☎ 44/269–5678), located in the former St. Nicholas Catholic Church, which was built at the turn of the century in the German-Gothic style.

International Center of Culture and Arts (⊠ 1 Institutsky, ☎ 44/228–7491 or 44/228–7491), Kiev's largest concert hall is located in a 19th-century finishing school for daughters of the nobility.

Philharmonic Society Concert Hall (⊠ 2 Volodymyrsky Uzviz, ☎ 44/229–6251). Classical music concerts are performed in the former Merchant's Hall, built in 1882.

Ukrainian Palace of Culture (⊠ 103 Chervonoarmiiska Vul., ☎ 44/268–9050). Contemporary ballet, musicals, and operas are featured here.

Opera and Ballet

The **Taras Shevchenko Opera and Ballet Theater** (⊠ 50 Volodymyrska Vul., ☎ 44/224–7165 or 44/229–1169), built in 1901, offers fine performances of Russian and Ukrainian operas and ballets in a gilded auditorium. The **State Operetta Theater** (⊠ 53/3 Chervonoarmiiska Vul., ☎ 44/227–2630 or 44/227–2241, FAX 44/220–8754) stages Ukrainian musical comedies. Try the **Tchaikovsky Conservatory** (⊠ 1/3 Vul. Gorodetskoho, ☎ 44/229–0792).

Theater

Lesya Ukrainka Russian Drama Theater (⊠ 5 Vul. Bogdana Khmelnitskoho, ☎ 44/224–4223 or 9063). Although the theater is named for a famous Ukrainian poetess, the repertoire is strictly Russian. Foreign dramas are occasionally performed, but only in Russian.

Ivan Franko Ukrainian Theater (⊠ 3 ploshcha Ivana Franka, ☎ 44/229–5991). Here you'll find Ukrainian classical and contemporary dramas, but only in Ukrainian.

Nightlife

For the latest in pop and folk music, check out the underground passageways of the subway stations on the Khreshchatik. Spontaneous performances of music and dance are given in these cavelike premises night and day, and crowds make the lively events hard to ignore.

Bars and Lounges

As in most cities in the former Soviet Union, nightlife still by and large centers around the city's restaurants and hotels, with their dining and dancing extravaganzas, which are usually not to the tastes of British and North American tourists. The only full-fledged bars are located in hotels catering to tourists; the Dnipro, Kyivska, and Rus have lively lobby bars. For late-night action, the best place is the snazzy **El Dorado** (☞ Dining, *below*), whose bar stays open until the last customer leaves. For quiet late-night conversation, the **Apollo** bar offers a rare haven from rowdy crowds in the hotel bars. Around town, small café-bars are increasing, and they stay open late.

In the last year a number of more adventurous, hybrid establishments have opened their doors, offering their patrons options that extend beyond just a drink and dinner: **River Palace** (⊠ Naberezhne Shosse, ☎ 44/416–8204, ⊘ daily 1 PM–8 AM, Metro: Dnipro), a popular new entertainment complex on the Dnieper, is a combination casino, restaurant, bistro, nightclub, and English-style pub. The live music is often quite good and the casino dance club differs from most in that it *doesn't* stage exotic dance shows. **Hollywood** (⊠ 134 Frunze Vul., ☎ 44/435–4068, ⊘ Daily 10 PM–5 AM) is where Ukraine's up-and-coming pop music stars all film their videos; here you'll find a disco, pool tables, casino, restaurant, bar, and floor show all under one roof. **Cowboy** (⊠ 1 Khreshchatik) features live (American) country music.

Casinos

Casinos are sprouting like mushrooms, and you'll find advertisements for them everywhere. Although you might get a kick out of these bits of Las Vegas, don't fool yourself or underestimate the atmosphere. It's not a good idea to play too loose or friendly or, of course, to deal in too much cash. If you're in the mood, you can check out **Casino Club First** in the Hotel Intourist (☎ 44/220–1978, ⊘ daily 8 PM–4 AM). **Playoffs International** is in the Hotel Libid (☎ 44/221–7674). **Club Flamingo** offers gaming in the Mir Hotel (☎ 44/264–9203, open daily 24 hours).

OUTDOOR ACTIVITIES AND SPORTS

Participant Sports

If you're a fitness fanatic, you'll have a hard time in Kiev, especially in winter. None of the major hotels has a fitness center. The Intourist Hotel's small pool, attached to its sauna, is too small to satisfy lap swimmers.

Access to Kiev's public indoor athletic facilities is restricted, just as it is in Moscow and St. Petersburg. The prerequisite "doctor's certificate" attesting to your good health would probably take more time to obtain than you plan to spend in Kiev. If you are visiting in summer, you're in luck, since the outdoor facilities are open to everyone.

Boating and Swimming
You can rent boats at Kiev's **Gidro Park,** which is easily reached by subway (Gidro Park Station); there is also a nice beach here. The most popular beach by far is on **Trukhanov Island,** which is connected to the right bank by a pedestrian footbridge (south of the main river terminal; Metro: Ploshcha Poshtova).

Running
You are welcome to try any of the city's parks and will probably feel comfortable on many of its wide, tree-lined streets—that is, if you can handle the hills. Or try the track at the **Central Republican Stadium** (⊠ 55 Chervonoarmiiska Vul.) or **Dynamo Stadium** (⊠ 3 Vul. Mikhaila Grushevskoho), which are free on days when there are no scheduled sports events.

Skiing and Skating
In winter you can rent skates and cross-country skis at the park on **Trukhanov Island** (☞ Boating and Swimming, *above*).

Tennis
There are public tennis courts in the park on **Trukhanov Island.**

Spectator Sports

Tickets to athletic events are sold at the sporting arena prior to the game, but popular events, especially soccer games, sell out far in advance. You may want to ask your hotel's excursion bureau for assistance in obtaining tickets. Kiev's main **ticket office** for sporting events is at 16 Chervonoarmiiska Vulytsya (☎ 44/225–3258 or 44/224–8234).

Hockey
Hockey is second in popularity only to soccer among Kievans. The home team, Kievskii Stroitel, plays at the **Central Republican Stadium** on Chervonoarmiiska Vulytsya (☎ 44/221–5775). The season is from October through March.

Soccer
Soccer is a national pastime, and Kiev's Dynamo team, along with its main rival, Moscow's Spartak, is one of the two most popular in the former Soviet Union; it has won several Soviet and European championships. You can watch them in action from March through September at the **Dynamo** (⊠ 3 Vul. Mikhaila Grushevskoho, ☎ 44/229–5252). The stadium, which seats 100,000, was built in 1941 but was not opened until after World War II. There is a monument here in honor of the Dynamo Soccer Team, which was forced to play against the Nazis—and then was shot for winning.

SHOPPING

You don't go to Kiev to shop, but still, to avoid frustration, think of shopping here as a way to acquaint yourself with the challenges facing Ukrainian citizens as their government tries to reform the economy. The old classification of stores by what they sell has been thrown out, and the stores themselves are in the process of rearranging themselves. Economic "reform" allows people to resell goods purchased in state-run stores—an activity once considered a capital crime. As a result, the streets are lined with makeshift kiosks offering a hodgepodge of goods, from caviar to nylons, and you'll often find an incongruous mix of items. Every subway station has several bookstands, where the selection is much better than it is in even the largest bookstores (you may even come across a book in English). The shopping center has traditionally been and remains the Khreshchatik, although you'll probably find just as much for sale in the streets and in all the new shops as you will in the huge department stores along its path.

Department Stores

Kiev's largest department store, the **TsUM Central Department Store,** is located just off the Khreshchatik (⊠ 2 Vul. Bogdana Khmelnit-skoho, ☎ 44/224–9505). The huge **Ukraina** (⊠ 1 Ploshcha Peremogi, ☎ 44/274–6017) is close to the Libid Hotel. To reach it, take any bus or trolleybus heading down the hill from the Universitet subway station. **Ditiachi Svet** (⊠ 3 Maliashka, ☎ 44/559–2170) is the children's department store.

Import Stores

Import stores sell high-quality imported goods, often a mix of foodstuffs and large consumer items, such as imported TVs, VCRs, or even cars. These stores generally accept either credit cards or Ukrainian hryvnia.

Candor (⊠ Spaska Vul., ☎ 44/416–1308) sells shoes, boots, cosmetics, TVs, washing machines, batteries, bottled water, coffee and tea, cigarettes, and liquor.

Nika Group Stores (⊠ 2 Bul. Tarasa Shevchenka, ☎ 44/225–0271) is a collection of shops that includes a large supermarket (with imported cheese and fresh bread sections), a clothing emporium, and an office-supply store that stocks foreign reading material.

Seagram (⊠ 4 Vul. Gorodetskoho) may be the world's most luxurious liquor store, offering premium wines and liquors from around the world.

Slavuta (⊠ 14 Vul. Gorkoho, ☎ 44/227–8464) is a hard-currency grocery with a good selection of imported foods, including frozen pizza, spaghetti, cereal, crackers, bottled water, coffee, canned goods, wine, beer, and alcohol. AE credit cards and traveler's checks are accepted.

Steilmann (⊠ 14 Chervonoarmiiska Vul.) sells men's and women's western clothing, shoes, and accessories.

Kashtan Stores

The Ukrainian variant of the state-run stores catering to tourists and operating only for dollars are named for Ukraine's national tree: the *kashtan* (chestnut). In these changed times, however, such stores are not really much different from the import shops (*above*). The largest Kashtan store (⊠ 24/26 Bulvar Lesi Ukrainki, ☎ 44/295–6127) sells souvenirs, snacks, food, clothing, and electronics.

Specialty Stores

Art Shops and Galleries

This is one area where Kiev has lots to offer. **Andriivskii Uvziv,** the twisting and winding street leading down the steep incline from St. Andrew's Church, is lined with art shops and galleries that sell works in all price ranges. Even if you're not in the market for Ukrainian art, you'll enjoy browsing.

Gallery Triptych (⊠ 34 Andriivskii Uzviz, ☎ 44/416–4453), owned by an association of well-known Kievan artists, sells paintings, handcrafted jewelry, embroidered vests, pottery, graphic art, and textiles.

Gonchari (⊠ 10A Andriivskii Uzviz, ☎ 44/416–1298) has a wide selection of pottery, including teapots of all shapes and sizes, teacups, chess sets, and ceramic animals.

Tsentralny Khudozhni Salon (⊠ 27 Vul. Bogdana Khmelnitskoho, ☎ 44/224–1660) is a former central art salon and sells a variety of handicrafts.

Tvorchistvo (⊠ 34A Andriivskii Uzviz, ☎ 44/228–3953) sells handcrafted Ukrainian souvenirs at very reasonable prices.

Virobi Maistriv Ukraine (⊠ 15 Khreshchatik, Passage, ☎ 44/228–5652) features an excellent selection of handmade items from Ukrainian artists.

Souvenir Stores

The state-run **Ukrainian Souvenir** (⊠ 23 Chervonoarmiiska Vul., ☎ 44/224–8516) has a surprisingly good selection of Ukrainian woodcrafts, tablecloths, bedspreads, and embroidered blouses. **Krystal** (⊠ 5A Vul. Lva Tolstoho, ☎ 44/227–3703) sells crystal and glass products, which make pretty gifts to bring home. The **House of Gifts** (⊠ 5 Bul. Lesi Ukrainki, ☎ 44/224–0590) showcases all manner of goods made only in Ukraine. The second remaining **Kashtan** store (⊠ 2 Bul. Tarasa Shevchenka, ☎ 44/224–7053) sells only gold and silver jewelry, created by artists from either Ukraine or other nations in the CIS. When you're visiting the Monastery of the Caves, you might want to stop by the **Ukrainian Folk Art Shop** (⊠ Building No. 5 in the Upper Lavra, ☎ 44/290–1249).

Street Markets

Kiev's largest farmers' market is the **Kriti Rynok** on Bessarabska Ploshcha at the western end of the Khreshchatik. Inside the domed building you'll find rows of private farmers selling fresh fruit and vegetables, cheeses, and fine cuts of meat; Ukrainian souvenirs are occasionally sold. Be aware that you are expected to bargain. There is also the **Volodirmirska** market at 115 Vul. Gorkoho and the **Lukianivsky** market at 1 Melnikova Vulytsya.

SIDE TRIP FROM KIEV

Folk Architecture Museum

The open-air **Folk Architecture Museum** of peasant homes is set in a vast field dotted with cottages, windmills, and wooden churches. Located near the village of Pirogova, it is a lovely place to spend a hot summer day. A visit in winter, however, or on one of Kiev's wet and rainy spring days, can be dispiriting: the buildings are far apart and a visit involves a lot of walking along dirt (or muddy) roads.

The museum occupies a territory of 120 hectares (297 acres), and its nine sections cover various regions of Ukraine from the 18th–20th centuries. Each section re-creates a Ukrainian village, with thatch-roof whitewashed cottages, windmills, wells, and wooden churches, most of which were brought from the region on display. The cottages are furnished and arranged to show how people actually lived and feature authentic household objects, including wooden utensils and cast-iron pots, embroidered linens, and wooden furnishings. The last section shows the architecture and lifestyle typical of a modern Ukrainian village. The museum is both fun and educational for young ones, with the added advantage of letting them stretch their legs. It's best to go in the good-weather months, however.

The museum administration organizes a variety of festivals and special events throughout the year, including Ukrainian Independence Day (August 24) and the festive Ivan Kupallo Day (June 6), a celebration of midsummer night that dates back to Kiev's pre-Christian era. The 17th-century wooden church transferred here from the village of Doroginka now holds services on church holidays, and weddings are occasionally performed here. To find out what's going on, call the museum. You can reach it by public transportation, although a guided excursion is advised, since there are few signs in English explaining the exhibits. Both Intourist-Kievska and the Slavutich excursion bureau (☞ Guided Tours *in* Kiev A to Z, *below*) offer tours. To reach the museum, take the subway to Lybedskaya. From there take Trolleybus 11 to the VDNKh stop and transfer to bus 24. ⊠ *Village of Pirogova,* ☏ *44/266–5542.* ☉ *Winter, Thurs.–Tues. 10–4; summer, Thurs.–Tues. 10–5.*

KIEV A TO Z

Arriving and Departing

By Boat

Kiev is a river city, and there is passenger service to several other cities on the Dnieper and the Black Sea, into which it runs. The River Terminal is located at Ploshcha Poshtova (for which there is a subway stop of the same name). For tickets, you can go there in person, or you may inquire at your service bureau.

By Car

It is possible to drive to Kiev from Moscow (via the M4 Highway through Orel) or from Poland, Slovakia, the Czech Republic, and Hungary. Be aware, however, that roads are poorly maintained, repair shops are few and far between, and there is a possibility of fuel shortages.

By Plane

AIRPORTS AND AIRLINES

Visitors arriving at Kiev's **Borispol International Airport** (☏ 44/295–6701), located 29 kilometers (18 miles) east of Kiev, are in for a pleasant surprise. The airport, in a priority project, has been completely renovated to modern standards and is clean, well lighted, and easy to navigate, with a large terminal and signs in English as well as Ukrainian.

After you disembark, before passport control, you may obtain a visa if you have arrived without one and possess the proper documents (☞ Passports and Visas *in* the Gold Guide). Baggage carousels are located just beyond passport control. Here you will also complete a customs declaration and exit via Customs in the adjacent room. You should be meticulous in declaring all goods of value, including personal items such as jewelry and cameras.

Some domestic flights depart from the small **Zhulyany** airport (☏ 44/272–1201 or 44/272–1202) located on the city outskirts.

The international Ukrainian carriers are **Air Ukraine** (☏ 44/216–7040) and **Ukraine International** (☏ 44/221–8380, 44/224–2905, or 44/296–7455). Each flies between several European capitals, and Air Ukraine also has routes to the U.S. and Canada. From Russia, you can use **Aeroflot** (☏ 44/255–4165) or **Transaero** (☏ 44/225–0640), which has more flights, including four daily between Moscow and Kiev. Airlines from other countries include Aerosweet (44/223–4546 or 44/221–8194), **Air France** (☎ 44/296–7050 or 44/229–1395), **Austrian Airlines** (☎ 44/296–7697), **Balkan Bulgarian Airlines** (☎ 44/229–7203), **British Airways** (44/225–0640 or 44/240–0212), **CSA Airlines** (☎ 44/228–0296), **Egyptair** (44/228–2343 or 44/228–4789), **Estonian Air** (44/274–9997), **Finnair** (☎ 44/229–4363), **KLM** (☎ 44/268–9023), **LOT Polish Airlines** (☎ 44/228–7150), **Lufthansa** (☎ 44/296–7686 or 44/229–6297), **Malev Hungarian Airlines** (☎ 44/229–3661), **SAS** (☎ 44/296–7697), **Swissair** (☎ 44/296–7697), and **Turkish Airlines** (☎ 44/229–1550).

BETWEEN THE AIRPORT AND DOWNTOWN

It is best to have made advance arrangements for your transfer from the airport, particularly as it is outside Kiev's city limits. If you have flown Air Ukraine, you may use their coach service between the airport and the Rus Hotel, by booking a ticket at the same time as your plane ticket; business-class passengers and babies (under 2) may use this service for free; space on the coach is not guaranteed without an advance reservation.

There is also an express bus service—**Polet**—that will take you to Ploshcha Peremogi in the center of town. Departures are scheduled every 20 minutes. The ride takes one hour. Taxis and private cars are available, and you will no doubt encounter a mob of drivers as you exit, but it is up to you to decide if this is the best way to get into Kiev.

By Train

Train is by far the most convenient mode of traveling to other points in the CIS. There are several overnight trains daily to and from Moscow; the trip takes about 12 hours. There is also a daily train to St. Petersburg, but the ride is 30 hours long. The train station is located at 1 Vokzalna Ploshcha (☎ 44/265–0430); there's a connecting subway station (Vokzalnaya), so it is easily accessible by public transportation. For information on arrival and departure schedules, call 005. The ticket office is at 38 Vulytsya Tarasa Shevchenka, but it's easiest to buy them through the service bureau of your hotel.

Trains can lack heat and hot water. In general, they are likely to be less comfortable than those between Moscow and St. Petersburg, for instance. Bring along some drinking water and light snacks. Also be aware that unless you and your group have purchased tickets to an entire compartment, there can be up to four travelers per wagon-car, and there is no segregation by sex on overnight trains. Your trainmates, if male, are also likely to consume several bottles of alcohol until journey's end. Courteous behavior is always proclaimed the standard—but heavy drinking is common—so consider what you want from a train trip before you get a ticket. There is no official border check between Ukraine and Russia, but Russian officials occasionally check the documents of foreign passengers upon arrival in Moscow and St. Petersburg. Traveling to Russia without a valid Russian visa carries a fine of up to $300.

Getting Around

Kiev is divided into 12 districts, but most of its historical sites are concentrated in the **Verkhny Gorod** (Old Town), **Podol** and **Pechersk** districts, and along the **Khreshchatik,** the principal thoroughfare. Although the main tourist attractions are far apart, they are all easily reached by subway.

By Bus, Tram, and Trolley

Buses, trams, and trolleys operate on the honor system. Upon entering, you validate your ticket by canceling it, using one of the machines on the wall of the vehicle. You can purchase tickets at yellow kiosks throughout the city (but not from the driver). The ticket is valid for one ride only; if you change buses, you must pay another fare. Buses, trams, and trolleys operate on the same schedule as the subway, although service in the late evening hours and Sundays tends to be unreliable.

Kiev has an extensive surface transportation system, but fuel shortages have led to cutbacks on many routes, so service may be somewhat slower than in Moscow or St. Petersburg. However, the vehicles here are in much better condition. During rush hours the word "crowded" acquires new meaning, as passengers squeeze into already jam-packed trams and trolleys.

By Car
Car rental is limited, and it is recommended that you stick to public transport. If you do opt to drive, you will at least find the roads much easier to navigate than those in the larger Russian cities. **Prostor** (⊠ 23 Lvivska Vul., ☎ 44/450–9261) rents to tourists. You will need a valid driver's license and an international license; payment is made in hryvnia.

By Subway
It pales by comparison with the elaborate and extensive metro of Moscow and St. Petersburg, but Kiev's subway system is efficient and well maintained. Three lines radiate from the Khreshchatik, connecting the city's historical center to the newer residential districts on the left bank of the Dnieper.

Purchase a token and insert it into the slot at the turnstile. Tokens are available at all stations. The fare is the same regardless of distance. If you are in Kiev at the beginning of the month, you may choose to purchase a monthly pass, good on all public transportation. They go on sale at the end of the month and are available through the first week. The subway operates from 5:30 AM to midnight and is best avoided during rush hour, when trains can be very crowded.

By Taxi
Official taxis roam much more frequently here than in Moscow and St. Petersburg. You will see them at most major sites, or you may wave them down on the street, where you should negotiate a price before getting in. To order a cab by phone, call 058. All the major hotels offer car service, available at inflated prices.

Contacts and Resources

Dentists
Dental care is available at this center as well (☎ 44/227–9240). You may also try **Cabot Dental Services,** which has two locations. The first is at 67 Honchara Vulytsya, across from the German embassy (☎ 44/244–4682 or 44/219–1679) and is open weekdays 9–9, Sat. 9–2. The second is at 9 Khmelnitskoho Vulytsya (☎ 44/224–0468), open weekdays 9–9, Sat. 9–6.

Embassies
United States (⊠ 10 Vul. Yuria Kotsyubinskoho, ☎ 44/244–7344, FAX 44/244–7350); **Canada** (⊠ 31 Yaroslaviv Val, ☎ 44/212–2235, FAX 44/212–0212); and **United Kingdom** (⊠ 9 Desyatinna Vul., ☎ 44/462–0011, FAX 44/462–0014).

Emergencies
Fire (☎ 01), **police** (☎ 02), **ambulance** (☎ 03). As in Moscow and St. Petersburg, you are unlikely to get an English-speaking operator if you call these emergency numbers. Medical facilities are far below world

standards, and Kiev is plagued by even more shortages in basic medical supplies and equipment than can afflict Moscow and St. Petersburg. In a true emergency, evacuation to Finland or Western Europe should be considered.

English-Language Bookstores
Druzhba (⊠ 30 Khreshchatik, 44/224–0373) and **Inostrannaya Kniga** (⊠ 48 Chervonoarmiiska, ☎ 44/227–0088) have English-language sections, but the selection is meager, and bookshelves are usually lined with Ukrainian souvenirs. The art-book shop **Mistetstvo** (⊠ 24 Khreshchatik, ☎ 44/228–2526) has the best selection of the state-run stores. You'll find an occasional guidebook or art book on Kiev in street kiosks and in the cavelike passageways of the subway (a favorite spot for budding entrepreneurs). American and British newspapers and magazines (*USA Today, Financial Times, Wall Street Journal*) are available at the lobby kiosks of the hotels Dnipro, Intourist, and Rus.

Guided Tours
Intourist-Kyivska (⊠ Gospitalna Vul., in the Kyivska Hotel, ☎ 44/224–7345) is the Ukrainian branch of the defunct Intourist. It will arrange excursions to any site in or around Kiev. It will also assist you with travel and hotel arrangements to other cities in Ukraine.

The city excursion bureau **Slavutich** (⊠ 22 Vul. Sichnevoho Povstannya, ☎ 44/290–8680) also offers excursions in and around Kiev on virtually any theme (historical, architectural, etc.). The agency can provide English-speaking guides and translators and assistance in booking low-budget accommodations.

Sputnik (⊠ 4/6 Desyatinna Vul., ☎ 44/212–2586) is another full-service agency that can arrange excursions as well as travel ticketing. Ask for English-language guides and programs.

Hospitals and Clinics
The U.S. Embassy suggests calling **Life Medical** (⊠ 17 Tychyni Vul., ☎ 44/553–7416, ℻ 44/553–9787). The Ukrainian staff works under the instruction of U.S. doctors; U.S. missionary workers there include hospital adminstrators and a nurse. Another option for emergency care is the **American Medical Center** (⊠ 1 Berdichevska Vul., ☎ 44/211–6555 or 44/211–6556, ℻ 44/211-6557).

For referrals to Ukrainian facilities you may also call **Ukrainian Medical Services** (☎ 44/440–6344), a 24-hour service with English-speaking operators. They can make arrangements for you and send a doctor, ambulance, and interpreter as necessary. Be prepared to pay any medical costs up front and in cash (US$).

In all likelihood, further clinics, such as an American Medical Center like the one in Moscow, will open no later than 1996. If you call an ordinary ambulance (03), you will probably end up at **the Emergency Care Center** (⊠ 1/29 Vul. Mechnikova, ☎ 44/224–7364). It enjoys a good reputation, partly because foreigners have always been sent here for treatment.

Pharmacies
Drugs and medicines are not necessarily readily available in Kiev. The foreign-currency pharmacies **Farma** (⊠ 3 Vul. Prorizna, ☎ 44/228–2871), **Shance** (⊠ 15 Kreshatik, ☎ 44/228–3249), and **Cabot Kyiv** (⊠ 67 Honchara Vul., ☎ 44/216–4562) do sell drugs and medicines and are generally better stocked than the state-run pharmacies. **Biocon** operates two pharmacies out of district hospitals—Starokiev (⊠ 100 Vul. Saksahanskoho, 1st fl., ☎ 44/228–1518) and Moskovsky (⊠ 104

Chervonoarmiiska Vul., 1st fl., ☏ 44/212–8293). They stock Western medicine and are open also on Saturday 9–3.

Visitor Information

The closest thing Kiev has to a tourist information bureau is the former Ukrainian branch of Soviet Intourist, now known as **Intourist-Kyivska** (✉ 12 Vul. Gospitalna, in the Kyivska Hotel, ☏ 44/224–7345 or 44/225–3243). You can also obtain tourist information at the excursion bureaus of major hotels, or consult one of the three agencies listed below. Most of the printed materials available are outdated, Soviet-produced booklets, which are heavy on propaganda and scant on information, but this is changing.

Where to Change Money

All of the major hotels have exchange bureaus, which are generally open from 9 to 6, with an hour break for lunch.

You may also use some of the Ukrainian banks, including **Ukrinbank** (✉ 26 Bulvar Lesi Ukrainski, ☏ 44/294–6009) or **Inko Bank** (✉ 10/2 Mechnikova Vul., ☏ 44/290–7130), which also accepts American Express traveler's checks. **Dendi** Currency Exchange points can be found throughout the city (✉ 3 Bulvar Khmelnitskoho, ☏ 44/228–6595). The hotel **Lybid** (☏ 44/221–7731) can handle transactions involving most credit cards as well as American Express and Thomas Cook traveler's checks, and can also arrange Western Union money transfers.

English-
Russian
Vocabulary

ENGLISH-RUSSIAN VOCABULARY

Although we have tried to be consistent about the spelling of Russian names in this book, we find the Soviet authorities are not consistent about transliteration of the Cyrillic alphabet into our familiar Latin letters. In Moscow, for example, In-tourist spells a street name "Chaikovsky," but in St. Petersburg it's "Tchaikovsky." We've tried to stick to internationally recognized U.S. and British systems of transliteration, but don't be surprised if you occasionally come across differences like Chekhov and Tchekov, Tolstoy and Tolstoi, Baykal and Baikal, Tartar and Tatar, rouble and ruble—to say nothing of icon and ikon!

We give here some hints on the vital matter of reading Russian signs and on pronunciation, as well as a general English-Russian tourist vocabulary. Reading street names is probably the most important use for even a small knowledge of the Cyrillic alphabet. To help you, a word or two about how they work in Russian. Many Russian streets and squares are named after *people,* but the people's names may appear in different spellings—often they are made into adjectives. Suppose we have a street called Pushkin street, after the poet. The word street, ULITSA in Russian, is feminine (all Russian nouns have a gender; masculine nouns usually ending consonants, feminine in "a" and neuter in "o" or "e"). So you will see the street name as *Pushkinskaya ulitsa,* a feminine form of Pushkin. Pushkin Avenue would be *Pushkinsky Prospekt* in Russian (the word for avenue is masculine). Pushkin Chaussée would be *Pushkinskoye Shosse* (Chaussée is neuter). Don't be worried if you see one of these signs when our guide tells you you are on *Pushkin* street, avenue, etc.—it's the same thing! Almost every Soviet town has its *Leninsky Prospekt*—Lenin Avenue. As a general rule, once you have deciphered the first few letters, you will recognize the name—don't worry about the ending!

Another common way of naming streets is to say, for example, "Street of Pushkin," "Avenue of Lenin," etc.—*Ulitsa Pushkina, Prospekt Lenina* and so on. Here again, the *name* is easy to spot—its ending is not a spelling mistake, just a genitive case form of Pushkin, Lenin, etc. If you do get lost, most passers-by will understand if you ask for a street by its English name.

We owe a debt of gratitude to the Government Affairs Institute, Washington, D.C., for their permission to reproduce the Tables of the Russian Alphabet which follow.

THE RUSSIAN ALPHABET

А а	И и	С с	Ъ ъ
Б б	Й й	Т т	Ы ы
В в	К к	У у	Ь ь
Г г	Л л	Ф ф	Э э
Д д	М м	Х х	Ю ю
Е е	Н н	Ц ц	Я я
Ё ё	О о	Ч ч	
Ж ж	П п	Ш ш	
З з	Р р	Щ щ	

The Sound of Russian

Category 1:
Russian Consonants that Look and Sound like English

Russian Letter (Capital)	Russian Letter (Small)	English Letter
Б	б	b
К	к	k
М	м	m
Т	т	t
З	з	z

Category 2:
Russian Consonants that Look Different from Their English Equivalents

Russian Letter (Capital)	Russian Letter (Small)	English Letter
Д	д	d
Ф	ф	f
Г	г	g
Л	л	l
Н	н	n
П	п	p
Р	р	r
С	с	s
В	в	v
Й	й	y

Category 3:
Russian Consonants that Have No English Equivalents

Russian Letter (Capital)	Russian Letter (Small)	Sound
Ч	ч	ch
Х	х	kh
Ш	ш	sh
Щ	щ	shch
Ц	ц	ts
Ж	ж	zh
	ь	soft sign

The Russian Vowels

Russian Letter (Capital)	Russian Letter (Small)	Sound
А	а	ah
Я	я	yah
Э	э	eh
Е	е	yeh
Ы	ы	ih
И	и	i (ee)
О	о	oh
Ё	ё	yo
У	у	u (oo)
Ю	ю	yu

EVERYDAY WORDS AND PHRASES

The most important phrase to know (one that may make it unnecessary to know any others) is: "Do you speak English?" — *Gavaree'te lee vy pa anglee'skee?* If the answer is "Nyet," then you may have recourse to the lists below:

Please	Пожа́луйста	pazhah'lsta
Thank you	Спаси́бо	spasee'ba
Good	Хорошо́	kharasho'
Bad	Пло́хо	plo'kha
I	Я	ya
You	Вы	vy
He	Он	on
She	Она́	anah'
We	Мы	my
They	Они́	anee'
Yes	Да	da
No	Нет	nyet
Perhaps	Мо́жет быть	mo'zhet byt
I do not understand	Я не понима́ю	ya ne paneemah'yoo
Straight	Пря́мо	pryah'ma
Forward	Вперёд	fperyo't
Back	Наза́д	nazah't
To (on) the right	Напра́во	naprah'va
To (on) the left	Нале́во	nale'va
Hullo!	Здра́вствуйте!	zdrah'stvooite!
Good morning!	До́брое у́тро!	do'braye oo'tra!
Good day (evening)!	До́брый день (ве́чер)!	do'bree den (ve'cher)!
Pleased to meet you!	Очень рад с ва́ми познако́миться!	o'chen rat s vah'mee paznako'meetsa!
I am from USA (Britain)	Я прие́хал из США (Англии)	ya preeye'khal eez sshah' (ah'nglee ee)
I speak only English	Я говорю́ то́лько по-англи́йски	ya gavaryoo' to'lka pa anglee'skee
Do you speak English?	Говори́те ли вы по-англи́йски?	gavaree'te lee vy pa anglee'skee?
Be so kind as to show (explain, translate)	Бу́дьте добры́ по- кажи́те (объясни́те, переведи́те)	boo'te dobry' paka- zhee'te (abyasnee'te, perevedee'te)
Excuse my poor pronunciation	Извини́те моё плохо́е произношѐние	eezveenee'te mayo'pla- kho'ye praeeznashe'nye
I beg your pardon	Прости́те	prastee'te
I want to post a letter	Мне ну́жно отпра́вить письмо́	mne noo'zhna atprah'- veet peesmo'
Postcard	Почто́вая ка́рточка	pachto'vaya kah'rtachka

DAYS OF THE WEEK

Monday	Понеде́льник	panede'lneek
Tuesday	Вто́рник	fto'rneek
Wednesday	Среда́	sredah'
Thursday	Четве́рг	chetve'rk

Friday	Пя́тница	pyah'tneetsa
Saturday	Суббо́та	soobo'ta
Sunday	Воскресе́нье	vaskrese'nye
Holiday, feast	Пра́здник	prah'zneek
Today	Сего́дня	sevo'dnya
Tomorrow	За́втра	zah'ftra
Yesterday	Вчера́	vcherah'

NUMBERS

How many?	Ско́лько?	sko'lka?
1	оди́н	adee'n
2	два	dva
3	три	tree
4	четы́ре	chety're
5	пять	pyat
6	шесть	shest
7	семь	sem
8	во́семь	vo'sem
9	де́вять	de'vyat
10	де́сять	de'syat
11	оди́ннадцать	adee'natsat
12	двена́дцать	dvenah'tsat
13	трина́дцать	treenah'tsat
14	четы́рнадцать	chety'rnatsat
15	пятна́дцать	pyatnah'tsat
16	шестна́дцать	shesnah'tsat
17	семна́дцать	semnah'tsat
18	восемна́дцать	vasemnah'tsat
19	девятна́дцать	devyatnah'tsat
20	два́дцать	dvah'tsat
30	три́дцать	tree'tsat
40	со́рок	so'rak
50	пятьдеся́т	pyadesyah't
60	шестьдеся́т	shezdesyah't
70	се́мьдесят	se'mdesyat
80	во́семьдесят	vo'semdesyat
90	девяно́сто	deveno'sta
100	сто	sto
1000	ты́сяча	ty'syacha

INFORMATION SIGNS

Toilet (Gentlemen) (Ladies)	Туале́т (М) (Ж)	tooale't
No smoking!	Не кури́ть!	ne kooree't!
Taxi rank	Стоя́нка такси́	stayah'nka taksee'
Entrance	Вход	fkhot
Exit	Вы́ход	vy'khat
No exit	Вы́хода нет	vy'khada net
Emergency exit	Запасно́й вы́ход	zapasnoi' vy'khat
Stop!	Стоп!	stop!

Drinks

cold water	холо́дной воды́	khalo'dnoi vady'
mineral water	минера́льной воды́	meenerah'lnoi vady'
grape, tomato juice	виногра́дного, тома́т- ного со́ка	veenagrah'dnava, tamah'tnava so'ka
whisky, vodka	ви́ски, во́дка	vee'skee, vod'ka
liqueur	ликёр	leekyo'r
lemonade	лимона́д	leemanah't
beer	пи́во	pee'va
tea, coffee, cocoa, milk	чай, ко́фе, кака́о, молоко́	chai, ko'fe, kakah'o, malako'
fruit juice	сок	so'kee

Meat

steak	бифште́кс	beefshte'ks
roast beef	ро́стбиф	ro'stbeef
veal chops	отбивну́ю теля́чью котле́ту	atbeevnoo'yoo telyah'- chyoo katle'too
pork chops	свину́ю котле́ту	sveenoo'yoo katle'too
ham	ветчину́	vecheenoo'
sausage	колбасу́	kalbasoo'

Poultry

chicken	цыплёнка	tsyplyo'nka
hazel-grouse	ря́бчика	ryah'pcheeka
partridge	куропа́тку	koorapah'tkoo
duck	у́тку	oo'tkoo

Fish

soft caviar	зерни́стой икры́	zernee'stoi eekry'
pressed caviar	па́юсной икры́	pah'yoosnoi eekry'
salmon	лососи́ны	lasasee'ny
cold sturgeon	холо́дной осетри́ны	khalo'dnoi asetree'ny

Vegetables

green peas	зелёный горо́шек	zelyo'nee garo'shek
radishes	реди́ску	redee'skoo
tomatoes	помидо́ры	pameedo'ry
potatoes	карто́шка	karto'shka

Desserts

cake	пиро́жное	peero'zhnaye
fruit	фру́ктов	froo'ktaf
pears	груш	groosh
mandarines	мандари́нов	mandaree'naf
grapes	виногра́ду	veenagrah'doo
bananas	бана́нов	banah'naf

white and rye bread	бе́лый и чёрный хлеб	be'lee ee cho'rnee khlep
butter	ма́сло	mah'sla
cheese	сыр	syr
soft-boiled eggs	яйца всмя́тку	yai'tsa fsmyah'tkoo
hard-boiled eggs	яйца вкруту́ю	yai'tsa fkrootoo'voo
an omelette	омле́т	amle't

SHOPPING

Description

good	хоро́ший	kharo'shee
bad	плохо́й	plakhoi'
beautiful	краси́вый	krasee'vee
dear	дорого́й	daragoi'
cheap	дешёвый	desho'vee
old	ста́рый	sta'ree
new	но́вый	no'vee

Colors

white	бе́лый	be'lee
black	чёрный	chyo'rnee
red	кра́сный	krah'snee
pink	ро́зовый	ro'zavee
orange	ора́нжевый	arah'nzhevee
yellow	жёлтый	zho'ltee
brown	кори́чневый	karee'chnevee
green	зелёный	zelyo'nee
light blue	голубо́й	galooboi'
blue	си́ний	see'nee
violet	фиоле́товый	feeale'tavee
grey	се́рый	se'ree
golden	золото́й	zalatoi'
silver	сере́бряный	sere'bryanee

In the shop

Baker's	Бу́лочная	boo'lachnaya
Confectioner's	Конди́терская	kandee'terskaya
Food Store	Гастроно́м	gastrano'm
Grocer's	Бакале́я	bakale'ya
Delivery Counter	Стол зака́зов	stol zakah'zaf
Wine and Spirits	Ви́на—коньяки́	vee'na — kanyakee'
Fruit and Vegetables	Овощи—фру́кты	o'vashshee — froo'kty

INDEX

X = *restaurant*, ⌦ = *hotel*

234   Index

NOTES

NOTES

NOTES

NOTES

NOTES

NOTES

NOTES

NOTES

NOTES

NOTES

Fodor's Travel Publications

Available at bookstores everywhere, or call 1–800–533–6478, 24 hours a day.

Gold Guides
U.S.

Alaska

Arizona

Boston

California

Cape Cod, Martha's
Vineyard, Nantucket

The Carolinas & the
Georgia Coast

Chicago

Colorado

Florida

Hawai'i

Las Vegas, Reno,
Tahoe

Los Angeles

Maine, Vermont,
New Hampshire

Maui & Lāna'i

Miami & the Keys

New England

New Orleans

New York City

Pacific North Coast

Philadelphia & the
Pennsylvania Dutch
Country

The Rockies

San Diego

San Francisco

Santa Fe, Taos,
Albuquerque

Seattle & Vancouver

The South

U.S. & British Virgin
Islands

USA

Virginia & Maryland

Washington, D.C.

Foreign

Australia

Austria

The Bahamas

Belize & Guatemala

Bermuda

Canada

Cancún, Cozumel,
Yucatán Peninsula

Caribbean

China

Costa Rica

Cuba

The Czech Republic
& Slovakia

Eastern &
Central Europe

Europe

Florence, Tuscany
& Umbria

France

Germany

Great Britain

Greece

Hong Kong

India

Ireland

Israel

Italy

Japan

London

Madrid & Barcelona

Mexico

Montréal &
Québec City

Moscow, St.
Petersburg, Kiev

The Netherlands,
Belgium &
Luxembourg

New Zealand

Norway

Nova Scotia, New
Brunswick, Prince
Edward Island

Paris

Portugal

Provence &
the Riviera

Scandinavia

Scotland

Singapore

South Africa

South America

Southeast Asia

Spain

Sweden

Switzerland

Thailand

Tokyo

Toronto

Turkey

Vienna & the Danube

Fodor's Special-Interest Guides

Alaska Ports of Call

Caribbean Ports
of Call

The Complete Guide
to America's
National Parks

Family Adventures

Fodor's Gay Guide
to the USA

Halliday's New
England Food
Explorer

Halliday's New
Orleans Food
Explorer

Healthy Escapes

Ballpark Vacations

Kodak Guide to
Shooting Great
Travel Pictures

Nights to Imagine

Rock & Roll Traveler
USA

Sunday in New York

Sunday in
San Francisco

Walt Disney World,
Universal Studios
and Orlando

Walt Disney World
for Adults

Wendy Perrin's
Secrets Every Smart
Traveler Should
Know

Where Should We
Take the Kids?
California

Where Should We
Take the Kids?
Northeast

Worldwide Cruises
and Ports of Call